# Flesh and Steel during the Great War

*To Anne, Marc-Antoine, Victor and Pierre-Alexandre*

# Flesh and Steel during the Great War

## The Transformation of the French Army and the Invention of Modern Warfare

Michel Goya

Translated by
Andrew Uffindell

Foreword by
Sir Hew Strachan

Pen & Sword
**MILITARY**

First published in French by **Éditions Tallandier in 2004**
English edition first published in Great Britain in 2018 by
Pen & Sword Military
an imprint of
Pen & Sword Books Ltd
47 Church Street
Barnsley
South Yorkshire
S70 2AS

Copyright © Éditions Tallandier, 2004 and 2014
This edition published by arrangement with Éditions Tallandier in conjunction
with their duly appointed agent L'Autre agence, Paris, France and co-agent
The St Marks Agency, London, United Kingdom.

Copyright English translation © Pen & Sword Books Ltd 2018

ISBN 978 1 47388 696 4

A CIP catalogue record for this book is available from the British Library

Typeset in Sabon 10/12
Typeset by Aura Technology and Software Services, India

Printed and bound in UK by TJ International

Pen & Sword Books Ltd incorporates the imprints of Pen & Sword Archaeology,
Atlas, Aviation, Battleground, Discovery, Family History, History, Maritime,
Military, Naval, Politics, Railways, Select, Social History, Transport, True Crime,
and Claymore Press, Frontline Books, Leo Cooper, Praetorian Press, Remember
When, Seaforth Publishing and Wharncliffe.

For a complete list of Pen & Sword titles please contact
PEN & SWORD BOOKS LIMITED
47 Church Street, Barnsley, South Yorkshire, S70 2AS, England
E-mail: enquiries@pen-and-sword.co.uk
Website: www.pen-and-sword.co.uk

# Contents

List of Tables..................................................................................vii

List of Maps and Diagrams...........................................................vii

Acknowledgements ........................................................................viii

Publishing History ...........................................................................ix

Foreword ............................................................................................x

Preface ............................................................................................xiv

Chapter 1     The Masterminds of *La Revanche* ...................................1

                  Five Heads for One Thought ...............................................2

                  Creating an Intellectual Aristocracy....................................11

                  Modes of Thought...............................................................17

                  The 'Offensive-Minded' Men ..............................................24

Chapter 2     In Search of a Doctrine.......................................................32

                  War Under the Microscope .................................................32

                  The 'Napoleonic Men' ........................................................39

                  Offensive Combat at the Dawn of the Twentieth Century ...........45

                  Modern Style and New School ...........................................53

Chapter 3     The Flaws in the Learning Process.....................................61

                  Officer-Training ..................................................................61

                  Training Insufficiencies ......................................................65

                  On the Eve of the War........................................................75

Chapter 4     The Choice of Arms............................................................79

                  The 'Bayonet Men' .............................................................79

                  The Virtuosos .....................................................................82

                  The Strange Case of the Heavy Artillery.............................87

                  Twilight of the Cavalry .......................................................92

                  Assaulting the Sky ..............................................................95

Chapter 5     The Test of Fire ..................................................................99

                  The Cost of Confusion .......................................................99

                  Origins of the Shortcomings .............................................103

                  The Turnaround ................................................................104

Chapter 6     The Pressure of the Front .................................................117

                  Micro-Transformations.......................................................117

                  The Model of Scrabble ......................................................123

Dynamic of the Tactical Innovations .................................... 127
The Restraints on Change .................................... 130
Unsettled Time.................................... 134

Chapter 7    GHQ and Tactical Change .................................... 137
The Reshaping of Roles.................................... 137
The Assimilation Through Training .................................... 143
The Lost Paradigms.................................... 149

Chapter 8    Confronting the Trenches .................................... 164
The Industrialization of the Infantry.................................... 165
Prisoners of Glory .................................... 172
The Transformations of the Artillery .................................... 175
Cavalry of the Skies.................................... 180

Chapter 9    In the Death Zone .................................... 185
Surviving in a Nightmare.................................... 185
Courage.................................... 192
Holding on .................................... 201

Chapter 10   The Steel Fist .................................... 204
Why did Estienne's Project Succeed?.................................... 204
Painful Apprenticeship.................................... 208
The Assault Artillery Reaches Maturity .................................... 216

Chapter 11   The Grand Army of 1918.................................... 230
Preparing for a New Form of Warfare.................................... 230
France's Shock Troops.................................... 236
Mastery of the Deep Battle.................................... 241
The Combined-Arms Battlefield.................................... 244
The Model Battle.................................... 252

Conclusion.................................... 259
Appendix 1   Timeline of Operations.................................... 262
Appendix 2   Analysis of the 13th Infantry Division's Actions.................................... 267
Appendix 3   Statistical Data .................................... 274
References.................................... 276
Sources.................................... 306
Printed Sources .................................... 308
Bibliography.................................... 311
Index.................................... 320

# List of Tables

1. Changes in military appropriations for the purchase of materiel.  89
2. Materiel as a proportion of men armed with rifles.  171
3. Comparison of the Schneider and the Saint-Chamond tank.  210
4. French light tank engagements, 1918.  223
5. The actions of the 13th Infantry Division.  270
6. Density of the 13th Infantry Division's firepower per km of front and per day of engagement.  272
7. Equipment allocations of the French armies.  274
8. Relative importance of the arms.  274
9. Losses of each arm.  275

# List of Maps and Diagrams

1. The 4th Army at the Battle of the Ardennes, 22 August 1914.  101
2. Layout of the ground for a divisional attack, as prescribed in the *Instruction on the aim and conditions of a general offensive action* (16 April 1915).  155
3. The French sector at the Battle of the Somme, 1 July 1916.  161
4. Second Battle of Artois, May-June 1915.  169
5. The 36th Infantry Division at Courcelles-Méry, 9 June 1918.  234
6. Battle of Montdidier, August 1918.  253

# Acknowledgements

For their kind consideration and valuable advice, I must thank Professor Georges-Henri Soutou of the Paris-Sorbonne University (Paris IV) and Colonel Frédéric Guelton, head of the research department of the French army's historical branch. I am also grateful to the research department's personnel as a whole, especially *Monsieur* Henry Vaudable, who welcomed me on numerous occasions and whose knowledge of the archives has been particularly useful. Nor can I omit to mention Laurent Henninger, of the French Centre for Historical Defence Studies, for his constant support and for the intellectual stimulation resulting from discussions with him.

# Publishing History

This book first appeared in 2004, under the title *La chair et l'acier: l'invention de la guerre moderne, 1914-1918* ('Flesh and steel: the invention of modern warfare, 1914-1918'). Its publisher, Tallandier, reissued it in 2014 as *L'invention de la guerre moderne: du pantalon rouge au char d'assaut, 1871-1918* ('The invention of modern warfare: from red trousers to tanks'). *Flesh and steel* is the first English translation of this classic work.

# Foreword

by Sir Hew Strachan

French scholarship on the First World War is in rude health, and has been so for at least two or three decades. Those who visit the British cemeteries on the Somme will be aware of the Historial de la Grande Guerre in Péronne, which houses not only a museum but also a research centre and archive. It has hosted workshops and conferences, and brought on a whole generation of younger scholars. Some of the works of its now more senior figures, such as Annette Becker and Stéphane Audoin-Rouzeau, have been translated into English, and its output has found reflection in, and also been fed by, English-speaking authors like John Horne, Leonard Smith and Jay Winter. Their preoccupations have been with the experience of war, its impact on civilians as well as soldiers, its implications for understandings of gender and identity, and its legacies in memorials and culture. They have reconfigured the debate on these issues and created fresh agendas for discussion.

For those interested in military history more traditionally defined, in tactics and operations, in command and strategy, the impact of French research in the English-speaking world has been more muted. None of the more important books has found its way into English. And yet here too the scholarly landscape has been changed, principally thanks to the opening and exploitation of the army's records in the Château de Vincennes. In 1967 Guy Pedroncini produced the first archivally-based account of the French army's mutinies of 1917 in a book dedicated to the memory of Pierre Renouvin. Renouvin, who had served as an infantryman in the First World War and lost an arm in the conflict, bestrode French scholarship on the topic from the 1920s until his death in 1974. That was the year in which Pedroncini followed his history of the mutinies with a definitive and revealing account of Philippe Pétain as the army's commander-in-chief between 1917 and 1918, a record of remobilisation and victory which had been obscured by the humiliation of 1940 and Vichy.

Michel Goya's *La chair et l'acier: l'invention de la guerre moderne (1914–1918)* was published in 2004. Amidst its many other contributions, it developed and extended the points about the French army in 1918 which Pedroncini had made. Goya, however, is not primarily an academic. He served as a career soldier in the French army from 1983 until 2009, being commissioned from the ranks into the marine infantry and reaching the rank of colonel. He was responsible for the development of French military doctrine in the wars after the 9/11 attacks, and was director of a group responsible for studying new forms of war at IRSEM, l'Institut de Recherche Stratégique de l'Ecole Militaire (the institute for strategic research at the military school) in Paris. He has published on the war in Iraq and the experience of front-line combat, and while still in uniform wrote trenchant pieces on France's strategy in the national press.

The fact that he was also able to undertake the doctoral work which produced *Flesh and Steel during the Great War* (to use its English title) shows how different from the British army is that of France in its approach both to military education and to military history. For Goya is not alone. Over the last ten years André Bach, Frédéric Guelton and Rémy Porte have all deepened our knowledge of the First World War through important and scholarly works written while serving in the French army. Moreover, as Goya's *Flesh and Steel during the Great War* demonstrates, those who have both military experience and academic training bring to military history perspectives which inform both callings. On the one hand they produce insights derived from current warfare which illuminate our understanding of the past, and on the other they give depth and context to the immediacies and experiences of armed conflict in our own times. There can be no doubt as to Goya's standards as a historian. He was supervised by Georges-Henri Soutou, a world-class historian whose book on the economic war aims of the First World War, *L'or et le sang*, ought also to have been translated long ago.

Goya also brings to *Flesh and Steel during the Great War* the insights of the sociologist or anthropologist, and does so in two ways. Look first at the preface, which ends with an analogy from sport (Michel Goya was a keen rugby player). It asks how a team learns from its first match: how it adapts and formalises things that have worked but which have not been planned and have emerged spontaneously on the field of play. The team then also has to take on board the instructions from its coach, who realises that its second game may make different demands. Goya's theme here is that of innovation. How do armies become (to use a title beloved of the US army in its adaptation to the Iraq and Afghan wars) 'learning organisations'? Armies are hierarchical organisations with top-down management structures undergirded by the principles of command and leadership. Michel Goya knows that by dint of over 25 years of military service. So that is his second set of insights: those which embrace the culture of armies.

In 1914 the French army was a thinking organisation but it was not an army with a coherent doctrine. That point has been recognised by others. Douglas Porch made it in *The march to the Marne: the French army 1871–1914*, published in 1981, and more recently – with a different set of arguments – so did Dimitry Queloz in *De la manoeuvre napoléonienne à l'offensive à outrance: la tactique générale de l'armée française 1817–1914*. Queloz published his book in 2009 and so benefited from reading Goya. Queloz describes *Flesh and Steel during the Great War* as 'without doubt the best book dealing with the tactics of the French army before and during the course of the First World War'. Goya and Queloz identify an organisation that was almost thinking too much as it approached the outbreak of war. For Queloz, as for Porch, the problem was that nothing had been settled by 1914: how the army might fight was still the subject of debate. For Goya, the explanation for this diversity was as much structural as intellectual. Too many units, commands and branches of the service were entitled to develop their own solutions, and not until 1911 – too late to be effective – was there a centralised general staff with the authority to pull everything together. There is a point when debate has to end and be replaced by a set of common operating procedures and tactical drills.

Neither Porch nor Queloz took their studies beyond the outbreak of the war. For that the only available work until Goya's was *L'évolution des idées tactiques en France et en Allemagne pendant la guerre de 1914–1918*, by Colonel Lucas, the second edition of which was published as long ago as 1924. Lucas provides an excellent summary of the tactical regulations, but – as Goya rightly points out – he does not discuss if or how they were implemented. Documents can tell us only so much. We need to know who read them, how they were disseminated, and in particular how training in the principles they promulgated was organised and conducted.

Goya shows how, over the four years of the First World War, the French army moved from being a thinking army to becoming a 'learning organisation'. In a battlefield defined in linear terms, by trench lines and by the curtains of artillery fire, command also worked in a linear fashion. Put crudely and over-simplistically, the front line ran vertically from north to south, while the command chain ran from east to west. Conventional wisdom might reverse that last orientation, arguing that France's commanders, being to the rear of the front, lay to the west, and the formations for which they were responsible to the east. But that is the point. The process was initiated from the 'bottom up'. Because higher command of mass armies required them to be behind the front, those who exercised junior command were much more aware of the demands of contemporary warfare and developed solutions to address them. The job of the generals was to collect the lessons their juniors had learned, to collate them, to draft them into potential doctrine, to test them in combat, and then to revise them once again. Only when that process was completed could the final product be endorsed and then adopted in the innumerable schools and training courses which would ensure its effective application in the field.

This process was continuous and conducted at high tempo. It had to be. Technological innovation was rapid, the move from prototype to series production being achieved in months rather than (as in peacetime) decades – from the perfection of artillery and aircraft to the introduction of gas and tanks. Even more pressing were the responses of the enemy: what mattered in tactics was relative advantage more than perfection – the ability to be better than the Germans on the day. The latter were innovating too, turning the western front into a constant cycle of change and adaptation. Those who best embodied the new approaches, not only Pétain but also Foch, confronted a further obstacle – the opposition of senior officers who still subscribed to the legacies of the pre-war doctrines which earlier historians castigated (unhelpfully) as the 'spirit of the offensive'. Those who still cleaved to that sort of thinking also resisted defence in depth and sought to undermine the efforts of both Pétain and Foch, with disastrous consequences on 27 May 1918. It was precisely that defeat which gave the new regime the authority to lead France and its allies to victory on 11 November 1918.

Goya begins his book with a bold claim: by the war's end the French army was 'the most modern in the world'. For British historians caught in a more insular narrative, this is a bold and provocative claim (as was no doubt intended). First, they have been inclined to treat 'the learning curve' as a process undergone uniquely by the British army. As not only Goya but also – more recently – Aimée Fox (in *Learning to fight: military innovation and change in the British army, 1914–1918*) have made clear, the two allies learned from each other. Goya's statement also challenges a second common perception, one which dates back to the arguments of John Terraine: that the British army won the battles of the 'Hundred Days' single-handedly.

One reason for the importance of this English translation of *La chair et l'acier* lies precisely here: it puts to bed the notion that the French army, broken by Verdun in 1916 and the Nivelle offensive in April 1917, never fully recovered after the mutinies in June. Douglas Haig laid the foundations of this argument. He complained about the failure of Pétain to support him after the German offensive of 21 March 1918, when in reality over 20 French divisions were rushing to close the gap created by the defeat of the British 5th Army, and in October 1918 he described the French army as exhausted when putting the case for accepting the armistice.

Michel Goya formulates sophisticated arguments for understanding how armies learn, change and adapt which have ongoing resonances and relevance. I have been urging British publishers to translate *La chair et l'acier* since it first came out, and congratulate Pen and Sword not only on doing so but also on securing Andrew Uffindell to do the work. He has produced a text that is accurate and fluent. In its new incarnation *Flesh and Steel during the Great War* will attract fresh readers, among them not only historians of the First World War but also those concerned with the continuing challenges of military innovation and the processes by which it is achieved.

# Preface

By the time the Armistice rang out on 11 November 1918, the victorious French army was more modernized than any other army in the world. No longer did its infantry have to go on foot in order to move from one point of the front to another. When it attacked, it did so with light tanks acting in conjunction with *groupes de combat* (tactical sub-units of between fifteen and twenty men) that were equipped with powerful weapons and surrounded by accurate fire from machine-gun sections, mortars and 37mm guns. Overhead flew squadrons of airplanes, harassing the enemy, blinding him with smoke bombs, or locating him for the artillery that could be found everywhere. If the enemy fell back, armoured cars or bomber airplanes set off in pursuit.

Compared to this 'industrial' army, the big battalions of August 1914 belonged to a different century. Back then, reconnaissance was done by squadrons mounted on horseback and armed with lances. To support the infantry, the artillery normally used direct fire. The infantrymen in their red trousers charged in mass with fixed bayonets, in a manner akin to that of the *grognards,* the 'grumbling' footsoldiers of the First Empire.

In short, the French army had been forced by a tremendous challenge to catch up with history in the space of just a few years, and had finally fallen into step with the technical transformations of its time. Faced with an opponent who had superior means at his disposal, and whose military effectiveness was formidable, the French army had managed to deploy considerable resources of imagination and willpower, and had thereby prevailed in the end. It is this endeavour by the French army to adapt its methods and means of combat, this process of tactical evolution, that I have done my best to analyse.

It is not a matter of studying the conduct of operations, nor of describing the soldiers' daily lives and sufferings. Plenty of writings already exist on those subjects. My objective is different. I have set out to describe the process that made it possible to take an organization containing several millions of men – men whose entire culture bound them to the nineteenth century – and to transform it radically into a remarkably modern force.

How does an army evolve? What accelerates or slows down this evolution? Can we distinguish a process specific to peacetime that differs from that of wartime? What are the tactical and doctrinal agents of change? These are some of the questions that I will address.

\*

The subject is an ambitious one, and it will encounter current-day concerns since one of NATO's two main military commands is now fully devoted to managing 'tactical transformation'. It is also a complex subject and some precautionary steps are necessary, the most important of which is to define the scope of the subject as precisely as possible. If we are to explain the victory of 1918, we must go back to the disaster of 1871, so deeply did that disaster mark men's minds and lay the foundations on which the modern French army was built. The naval war will be excluded from this study, since it had only a secondary importance on the operations of the First World War. As for the land forces, I will focus on the action of those arms that had a direct impact on the enemy. This is why I will say nothing about sappers, or about second-line or fortress troops, unless they had a direct effect on the operations.

Another problem is deciding the scale of study. In economics, there is a fairly clear-cut distinction between macroeconomics, with its big aggregates, and microeconomics, which is concerned with how the 'fundamental particles' behave. The same separation can often be found in military history, between the description of major operations and that of the daily life of the troops. I have no desire to carry out yet another exploration of one of these levels, but rather to see how they related to each other in the particular field of tactics. I have therefore decided to navigate between three echelons: the troops, the high command and the arms (infantry, cavalry, artillery and two specific sub-divisions, namely aviation and tanks). Since my subject is not tactics in themselves, but rather the process of tactical evolution, I have no intention of describing all of the French army's combat methods in detail.

*

This study straddles the line between history and the sociology of organizations. It was therefore logical to borrow some interpretative templates from sociology.[1] I have used these templates to examine three main sources of historical evidence. I started with the archives of the French army's historical branch, which provided me with priceless information about the war as seen by the high command, and especially by the Third Department (Operations) of the General Headquarters (GHQ). I then drew on two groups of authors from that time: the pre-1914 theorists and the Great War veterans. Among the veterans, two authors proved particularly useful. Colonel Pascal-Marie-Henri Lucas' book, *The evolution of tactical ideas in France and Germany during the war of 1914-1918,* first published in 1923, provided me with an overall picture of the various doctrines that emerged during the war. But Lucas described only indirectly the way in which ideas were born and he barely touched on the period before the war. I admit to a certain affection for the second author, Emile Laure, a prolific writer with an inquiring mind who analysed his profession throughout a packed career. Before the war, he was a fervent supporter of the offensive, and then in 1917-18 he was a meticulous observer of GHQ and of tactical – and even micro-tactical – evolutions. He later wrote a fascinating joint study with Major Jacottet on how the 13th Infantry Division evolved during the war. My third source of historical evidence, after the archive documents from GHQ and the writings of theorists and veterans, were the military regulations, and it goes without saying that I paid particular attention to them.

*

In fitting together all the pieces of this multi-dimensional puzzle, I found that my personal experience of serving more than twenty years in the French army was invaluable, ranging as it did from command of a *groupe de combat* to the Joint Services Defence College. Working on the assumption that the behaviour of present-day French soldiers might be similar to that of their 'seniors' of the early twentieth century, I found this 'empathetic' method most useful.[2]

*

Having established this methodological framework, how was I to tackle the question of tactical change? I started by taking the example of a sports team that after playing its first match is preparing for the next one. It has played the first match by applying a number of tactical procedures. Some of these procedures have turned out to be ineffective, or have not been properly adopted by the team. Others may have appeared spontaneously during the game. Others again need to be devised to take on the new opponent, or in order to adapt to new rules. What is required, therefore, is the management of a tactical evolution. This will largely be the mission of the coach and his assistants, but some of the players, such as the team captain, might play a role in it. The management of this tactical evolution begins with a detailed analysis of the changes that have to be made, using as a basis what has been seen of the preceding match – seen either in the heat of the action during the match itself, or in the cold light of day using video. This analysis also entails studying the prospective opponent, the pitch, the referee and other elements. From this study, a certain number of procedures are conceived, which must then be spelled out to the players. Above all, the players must be made to adopt these procedures.

Ensuring that these new methods become firmly embedded in the way the team plays means that specific training has to be organized, including pitches, particular equipment and training session records. Some players may be sceptical about the relevance of new practices. Others might fear for their place on the team, and others besides might miss the training periods. When the match day comes, the extent to which the new practices have been taken on board remains uncertain, as does the question of whether they will prove effective. It is the start of the game that reveals the value of the efforts that have been made. If deficiencies become apparent, the only time left for putting them right is the actual duration of the match. A new, and far quicker, process now begins. It is the players who now have the lead role in analysing what is happening and in devising new methods. The coach on the touchline supports the process with his exhortations, with advice during stoppages in play and with replacement players.

This sporting metaphor has served as my guiding theme. Between 1871 and 1918, the French army resembled this sports team. It had just suffered a bitter defeat in 1870-1, and had to prepare for *la revanche* – a conflict to avenge that humiliation. But if in its quest for revenge it was to avoid another defeat, it had no option but to evolve. Using this as my starting point, I tried to identify those men who brought about the transformation, and to ascertain their mental framework, the analytical methods they used and the way in which they grasped the changes in the long term. I then had to work out what procedures were used to ensure the outcome of this thinking was incorporated into actual practice, and to what extent it was taken on board before the outbreak of the war. I have paid particular interest to the circulation of ideas between the various echelons of the military organization and within each echelon itself.

# Chapter 1

# The Masterminds of *La Revanche*

In 1912, Lieutenant Emile Laure, writing in his book *The French offensive*, reckoned that 'the throbbings of the offensive determination have reached a peak of intensity'.[1] To his fellow officers he issued a vibrant appeal:

> All of you my comrades, all of you who feel French hearts beating inside your soldierly chests, I entreat you, join me in yelling this war cry that your temperament instinctively inspires in you: 'We want to conquer', and its natural upshot: THE OFFENSIVE! ...
>
> Hurrah for the manly, energetic and resolute leader, set in his offensive determination, whose superb propaganda seeks to extend such a doctrine to the entire nation.
>
> Hurrah for the breakthrough!
>
> Hurrah for the FRENCH OFFENSIVE![2]

A year later, Captain Marie Marcel André Billard took an even more extremist line in his *Infantry education:*

> In war, being skilful is far less important than being brave. Knowledge will always take second place to loyalty and comradeship. Every last soldier will therefore need to be imbued first and foremost with a superior spirit of sacrifice, a spirit that will instantly reveal itself through the offensive, through the drive for the frontier ... through the forwardness that scorns the humanitarian trench – a trench that may offer safety to individuals, but will inevitably become a coffin for nations.[3]

Forty years earlier, the French defeat of 1871 had universally been seen as an intellectual defeat. The Prussian army had managed to harness together the creative energies of its officers, and the superiority of this approach over the muddled inspirations of the French had become firmly established during the war.

Stung by that humiliation, the army of the new French Republic became absorbed in searching in a scientific manner for the 'secrets of victory'. A vast movement of intellectualization of the officer corps began. The result was a remarkable profusion of writings that is probably unique in the history of the French army. Yet time passed and in the last few years before the war these writings were no longer advocating anything other than the offensive, sacrifice and scorn for material factors.

Before we examine how the doctrines for the use of the arms were formulated, and how they were combined into a so-called 'operational' doctrine, we should think about the key players in this process. Who were the men in charge of thought and of the management of change? How were they selected and trained? Ultimately, we need to understand how an initial, positivist methodology could lead to such mystical tactical considerations that we find in the writings of those young officers, Laure and Billard. We will discover a growing contradiction between on the one hand a high command that was incapable of controlling change and on the other hand an intellectual élite of officers, self-confident but at odds with each other, whose theories gradually lost touch with the industrial reality of the time.

## Five Heads for One Thought

Rebuilding the French army after the 'dreadful year' of 1871 was an immense task. Organizational structures, institutions and mindsets all had to be changed.

The victorious Germans made a clear-cut distinction between the administrative sphere, under their Ministry of War, and the tactical sphere, which was the preserve of a highly independent General Staff. But for all the allure exerted by the Prussian model, this solution seemed too dangerous for the new French Third Republic, given the political background to the regime's birth. The head of the army had to be answerable to parliament, and this meant he could be nobody other than the Minister of War. The speed with which the French forces were rebuilt in material terms demonstrated the effectiveness of their administrative management. But tactical thought was soon hampered by the absence of a stable, centralized body. The result was a succession of different 'poles' of thought, and although some of these poles were more productive than others, none was capable of imposing the much sought-after doctrinal unity.

### A three-headed high command

If the Ministry of War was to be made the army's high command, it first needed to be thoroughly reorganized. At that time, the Ministry was a purely administrative body, divided into ten directorates under civilian directors, and into five advisory committees for the staff and the four arms (infantry, cavalry, artillery and engineers). The institution as a whole was compartmentalized and largely divorced from military needs.

The reform of the Ministry of War was carried out by two ministers, Generals Ernest Courtot de Cissey and François-Charles du Barail, both of whom had been outstanding officers during the Second Empire. Their efforts had two main thrusts. The first was to try and transfer some of the powers of the directorates to the army corps and to the Minister of War himself. The second was to 'remilitarize' the Ministry by creating the General Staff in 1871 and the directorates of arms in 1878. These directorates of arms had the support of specialised technical committees, and were placed under military, not civilian, directors. For instance, the engineers, who were notoriously uncooperative with other arms, were given General Raymond Séré de Rivières as their director. But in the end, these reforms had only a limited success. The technical committees were used by ambitious men as springboards to further their careers, and they increased in number despite regular attempts by Ministers of War to create a more rational organization. The problem was that the turnover of Ministers was too high. In the period of interest to us, forty-three Ministers of War held office in succession, or an average of one every year.[4] Under these conditions, the vast majority of them were unable to monitor the proposed reforms, and the new directors resumed their predecessors' habits of independence.

The post of Minister of War required authority and competence. Hence it was initially held, logically enough, by soldiers. These men at first were apolitical technicians, although they then became increasingly close to the Republican regime. But it proved difficult to find senior officers who were willing to forgo a major command in order to venture into the political sphere for several months. The lack of anyone more suitable often resulted in the appointment of a 'young' general, such as Jean-Baptiste Marie Edouard Campenon, Georges Boulanger, or Jules-Louis Lewal, but such men lacked authority over generals of the same rank who were senior to them owing to their length of service. (The highest rank to which it was possible to be promoted was *général de division*.) In 1888, Charles de Freycinet was the first civilian to become Minister of War. An interlude occurred from 1899 to 1905, during which the Ministers were two generals who brought the Dreyfus Affair to an end. An almost uninterrupted succession of civilians then held the post again up until the war. These civilians needed stable military advisers.

*

It was realized early on that France had to have a generalissimo who could take command of the army in the field. But until 1911 political wariness ensured that this role was kept carefully separate from that of the Minister of War's chief-of-staff. The future commander-in-chief was also submerged in a Supreme War Council that contained the army's foremost generals. The Supreme War Council went through many metamorphoses. Created in July 1872 with around twenty members, it was responsible for examining in a very broad way any issue relating to the army and defence. It met thirty-six times and made a major contribution to the work of reorganizing the army, but did not concern itself with issues of doctrine. The Supreme War Council increasingly found itself vying with parliament, which was growing in importance, and it lapsed into inactivity in March 1874. But in 1888 it was reborn at Freycinet's instigation. It consisted of the Minister of War and his chief-of-staff, as well as the chairmen of the advisory committees of the artillery and engineers, and also eight *généraux de division* who were earmarked for major commands in wartime. The Supreme War Council was consulted on any important matter regarding the preparation for war. Its members were also inspectors-general. They were each responsible for keeping the Minister of War informed about the state of the army within a specific inspection district, with a particular focus on war preparations. They might also receive special missions, or supervise the large-scale manœuvres. It was the vice-chairman of the Supreme War Council who had the role of commander-in-chief designate, and he was appointed annually.

In 1900, a new and controversial Minister of War, General Louis André, regarded this board of generals with suspicion. As a result, the permanent inspectors-general became 'special, or temporary, inspectors' and returned to Paris. The role of commander-in-chief was retained, despite being seen as a threat by many radicals, but was kept within strict bounds. The vice-chairman of the Supreme War Council had no authority over the army commanders (except for some map manœuvres, if the Minister of War approved), nor over the General Staff.[5] The Supreme War Council was deprived of any substance, and was not even consulted about the plan to reduce the length of military service to two years.

*

The Minister of War and the commander-in-chief designate were two of the French high command's three heads. The third was the General Staff. Created in June 1871, this staff began as no more than an expanded cabinet, or personal office, of the Minister of War. The chief-of-staff changed whenever a new Minister was appointed, so the first fourteen years saw a succession of as many as twelve chiefs. Specialized staff 'departments' were created in 1874.[6] But, as in other matters, it took Freycinet's arrival in 1888 for the Minister of War's staff to become the truly 'General Staff' of the army. Its chief now became responsible for 'examining issues relating to the general defence of the country and to the preparation of war operations'. A decree of 1895 also made the directorates of arms subordinate to him in matters affecting the preparation for war.[7] But in reality, according to General Henri Bonnal, the General Staff was 'largely distracted from its vital task by looking into a host of issues connected with routine duties. The chief of the General Staff exerted no real control over its personnel, and remained imprisoned in paperwork.'[8] The chief of the General Staff often took second place to the vice-chairman of the Supreme War Council, and had practically no authority over the directorates of arms.

A decree of 31 July 1888 tried to rationalize the work of the Ministry of War's directorates, which were still cluttered with multiple advisory committees and technical branches. These cells were replaced by several 'technical committees', which, although under the nominal authority of the directors of arms, could be consulted by the Minister of War on 'the organization of the arm or of the service, on the rules or methods that govern how it functions, on the improvements to be made to the materiel, on the work to be carried out – in short on anything concerning the adaptation of the arm.'[9]

Freycinet hoped that this would result in a clearer separation of the administrative role that had been assigned to the directorates, and the role of technical and tactical thought that belonged to the technical committees. A decision of 23 October 1887 also created a review commission for inventions that concerned the army.

*

By fragmenting the high command, the Republican regime may have reduced the supposed threat of a military *coup d'état*, but also prevented military thought from being centralized. Military thought was stimulated by the desire for revenge against Germany, and the arena in which it could take place was initially filled by the directorates of arms, which had specially-formed commissions rewrite the regulations using lessons drawn from the war of 1870. New training regulations were issued for the infantry, for example, in 1875, and for the cavalry in 1876.

The arms' organizational structures of change were based on 'tactical laboratories'. These were mostly schools of advanced training, such as the Cavalry School at Saumur in the Loire valley. In addition, the scientific arms could depend on the technical schools of the various army corps. The School of Poitiers, and later that of Mailly in particular, were where the main artillery experiments were carried out. The school of the 5th Regiment of Engineers at Versailles was the Railway School. Although the infantry had no school of advanced training, it did have the Musketry Training School at Châlons in Champagne for experimenting with small-arms and clarifying how they should be used in combat. For experiments of a more tactical nature, the infantry used the battalions of foot *chasseurs* (light troops).

### A conservative shield: the army corps generals

The Law of 27 July 1873 was one of the great pieces of legislation for reorganizing the army. It created permanent army corps on the Prussian model, which existed even in peacetime and were each linked to a specific military district. But the commanders of these army corps were answerable at this time only to unstable governments. They were therefore quick to acquire habits of independence, just as were the directors of arms and directors of services. Their habitual independence was strengthened by the fact that they were responsible for appraising all officers, including those of the General Staff. The sole instance of their independence being disputed was short-lived. It happened in 1898, when the Minister of War, Freycinet, tried to place members of the Supreme War Council above them as inspectors-general. These inspectors were to provide objective information on 'the fitness of the instrument of war that has been prepared in this way'.[10] But the inspectorates-general were disbanded in 1901 by a subsequent Minister of War, General André, on the principle that the real inspector of troops 'is the man who commands them. It is for him to ensure they are constantly ready to fight.'[11] Not until 1912 did a new decree stipulate once more that the ten generals belonging to the Supreme War Council were to be entrusted, in peacetime, with permanently inspecting the army corps and cavalry divisions, as well as with supervising the annual large-scale manœuvres.

Bolstered by their independence, the army corps commanders took charge of the large-scale manœuvres from the outset. In the absence of regulations, they themselves issued tactical directives for the units in these manœuvres, and this practice lasted until the start of the twentieth century. These generals had been nurtured in the anti-intellectualism of the army of the Second Empire, and for decades only a few personalities among them took much part in theoretical thought. With an average age of well over 60 years, these men at the peak of their careers made no effort to keep themselves up to the tactical level corresponding to the rapid technical developments of the time. Often imbued with the idea that 'war can be learnt only in war', they largely scorned the regulatory manuals produced by the 'young men' of the directorates, schools or staffs. We must remember that it was the army corps commanders who appraised these young men. Since these commanders were also in charge of supervising the instruction and training of the troops, we can already see why the doctrine decided upon at the top might not be reflected in actual reality. We can also see why a gap opened between these conservative men who held power and the young, qualified staff officers who in the mid-1880s started to assist and observe them.

Shortly before the war, the generation of 'Empire men' gave way to that of the first qualified staff officers produced by the initial classes of the Staff College (or by the advanced staff courses from which the College emerged). This new generation of generals had received a training that was still badly flawed, and did not supplement its training later. It was a more politicized generation than its predecessor and was barely any more innovative. Three-quarters of its members would be *limogés* (dismissed) for blatant incompetence, starting in the opening weeks of the Great War.

### The golden age of the Staff College
One of the priorities in the wake of the defeat of 1871 seemed to be a reform of the French staff corps. Yet it took nine years of discussion and the labours of two commissions to create an equivalent of the Prussian *Kriegsakademie,* or War Academy.

The fact is that much dithering occurred over what objective should be given to this future institution. Should it train staff officers, or produce élites destined for the high command? In February 1875, the Minister of War, General de Cissey, decided on the creation of special, two-year courses of advanced training. In March 1880, these courses became the *Ecole supérieure de guerre,* or Staff College. Its objectives were in line with those set out in 1874 by a commission chaired by General Henri Castelnau: 'To give a broad and detailed education in the higher branches of the art of war to those officers of any arm who are deemed capable ... In addition, to train officers for staff duties.'[12]

This dual purpose, which did not yet seem contradictory, was offset for the time being by a first-rate teaching body that attracted all the military intellectuals of that era. These professors occupied the doctrinal void that the officers of the Ministry of War or of the army corps had not been able to fill. The first generation of professors was dominated by the personality of General Lewal. It proceeded by trial and error, and explored in a rather anarchic way all the available military literature, especially the writings of the Prussian victors of the war of 1870. But then the ideas and methods became more focused, and this was due to the succession of officers who were in charge of the military history and general tactics course between 1885 and 1901: Major Louis-Adolphe Goujat dit Maillard, Colonel Henri Bonnal and Lieutenant-Colonel Ferdinand Foch. They adopted the Prussian methods of concrete examples, which meant studying specific wartime actions and then extrapolating what was learnt in order to establish a practical doctrine. This approach had much in common with the experimental sciences that were flourishing at that time, and it proved highly fruitful. Many witnesses reckoned that Maillard's course, especially his analyses of the Battle of Saint-Privat (18 August 1870), marked a turning point in the evolution of the art of war in France by laying the foundations of general tactics (in other words, tactics of the three arms used in combination.)

In 1892, Bonnal took over the course from Maillard. He introduced the *Kriegspiel,* or wargame, to the Staff College, and continued Maillard's work by raising it to the level at which army corps, or even armies, operated. In common with Maillard, he drew on examples taken from the war of 1870, but he also drew, to an even greater extent, on his study of Napoleon's campaigns, using as a starting point the Emperor's correspondence that had been published during the Second Empire. Bonnal had considerable influence. His ideas served as a basis for the 1895 *Field service regulation,* the first real doctrinal document produced by the French that described the manœuvre of army corps and armies (the level of 'large units', or in simpler terms the operational level). Bonnal even had a hand in designing Plan XIV (1898) for the army's mobilization in the event of war.

Apart from their studies of operational doctrine, the professors of tactics had a major influence on how the arms evolved. They supplanted the personnel of the directorates in this role. Examples include Major Hippolyte Langlois, who in 1892 published *The field artillery in cooperation with the other arms,* or Colonels Pierre-Joseph-Maxime Cherfils and Frédéric-Edmond Bourdériat for the cavalry.

Yet the Staff College's great influence produced internal contradictions. The College was a centre of teaching, but also a pole of thought. The regulations of the period 1885-1902 were both its work and the basis of its teaching. But freedom of debate, which was vital for the regular reconsideration of the paradigm, fitted awkwardly with the respect due to the teaching of the same paradigm. Furthermore, the teaching, which at first had been essentially tactical, had come to occupy the operational, or even strategic, plane. Two levels of teaching therefore existed at the same location. The military history and general tactics course described actions at the level of large units, whereas the courses of the arms described engagements smaller than those of a division. Although this combination might seem complementary, in reality it soon became discordant. Nor did the professors have any specific authority. In the absence of a centralized body, their ideas spread only by influence, and that influence declined as those professors who had seen action during the Second Empire were replaced by men who lacked a reputation. Ideas about how the arms should be used might therefore be at odds with the ideas of the directorates, committees or schools, not to mention with what was actually happening in the corps.

The Staff College's operational ideas might seem more difficult to question, given the weakness of the high command. Even so, they came under attack from three sides. The first attack came from certain generals, and drew on the evidence of the South African war (1899-1902). General François-Oscar de Négrier had six articles published in the *Revue des deux mondes* between 1 September 1901 and 1 March 1904, although he had to do so anonymously as 'XXX' despite being an outstanding soldier and a member of the Supreme War Council. In his view, the firepower of modern weapons made Napoleonic schemes unrealistic at any level of warfare. General Charles Kessler shared this view. In common with the British and Germans, Kessler and Négrier advocated caution and the decentralization of decision-making at the tactical level, along with the systematic use of outflanking movements on broad fronts at the operational level. The notion of the 'impregnability of fronts' spread, and some men even described future conflict as a long siege war.

Such ideas were taken up by a group at the very heart of the Staff College, namely the professors of infantry tactics. From the start of the twentieth century, the infantry tactics course was run by three former lieutenants of the 3rd Battalion of Foot *Chasseurs:* Louis de Maud'huy, Philippe Pétain and Eugène Debeney. (Debeney was also a relative of General de Négrier, who was himself a former *chasseur.*) The foot *chasseurs* had a culture that favoured fire and decentralized combat rather than actions in mass. Some of the ideas of these two streams of dissent – the professors of infantry tactics and some generals – found concrete expression in the 1904 *Infantry training regulation.* As a result, it occasionally contradicted the 1895 *Field service regulation.*

### The 'Forum'

The third challenge to the Staff College's predominance came from young, qualified staff officers. The complete reorganization of the French military machine in the 1870s had been a time of intellectual ferment encouraged by the senior ranks. According to General Kessler:

> The high command, keen to foster the flow of ideas and the development of individual initiative, elicited the views of officers of every rank on issues that had hitherto been regarded as sacrosanct. Since this interplay of opinions produced the best results for the development of the main military regulations, the same methods of gleaning feedback were used thereafter in order to settle issues concerning either tactics or national defence.[13]

The Minister of War, General de Cissey, initiated the founding of a network of officer gatherings and garrison libraries – 200 of these libraries existed by 1914 – where the officers were required to give lectures and publish works, especially during the winter period. At the same time, many military reviews were founded or revived. As early as 1872, the *Revue militaire des armées étrangères,* edited by the General Staff, was meticulously using whatever 'unrestricted' documentation was available about foreign armies and various conflicts. From 1873, each arm started its own monthly review. The beginning of the twentieth century saw the creation of reviews of more advanced thought, such as the *Revue des deux mondes,* or the *Revue militaire générale.* The latter was founded in 1907 by General Hippolyte Langlois, a former Staff College professor who was a member at that time of the *Académie française* – the prestigious body that regulates the French language. One of his successors at the Staff College, General Henri de Lacroix, reckoned that the *Revue militaire générale:*

> seeks to inculcate a doctrine among its readers, but this does not mean that the *Revue* is closed to those who fail to share its ideas. On the contrary, it is an organ of free discussion, of candidly open discussion. Here, we are not on an execution ground where obedience must be absolute.[14]

Some of the articles in the *Revue militaire générale* were subsequently reissued as monographs by specialized booksellers such as Chapelot or Berger-Levrault, which also published many books by officers. If we bear in mind that military men could also be published by the civilian press, we can see that the intellectual output was abundant. As General Henri Bonnal noted, 'since the last war in particular, there have been so many books and pamphlets concerning the various methods of using infantry that it would be difficult to estimate their number, even roughly.'[15]

From the 1880s, newly qualified graduates of the Staff College became more and more prevalent in this network and ended up composing almost the whole of it. In the Berger-Levrault catalogue for 1914, the subject heading of the 'art of war' contained 128 publications written by seventy-four different officers, and almost every one of those officers had the designation of 'qualified staff officer' next to the rank. From this profusion emerged not a doctrine so much as complex and diverse ideas that reflected the various trends of opinion among the officers.

By 1909-10, the problems of internal politics were causing less heated debate, and the outbreak of war seemed imminent. Many officers now began to rail against the official doctrine concerning operational matters. They sought to supplant a paralysed high command and overturn the conformity of the units. These 'Young Turks' – a reference to the officers who had imposed their ideas on Sultan Abdul Hamid II by a *coup d'état* in 1909 – were helped by the acceptance they received from the General Staff, which had hitherto been an intellectually empty shell but now suddenly became important.

### The General Staff: a new pole of thought

As the international situation grew more threatening, a new French government discarded the illusion that an 'annual minister' – the average tenure of office of a Minister of War was just a year – could be an adequate substitute for a commander-in-chief. A decree of 28 July 1911 on the structure of the high command substantially increased the power of the chief of the General Staff. He became vice-chairman of the Supreme War Council and hence the commander-in-chief designate. He also took under his control the Staff College and the Centre for Advanced Military Studies.

The Centre for Advanced Military Studies had been created in 1910. It admitted classes of about twenty-five lieutenant-colonels and gave them six months of training in the operational management of armies. The Centre for Advanced Military Studies was meant to become the new centre of operational thought, but had too short an existence before the outbreak of the war to exert a real influence.

The Supreme War Council also took on a new importance as a result of a decree of 20 January 1912. Its members were earmarked to take up army commands and several of them were inspectors of arms, which meant they could monitor unit efficiency. Furthermore, in 1912, an embryonic staff was set up for each of them, and the chiefs of these embryonic staffs composed a committee under the immediate control of the chief of the General Staff. This committee took an active part in both the preparation of future operations and the training at the Centre for Advanced Military Studies.

Yet limits remained to the future commander-in-chief's independence. The Ministers of War retained the habit of taking decisions without consulting him, and above all they excluded him from all political matters. For example, the General Staff was forbidden to contemplate any pre-emptive action on Belgian territory.[16] Nor did the chief of the General Staff have any authority over the directorates and technical committees. Yet the number of committees had begun to rise again. By 1910, the Ministry of War had become a conglomerate of fourteen services and directorates, eleven technical committees and 100 temporary committees. Freycinet had wanted to separate pure administration, which was to be undertaken by the directorates, from technical-tactical thought, which was to be the province of the committees and commissions. But this separation had proved illusory, if only because the work of the committees had financial implications that required the involvement of the directorates. Besides, the technical committees failed to accomplish much.[17] Under a decree of 22 October 1910 they were either abolished or attached to the directorates. The directorates therefore gained in importance, but without coming under the commander-in-chief's control. Nevertheless, a considerable step forward had been taken, making it possible to unite most of the bodies responsible for war preparations and operational thought.

This background situation made it crucial to select the right chief of the General Staff. The government considered General Joseph Galliéni and General Paul Pau, but in the end picked Joseph Joffre. A first-rate engineer, Joffre had spent much of his career constructing fortifications in the colonies. He had an excellent grasp of transportation, having been 'Director of the Rear Area' in 1910, but he had little experience of either staff work or tactical problems. He had played no part in the various doctrinal debates that had constantly ruffled the military world up to 1914, and these debates appear to have been of little interest to him. He did not lack character, as the war would show, but he did lack ideas that would enable him to surmount the prevailing confusion.

Joffre therefore allowed his young subordinates within the General Staff much initiative in matters of doctrinal thought. They were soon dubbed the 'captain-issimos'. Their figurehead was Lieutenant-Colonel Louis Loyzeau de Grandmaison, a former head of the Third Department, whose two lectures at the Centre for Advanced Military Studies in 1911 had marked the start of the domination of doctrine by the 'Young Turks' – a domination that would last until the end of 1915. The body of doctrine that they developed was embodied in 1913 in a *Regulation on the handling of large units* and a *Field service regulation*. These two manuals – which stated that the army 'now recognizes no rule in the conduct of operations other than the offensive' – served as a basis for advanced military teaching and for the compilation of training regulations for the various arms.

\*

Yet this centralization of the high command from 1911 onwards came too late to be effective. Instead, different poles of thought supplanted one another. Some of these poles were powerful but lacked the capacity for steady, deep thought, namely the Supreme War Council, the directorates and (until 1911) the General Staff. The others – the Staff College and the Forum – were richly endowed in intellectual terms, but lacked any power apart from their moral authority. Military thought therefore became erratic and owed almost everything to the quality of the individuals who contributed to it. This quality was largely the result of the new system of officer-training.

## Creating an Intellectual Aristocracy

### A compartmentalized officer corps

From its earliest years, the Third Republic undertook a thorough reform of its officer recruitment and training system. It had to provide the large numbers of officers required by a conscript army, while ensuring they had the quality needed for modern warfare.

The system remained aristocratic in character, despite the democratic nature of the entrance competition and the generous provision of scholarships. Notions of duty were prevalent at this time, and so nothing in the competitions was designed to ascertain the moral qualities of the officer candidates. Moral qualities seemed to form an integral part of the 'officer social order', just as they were associated with the 'social order of the nobility', and they were picked up by cultural infection. We must remember that a military career remained the favoured path of those sections of society that had an aristocratic lineage. Between one-third and one-quarter of the generals had such a background.[18] Almost all the other generals came from a bourgeoisie that had absorbed many aspects of aristocratic conduct.

Duties were bound up with a strict classification between what was noble and what was base. Noble meant seeking a duel with the enemy, standing stoically upright whilst under fire, or sacrificing oneself (which meant much the same thing). Base meant crawling, digging, taking cover, or falling back.[19] Duties therefore had a prescriptive force far stronger than that of the regulations. The same *Ancien régime* model meant that the troops were assumed to lack these noble qualities, regardless of whether they were professional soldiers recruited from the lowest sections of society or conscripts. (The one break with the past was that there was now a belief in the value of education, and hence in the possibility of instilling a few noble notions in the troops.) Since moral worth meant the same thing as professional quality, and was part and parcel of being an officer, it was pointless to try and detect it in competitive examinations. The exams consisted almost exclusively of intellectual tests. They also enabled officers to be arranged in tiers, in a way similar to that seen under the *Ancien régime*.

The new French army of the Third Republic concentrated on recruiting officers by direct, competitive entry to the School of Saint-Cyr and the *Ecole polytechnique*. As a result, the proportion of officers who were direct-entrants rose from 30 to 50 per cent. Then, from 1875, a second system was set up with the creation of NCO schools for the various arms specifically to enable young NCOs to gain an officer's epaulettes by doing appropriate training.[20] Thereafter, 90 per cent of officers came from either these NCO schools or the School of Saint-Cyr or the *Ecole polytechnique*. Yet promotion prospects differed sharply between these two entry methods, despite the fact that the methods produced officers largely similar in both age and social origin. In 1905, 55 per cent of the lieutenants were direct-entry officers, and 45 per cent came from the ranks. Yet of the colonels at that same time, 95 per cent were direct-entry officers, and just 5 per cent were former NCOs.[21] At the Staff College, seventy-seven of the eighty-six admitted to the final class before the war were direct-entry officers.[22]

This exclusivity affected the evolution of tactics in several ways. Firstly, it made promotion dependent on criteria besides that of merit. Many elected politicians, and even some ministers such as Adolphe Messimy, objected to a selection method they deemed 'blind and stupid', and in which:

> completely unknown candidates are ranked solely by whether they happen to give the right reply. This one-off competition stands on the path of life like the monumental gate of a sacred enclosure. Whoever has passed through it – even if he manages to do so contrary to expectations – is proclaimed fit to glide through a successful career. But whoever sees this gate close in his face finds only a stony path to take him to his goal, and can tell himself that he will always lack a kind of investiture.[23]

The discrimination between the two officer-entry methods robbed tactical thought of about half the number of minds that existed, and placed a constraint on the dissemination of ideas. Officers who had spent fifteen years as company commanders were not necessarily prepared to disturb the monotony of their lives in order to apply new regulations devised by high-flying staff officers who had come from a different school culture. Since their own promotion was so slow and restricted, the only motivation they had for applying those new regulations was their professional conscience. The same gulf existed between officers of the active army and reservist officers. Officers of the active army tended to regard the others as members of an inferior category. The effects of this additional split were particularly evident during the war, when half of the officers were reservists.

The body of those officers who had been educated at the top, prestigious schools was also divided into two distinct categories. On one side were the *Polytechniciens* – the graduates of the *Ecole polytechnique* – who had a solid, scientific training and served in the scientific arms, namely the artillery or engineers. On the other side were the *Saint-Cyriens*, who had graduated from the School of Saint-Cyr: since they did not have such a technical training, they instead entered the infantry and cavalry. The result was two groups with different cultures. This additional compartmentalization – the *Polytechniciens* had a tradition of saluting only officers of the artillery and engineers[24] – favoured neither the exchange of ideas nor the cooperation that was necessary between the infantry and artillery. Above all, the fact that the officers of the combat arms lacked a technical culture resulted in their ideas constantly lagging behind the innovations of the time.

The rivalry between the graduates of these two schools gradually swung in favour of the *Saint-Cyriens*, since the *Polytechniciens* showed an increasingly marked preference for civil careers. Two factors hastened this process. The first was that a large proportion of entrants to the Staff College were initially *Polytechniciens* (45 per cent in 1883). Many *Saint-Cyriens* soon became concerned that the *Polytechniciens* might therefore monopolise the positions of command. Hence the purely scientific parts of the entrance examination were removed, and quotas were applied for each arm.

The second factor was the bad atmosphere that prevailed in the army at the start of the twentieth century. It drove the *Polytechniciens* to leave the service in mass. As a result, the proportion of second-lieutenants in the artillery who had come from the *Ecole polytechnique* declined from 42 per cent in 1900 to 20 per cent in 1913.[25] By the eve of the war, the intellectual aristocracy consisted predominantly of *Saint-Cyriens*. Out of the seventy-seven direct-entry officers in the 38th class of the Staff College (1912-14), only nine were *Polytechniciens*.[26]

To these splits between direct-entry officers and those who had come from the ranks, between active army and reservist officers, and between *Saint-Cyriens* and *Polytechniciens*, can be added the split between staff officers and regimental officers. These divisions did not make for a strong 'idea economy'. Furthermore, the arrangement of officers in levels in accordance with their origin was reflected in the way that responsibility and honours were allocated, and also in the distribution of values and thinking. The doctrinal speculations and tactical thoughts published in reviews or by military booksellers were reserved for the 'nobility of the competitive examination'. The other officers merely took part in technical commissions and more obscure tasks. This compartmentalization was unwritten but it was also unbending.

Few senior officers wrote a book of doctrine. The number of 'noble' officers who prided themselves on knowledge of a purely technical nature – a lowly field compared with Clausewitzian speculations – became fewer and fewer after the departure of the *Polytechniciens*. Two different worlds existed side-by-side. In one, there was much discussion, but not about technical innovations. In the other, the technical innovations were tested, but there were no means of discussing them. The lack of interest felt by the first of these worlds in technical matters made a certain freedom of experimentation possible in the second.

Ideas, therefore, had to cross barriers. If they did not fit in with the values and habits of the 'next-door' group, they would find it difficult to pass. This was the case, for example, with the abandonment of close order in training, as we shall see in due course. (Formations in close order have tightly-packed ranks.) Conversely, ideas might win supporters 'next-door' but be transformed, or even developed. On the other hand, horizontal communication between men of the same category was eased by the fact that the officers concerned had common bonds: a shared culture that had been inculcated at the same military school, and possibly additional ties from having been in the same class at that school.

To this social compartmentalization must be added the different cultures of the arms, the uniqueness of the colonial army, and also the political 'chapels' that I will explain in due course. The French officer corps was a mosaic that generated a whole variety of ideas.

### Educated minds

The competitive entrance examinations to Saint-Cyr and the *Ecole polytechnique* sought simply to pick educated minds from among the 'enlightened classes', namely the old aristocracy, and the upper and middle bourgeoisie of public officials and employees in the liberal professions. The average level of knowledge was certainly higher than it had been during the Second Empire, but the entrance examinations did not reveal the qualities of imagination and authority, a spirit of initiative or an openness to change.

Military qualities were therefore supposed to be picked up in practical training exercises that were carefully thought-out, including musketry, working with drill units, camps and demonstrations. In 1905, these exercises began to be supplemented by a year spent serving in units, in order to close the divide that existed between the officers from the military schools and the recruits. Those pupils who were intended for the cavalry were selected when they entered Saint-Cyr, through their own choice and practical tests, and formed a squadron of around seventy-five men. As for the rest of the training, the historian Raoul Girardet described it as:

> purely academic and without much openness to the outside world. ... The prospective officers were given an authoritative teaching that sought to increase their knowledge. It required considerable efforts of memory, but seemed in no way to favour research or work on their own initiative. The mindset that tended to be formed there – the mindset of a good pupil, of a good, docile subject, submissive and passive – was bound to run the risk of developing, in the empty monotony of garrison life, into the mindset of a timid and routine-ridden little bureaucrat.[27]

There was no inclination to intellectual boldness. Nor does this theoretical teaching appear to have been particularly successful with the pupils, especially at Saint-Cyr. A 'cold jail that closed in on the teenager'[28] was how Lieutenant-Colonel Jean-Baptiste Montaigne remembered Saint-Cyr, and good pupils were bullied by their comrades, at least until the end of the nineteenth century.[29]

Unless they were infantrymen, officers on leaving their school of initial training had to attend the advanced training schools run by the various arms, for periods that changed with the passage of time. Until 1912, graduates of the *Ecole polytechnique* had to spend a year at the Applied School of Artillery and Engineers at Fontainebleau,[30] in order to acquire the technical training they needed as well as further military training. Cavalry officers went to Saumur. Officers who came from the ranks were trained directly in the NCO schools of the arms. These various schools were under the authority of the Ministry of War's directorates. As such, they were the guardians not only of their arm's technical knowledge but also – and probably to an even greater extent – of its traditions and culture. They therefore shared a spirit of parochialism that was all the stronger because of the rarity with which officers from different arms met.

The vast majority of officers received no other training during their career than what they had been taught at their school. But those officers who had higher ambitions could apply to the Staff College. Its competitive entrance examination was open to soldiers who had been an officer for at least five years, including three spent serving in a unit. Between eighty and 100 places were available in each annual class. (It was also possible for a few top-notch captains or field officers, such as Galliéni, to be awarded a direct Staff College certificate, if they took a special examination that was equivalent to the graduation tests.) At first, since appraisal was decentralized to army corps level, the most outstanding officers preferred to make sure they were promoted by remaining in their regiments rather than passing the Staff College's entrance examination. This meant that the Staff College was initially a 'school for the second-rate'. The only way of shedding this reputation was openly to advance the careers of qualified staff officers. This resulted in a rapid rise in the Staff College's selection rate,[31] and a corresponding rise in resentment directed at qualified staff officers. We should note in passing that the supposedly 'second-rate' officers of the Staff College would be the ones in control in 1914.

Preparing for the Staff College's competitive entrance examination – and this was also the case for admission to Saint-Cyr – required learning almost by heart 'a vast amount of specialized knowledge that was as indigestible as it was pointless', or so Bonnal reckoned.[32] This knowledge had little relevance to the daily routine of these young officers for many years to come. For example, the entrance examination of 1906 required candidates to describe an historical campaign (a choice between the 1807 campaign up to the Battle of Friedland and the German 3rd Army's operations on 19 August 1870), write a paper in German, draw a map of the Alps or Pyrenees, and describe a problem of political geography – the subject nationalities of the Austro-Hungarian empire or the positioning of the British colonies to facilitate naval movements. The candidates were also asked to describe the peacetime organization of the four arms and of an army corps, explain the role of forts and intermediate defensive works, and resolve a tactical problem.[33] As in the competitive examinations for direct-entry officers to Saint-Cyr, no attention was paid to qualities of character or command, even though, paradoxically, manuals and lectures were full of notions of morale or *cran* (guts).

Each of the two years that an officer spent studying at the Staff College was divided into six months of theoretical courses and six months of work outdoors. The theoretical courses focused on analysing examples of situations that had actually occurred in war, and almost all of these examples were drawn from Napoleon's campaigns and the war of 1870. Between 1900 and 1910, these tactical studies took up about 40 per cent of the time, with the rest being devoted to staff work, such as mobilization, railways and geography. The summer term was used to visit the eastern frontiers of France and study the battles of 1870-1 on the terrain where they had been fought. During this term, the officers also took part in various simulations and 'staff rides' (exercises designed to study tactical problems on the ground), and they observed the annual, large-scale manœuvres.[34]

Despite its fullness, this training programme was too short and theoretical to produce military commanders. By the end of their training, the newly qualified staff officers had an average age of barely more than 30 years. Their practical experience amounted to a few years in a company or a battery, while their theoretical knowledge consisted of two years spent studying high-level actions. This mismatch between what they had experienced and what they had learned produced several misunderstandings. The qualified staff officers tended either to extrapolate tactical considerations to the operational level or else, in contrast, to speculate in an abstract way on spheres that they did not encounter for real until at least twenty years after leaving the Staff College. In the meantime, they were obliged to spend a period serving on the staff, in accordance with a law passed in 1889. They therefore had an abrupt transition from Napoleon's dazzling campaigns to years of purely administrative labours or 'office-work'. Although the holding of high commands was the second objective of the Staff College training, officers did not attain these positions until long after they had been taught. By then, what they had learned at the Staff College might no longer be appropriate, and in many cases it had gone stale. Bonnal reckoned that 'office-work took a keen, vigorous officer, highly intelligent and enthusiastic, and turned him into a needy man who could not think for himself and who would look for answers in the *Journal militaire* or in archival documents instead of using his own judgement'.[35]

According to Bonnal, it was necessary to distinguish, as the Germans did, between staff officers in the real sense of the term, who would assist generals with their work in wartime, and mere archivists who were fit for office-work. In 1906, the Germans had 250 real staff officers and 500 assistants, whereas the French had 950 officers, including 650 qualified staff officers, who attended to the whole range of bureaucratic tasks.[36] In Germany, officers spent three years studying at the *Kriegsakademie*, where the teaching was more tactical than at the French Staff College. The best graduates from the *Kriegsakademie* then served tours of probationary duty on the General Staff. In France, an attempt was made to add a third year to the Staff College course, for the best of the officers who were in training. But this attempt was aborted, so there was no additional training until the Centre for Advanced Military Studies was created in 1910, and just four annual classes studied at the Centre before war broke out. Nevertheless, the qualified staff officers, and in particular those who served in the prestigious staffs of the Ministry of War or of the army corps of eastern France, tended to consider themselves 'the High Priests of the profession, the repositories of the True Faith'.[37] That was the opinion of the British General Edward Spears, who had long dealings with them. This caste was not exactly esteemed by the rest of the army. But within this caste was an entire intellectual élite – and since this élite was unable to seek glory on the battlefield, as it now had few chances of finding itself on one, it instead sought recognition through what it wrote.

### The colonial school

At the same time as the officer corps was arranged in tiers by military schools and competitive examinations, part of it was acquiring campaign experience once more during the new colonial venture that continued in the main from 1880 to 1905. The experience of colonial warfare would have a delayed and indirect impact on the evolution of the French army's tactical concepts.

The colonial troops were initially naval troops, or marines. Until 1880, they were not held in particularly high regard, and their officers were picked from the bottom quarter of the names as they were ranked by the military schools. But in 1881, the allure of expeditions in Africa or Indochina began to attract those who were at the top of their class,[38] along with some talented, regular officers such as Lieutenant Hubert Lyautey. Since the colonial troops were far more open to the lower classes,[39] the *marsouins* and *bigors* (as the colonial infantry and artillerymen were nicknamed), soon acquired a reputation as hooligans. They reinforced that reputation through their habits of independence, or even outright disobedience, while on overseas expeditions.

Yet colonial actions were of little interest in mainland France. They were often one-sided and limited in scale. The methods that were used – flying columns and pacification, including the 'oil-stain' approach of progressively expanding areas that had already been pacified – were nowhere to be found on the curriculum in military schools.[40] In Berger-Levrault's catalogue for 1914, just seven historical works out of 169 were devoted to the colonial actions of any country. General Bonnal even commented ironically about the articles by General de Négrier that appeared in the *Revue des deux mondes:* 'Would he want the operations of the great Balmaceda or the retreat from Bang-Bo to be studied in depth at the Staff College?'[41] Nevertheless, Bonnal conceded that tactical understanding:

> develops better and more quickly among young officers who have been on campaign in our distant possessions, when compared with their less fortunate comrades. While on exercises and manœuvres, officers with campaign experience generally show a high degree of decisiveness and ability to take in a situation at a glance. Once acquired, these qualities last until the end of a career.[42]

Colonial officers found themselves faced with a whole range of situations, and developed a pragmatism in striking contrast to the formalism of the home army – a formalism that they regarded as 'Prussian'. Officers serving overseas learned the importance of logistics and were able to carry out combined-arms operations for real, even if on a modest scale. They discovered the importance of moral aspects in command: character and charisma. The failure of Colonel Paul-Gustave Herbinger – a former Staff College instructor who lost his head and ordered the retreat from Lang Son in 1885 – simply reinforced a certain anti-intellectualism.

By 1905, campaigns in far-off corners of the world had more or less come to an end. The colonial army re-focused on the French mainland, particularly as colonial officers were obliged under the Law of 1900 to return to the home country every two years before they left again for another colony. Their spell in France, at a time of turmoil, embittered them and strengthened their belief that the army, if not the country, would benefit from a good injection of colonial spirit – action, imagination, a readiness to take risks and the spirit of initiative and self-sacrifice.[43] In this way, the colonial officers helped to develop the 'super-offensive' spirit.

The colonial army supplied France with black manpower, the so-called *force noire,* although it would be 1916 before this manpower really materialized. The colonial army also provided men who had gained combat experience and had avoided the political turbulence of the turn of the century. Many officers – Galliéni, Henri Gouraud, Paul Henrys, Louis Franchet d'Espèrey and even Charles Mangin – would prove their worth after having had the opportunity to complement their experience with a solid, theoretic training. The colonials may not have had much influence on the pre-war debates, but they would contribute to the answers to be found to the challenges of European warfare.


## Modes of Thought

No censorship hindered the participants in the debate about ideas, except perhaps the self-censorship that stemmed from fear about the possible damage they might do to their career. Even so, a certain conformity can be seen in both the subjects they addressed and the literary form they adopted. No officer could completely shed his specific heritage, whether it was the culture of the military school where he had trained or that of the arm to which he belonged. Furthermore, he was influenced by models, modes of thought and passions. These influences were not the result of chance. Most of them stemmed from the shock of 1870.

*The humiliation of the 'dreadful year': the womb of military thought*

The defeat of 1870-1 was a key feature in the collective imagination of the officer corps. The events of the 'dreadful year' left deep scars and a profound feeling of humiliation. So great was the trauma that all tactical and strategic thought was linked, directly or indirectly, consciously or unconsciously, to this disaster.

Studying the 1870 campaign in detail made it possible to correct some deficiencies. Since the staffs had proved inadequate, the Staff College was created. Whereas the mobilization had been a shambles in 1870, it was organized flawlessly in 1914. Railways had been exploited in a clumsy way in 1870, but their use then became outstanding.

Despite these corrections, the military institution kept the trauma of 1870 alive by endlessly returning to the battles of that year, like a man who has suffered a shock and whose mind is constantly mulling over what has thrown him into disarray. The battles of 1870 were required knowledge for candidates seeking admission to the Staff College. They were the subject of every wargame and provided the foundation of the military training. The French flaws of that time – the foremost of which had been passivity – became an obsession and a spur to act in precisely the opposite way. This pendulum effect resulted in excessive caution becoming 'the dreadful hydra of the defensive'.[44] (A hydra is something that is difficult to eradicate.) Caution therefore gave way to the all-out attack. Confidence in weaponry was replaced with absolute faith in morale.[45] The former attraction to superb defensive positions turned into a resolve 'to attack the enemy wherever he is encountered'.[46] The possibility that France might again be invaded acted as a spur to seek out the enemy on his own soil with a vigorous offensive. The attachment to brightly-coloured uniforms can even be attributed in part to an unconscious desire to avenge 1870 whilst wearing uniforms similar to those of that catastrophic year, to link the future victory with the past, as if the defeat had been just the first phase of one and the same action. Lieutenant Laure reckoned in 1912 that 'the impressionability of our national temperament still prevents us from having recovered from the terrible shocks experienced more than forty years ago.'[47]

As late as 1914, out of the 169 historical works in the Berger-Levrault catalogue, seventy-nine were devoted to the war of 1870.[48] Even in 1917, after three years of fighting on a far greater scale, some men still talked of 'a return to 1870' as a way of criticizing the defence-in-depth that Pétain advocated.

Another consequence of the defeat of 1870 was that it turned the seemingly invincible Prussian military machine into a model for imitation. For the next few years, the French were content to copy that machine's institutions. The Law of 27 July 1872 introduced compulsory military service. The Law of 23 July 1873 created eighteen permanent army corps, each of which was linked to a military region. But a more cautious approach was taken in terms of setting up an organizational structure for tactical evolution. The French army adopted the methods of experimentation and thought (large-scale manœuvres, wargames and case studies drawn from historical reality), but it did so long before it adopted bodies that were capable of making the best use of these methods. The Staff College – the equivalent of the *Kriegsakademie* – was created only in 1880, and it was 1911 before the General Staff began to resemble that of the German Empire.

On the other hand, the intellectual agitation of the 1870s and the quest for the secrets of victory saw the French avidly studying German authors. This was the period when French officers were required to be able to speak German, and when Lieutenant-Colonel Jean-Baptiste Montaigne admitted to having had a revelation when as a young officer he had read the *History of the war of 1870-1871*, produced by the German General Staff.[49] When French officers wrote anything for publication, they felt almost obliged to quote German authors. The most frequently quoted of these authors were Helmuth von Moltke the Elder, Friedrich von Bernhardi and in particular Colmar von der Goltz, the author of *The nation in arms* (1884) and *The conduct of war* (1900).

Carl von Clausewitz was accorded particular esteem. He was quoted by Maillard in his course and became especially important after being translated by Lieutenant-Colonel Marc-Joseph-Edgard Bourdon de Vatry in 1887, and after Captain Georges Gilbert published a thorough analysis of him. Another point in Clausewitz's favour was that he had studied Napoleon's campaigns. The light he shone on that period was distorted by the trauma of 1870 and resulted in an emphasis being placed on the idea of a huge, decisive battle that would decide the fate of nations. Clausewitz's notion that moral strength was superior to material strength also proved highly popular.

In more pragmatic terms, the French closely studied the German large-scale exercises and in particular their regulations. The 1887 *Felddienst Ordnung*, which was far superior to the French army's *Field service regulation* issued in 1883, stimulated operational thought at the Staff College. The 1907 *Felddienst Ordnung* helped provoke the French into developing ideas of the all-out offensive. The German model made such an impression that Colonel Arthur Boucher noted in 1911: 'We are still so affected by our defeats of 1870 and think our neighbours are so strong that the possibility of carrying the theatre of war into Alsace-Lorraine from the outset has never, we believe, been seriously considered.'[50]

The Boer and British methods during the South African war briefly aroused interest. Then the French army found another model in the Japanese army, which in the view of Lieutenant Laure 'gives us this complete paragon as an example, this deification of the soldier that is the Japanese man'.[51]

## The dogma of the offensive

Even the most prudent of soldiers thought that, as Colonel Jean Colin wrote in 1911, 'anyone who wants to win must take the offensive'.[52] They could not forget the aggressiveness of the Prussians in 1870, nor the earlier *furia francese*, or 'French fury', that had defeated the Austrians at the Battle of Solferino in Italy in 1859. Belief in the offensive, the 'perfect and victorious form of warfare',[53] found further support in studies of recent wars. The side that had taken the offensive, it was noted, had invariably prevailed: the Prussians over the Austrians in 1866 and over the French in 1870, the Russians over the Turks in 1877, the British over the Boers in 1899-1902 and the Japanese over the Russians in 1904-5.

Hence the offensive rapidly crystallized into a dogma. The 1904 *Infantry training regulation,* which in this respect echoed all the preceding regulations, reckoned that 'the offensive stimulates moral strength to the greatest degree, and suits the French temperament perfectly'.[54] Every soldier must 'ardently long for the assault'.[55] If all the prescriptions about defence in the 1904 regulation are collected together, they fill no more than five of the 105 pages.[56] So fully did the dogma of the offensive fill men's minds that it distorted almost every tactical analysis and acted as a filter for innovations. Any change in method, materiel or organizational structure now had to have an offensive gloss if it was to be accepted. Every regulation since 1875 stated that 'the passive defensive is doomed to inevitable defeat; it must be absolutely rejected. Only an aggressive defensive produces results.'[57] The regulations added that the best way of countering an assault was to launch a counter-attack with the bayonet immediately before the enemy could crash into the defenders. If the defensive was used, it could only be as a way of conserving manpower: its sole justification was to enable the main body of the troops to act offensively under more favourable conditions.[58] If ground was lost, it was to be retaken with vigorous counter-attacks.[59] In every case, the defensive was an exceptional method. It had to be no more than a way of filling in time, as the prelude for the offensive.[60] Major de Grandmaison and Captain Billard believed that 'you defend only when you have received the order not to attack, or when it is impossible to attack.'[61] Lieutenant-Colonel Montaigne argued: 'In speculations about war, the idea of defence must be absolutely rejected.'[62]

When it came to knowing whether the development of weaponry favoured the attack or the defence, almost every author had the same answer as Foch: 'The improvement of firearms adds to the strength of the offensive and of the intelligently-led attack. History shows this. Logic explains it.'[63] In his book, *The principles of war,* Foch described a situation in which 2,000 men were attacking 1,000. If the rate of fire increased from one shot to ten shots a minute, the difference in the volume of fire being exchanged by the defenders and the attackers would increase from 1,000 bullets to 10,000. (The attackers would now be firing 20,000 bullets a minute and the defenders just 10,000.)[64] But Foch was thinking in terms of rifles rather than 'rifles plus men'. The problem was that the effectiveness of a weapon when used in combat conditions differed from that observed on a firing range, and the defender enjoyed a clear-cut advantage in both material and psychological terms. Furthermore, the powerful weapons that appeared at the start of the twentieth century – machine-guns and quick-firing artillery – were more difficult to use in the offensive than when defending a position.

In 1902, General Kessler boldly made an even more dangerous assertion. He stated that the primacy of the offensive remained valid, despite being complicated by the new weapons, for 'history, experience and logic show irrefutably that modern wars will be less murderous than those of the past'.[65] Every author subsequently adopted this same notion.[66] The explanation for its seemingly paradoxical nature must be sought in the adaptation of combat methods (decentralization and the use of more flexible and widely-spaced formations) and in the resulting increase in the duration of battles. The number of men lost in every hour of combat fell at the same pace as firearms improved. In Manchuria during the Russo-Japanese war of 1904-5, the hourly loss rate did not exceed 0.1 – 0.2 per cent of the combat strength, or ten times lower than the figure for 1870.[67] In addition, these statistical studies invariably indicated that the artillery caused just 15 per cent of the losses, compared with 85 per cent inflicted by infantry weapons.[68] The fact that bladed weapons never caused more than 1 per cent of the total losses did not worry the advocates of bayonet fighting, though admittedly they saw the bayonet as primarily a psychological weapon. Similarly, although artillery fire made a powerful impression in combat, it did so 'less by the losses it inflicted than by its deafening din'.[69]

In looking to the future, therefore, all authors favoured 'musketry' in their analyses. When they wrote of the increase in firepower, they were thinking of long-range, repeating rifles. But their predictions were seriously flawed, since three-quarters of the losses in the Great War would in fact be inflicted by artillery.[70]

Losses may have fallen, but the men became the target of more and more powerful fires that might continue for days on end. They were therefore subjected to a far greater psychological pressure than before. Moral considerations became fundamentally important. When men talked of the power of modern weaponry, it was this terrible pressure that they had in mind. Some reckoned it was impossible to handle the pressure, whereas others asserted the opposite. Grandmaison took the view that 'the improved weapons are to be feared. They have to be reckoned with, not because they are more deadly – for the opposite is in fact true – but because they make a greater impression.'[71]

What was important, therefore, was how the moral strengths of the two sides measured up against each other. The study of human nature using the social sciences, or pseudo-social sciences, that were flourishing at that time became the predominant, if not exclusive, feature in the Forum's debates. This was both a cause and a consequence of the importance accorded to moral strength.

### The attraction of the social sciences

Every school of tactical thought since the end of the Napoleonic wars had emphasized the human factor. Believers in the supremacy of firepower argued in favour of light troops fighting in extended order, but this required the men to be trained to show initiative and individual bravery. Supporters of shock, which was produced by using troops in mass, believed that high morale was essential to overcome the hostile fire.[72] Shortly before 1870, Colonel Charles Ardant du Picq described combats as places of fear and confusion – feelings that were heightened owing to the dispersion made necessary by the effectiveness of modern weapons. In order to try and control this disorder, he advocated a new discipline based on a solid moral education, or even indoctrination. His ideas found echos in Germany (*Innereführung*) and in Great Britain ('inner leadership').[73] Even forty-five years later, when the *Infantry NCO's manual* was issued in 1914, it opened with a sentence taken from Ardant du Picq's *Battle studies:* 'The study of combat must be based on a knowledge of men. It is not the weapon, but the human heart, that has to be the starting point for everything in war.'[74]

The social sciences took off in the final thirty-odd years of the nineteenth century, and went through considerable development and diversification. Théodule Ribot's books, which began to appear in 1870, encouraged people to think of psychology as a science, and 1895 saw the publication of a work that made an enormous stir, Gustave Le Bon's *Psychology of crowds*. The twenty years leading up to the First World War saw the almost simultaneous development of psycho-analysis, Taylorism, Ivan Pavlov's behaviour analysis and behaviourism.

This intellectual ferment influenced the French officers of the time in several ways. An initial trend might be termed 'culturalist'. It drew on Charles Darwin's work, on Friedrich Ratzel's anthropogeography (mankind's geographical distribution and interaction with its environment) and on a host of pseudo-scientific authors. It was constantly drawing on biology. General Bonnal stated at the turn of the twentieth century:

> Biology has made such progress in the past fifty years that it has become a reliable guide for statesmen anxious to increase their country's greatness. If the high command is to fulfil its purpose, it must therefore be based on biology.[75]

These ideas, when combined with an intense nationalism, produced notions of national character that then rubbed off on tactics.[76] Conscript armies were supposed to be representative of society and the national spirit. Tactics, therefore, had to fit the national temperament. 'An infantryman is a man, a man of a race', argued Colonel Louis de Maud'huy. 'The race must therefore be studied, since that is what will determine the organization, training and tactics.'[77]

The French soldier was reckoned to be keen, fiery and full of initiative. Enthusiasm and flexibility, therefore, had to be the basis of French methods, against the supposed rigidity of the Germans. Lieutenant-Colonel Montaigne described the battle of the future: 'The German masses move slowly and with difficulty. Every movement costs them significant losses, whereas the light and flexible French maniples [tactical units] manœuvre with ease, strike accurately and evade every battering.'[78]

Another trend, which extended this initial, 'culturalist' trend, focused on the analysis of individual and collective behaviour. Typical of this school of thought was a book published in 1911 under the title *Infantry*. It was written by Colonel de Maud'huy, a professor of infantry tactics at the Staff College. The book was a mixture of historical studies, reflections on fear in action (which took up one-third of the book) and thoughts on physical education. The recommendations that Maud'huy made in his general reflections included reading books on psychology, physical education and educational psychology.[79] One of its parts was entitled 'Crowds and troops' and set out to apply the *Psychology of crowds* to the military. (Maud'huy corresponded with its author, Le Bon.)[80] He described troops as a crowd transformed into an organized group, and 'inversely every possible means will always be used to try and turn the enemy troops into a crowd'.[81] Combat was primarily, therefore, a psychological confrontation. It was against fear that the infantry fought in war. Nothing other than fear, therefore, was the real enemy of the infantry.[82] The notion that it was possible to control human behaviour scientifically began to emerge.

### The technical backwardness of the Forum's members

At the same time as this passion existed for the social sciences, the officers of the Forum were increasingly out of touch with the technical innovations of their era. In 1911, the President of the Republic, Armand Fallières, told Joffre, the newly-appointed commander-in-chief designate: 'I am pleased to see an engineer officer at the head of the army. War, in my view, has become the art of an engineer.'[83] Yet when we examine the many writings, regulations and works by influential military authors that appeared in the five years leading up to the war, what strikes us is the absence – or at least the extreme rarity – of certain words such as airplane or motor-vehicle. Such materiel would be crucially important in the coming years, yet the military writers actually described a conflict fought with the means that were available at the end of the nineteenth century, such as melinite (an explosive containing picrid acid), smokeless powder, new types of steel, aiming devices and long-range repeating rifles. Maud'huy, Montaigne and Grandmaison thought of infantry combat as exchanges of rifle fire, supported by direct fire from field artillery. Machine-guns, in contrast, were never mentioned, and the new power of quick-firing artillery pieces such as the French 75mm was under-estimated.

In short, these officers were describing what they had personally experienced while serving in a company or battalion, generally in the years between 1900 and 1905. We can also detect the effects of a Staff College education. Some 200 lectures were given at the Staff College during the two-year course. In 1914, just three of those lectures concerned the siege artillery of de Bange's system. (France had a total of 7,500 de Bange guns.) No courses existed on ballistics, nor on the communications equipment and technical aspects of liaison between the arms.[84] The course on topography, or terrain science, was discontinued in 1900.[85] Since 'men overrate those elements of knowledge they possess and underrate those they do not',[86] it was unsurprising that these *Saint-Cyriens* imagined combat in a way that neglected the artillery and reduced it to a mere support role for the infantry, with the infantry's fervour being seen as the key to victory.

The start of the twentieth century saw innovations appear at a faster pace. They included motorization, radio communications and the conquest of the air. Yet little thought was given to taking advantage of these numerous technical innovations instead of focusing on the use of human resources. The infantry remained ill-equipped. Before 1914, it had no range-finders, few good pairs of binoculars, no rifles with telescopic sights, no telephones and no mobile field kitchens. The artillery was deliberately limited to the 'harmonious' proportion of one battery for every battalion in an army corps. The priority given to the numbers of infantrymen stifled the development of the technical arms. It was extremely difficult to find the necessary men for the small branch of heavy field artillery that was formed in 1914. The very word 'artillery' was almost nowhere to be found in the 1913 *Field service regulation,* in the 1914 *Infantry training regulation* or even in the 1906 *Practical instruction on fieldworks for the use of infantry units.*[87]

The paradox was that the French army made many experiments. The annual, large-scale manœuvres saw the successive appearance of machine-guns in 1902, field telephones in 1906,[88] a dirigible airship in 1907 and airplanes in 1910 – just seven years after the Wright brothers had made their first successful flight. The 1907 manœuvres alone saw several innovations being tried out, including a new uniform, light bridging equipment, wireless telegraphy using a captive balloon and posts equipped with masts, and the transport of machine-guns on baggage animals or on vehicles pulled by teams of animals. The mobile field kitchens that were tried out performed superbly, as did two logistical convoys with forty-two lorries, most of which had been hired.[89] These numerous experimentations were a stark contrast with the literature on the art of war, in which they were almost completely ignored.[90]

This inconsistency stemmed from the fact that the Forum's members concerned themselves with 'noble' issues and favoured a 'social science' approach to tactical problems. They were encouraged to do so by the cautionary example of 1870, when one of the reasons for the French army's general passivity had been a so-called 'materialist' doctrine, reliant as it was on the effectiveness of the new Chassepot rifle. They also found affirmation in the words of Clausewitz, which made them think of moral strength as a somewhat metaphysical entity that was capable on its own of gaining victory. Since the proportion of qualified staff officers who had come from the *Ecole polytechnique* was in rapid decline, there was no new generation to take the place of the talented technicians of the years immediately after 1870 – General Jean-Baptiste Verchère de Reffye, Colonel Charles Ragon de Bange and General Raymond Séré de Rivières. The combat arms – the infantry and cavalry – became technical deserts and lagged further and further behind progress.

The principle that technical developments could lead to a rapid and permanent change in the art of war was a recent notion. It only really started to appear in the 1890s.[91] Many officers of the early years of the Third Republic still did not fully accept this notion, and were convinced that war could be learned only on the actual battlefield and not in a study. Some of these men would find themselves in command of large units in 1914, and would then make up the bulk of the *limogés*, the senior officers who were dismissed. Many of the qualified staff officers also made no effort to keep abreast of the art of war. The problem was that there was no continuous training. This meant that most reservist officers were likely to be even more backward, as were the majority of those generals who were recalled from retirement in 1914 to take up commands only to find themselves unfamiliar with the equipment that had been tried out during the arms race.

New psychological phenomena also appeared. The profession of arms was a vocation. This vocation often took shape in adolescent dreams, based on the model that existed at that time. But officers were now finding when they reached maturity that their profession no longer really matched what they had imagined it to be. Furthermore, since the war was expected to be short, the notion of technical adaptation during the course of the conflict simply did not exist. These gaps were starkly exposed once the fighting began. A revealing story was told by Captain Maurice Maugars, an engineer who had graduated from the prestigious *Ecole centrale* in Paris and had been mobilized to serve in the artillery. In November 1914, he was establishing a telephone switchboard in a post office, when a general came in and protested: 'My compliments, gentlemen, but this is hardly the time for playing music!'[92]

## The 'Offensive-Minded' Men

The intellectual background at the start of the twentieth century abounded with uncertainty, and the positivist approach was under attack from all sides. The exact sciences came to be seen as 'strange' following the appearance of relativistic mechanics or the publication in 1910-13 of Bertrand Russell's *Principia mathematica*. Instincts and the subconscious made a powerful comeback with Sigmund Freud and in particular Henri Bergson. Science and materialism were often portrayed as the reasons for the supposed decline of the West, and the attacks on them were loudly repeated in officer circles. The attacks coincided with a revival of the Catholic faith, which was reflected in the life and writings of the soldier-monk Lieutenant Ernest Psichari. Another sign of this religious revival could be found among the army's captains and majors. These ranks were now starting to be reached by some of the large numbers of men with a religious education who in the 1880s had entered the *Ecole polytechnique* and to an even greater extent the School of Saint-Cyr. (In 1887, pupils with a religious education had formed 18 per cent of the class at the *Ecole polytechnique*. The corresponding figure for Saint-Cyr had been 34 per cent, compared with under 1 per cent in 1847.)[93] This growing spiritualism was linked to a deep concern about the French army's inferiority in the face of the growing threat from Germany and frustration over the high command's inability to confront that threat.

### The 'Young Turks' movement

The movement that led to the notion of the all-out offensive dominating the army's intellectual landscape began as an officer revolt arising out of the discontent of the radical years 1899-1909. The tactical concepts generated by the Staff College or by the directorates of arms caused much controversy at that time, and a lack of clarity prevailed as to what changes were necessary. A rift opened between the corps of generals, which was highly politicized, and the young officers. This was the period when 'Captain Jibé' noted that 'the current generation of captains, or even field officers, is most astonished to see how little its tactical notions conform with those of most of our generals. In this respect, unity of doctrine in our army is far from being attained.'[94]

After the war, Joffre's memoirs – which were undoubtedly ghost-written by officers – described the turn of the century as a time when:

> the high command's notions had become antiquated as it grew old. A period of turbulent politics had made it wary, and its scepticism and impotence were evident. It was against this backdrop that a young, fervent body of opinion believed it had constructed a body of doctrine in keeping with the traditions of war, and it let itself be carried away by its faith and enthusiasm into dangerous exaggerations.[95]

Joffre then described 'a small core of soldiers, bold, educated and hard-working, who revered energy and the mastery of character'.[96] These men decided to shake the high command out of its inertia and revitalize some apathetic units. During an exercise in 1907, Lieutenant-Colonel de Grandmaison told General Alexandre Percin:

> The regulation will be changed. There are a number of us young officers who are strongly convinced of the correctness of our ideas, and of the superiority of our theories and methods, and we are firmly resolved to make them prevail despite all opposition.[97]

This movement gained strength from the surge in nationalism that followed the Agadir affair of 1911. It benefitted from political changes (Raymond Poincaré became President of the Council of Ministers in 1912 and President of the Republic the following year.) But in no sense can the movement be seen as the expression of a reactionary army that had regained favour. Instead, in everything they wrote, these officers carefully avoided any political or social debates, and sought a national consensus in the face of the growing threats.

## The case of Grandmaison

In the beginning was the word of Lieutenant-Colonel Louis Loyzeau de Grandmaison. This is how he was later described by General Debeney, who at this time was a professor at the Staff College and an opponent of his ideas:

> It's impossible to think of a more persuasive man than Grandmaison. With his sharp mind, fiery temperament and generous character, he had great personal magnetism. But he was carried away by his vivid imagination, and the truth was that he had subordinated his judgement to his temperament. Unfortunately, so gifted a man wielded major influence, and his influence created an alluring school for mediocre minds that loved precepts.[98]

Grandmaison was typical of the young, qualified staff officers who took part in the Forum in the ten years leading up to the First World War. He was influenced by the pre-social sciences, especially by the psychology of crowds. Moral factors, 'the only ones that count in war', could be found on almost every page of his writings. He referred to the South African war, as an illustration of what not to do, and to the Russo-Japanese war in Manchuria, in which he always held up the Japanese army as the model to be imitated. But it is clear that he was drawing examples from these wars purely to support his theories and not to serve as the basis for a debate.[99] At a time when he had commanded nothing larger than a battalion, he was speculating about how large units – army corps or armies – should fight. We therefore find a mix of concepts drawn from his time as a battalion commander and broadened with abstract, or even philosophical, considerations. He also mistrusted any solution based on new technology. The words 'airplanes', 'machine-guns' or 'heavy artillery' never appeared in his writings. When he asserted in 1911 that reserves would never be able to come up in time if they were kept in the rear, he failed to consider motor-lorries or even railways.

In his book, *Infantry training for offensive combat,* first published in 1906, Grandmaison summarized the experience he had acquired whilst commanding the 1st Battalion of the 30th Infantry Regiment, and attacked the formalism that prevailed in most units. His conclusions were hardly original: ultimately, modern combat was more terrifying than deadly, and the offensive was still possible under certain, strict conditions. What was needed was a combination of permanent, massive firepower support, from artillery in particular, and an aggressive spirit fostered right down to the lowest echelon. The difficulty in exercising command under fire meant there was little point in fussing over combat formations. What was really important was to elevate the men's morale, so they carried the fight through to hand-to-hand combat.[100] Grandmaison pressed for more realistic training, especially where musketry was concerned.

Grandmaison was bolder in the two lectures he gave at the Centre for Advanced Military Studies, which were published in 1911. He criticized the 1895 *Field service regulation,* and in particular the advanced-guard method that had been developed at the Staff College. He thought this method would be dangerous in the face of the outflanking movements used by the Germans. Instead, he advocated achieving security by concentrating the attacking troops well forward, and by being audacious in the offensive so as to upset the Germans' preconceived timetable and dislocate their strict march procedures.[101] 'In the offensive', he argued, 'rashness is the best safeguard.'[102]

To catch his audience's imagination, Grandmaison developed a simplistic and uncompromising way of expressing himself. He used arresting phrases, most famously of all when he concluded one of his lectures with the words: 'Let's go to extremes, for it is possible even that may not be enough.'[103] It is important to note that at the same time as he was openly criticizing the 1895 *Field service regulation,* he was head of the Third Department of the General Staff – the body responsible for implementing that very same regulation. On being mobilized in 1914, he commanded the 153rd Infantry Regiment. He was wounded, but returned to the front to command the 105th Brigade, then the 53rd Division and finally the 5th Group of Reserve Divisions. In each of these commands, he demonstrated sound, prudent judgement.[104] He was killed in 1915 outside Soissons. Few other officers holding so high a position fell in action. He was one of the nine colonels in command of regiments at the start of the war who became *généraux de division* by the end of 1914. That was rapid promotion, at a time when anyone who gave signs of being incapable suffered immediate consequences. Grandmaison had a certain competence, and even if historians have made him carry the burden of blame for the excesses of the offensive, it is notable that he was never officially censured on that score. He was proved right in some of what he said, such as the superiority of the German advanced-guards or the weakness of the musketry training. Grandmaison was a mere colonel in 1914 and can not be saddled with all the blame for the initial setbacks. It was a collective responsibility.

### The spiritualist context

The General Staff's predominance from 1911, and the influence the 'Young Turks' had on Joffre, helped ensure that Grandmaison's ideas served as a basis for the *Regulation on the handling of large units* and the *Field service regulation,* both issued in 1913. This official adoption of his ideas met the expectations of much of the officer corps. It sparked an enthusiasm that Lieutenant Laure claimed 'to have felt was shared by many friends, [and] to have seen encouraged by more than one commander'.[105]

But the tactical concepts of Grandmaison and of the 'Young Turks' became distorted by extremism when they encountered spiritualist movements. This distortion was exemplified by Lieutenant-Colonel Jean-Baptiste Montaigne's treatise, *To win,* published in 1913. Montaigne exaggerated the 'preponderance of moral values in war and the decisive, and almost exclusive, contribution they make to victory'. Montaigne reserved particular condemnation for 'industrial war, where the generals are engineers and the officers are workshop supervisors'.[106] In his view, 'salvation lies in the revolt of the will against reason',[107] and he pointed to the examples of Joan of Arc and the French Revolution.

Lieutenant Laure, for his part, rejected 'the progress in science and in thought, which cultivates at the heart of the most civilized nations the microbe of utopian notions and the germ of personality flaws.'[108] He lambasted public opinion, noting that 'popular support fastens on the mysterious powers of advanced weaponry. ... What an exaggerated importance it readily gives to the scientific nature of battles to come, and to the so-called scientific arms that it reckons will play the leading role in them.'[109]

Montaigne and Laure were not alone in their anti-materialism. Percin condemned the excessive confidence that resulted from the improvements made in firearms – 'a confidence that caused our disasters of 1870'[110] – and he regretted 'the frame of mind of a people who could be given confidence simply by being told a full stock of war supplies existed'.[111]

Some of these writers in particular ended up glorifying self-sacrifice. Montaigne thought that the spirit of sacrifice and the will to win guaranteed success.[112] Captain Billard went even further:

> Dying usefully, that's what the art of war is all about. You die usefully by attacking. If you have enough space (an advanced-guard or a detachment ...), attack immediately by turning a flank. If you lack space, attack immediately by feeding in reinforcements in rapid succession ... So attack, officer of France, and die.[113]

The role of officers, therefore, was to turn soldiers into men who were prepared to get themselves killed.[114] Laure praised those who 'could impassively watch the reaping of thousands of human lives [and] who, with their finger on a map, could suppress the emotions of their heart and give orders in their impassive way: Here we will die, there we will kill!'[115]

In December 1913, during a lecture at the officers' mess at Nancy, Major Firmin Emile Gascouin presented the conclusions of his book, which had been published in 1908 under the title *French infantry and German artillery*. The book explained how losses could be kept low in the presence of hostile artillery. But the chairman of the meeting, a general, took offence, rose to his feet and declared that at Nancy the army was not afraid of incurring losses.[116]

Gascouin's book was deemed too mathematical and proved a failure.[117] After the Russo-Japanese war, the Russians placed orders in France for 100,000 breastplates and belly-protectors made of a special steel that could stop bullets fired from several hundred metres away.[118] The French had no thought of following their example. The steel helmet, whose introduction Langlois had been demanding since 1892, was ignored. The gun shield for the 75mm artillery piece was adopted only belatedly and after much resistance. The individual first-aid kits issued to soldiers were inadequate.[119] Nor was this state of mind found only in France. The German field artillery neglected indirect fire, despite having the necessary technical capabilities, for it was loathe to give the impression of being afraid of hostile fire.[120]

Willpower and the spirit of sacrifice were supposed to pit the superior French temperament against the German superiority in numbers and material means.[121] By 1914, France was making unprecedented exertions in terms of manpower. It was conscripting 5,620 men for every 1 million of its inhabitants, compared with the German figure of 4,120. At the same time, according to Adolphe Messimy, the Minister of War, military expenditure accounted for 36 per cent of the French national budget, compared with 20 per cent in Germany. Yet in absolute terms, it was the French who were inferior to the Germans.

Since the Germans kept extensive resources in reserve, the French ideally needed to win a quick victory.[122] The fervent desire for the assault, as expressed in the 1904 *Infantry training regulation,* had to become what bound a unit's members together and constantly drove them on. The aim was therefore to create an 'offensive-minded man', somewhat akin to the concept of the 'Soviet man' that would subsequently appear in the Soviet Union. This meant that tactical training had to be primarily psychological training[123] and 'the art of touching men's hearts'. Captain Billard even proposed a 'catechism' for the use of young soldiers, assembling maxims that had to be absorbed subconsciously. These maxims included:

- winning means attacking and sticking your bayonet in the enemy's belly;
- victory goes to those who are the readiest to die;
- pitch in, and try to pitch in all together;
- if you no longer know what to do, attack or give it further thought while attacking;
- you must always take action or sacrifice yourself for the others;
- the only good formation is [to exploit] the terrain. Otherwise, be fast, and quick to take cover or fire.[124]

This doctrine also had the benefit of simplicity: 'The beauty of FRENCH MANŒUVRE consists of the simple, direct and powerful OFFENSIVE.'[125]

### A national doctrine

This was also intended to be a totally national doctrine. It rejected the German model. Grandmaison stated in one of his lectures:

> We could not be more removed from the feeling of blind admiration for anything German, which is a degrading feeling. We want to know what they are thinking and doing, not in order to fight like them, but in order to fight against them. Therefore we will not turn to their instructional writings to look for models or train our minds.[126]

The inspiration had to be French. It consisted of a mixed-bag of the Crusades, Joan of Arc, the Napoleonic era, the *furia francese* of Magenta and Solferino in 1859, and above all the *Patrie en danger* – the rallying cry of Revolutionary France that the ancestral homeland was in danger from invasion. The exploits of the Army of the North and the Army of Italy between 1792 and 1799 were inflated to a greater or lesser extent into myths. These exploits had the advantage of being part of Republican ideological baggage and of being shared by every political group. Inspiration was found by glorifying shock actions with fixed bayonets. Laure thought that these bayonet attacks were the main asset of the soldiers of 1793-4, compared with 'such slow, cautious and feeble operations of most wars in previous centuries'.[127] In this respect, Laure was echoing not only the anti-clerical Captain André Chalmandrey, but also Foch, who was a Catholic. Chalmandrey spoke in 1904 about 'returning in a carefully thought-through manner to the victorious traditions of the great Republican era'.[128] Similarly, Foch reckoned in 1906 that:

> denying the change that has happened in warfare is to deny the Revolution, which ... dared to declare war on kings and tyrants and successfully to oppose the

thoroughly and rigidly trained armies of the old Europe with the inexperienced bands of the *levée en masse* that were instead driven by violent passions.[129]

In keeping with the culturalist mindset of the time, men such as Laure concluded that:

> it is in the offensive manœuvre itself ... that we shall find the fighting conditions that best suit the impetuous French temperament. What is its essential characteristic? The answer is the superiority of moral strength.[130]

### The offensive is fashionable

The ideas of the 'Young Turks' rippled outwards through the rest of the officer corps. The network of officer gatherings helped them spread. So, too, did much of the press, which talked up the movement in the often extreme style of that era. A columnist in the *Gazette de l'armée* noted on 28 March 1912:

> Never has offensive-mindedness been so deep and vibrant as in the last few months, and we must join the whole country in rejoicing at this. Everyone feels that nothing other than the heedless offensive will enable our army to triumph in the future struggles, making full use of the energetic vitality of our race, and the fervent temperament of the soldier of Latin origin opposed to the heavy temperament of the soldier of Germanic origin.
>
> This salutary reaction, which has originated in the dangers of these insecure times and in a great quiver of patriotism, has managed to win over every heart and every section of society, to extend its influence right down to the smallest cogs of the army, and to shake up the regulations that were slumbering in a blind pedantry. Everyone has set to work. Our officers have realized that they must exploit this national rebirth of affection for the offensive in order to work with a will to reform their training methods and the combat techniques of their arms.

The same writer reckoned that the allocation of motor-vehicles would be a pointless burden on the infantry, would congest the roads and turn the French armies into 'Darius' armies' (a reference to a king of the Achaemenid Empire). 'We have no need of our cars', he concluded. 'Burn them if they hinder you.'

Ideas of the offensive changed and became simpler as they spread through the compartments of the officer corps. There was the 'all-out offensive' of the qualified staff officers of the Forum, where coherent tactical thoughts overlapped with bouts of exaltation. But there was also the 'offensive' of the regimental officers, who remembered primarily its moral aspect owing to a lack of education and the limited means of training. Finally, there was the offensive reduced to its simplest expression, and that was the offensive of the reservist officers, who formed half of the *section* leaders on mobilization.

Despite generating great enthusiasm, the theories of the all-out offensive did not win universal approval. Many officers – qualified staff officers and others – did not accept them. Most of the army and army corps commanders were opposed, since they had been directly impugned by the Young Turks. General Charles Louis Raoul Marion, a member of the Supreme War Council, concluded his report on the 1912 manœuvres: 'The experience of the army manœuvres has dealt a blow to certain tactical theories, which have been trying to take root for the past eighteen months. The time has come to stamp out these theories once and for all.'[131]

General Franchet d'Espèrey, who had been in charge of the 1st Army Corps since December 1913, was among those who refused to join the new school. He had a methodical style of combat and set a high value on improvised fortifications. Further down the hierarchy, opinions became more polarized. In August 1914, Major Maurice Larcher of the 10th Army Corps described the tactical views of two *généraux de division*:

> In the 19th Division, commanded by General Bonnier, the approach was close to that which Colonel de Grandmaison had advocated so eloquently. ... In contrast, the 20th Division under General Boë looked more to precise orders, a methodical advance and cooperation between the arms. In this respect, it remembered what it had been taught by its former commander, General Lanrezac.[132]

The Staff College was another group that refused to conform, despite today's widespread belief to the contrary. Grandmaison's lectures at the Centre for Advanced Military Studies were direct attacks on the system of advanced-guards that Bonnal had devised and Foch had then developed. (Foch was the commandant of the Staff College at the time that Grandmaison gave his lectures.) Debeney, who was in charge of the infantry course, reckoned:

> during the four years that preceded the war, a period of permissiveness was at its height and the focus was on training officers rather than formulating a doctrine. The notions of all-out offensive, as developed by Colonel de Grandmaison, the head of the Third Department of the General Staff, directly contradicted the notions about the supremacy of firepower that Colonel Pétain and others taught at the Staff College.[133]

The operational regulations of 1913 drew heavy criticism from the former professors of tactics, Pétain, Maud'huy and Emile Fayolle, who faulted them for failing to take enough account of the impact of firepower. As for Debeney, he regarded them as just abstract regulations: 'The ideas did not stem from any experience of war, nor were they produced by an advance in weaponry. They simply came from a concept.'[134]

But according to General Firmin Emile Gascouin, the Staff College at this time was:

> under the strict control of the Military Staff Committee and of the Supreme War Council. It was no longer the College of Military Criticism that it had once been, with some brilliance, shortly after being set up. No longer, therefore, was it a contributor to tactical progress, nor a source of new ideas.[135]

In the years leading up to 1914, France had an outstanding group of intellectual officers. But this group lacked firm leadership and was divided into numerous 'chapels'. Tactical thought tended to be akin to a series of trials of strength, with the smoothness of the debates being undermined by the extremeness of what was said and by the manœuvring to gain political or military support.

*Chapter 2*

# In Search of a Doctrine

In 1900, Lieutenant-Colonel Ferdinand Foch was teaching the Staff College's prestigious course of general tactics. He wondered how it was possible to 'shape the preparation for war, an activity that occurs on battlefields amidst danger and the unexpected, ... by means of this other activity – study – which requires calm, method, reflection, reasoning and reason.'[1]

The French strove to resolve this contradiction, and to define a coherent policy intended to guide the way their forces acted. Their defeat of 1870-1 made it logical for them to replicate at least the tools that had enabled the victorious Prussians to develop their own such policy. By the mid-1880s the French had adopted these tools. Their doctrinal thought was then able to leave behind the trial-and-error approach of the previous decade and establish a body of thinking that seemed solid and coherent. Yet this edifice began to totter several years later, when the methods that the Prussians had inspired proved inadequate for grasping rapid technical changes. Even though it collapsed almost completely on the eve of the war, it was not replaced by a universally-accepted paradigm.[2]

## War Under the Microscope

On 14 February 1912, the mathematician Henri Poincaré gave a speech at the funeral of General Hippolyte Langlois, a former professor and commandant of the Staff College. The science of war, Poincaré said, ought to be experimental, but 'experiments in war were too costly to be repeated without necessity and progress was so rapid that yesterday's experiments soon became unreliable'.

To get around this difficulty, the Prussians had created a sort of imaginary front, from which they drew lessons as well as practical experience. This experimental front was in fact a collection of incidents drawn from recent and historical wars and also from simulations such as wargames and large-scale manœuvres. It constituted a source of information for theoretical thought, as well as a means of testing hypotheses. Each of the successive poles of thought mentioned in the previous chapter favoured one of these tools as a way of drawing on the evidence it needed to impose its ideas.

### What is a doctrine?

We can understand the art of war only if we divide it into different levels of study, each corresponding to an appropriate command. These are the divisions that are used:

- the tactical level applies to the three main arms – infantry, cavalry and artillery – acting either on their own or in combination to accomplish specific missions within the framework of a battle. This level corresponds to a spectrum ranging from battalion to army corps, or possibly even army;
- the operational level (although this term was not in use at the time) applies to the combination of forces for fighting a specific battle that is large enough for its name to be recorded, such as the Marne or Verdun. The corresponding level of command is the army or army group;
- the strategic level applies to the conduct of war in a theatre of operations. This level is not directly relevant here.

Each level has its own 'physique'. Doctrine is the combination of all the concepts that enable the means to be used to best effect at a particular level. We must therefore draw a distinction between operational doctrine and doctrines for the use of arms. Doctrines for the use of arms show what the high command would like the forces to be capable of doing and how it counts on using them.[3] They are the subject of specific training regulations, such as the 1875 *Infantry training regulation.*

Operational doctrine, on the other hand, is more difficult to define. Foch reckoned that operational doctrine, or simply doctrine, was a collection of indisputable principles, 'whose application varies according to circumstances ... but is always pointed in the same direction'.[4] Foch added: 'The same way of looking will first result in the same way of seeing. This shared way of seeing will result in the same way of acting. Soon this way of acting will itself become instinctive.'[5]

The operational doctrine, which more or less amounted to a paradigm, found concrete expression in *Regulations on the handling of large units,* or in *Field service regulations.* These regulations described the combat of army corps – and of armies from 1913 – as well as the general role of each arm in the overall disposition.

The distinction between operational doctrine and doctrines for the use of arms was somewhat arbitrary in nature, for the various levels were not separated by impermeable partitions. Confusion was only to be expected in an era when young, qualified staff captains were required to ponder army manœuvres.

A second source of confusion stemmed from the duration of the validity of each of these doctrines. It was essential that the operational regulations, which described general principles, could be applied to varied situations, and not quickly become out-of-date as a result of technical progress. General Henri Bonnal, the guiding light behind the 1895 *Field service regulation,* frequently referred to Napoleonic principles, which were regarded as timeless. As for the regulations of arms, they laboured under a double constraint. They had to take a lead from the operational doctrine so as to ensure a degree of coherence, but at the same time they were undermined by the speed of technical progress. This speed can be seen in tangible form in the regularity with which the *Infantry training regulations* appeared every ten years between the two wars: 1875, 1884, 1894, 1904 and 1914. The same period saw the issue of just three operational regulations, in 1883, 1895 and 1913.

If we borrow a word from economics, we might say that the various levels of the art of war had a different 'elasticity'. There was a risk of these levels being out of step, or even contradicting each other. The risk was greater if the operational regulation was prescriptive and hence inflexible. Furthermore, in the French intellectual military system, those who devised the various doctrines (the Supreme War Council, the Staff College, the General Staff and the directors of arms) were akin to 'barons', whose relations with each other were based on negotiation and influence. Concerns about rationality often took second place to power politics. The first limitation was therefore one of overall coherence, or 'unity of doctrine' as it is known. But the regulations were also limited by the need for them to be actually adopted by the units. This was something that rarely happened, despite the prescriptive nature of the regulations.

### Setting up the imaginary front

The annual, large-scale manœuvres were the first method of simulation. Starting in 1874, they were based on the German model. Every autumn, large units confronted each other, using tactical scenarios that were often inspired by the war of 1870. In the early years, these large units were a couple of army corps, but from 1900 onwards they consisted of two armies. All the other army corps held their own, separate exercises at the same time. The progress of the large-scale manœuvres was supervised by members of the Supreme War Council assisted by about 100 umpires who were responsible for deciding the outcome of the simulated combats. These manœuvres were central to the system of training and development. They appeared not only to provide excellent training for the staffs, but also to be laboratories on a real-life scale for trying out new materiel and procedures.

Yet the system had its faults. In France, it was instituted before any doctrine existed and even before a stable high command had been created. Apart from the doctrinal independence of the manœuvre directors, already mentioned, the very organization of the exercises contained many unrealistic features. The manœuvres stopped each day around 10.00 or 11.00 am to allow the troops to eat and find billets for the night. In many cases, the corps that were taking part had been given the scenarios five or six months beforehand, and had therefore had plenty of time to prepare. In the German manœuvres, in contrast, instructions were received at the last moment, and no pauses occurred.[6] It is hardly surprising that many observers condemned what they saw at the French manœuvres for being unrealistic. This is how the newspaper *Le Matin* described the combats that occurred during the large-scale manœuvres up to 1908:

> When two forces made contact, the operations became completely implausible and ridiculous. Battalions could be seen dashing with serene impetuosity to assault entrenched positions that would have been impregnable in wartime. Regiments could be seen marching across open fields with magnificent disdain for the gusts of fire the enemy was raining down on them. Squadrons could be seen charging against an entire army corps with a fury that was all the more spectacular in that it lacked any danger.[7]

As time passed, these exercises took on the aspect of major shows for the prominent figures, civil and military, French and foreign, who came to watch them. General Alexandre Percin reckoned that:

What the troops did well was not what delighted a public eager for military thrills. Nor was it what gave the greatest pleasure to the surfeit of excessively senior figures who for some years past had been invited to watch the autumn manœuvres. Instead, it was the ways in which the troops infringed the regulation. It was the bold marches under fire, carried out in implausible formations and followed by furious hand-to-hand fighting.[8]

During this same period, Lieutenant Emile Laure added that: 'Our manœuvres – both map manœuvres and those carried out on the ground – will cease being childish exercises on the day when we stop regarding them as a little war in which everyone strives to reap laurels.'[9]

Under these conditions, the effect of the large-scale manœuvres on the training of the troops and their cadres could be counter-productive. This was clear to authors as far apart as Joseph Monteilhet and General Bonnal. In Monteilhet's opinion:

The large-scale manœuvres were the very opposite of an education. Everything about them was conventional, fictional and incoherent. Officers learned nothing, and the soldiers even less. In fact, it was worse than that. They formed bad habits, whilst their senior commanders learned to be content with appearances and with vagueness, and to be taken in by illusions.[10]

Bonnal thought that:

At the autumn manœuvres, the subordinate units applied what they had been taught, but more often than not with a haste and confusion that were detrimental to their proper training for war. The problem was that these manœuvres were trying to carry out in just a few hours a series of operations that would require entire days in actual conflict. This resulted in countless implausibilities and the overturning of sound ideas that had previously been picked up about approach marches, the use of ground cover, fire control and so on.[11]

It took two or three months for the lessons drawn from the exercises to reach the units, and this lessened their impact. In 1912 and 1913, the large-scale manœuvres even became a sort of ceremony of 'clearing out the cadres'. Generals suspected of incompetence were picked to command the opposing sides, or to act as umpires on horseback instead of in motor-cars. This starkly exposed their incapability, and made it easier to place them in retirement, but the end result was to discredit these manœuvres as a serious tool for preparing for war.

There was more to the imaginary front than simply analysing incidents from past wars. It included another component, which had likewise been inspired by the Prussians, namely the wargame, or *Kriegspiel*. A wargame in the true sense of the word consisted of exercises carried out on special, large-scale topographic maps, using small, lead cubes in red or blue to represent the various units of each arm. Two sides confronted each other, and an umpire decided the outcome of clashes in accordance with specific rules.[12] Variations existed in the form of simple directed exercises or competitive exercises (two opposing players), either on a map or on a 'staff ride' on the ground.

Wargames were popular in the officer gatherings from 1874-5. But in the absence of any official encouragement, and in the face of the indifference of most generals, they then gradually fell into disuse, except at the Staff College. However, Joffre had taken to wargames in Berger-Levrault's offices in 1904-5 under the guidance of General Langlois.[13] In 1911, he made them the preferred method for the rationalization of doctrine that he was undertaking, and the main instrument for training the staffs of large units. A very specific process was used: the army commanders designate did an initial map exercise with their staffs and then had the army corps belonging to their inspectorate play another map exercise on the same lines. The third stage consisted of the exercise being held again, but this time on the ground and with each command echelon playing its role. The results were codified into the regulations of 1911-14.[14] Two series of exercises were therefore organized every year by Captain Ferréol-François Bel. One series consisted of map exercises and was held in Paris during the winter. The other series was conducted on the ground in the spring, at Bar-le-Duc, Auxerre and Saint-Quentin.[15] During the first six months of 1914 alone, Joffre organized seventy training sessions that brought together the army commanders designate and their staffs.[16] Some of the simulated situations would actually become reality just months later, and the staff-work would be far easier than it would have been without those previous simulations.[17]

### The first regulations fail to take hold

In the 1870s, these tools had yet to come into habitual use. For the time being, they played less of a role in military thought than did memories of the war that had just concluded. At the tactical level, each arm sought to produce a rational summary of the lessons of the recent fighting. The work, which was carried out by commissions of the Ministry of War, resulted in the 1875 *Infantry training regulation* and corresponding regulations for the cavalry in 1876 and the artillery in 1878.

Operational doctrine took longer to formulate. The first generation of writers – such as Generals Jules-Louis Lewal, Jean-Auguste Berthaut, Victor-Bernard Derrécagaix and Edouard Pierron – explored every possible approach, while initially shying away from big, strategic principles and concentrating instead on the practical methods of handling large units. The influence of this early output was limited.

The first operational doctrine was the *Field service regulation* of 26 October 1883. It was issued in the wake of the new regulations of arms, and merely juxtaposed the combats of those arms. The cavalry was entrusted with intelligence-gathering, and so it first had to chase away the enemy cavalry. The artillery had to silence the opposing guns and prepare the infantry's action. The infantry came into play once the last gunshot had been fired. This compartmentalization was both the cause and the consequence of a particularism that the arms would continue to display up until 1914.

As for the regulations for the various arms, the 1876 cavalry regulation was rejected after being tried out at the large-scale manœuvres. The artillery regulation covered only the standing-gun drill for the 80 and 90mm pieces. The 1875 *Infantry training regulation,* on the other hand, deserves to be examined in more detail.

The thinking about infantry tactics fitted within the framework of a debate that had been going on ever since the invention of firearms – a debate that pitted the advocates of fire against those of shock. Advocates of fire reckoned that firepower was more important than anything else, and that tactics fundamentally consisted of exploiting your own firepower to the full whilst avoiding that of the enemy. Advocates of shock thought that there could never be a decisive outcome without a massed assault by troops intent on closing with the enemy. The problem had become more acute in 1849, when a foot *chasseur* called Claude-Etienne Minié invented the first rifled musket of practical use in the field. At a stroke, Minié's invention increased the effective range of the musket by a factor of six, to 300 metres. The 'death zone' within which the infantryman had to manœuvre was now considerably larger. This technical innovation seemed to confirm the evolution towards the dispersed forms of combat used by skirmishers or foot *chasseurs*. Yet this path led to a dead-end. Even when soldiers were advancing at the double, at the *pas gymnastique*,[18] they were exposed to fire for a long time. The problem, it was noted, was that troops in extended order, once established near the enemy line, were reluctant to launch the assault on their own initiative. In the 1840s, under the influence of General Thomas Robert Bugeaud, the first officer to make a detailed study of the role of psychology in combat, the French infantry returned to massed fire at short range, followed by a bayonet attack. These methods, which sometimes looked like flights towards rather than away from the enemy, made it possible to gain some successes in Crimea and in Italy. The victories of Magenta and Solferino in 1859, the last great battles won by the French before 1914, made a lasting impression. Losses were heavy and fear widespread, but the French, it was noted, had ultimately managed to overcome that fear.

The infantry regulation of 1867 stuck to an offensive method inspired by that of 1806:

- skirmisher fire to prepare the attack;
- 'decisive' fire, in volleys delivered by a solid line two ranks deep, with the front rank kneeling down and the rear rank standing up;
- change of formation to 'attack column', and attack with bayonets and beating drums.

But then, in 1875, a new regulation appeared. The commission that produced it was composed of officers influenced by their experience of combat in the recent war against the Germans. The commission's preliminary report to the Minister of War set out the principles that had guided the drafting of the regulation. These principles were summarized in true maxims of modern combat, maxims that would be seen again in various forms up until 1914:

- the overriding importance of fire as a method of action;
- the impossibility for any sizeable unit to move and fight in close order, in either line or column, within the enemy's effective zone of fire;
- in consequence, the need to split up the first-line units and have them act in extended order;
- the unavoidable shifting of the combat on to the skirmish line, which formerly had been tasked with just the preparation.[19]

The commission began by noting the complete failure of the three-stage method prescribed by the 1867 regulation. Fire from a two-rank line inflicted such losses that it generally brought the combat to an abrupt stop. On the rare occasions when assaults had been attempted in column in 1870-1, they had almost invariably been broken by fire. The commission concluded that troops massed in columns or in solid lines could no longer manœuvre, fight or even hold a position, when under fire.[20] These close-order formations incurred such losses that they did not even offer the advantage of moral support any more. Skirmisher fire, in contrast, had proved formidably effective in 1870-1 and in most cases had been delivered by men lying down, even though this had not been stipulated in the regulations. Hence this was the method of action that became established, using an 'extended order' in contrast to the 'close order' of lines and rigid columns. Extended order required extensive training of the junior leaders and the development of initiative among the men.[21]

To simplify command, a 'standard combat formation' was specified for the infantry battalion, enabling it to handle any situation. The battalion's four companies were arranged in a square pattern, with two in the first line and the other two 500 metres further back in reserve. Each of the foremost two companies manœuvred on a 150-metre front and with a depth of disposition of 500 metres: one of its *sections* (similar in size to a British platoon) was deployed in a 'chain' of skirmishers out in front, and was followed by a reinforcement *section* and two support *sections*.

Offensive combat, which followed an artillery preparation, consisted of several stages:

- between 2,000 and 800 metres from the enemy: the battalion, in 'standard combat formation' carried out an approach march under enemy artillery fire;
- between 800 and 300 metres: the leading companies advanced by rushes and rapid fires, in order to 'cover the enemy's position with a sheaf of bullets'. The captain in command of each company used his reinforcements and supports to keep the chain of skirmishers constantly 'fed';
- at about 300 metres: the combat line was reinforced by the last of the supports and if necessary by a reserve company. These additional troops produced a density of one man for every 1 metre of front, and 'give a vigorous impetus to the combat line, pulling it and carrying it along by example' up to a distance of 50 metres from the enemy;
- at 50 metres: 'the attack can normally be regarded as having succeeded. This is invariably the decisive moment, for hand-to-hand combat is extremely rare. One final effort, and the attacker will be inside the [enemy] position. The whole line hurls itself forward with the utmost vigour, with drums beating and bayonets lowered.'[22]
- the final reserve company either consolidated the conquered position against counter-attacks, or covered a withdrawal.

Offensive combat, therefore, consisted of 'constantly advancing fire', and the final assault simply translated into tangible reality the crushing ascendancy that fire had already acquired over the enemy. When acting on the defensive, a battalion fought in a 'square' disposition similar to that used for attack, and 'any thought of a passive defence was totally rejected'.[23]

This new tactical context made the company especially important. The company now became the basic combat unit. Its commander, a captain, was the 'conductor of the orchestra', using verbal orders to direct the fire and the movement of his troops. No longer did he merely supervise the execution of orders issued by his superior officer. Similarly, when his unit was in quarters, he became its instructor.

The 1875 *Infantry training regulation* ruptured the tactical formalism of that era. The rupture affected only the company's evolutions under fire, since close order remained the rule for everything else. Even so, it was enough to inspire misgivings. Extended order offended the values of most officers. What General Bonnal described as this 'vast game of hide-and-seek'[24] did not seem very manly. It certainly did not seem so to Captain Lucien Cardot, even though he had sat on the 1875 commission. Cardot was the apostle of shock combat, and was himself inspired by the Russian General Mikhail Ivanovich Dragomirov, who argued that 'bullets are erratic, but bayonets are clever'.[25] On 16 July 1880, Cardot wrote in the *Revue militaire de l'étranger*:

The French are ruining and wearing themselves out in the art of avoiding losses and using even the slightest cover afforded by the ground. They have become too forgetful of the élan, energy and boldness that are vital for decisive actions. ... French infantry today will not advance until the enemy falls back.

Cardot reckoned that 'any tactic that is not energetically and pitilessly directed towards hand-to-hand fighting is a backwards tactic'. Teaching men to take cover was a 'tactic for vendors of field-glasses', and was 'teaching cowardice and moral emptiness'.[26]

The ambition shown in the 1875 regulation to base the infantry's combat methods on actual experience ended up being crushed by the culture of centralized command. The advent of conscription had done nothing to dispel the traditional mistrust of the troops' capabilities. In fact, it had done quite the opposite. The army tripled in size within a few years, but lacked the necessary instructors and training infrastructure. Training was often limited to what had always been done, namely close-order drill on the parade ground, which had the advantage of strengthening cohesion and 'breaking in' the men. The high command was sceptical about the 1875 regulation, and made no effort to impose it. Nor did the intermediate echelons, which were unwilling to yield any of their power to the subaltern officers.

## The 'Napoleonic Men'

By the mid-1880s, the reorganization of the French army had been completed behind the protection of a modern system of frontier fortifications inspired by General Raymond Séré de Rivières. France's new military machine needed a more coherent doctrine than just a juxtaposition of combats of arms, especially as the level on which those combats were described was no higher than that of battalions, squadrons or *groupes* of batteries. At the Staff College, Major Maillard's course on tactics – which became the 'military history and general tactics course' under his successor, Colonel (later General) Henri Bonnal – gradually formulated a body of principles that became a regulation in 1895.

### Bonnal and the historical laboratory

In 1885, Major Louis-Adolphe Goujat dit Maillard laid the foundations for the teaching of tactics at the Staff College through the study of military history. Maillard drew inspiration from the methods of the Prussian General Eduard von Peucker. He himself used two complementary methods. One was the 'historical' method, which studied an example of an historical action in detail, in order to extract timeless principles from it.[27] The other method was the 'positive' method, which consisted of removing a combat from its historical context in order to study how it might be fought using modern equipment and technology. Infantry combat was difficult to analyse objectively, since moral factors played such an important role in it. Yet it should be possible, it was thought, to isolate these factors in a scientific way by making a progressively more detailed observation, as if with a microscope. 'Let's do some microbiology', suggested Foch, and 'then throughout our study the moral qualities of which we have heard so much will appear before our eyes in proportions impossible to predict.'[28] Colonel Louis de Maud'huy added: 'In order to understand an infantry combat, you have to descend into the details. You have to study the companies, the *sections* and even the individual soldier.'[29]

Maillard's successor, Colonel Henri Bonnal, gave a big boost to the historical method, but distorted its spirit with his forceful personality. Born in 1844, Bonnal studied at Saint-Cyr, was a veteran of 1870 and a qualified staff officer from the very first class of the Staff College. He was described by General Arthur Boucher as a man 'in love with his job, highly intelligent, hard-working'.[30] Unusually for an infantryman, he was a horse-trainer. This helped him devise a method of training troops based on them acquiring reflex actions through a process of endless repetition. His method sought to ensure that a soldier in combat, despite being afraid, was capable of acting 'as a simple automaton operated by his leaders'.[31] Bonnal was a staunch advocate of close-order drill and the strictest application of the manual of arms. He applied his methods, apparently with success, while commanding the Gymnastics Training School at Joinville-le-Pont near Paris and in due course an infantry regiment.

Bonnal was transferred to the Staff College in 1888 as assistant to the directorate of studies. Then, from 1892 to 1896, he was head of the military history and general tactics course. He adopted the methods of his predecessor, Maillard, and did much to build on the foundation he had laid. Turning himself into an historian, Bonnal strove to find out the secrets of the most famous of models – Napoleon himself – by going through the Emperor's military correspondence.[32] He studied one after the other the manœuvres of Jena, Landshut and Vilna (now the Lithuanian city of Vilnius), and concluded that he had discovered Napoleon's strategy, 'with which the French had been unfamiliar until then'.[33] From it, he deduced a body of principles that were timeless and intangible since they had come from the 'god of war'. Bonnal, like any good scientist, tested his hypotheses against the Prussian campaigns –

Sadowa in 1866, and Frœschwiller and Saint-Privat in 1870 – which, unsurprisingly, confirmed his theories, even if he saw Field Marshal Helmuth von Moltke the Elder as a mere imitator of Napoleon's methods, diligent but lacking in genius.

Bonnal's course had considerable success, backed up as it was with tactical exercises that he directed in a masterly manner. That success rubbed off on the professors of tactics, who fell into line with his ideas, and then spread beyond the confines of the Staff College. In the doctrinal void of that period, the system set out by Bonnal was completely dominant and served as a basis for the new *Field service regulation* of 28 May 1895. The qualified staff officers who filled the General Staff and who had taken Bonnal's military history course even managed to ensure that it was Bonnal who in 1898 devised Plan XIV for the concentration of the French army. Bonnal enjoyed such prestige that he was personally invited by the German *Kaiser,* Wilhelm II, to attend the imperial manœuvres. In short, the operational doctrine that the French army had been awaiting since 1871, and which would be replaced only at the end of 1913, was almost entirely the work of one man with a high degree of intelligence and a certain persuasiveness.

Bonnal's political views, and murky dealings in his private life, led to his dismissal. But he continued to defend his system against the innovators. In 1904, despite the lessons of the South African and Russo-Japanese wars, he thought that 'the methods of implementation have to be modified to keep pace with the advances in weaponry, but these advances do not invalidate in any way the basic principles for conducting a combat – principles that Napoleon's genius identified once and for all.'[34]

It was Foch who succeeded Bonnal in the chair of military history and general tactics. Foch held the post from 1897 to 1900, but did not make many changes in either form or substance. He took up the idea that modern warfare was derived from the ideas of Napoleon, 'the incomparable genius',[35] and he too analysed Napoleon's campaigns and those of the Prussians. He challenged no aspect of the operational system his predecessor had advocated, a system that was now enshrined in the regulations.

In his book, the *Principles of war*, Foch devoted ninety-six of the 330 pages to the advanced-guard combat that was so important to Bonnal. (As the basis for these sections, he studied the advanced-guard actions of Saalfeld in 1806 and Nachod in 1866.)[36] In common with everyone else, Foch often quoted Carl von Clausewitz, using the French translation of 1887 by Lieutenant-Colonel Marc-Joseph-Edgard Bourdon de Vatry, and emphasized the concept of 'national war; war waged with men; war waged violently and rapidly'.[37]

Yet the historical method provoked many criticisms, not least from General Eugène Debeney in 1937. Debeney was himself a former professor at the Staff College, and found it 'a bit childish to read Napoleon's correspondence in the hope of extracting maxims of war', especially when this was done by someone who lacked any training as an historian:

> From the historical documents, [Bonnal] gleaned those he thought were the most useful for a thesis that was already hovering in his mind. Its outlines were still not clearly drawn, and so, although he was totally sincere, what he was doing boiled down to picking those events that confirmed his thesis while clarifying it.[38]

Debeney was particularly critical of the notion that:

> Doctrine ... would be a bundle of principles containing the secret of victory. The doctrine emerges from either historical studies or quite simply didactic ones. The strategy and tactics of the great captains are analysed. The quintessence of their ideas are extracted from the distilling apparatus, and on the flasks are stuck labels reading 'principles'. These principles are then commented on, and adapted to the present moment. They are invested with an attention-grabbing form that is both technical and full of imagery, and the dish is served with 'Doctrine' sauce.[39]

Furthermore, the French theoreticians in using the historical method contributed to a degree of confusion. The problem was that they focused on the study of battles – Austerlitz, Waterloo, Wœrth and Saint-Privat – and then extended their conclusions to every level of warfare.[40] For Napoleon, tactics, operational art and strategy were practically one and the same, since he annihilated the main body of the enemy's forces in a single stroke and forced him to come to terms. As a result of using Napoleon as a model, the French theoreticians simply could not imagine clearly differentiated orientations being adopted at the various levels of the art of war. In 1870, the defensive was waged on every level, and in 1914 the offensive alone was undertaken. In addition, the concepts of offensive and defensive remained highly abstract. We should also note that the theoreticians concentrated solely on the campaigns of Napoleon and the Prussians, and so they came to think of operations as being exclusively mobile. Slow and methodical operations were ignored, such as those in Virginia in 1864 during the US Civil War. These were special cases, exceptions that did not call the general theory into question.

### The imperial paradigm

We shall now examine the Napoleonic system in detail, as Bonnal saw it, and as it was described in the 1895 *Field service regulation*. The cavalry was several days' march out in front of the disposition in which the army was manœuvring. It was responsible for scouting, and for providing a zone of protection around the infantry columns so as to prevent any surprise. It had to make contact with the enemy and reconnoitre his disposition. It was organized into autonomous cavalry divisions that were capable of either acting in mass to drive off the opposing cavalry or of seeking information by means of small detachments.

Some tens of kilometres behind the cavalry were the first-line security detachments, which consisted of strengthened battalions. These detachments complemented the cavalry's action and covered the army's deployment. Then came the columns, preceded by a combined-arms advanced-guard and covered by flank-guards. As Bonnal himself stated, advanced-guard combat 'dominated every doctrinal issue'.[41] It was a fairly complex subject and would cause bitter arguments. In the general tactics course of 1892, the advanced-guard was described as follows:

> The advanced-guard – regardless of whether it consists of a detachment, an army or even an army group – is a fraction entrusted with reconnoitring the enemy, with protecting the main body of its forces from surprise, with obtaining for

commanders the time and means to take action free from any interference, and with making possible the manœuvres that are intended to deliver the main attack against the enemy's weak point.[42]

Hence the advanced-guard was both an intelligence-gathering body and a shield behind which the commander, like a chess player, could deploy his forces and plan his manœuvre. By the time this preparatory phase came to an end, the commander had concentrated as many means as possible opposite the decisive point and could bring about the 'event'. After the bulk of the artillery had directed a hail of fire against the selected point, it was necessary, Foch argued, 'to pounce, but to pounce in strength and mass, for that is where safety lies'.[43] The last of the available reserves were then used to exploit the 'event', or to limit the consequences of a setback.

In short, it was a play in three acts: preparation, decisive action and exploitation. It conformed with the three principles that Foch set out in 1900, namely security, freedom of action and concentration of effort. This system had a universal appeal. For example, Plan XIV – the plan of concentration devised by Bonnal – envisaged one army assembled as a general advanced-guard near Nancy, three armies forming the main body on the front Epinal – Mirecourt – Commercy, and one army in reserve near Chaumont. This assembly disposition made it possible to respond to any eventuality.[44] The same procedures also existed at the level of the infantry division. They were fully in accord with the new regulations for the infantry, the so-called 'queen of battles'.

### Fifes and drums

In 1883, the Minister of War formed a commission to produce a new infantry regulation. This work led to the *Infantry training regulation* of 29 July 1884, the first in a long series of regulations, instructions, amendments and drafts issued in 1884, 1887, 1888, 1889, 1894, 1901 and 1902.

The 1884 regulation tried to correct a lack of precision and skill at manœuvre, and therefore sought to describe even the most minor of movements in abundant detail. As memories of the war of 1870 faded, the school of shock reappeared. Many of the leaders of this school were officers who had been captured at the start of the war and had not seen how Prussian tactics had then shifted towards a more cautious approach under fire.[45] These men reckoned that the extended order, described in the 1875 *Infantry training regulation,* was impossible to control. The result, in the words of General François-Oscar de Négrier, was a return to 'the linear spirit of the time of the Seven Years' War'.[46] Experiments carried out at Châlons camp in 1878 revealed how vulnerable a company was when disposed on a depth of a few hundred metres. Its reinforcement and support lines were therefore abolished. In the 1894 regulation, 'the entire company goes into the line, and can thereby open the action vigorously from the very outset'.[47] Since volley firing had been reintroduced, the company under the command of its captain became a battery of rifles, composed of four 'guns', namely the four *sections*. Pétain, who was a professor of infantry tactics at the Staff College from 1901 to 1911, thought that 'this is the complete negation of the lessons of 1870'.[48]

These manuals were primarily concerned with the assault, which had been neglected in 1875. The 1884 regulation, complemented by the 1887 *Combat instruction,* drew a clear-cut distinction between a firing line, which had just a preparatory role, and a shock unit. In 1911, Pétain described a shock unit as 'a sort of rising sea that must advance without flinching under fire, and assail the enemy in a continuous surge. This is attacking by means of throwing in men, as seen in its most brutal form, a sort of murderous game.'[49] Major Edmond Buat, who was an artilleryman, put this in a more scientific way:

> They are therefore basing the attack's prospects on its shockpower – the product of mass [M] multiplied by the square of velocity [V²]. MV²! Since V does not lend itself to being increased indefinitely – and it even sticks within the well-known lending limits – the completely instinctive idea of increasing M must naturally spring to mind. Sure enough this has happened, and at some autumn manœuvres it has been possible to see large blocks of troops launching an attack, in the open, behind a thin chain of skirmishers – and sometimes even without this mitigating measure – against well-defended and well-fortified positions.[50]

The 1894 regulation was more moderate than its predecessor. Even so, it condemned the excessive search for cover that wasted time, slowed down marches, caused combats to drag on and left the troops under fire for protracted periods. It stiffened the firing line, and within about a year entire battalions were manœuvring while formed in a single-rank line without intervals, followed by shock units in columns. It was thought that this would make the troops less vulnerable, but Pétain protested:

> When under fire, a unit will adopt neither one nor the other of these formations. Driven by the legitimate desire to restrict its losses, it will seek all the protection the terrain can offer, and with this goal in mind it will resort to procedures more akin to the subterfuges used by the Apaches than to the formations prescribed by the regulations.[51]

Since the firing line now had only a preparatory role, the decision about when to launch the final assault no longer belonged to the captains who commanded that line, or even the battalion commanders. Instead, the decision became a prerogative of the *général de brigade,* who was reckoned to be in a better position to choose the point of application that was most suited to bringing about the 'event'. This separation was in line with the stages described by the 1895 *Field service regulation.* When the commander of an infantry division was engaged in an offensive combat, he divided his battalions into preparation, shock and reserve units. The preparation force advanced as far as a 'main firing position', between 700 and 400 metres from the enemy line. It then opened a protracted fire-fight, whilst at the same time the artillery duelled with the opposing guns. The so-called manœuvre, or shock, echelon intervened when the commander gave the order. It either went round the firing line and attacked the enemy's wing or flank, or it 'propelled' the first line up to 300 or 250 metres of the enemy and delivered the assault against the decisive point that had been selected.[52]

The 1902 regulation produced a complete unity of doctrine by conforming with the 1895 *Field service regulation*. But since fifteen years had now been spent in a process of trial and error, the Minister of War required the new regulation to be tried out by the regiments before it was actually adopted. It was then hopelessly invalidated by the lessons of the South African war, which had just come to an end.

## Offensive Combat at the Dawn of the Twentieth Century

The neo-Napoleonic dogma of the Staff College was assumed to be sacrosanct, but after four years it began to totter. It was undermined from 'below', since it was no longer in step with infantry combat, and at the same time was assailed by an emerging doctrinal pole of the generals. But even if the tactical regulations changed, the operational doctrine endured.

### Swept away by 'Forwards!'

The initial rupture had technical origins. In 1886, a commission designed a new weapon, the Lebel rifle. It was a simple and robust model, but had some flaws, particularly in its reloading system, as a result of its hasty development.[53] It was this rifle, modified in 1893, that would be used by the infantrymen of 1914. Its rate of fire was fourteen shots a minute. Even though this was slower than the twenty-two shots a minute of the Mauser 98 issued to the Germans, it was twice the rate of fire of the Gras rifle that it replaced. The main innovation was the reduction in calibre from 11mm to 8mm. This was the result of the invention of *Poudre B*, which produced no smoke, left no residue and was three times as powerful as black powder. The 8mm bullets had a flatter, and hence more dangerous, trajectory than that of the 11mm bullet, which after travelling 600 metres reached a height of 2 metres above the ground and then started to fall. The effective range therefore increased from 400 to 800 metres, and the Lebel could hit a man standing as far away as 3,000 metres.[54] The lightness of the ammunition – which was also used for the machine-guns, the cavalry's musketoons and the artillery's carbines – made it possible to increase the allocations of rounds and reduce the weight of the weapon, since it did not need to be as robust to absorb the shock of the shots being fired. This amounted to a considerable evolution. At a stroke, the effectiveness of an infantryman's fire increased four times compared with what it had been using the Gras rifle (double the rate of fire, and double the range). In fact, the absence of smoke increased the effectiveness even further, for it allowed the infantryman to fire without hindrance and without giving away his location.

At the same time, the appearance of melinite and nitrate-based explosives made the artillery more powerful. A single battery could now devastate a battalion in combat formation at a range of 3,000 metres. These changes were known, but their tactical consequences remained hazy until the South African war, which pitted the Boers against the British from 1899 to 1901. This was the first conflict, apart from the combats of 1870, to be really analysed by the 'positive method' established by Maillard. Within the Forum, it became the tool of thought of those who were the first to criticize the official doctrine. For the infantry, the finding was simple. According to the commander of the 72nd Infantry Regiment, the South African war offered 'startling and dreadful examples of the power of quick-firing weapons'.[55] From now on:

> it must be regarded as a maxim that the terrain within 1,000 metres of well-posted infantry is so completely swept by the sheet of lead that it is out of bounds for any formation other than lines of skirmishers who are lying down and spaced widely apart. This long death zone of horizontal fire is the most powerful coefficient of modern combat.[56]

The regulatory manuals that the infantry was using at that time instantly became obsolete. In order to produce a new *Infantry training regulation*, the Minister of War organized a debate. When the members of the Supreme War Council summed up that debate, they highlighted several points:

- the vital need to make better use of the terrain for protection and concealment during the approach march, which now began some 3 or 4 km from the enemy;
- continuous fire support for movement, especially from the artillery, which was no longer merely to prepare the action;
- more or less disjointed action along the line of contact, by small sub-units making successive rushes and providing mutual support.

In contrast, the issue of the decisive assault proved contentious. The approach zone, which was now several kilometres deep, became a 'slowness zone'. Forward movements within that zone could take hours or even days. The transmission of orders and reports by runners was difficult. Concealment became the rule, so it was increasingly tricky to ascertain the enemy's exact location. Under these conditions, the commander-in-chief had difficulty identifying the point against which the decisive act was to be brought to bear.

Supporters of fire concluded that it was necessary to abandon this notion of the commander's role. They argued that 'the breach through which all the attack troops will dash will open in front of whichever unit is the best led and commanded, even if that unit is a subordinate one'.[57] No longer was the combat pushed forward by reserves that the commander sent against a point he had chosen. It was instead pulled forward from the front. This meant abandoning the concept of the commander as a chess-player, as described by Bonnal.

But Bonnal pointed to Napoleon's genius, and thought that the new weaponry actually confirmed the idea of the 'decisive act': 'The new artillery makes breaking through a point of the front ... a normal form of the decisive attack.'[58] Similarly, Langlois thought that achieving a breakthrough in combat became all the easier with more powerful weapons.[59]

The *Infantry training regulation* of 3 December 1904 was the outcome of this difficult debate. Replaced only in April 1914, this was the manual that guided the French infantry's preparation for war. It therefore deserves to be examined closely. In the foreword, the authors set out the reasons why it had been produced:

The training regulations have to be amended to keep pace with improvements in weaponry and changes made to the length of military service [which was reduced to two years in 1905]. They must also take account of the experience of the most recent wars.[60]

The authors recognized that:

The use of smokeless powder has introduced into combat a factor whose considerable impact is shown at the present time. The ever-increasing speed of the [infantry's] fire and flatness of the bullets' trajectories, and the power and rapidity of artillery fire, expose the troops to greater and greater destructive effects.[61]

The dispersion that had become necessary under fire, and the need to conform with the terrain, dictated 'the use of highly flexible formations that adjust themselves to suit the terrain closely, [as well as the] replacement of the old line of skirmishers with *groupes* spaced at irregular intervals along the combat front.'[62]

The basic tactical unit became the infantry *section* of fifty men. (A *section* was similar in size to a British platoon.) During the approach march, the *section* adapted its formation in accordance with the terrain, so as to keep its losses to a minimum while ensuring that the movement remained uninterrupted.[63] The *section* might advance either united, or by half-*sections*, by squads, or man-by-man. During the actual attack, the *section* advanced as a single unit, in a skirmish line, using rushes and collective fires, and it did so independently of the other *sections*.

This decentralization was in line with the ideas of the radical politicians in power at that time. The emphasis was on the lieutenant, whose role until now had been 'limited to staying in the rank, in his place as a file-closer, supervising the fire of his troops, closing up the ranks and files'.[64] Emphasis was also placed on the ordinary 'skirmisher – hardy, full of spirit, and familiar with his duties in combat – [who] brings to the fight the fervour, energy and intelligence that allow the commander to dare all'.[65] The aim was to make this isolated soldier, this heir of the skirmisher of 1792, act 'as an individual combatant, without the immediate supervision of his leaders'.[66]

In short, there was a desire to foster the spirit of initiative at every level, in order to achieve 'more flexibility and speed in the evolutions, and greater elasticity and variety in the combat formations'.[67] But this desire clashed with the concept of controlling the infantry's fire. Fire control remained highly centralized so as to avoid wastage of ammunition. The fires were executed on the orders of the *section* leader, and were normally collective, 'with counted rounds, either fired in rapid succession or in volleys'. Only on rare occasions was fire delivered freely, 'at will'. Since command at this time was exercised verbally, centralized fire control necessitated closed-up dispositions, with an interval of just one pace between each man. This was a far cry from the *Burentaktik*, the tactic used by the Boers, which allowed every man a high degree of initiative in firing and moving within extremely open dispositions. In Bonnal's view, the Boers' tactic could tempt only soldiers who were 'poorly trained or drawn to the fantastic'.[68]

The 1904 *Infantry training regulation* appeared, outwardly at least, to accept the guidance of the principles contained in the 1895 *Field service regulation:*

> [These principles are] conducive to establishing within the army the unity of doctrine that is vital for ensuring cooperation between the arms and the coordination of efforts on the battlefield. The way in which infantry is used in combat stems from these principles. Every officer should therefore be familiar with them and draw inspiration from them constantly.[69] [Nevertheless] infantry combat does not consist of fixed rules, and most of the time it confronts commanders with unexpected situations.[70]

Yet in actual fact, when the 1904 *Infantry training regulation* described the process of attack, it broke with the formalism of its predecessors. There was no longer any talk of preparation, nor of decisive action. The regulation instead spoke of a piecemeal combat left to the initiative of the officers who were on the spot. The final effort was unleashed by the leader against weak points that had been either spotted or created. The point of attack was no longer chosen, and instead had to be accepted. The 1904 *Infantry training regulation* was clearly inspired, therefore, by the 'school of fire', and it broke with the principles of the *Field service regulation* even while claiming to conform with it.

The *Artillery training regulation,* which was issued in 1903, reflected a similar philosophy. It never used the words 'preparation' or 'decision'. The artillery no longer opened the combat with a dramatic deployment. Instead, it slipped into the combat, and initiated scattered actions.[71]

The 1904 *Infantry training regulation* was a distinct improvement on its predecessors. Even so, it had its flaws. Issued while the Russo-Japanese war was still in progress, it failed to take sufficient account of either the defensive organization of the terrain or the intervention of machine-guns. Above all, it was introduced without any prior explanation, and it passed over the heads of most officers as a result of its overly abstract style.[72] It completely contradicted the previous regulation in terms of the flexibility of the formations and the wide scope for initiative that was given to the junior officers, NCOs and corporals. It shocked some field officers who linked it to political ideas that were around at the time. Furthermore, it was yet another addition to the unbroken string of regulatory manuals that had appeared since 1884. This profusion, which was an indication of uncertainty rather than of prolific thought, definitely reduced its impact.

### A new jump in firepower

The Russo-Japanese war of 1904-5 broadly matched the expected nature of the next war in Europe. The French were able to study it in detail, for they had military missions on the ground as well as contacts with their Russian allies. What emerged from this conflict, when compared with the South African war, was a jump in the increase in firepower. This resulted from the introduction of machine-guns, quick-firing artillery and field howitzers on to the battlefield. It was therefore concluded that the precautionary measures adopted during the various phases of the action had to be extended even further.

The approach march became longer as the effective artillery ranges increased. Since the main protection during this approach march consisted of the terrain, units had to be split up so they could make the best use of any cover and of any zones that were shielded from enemy observation and fire. When the fire became fiercer, the men clung to the ground. They did so using entrenchments strengthened – and this was a major innovation – with barbed-wire entanglements. Manchuria, the seat of the war, soon became 'furrowed with trenches that, if placed end-to-end, would be several thousands of kilometres long'.[73] The importance of the entrenching tool was universally acknowledged. A Russian officer, Captain Soloviev, stressed the need to 'construct trenches whenever possible'.[74] Lieutenant-Colonel Alexander Alexandrovich Neznamov reckoned:

Life and experience show that unit commanders must master the use of temporary field entrenchments in every detail. This obliges them to study the matter thoroughly, for, along with the present improvements in weaponry, it has become one of the main features of combat.[75]

In these circumstances, it was generally only if soldiers could be seen by the enemy that they were at risk of being killed. Every effort was made to reduce their visibility. The Second Department (Intelligence) of the French General Staff noted 'the pressing need to remove any shiny items from the uniforms ... to provide the officers with the same uniform as the troops and to adopt a single, neutral colour, at least for the headdress and jacket, even if not for the trousers.'[76]

Whereas the Japanese infantrymen had gone to war in blue uniforms with red shoulder-straps, they were issued with a khaki uniform in the course of the operations. The battlefield therefore tended to become empty. The Russian Captain Soloviev described battlefields where 'officers and soldiers spent several days in a position, were wounded, carried away and brought back to Russia, without even having seen a Japanese man'.[77] The actions in Manchuria might last for weeks, and 'élan' often had to take second place to obstinacy.

All these lessons were well known, but proved difficult to apply in France. The 1904 *Infantry training regulation* already set out the need to split units up during the approach march. But Major de Grandmaison felt obliged in 1908 to issue a reminder:

What is important is to employ a large number of small groups that move easily and make good use of the terrain, swift and irregular movements, and men who lie down whenever they are not completely under cover. ... As for big bodies of troops – dense lines one behind the other, or columns – the question of their vulnerability is fairly obvious. Regardless of their exact disposition, they will no longer be seen under the fire of an unshaken enemy.[78]

Camouflaged uniforms had been under consideration since 1899. But the 'Boer' uniform of 1903, the 'beige-blue' of 1905-6 and the grey-green 'reseda' of 1911-12 were all failures. Many French officers had reservations about such a change. In their eyes, the uniform was not 'practical work clothing', but rather a symbol of traditions and a source of pride. Other countries, notably Germany, harboured similar reservations, but between 1905 and 1914 subordinated them to tactical considerations. Only the French retained their old uniforms that stemmed from the reign of King Louis-Philippe (1830-48). A new 'horizon blue' colour was belatedly adopted under a law passed on 9 July 1914. The tardiness of the measure reflected the delays affecting the mobile field kitchens and the heavy field artillery, but was more than just a symptom of conservatism. Its prime cause seems to have been the practical difficulties that prevented the Ministry of War from implementing initiatives quickly.

The dispersion of units caused the combat to slip increasing out of the hands of the captain in command of the company. The *section*, as the 1904 *Infantry training regulation* indicated, now seemed to be the basic tactical unit. Some men thought that this decentralization did not go far enough. Grandmaison pointed out that even a *section* would be difficult to command if its lieutenant was obliged to go to ground like his men. He therefore proposed to go down another echelon and make the half-*section* of twenty to twenty-five men the basic fighting unit.[79] Debeney even talked about swarms of three or four skirmishers during his infantry tactics course in 1913.

For the time being, these ideas were deemed unrealistic, if only because on mobilization half of the lieutenants would be reservists with limited tactical training. The captain remained the mastermind. There was no question at that time of giving sergeants responsibility for making tactical decisions. Professional NCOs were far too rare. Nevertheless, it would have been possible to thin out the dispositions, as had happened in Manchuria where the interval between a couple of skirmishers was often as much as three paces. Lieutenant-Colonel Jean-Baptiste Montaigne advocated reducing the density of men:

> We accumulate reinforcements, supports and reserves, to a point when we have a depth of five or six men on every 1 metre of front. We undoubtedly do this out of fear or with a view to hand-to-hand fighting. But why not give pikes to those men? Pikes would be just as useful to them as rifles ... Having a density greater than one man for every 1 metre of front seems madness to me. Only the stubbornness of habit can lead to such blunders.[80]

On the other hand, many commentators – including Captain Marie Marcel André Billard in his *Infantry education* – thought that if the intervals were increased to two or three paces, 'the [men's] vulnerability would be reduced, but the *section* would become unmanageable and would come to a standstill'.[81]

Protection, it was thought, could be obtained by neutralizing the enemy with heavy fire, at least as much as by exploiting the terrain. Apart from General Cardot, who still believed that the notion of fire superiority was 'a terrible nonsense', every infantryman agreed that 'forward movement within the zone of effective fire becomes impossible if the attacker lacks fire superiority'[82] and that, as a consequence, 'you can advance only by fire'.[83] This fire came from the infantry itself, but also from the artillery, which was the 'real shield of the infantry'.[84] But, as with anything in the French army of that time, a debate occurred about the use of the artillery for this purpose. The conclusions of the debate were very reductive for the artillery. Hence the 1913 *Field service regulation* laid down that the artillery's main role was 'to support the infantry attacks by destroying anything that opposed the progress of these attacks'.[85] Countering the enemy artillery, although not ruled out, was a secondary mission. An artillery preparation before the attack was deemed unprofitable against dug-in positions, given the limitations of the 75mm gun. In order to use resources efficiently, it was thought better to concentrate on providing the attack with constant fire support – a long operation that required large amounts of ammunition. Furthermore, it was deemed ineffective to fire unless the enemy was visible, and the enemy would not reveal himself until he was attacked with infantry. The two actions – attack and support – seemed inextricably linked, and yet no firm decision was made as to how the two should be coordinated.

The issue of the final assault still remained unresolved. Every author agreed that only fire would make it possible to advance up to the zone of contact, in other words, up to about 200 metres from the enemy. But doubt still existed about how the assault should be delivered. The lessons of the Russo-Japanese war were contradictory on this subject. Adherents of the school of shock reckoned that the Japanese had succeeded in several, energetically-led, frontal attacks, notably at Liao-Yang. Captain Soloviev thought that the bayonet attack remained the infantry's *ultima ratio*, its final argument: 'The bayonet has been in regular use all the time. No combat of the least significance has failed to see the bayonet in use.'[86] On the other hand, Lieutenant-Colonel Neznamov stated that:

the bitter attacks, carried out repeatedly and with superior forces – notably on 14 and 15 October by the 'Iron' General Okou – all ended up breaking on the covered trenches that had been constructed to allow men to fire while standing up. This happened even though the covered trenches at that time still lacked even secondary defences [barbed-wire or other obstacles].[87]

Hence Neznamov recommended an advance using fire from chains of widely-spaced skirmishers. Similarly, General Jean Colin recalled how the Japanese incurred enormous losses whenever one of their units in close order, 'even just a company, ventured into the open at long range'.[88] He therefore cast doubt on the idea that the Japanese had made a success of their frontal attacks, and reckoned that they had simply occupied positions already abandoned by an enemy who had been expelled by fire. In Colin's view, which accorded with the 1875 *Infantry training regulation,* the act of closing with the enemy might clinch the victory, 'but fire is what produces it'.[89]

Other commentators, including Grandmaison, took issue with the 'lovers of ballistics', and instead advocated brute-force attacks:

To overcome [stiff resistance], you must advance. The only way you will be able to do so is brutally, without worrying about losses, without sparing anyone. That is what is meant by an attack using brute force. The Russo-Japanese war demonstrates that frontal attacks by brute force are both necessary and possible, and thus exempts us from any discussion.[90]

Yet Grandmaison conceded that this final assault was extremely difficult, and he set out strict conditions for success:

The enemy has already been shaken, and now shows signs of being about to give in to demoralization. The attack enjoys a very marked moral and physical superiority. Finally, the distance is relatively short. The principle, moreover, remains unchanged: it is always fire that ensures movement.[91]

The assault itself was about the psychology of crowds:[92] 'It's a matter of morale, and the prime aim of our tactical efforts will be to prepare this solution and make it possible, by pitting troops with superior morale up close against a foe who is depressed by the awareness of his inferiority and paralysed by fire.'[93]

The problem remained of working out who should initiate this final action. Debeney stated that the assault had always been delivered 'by the chain [of skirmishers], after the chain had been brought up to within a short distance'.[94] But Major Buat retorted:

> it is not the chain of skirmishers that, having been constantly reinforced, determines the initial success. It is not the chain that remains free to go over to the assault, if it reckons the time has come ... It is from the rear that the thrust comes to [the chain].[95]

Since minds were focused on the final crisis of the assault, the subsequent actions – exploitation and the defence of the conquered zone – were often neglected.

The final pre-war *Infantry training regulation*, dated 20 April 1914, failed to provide any definite answers to these issues. Debeney helped produce an initial, innovative, draft. But that draft was rejected. Instead, the 1904 *Infantry training regulation* was simply reiterated almost in its entirety, so as not to disrupt the units on the eve of a war whose imminence was sensed.[96] The work of revision focused almost wholly on rationalizing the part that was devoted to training. Hence the 1914 regulation retained the flaws of its predecessor. Manœuvre received scant attention, the excuse being that simplicity suited 'the temperament of the French soldier'.[97]

The 1914 regulation did not neglect defensive procedures. It clearly specified the need for trenches that were both deep and narrow. It described in detail how a defensive front should be organized by means of the creation of strongpoints, along with the provision of communications and unit emplacements. But there was no flexibility to the defence: 'everyone is to die where he stands rather than give up an inch of ground'.[98] The only use for the defensive remained a means of economizing on strength in a secondary sector in order to benefit the offensive in the main sector.

In short, the new *Infantry training regulation* gave the impression of having practically ignored the technical developments that had occurred between 1904 and 1914 – except in so far as a few of its articles addressed the use of machine-guns. It was compatible with the South African war, meaning that it focused on combat using rifles. The strength of the firepower seen in Manchuria did not shine through in the regulation. Yet even that firepower was inferior to what French or German troops could deliver, equipped with two or three times the proportion of machine-guns and artillery pieces available to the Russians and Japanese in 1905.

The increase in firepower was boosted by the money spent on the arms race, and was far more rapid than the evolution of doctrine. As a result, the two were dangerously out of step.

# Modern Style and New School

The transformation of the regulations of arms was more or less dictated by what was actually happening, and was managed at the level of the directorates of arms. But transforming the operational paradigm was more difficult. The authority of the Staff College, which was essentially no more than a moral authority, was in decline. The College was attacked first by the top brass and then by young field officers, in conflicting directions. Until 1913, the absence of strong leadership resulted in a process of evolution driven by crises. Ideas could become established only if they won converts, and so debates took a fierce and passionate turn. Appeals to the emotions and the use of invective intruded into a process that should have stuck to logic alone.

## The issue of the fronts

Some commentators thought that the rigid fronts of the South African war foreshadowed a vast 'stalemate'. Colonel Charles Berrot, the head of the Third Department of the General Staff, who was one of the few men to highlight the relevance of the US Civil War, asserted that from now on the cavalry would be unable to reconnoitre the enemy, while the artillery would be powerless to prepare the attack and the infantry to carry it out.[99] Lieutenant-Colonel Emile Mayer predicted that the front would extend from the North Sea to Belfort, and that a long, static conflict would then set in. His fellow-colonel, Louis de Maud'huy, explained as early as 1909 that any position where the troops came to a standstill would be rapidly fortified by means of digging, and that, with this happening on both sides, the result would be siege warfare.[100] In 1905, another Staff College professor, Lieutenant-Colonel Martial Justin Verraux, described a future war consisting of two phases. The first, consisting of 'mighty clashes', would give way to a second phase, in which the armies 'will wage siege warfare' for years on end.[101] Even earlier, in 1897, the Polish banker Jan Bloch, writing in *The future of war, in its technical, economic and political relations*, had already described:

> slaughter on so terrible a scale as to render it impossible to get troops to push the battle to a decisive issue ... [The war] will become a kind of stalemate, in which, neither army being able to get at the other, both armies will be maintained in opposition to each other, threatening each other, but never able to deliver a final and decisive attack. ... Everybody will be entrenched in the next war. It will be a great war of entrenchments.[102]

These authors described the trench warfare of the future fairly accurately, but none of them imagined any other outcome than mutual exhaustion. Their theories of the so-called 'impregnability of fronts' discounted any possibility that a great, decisive battle might end the war quickly.

Such theories sparked fierce criticism. The former professors of the Staff College had been enterprising in their day, but now defended the ideas that they had helped to establish. They regarded their opponents' outlook as a sort of disease, 'Transvaalitis'. They accused them of fostering 'the hidden instincts of self-preservation' and of undermining both the regulations and the officers' confidence in their leaders.[103] Above all, they refused to accept that the notion of 'decisive battle' was invalid. Cardot emphasized that there had to be slaughter, 'and the only reason men go on to the battlefield is to get themselves slaughtered'. Langlois refused to accept either enveloping attacks, or night attacks, or the notion of 'key' positions, or lines of troops stretched out 'like a rubber band'. In his opinion, war was an act of force, and 'you must seek battle and desire it with all your might'.[104] Similarly, Foch condemned the old ways: 'the old fencing, the outdated methods of the pre-Revolutionary era. Manœuvre boils down to seeking battle.'[105]

This 'Clausewitzian' school was able to use the Russo-Japanese war to support its case. Joffre saw in that conflict:

> a striking confirmation of General Langlois' words. At the Staff College, under the guidance of men such as Foch, Lanrezac and Bourdériat, the whole of the young, intellectual élite of that time discarded the entire phraseology that had disrupted the military world, and returned to a sound conception of the general conditions of war.[106]

Lieutenant-Colonel Montaigne concluded that what had happened in Manchuria had been 'too stark a refutation [of Bloch's theories] for it to be necessary to belabour the point'.[107]

At a lower and more operational level, Generals de Négrier and Charles Kessler, writing in 1901-2, developed ideas that were close to the notion of the 'impregnability of fronts' and that challenged the 1895 *Field service regulation*. They began by pointing out what had happened in the South African war. During that conflict, the British had applied principles similar to those of the French, but at no point had they managed to conduct a coherent combat by their advanced-guards or their various echelonned bodies of troops. The British had subsequently won only by means of a mobile and decentralized combat that had systematically sought to outflank pockets of enemy resistance. 'The small-calibre bullet has blown apart the old order of battle', concluded Négrier. 'It has fragmented the combat and caused its conduct to pass from the leader's brain to the soldier's heart.'[108]

Hence Négrier recommended an *art nouveau*, a 'new art' of British-style warfare, with a 'war of screens' replacing the old 'war of masses'. The 'screens' were combined-arms *groupements* ('groupings') of cavalrymen, gunners and cyclists, and they would act in front of the main body so as to create a zone of security around it. Behind the cover of these screens, the columns would advance on a wide front, so they could rapidly envelop any enemy force they encountered. If this envelopment failed, the infantry columns would be committed in widely-spaced and independent swarms. These swarms would form a line of fire of variable density. They would advance by combining fire, movement and the digging of entrenchments, so as to discover the weak points in the enemy line. The reserves would be held back until this moment and would then be brought forward, along routes out of the enemy's sight, in order to reach the points of breakthrough. Once they arrived, they would finish the work begun by the swarms and cause the enemy to disintegrate completely.[109]

These theories were fiercely attacked by the former professors of the Staff College, especially Bonnal and Langlois. In his book, *Lessons of two recent wars,* Langlois denied that the South African war was a valid example. He reckoned that the British could blame their initial failure largely on their incapabilities. They launched attacks prematurely, without any preliminary reconnaissances and after a phase of preparation that consisted of no more than a few ineffective bombardments. The attack itself was not helped by the absence of any cooperation between the arms. Hence the setbacks of the start of the war were hardly surprising, and did not call into question the principles of the 1895 *Field service regulation*. As for the second part of the conflict, the conclusions that had been drawn had been distorted by the crushing superiority of the British, and the purely defensive tactics of the Boers. Frontal attacks were still possible, Langlois thought, provided the attackers had fire superiority, their morale was as tough as steel and their various arms cooperated.

The system of screens was twice put to the test in France. It was first tried out during the large-scale manœuvres held in the central region of the country in 1903, apparently with mixed results. The combined-arms *groupements* that formed the screens lacked cohesion and were difficult to command. General Langlois then arranged a *Kriegspiel,* which pitted two armies against each other, each composed of four corps. The Army of the South was organized in a diamond formation, preceded by combined-arms advanced-guards, in accordance with the 1895 *Field service regulation*. It faced a modern-style Army of the North, which advanced on a single front with divisional columns covered by 'screens'. The advanced-guard of the Army of the South managed to penetrate the screens and ascertain the location of the Army of the North. In doing so, it detected the movement of an enemy army corps that was making a long detour to avoid a forest and to turn the 'Southeners'. This movement caused a gap to open in the Army of the North's disposition. Through this gap, the Southern player sent a strengthened army corps that decided the outcome.[110] The 1895 regulation therefore remained unchanged in the wake of this first onslaught against it.

### The new school

The French were not alone in updating their regulations at this time. The Germans did the same between 1906 and 1908. The principles of their 1908 *Felddienst Ordnung,* ('Field service regulation') were an attempt to adapt the ideas of Field Marshal Helmuth von Moltke the Elder in the light of the lessons of recent wars. The basic method was *Festhalten und umfassen,* which meant to 'fix and outflank'. As soon as the Germans made contact with the enemy, their commander systematically opened two actions – and this held true regardless of whether he was commanding a mere company or the entire army. One of these two actions was a frontal action to fix the enemy. The other, a turning move, sought a decisive outcome on a wing of the enemy disposition. The frontal action might be either offensive or defensive, but it was always a fire action, with artillery and machine-guns used as rapidly as possible, whereas the French in such a situation would favour a shock action.

Another difference, which applied equally to a frontal or a flank action, was that whereas the French often neglected the terrain, the Germans used it to the full, exploiting the opportunities it offered for defence or infiltration. Furthermore, the German methods were based on universally-known models that required subordinates to react automatically on a decentralized basis. Everyone knew what he was expected to do in specific situations, and everyone was actively encouraged to use his initiative, even if in doing so he was disregarding the initial orders he had received. In contrast, the French fought highly-centralized combats and stuck to the notion of the commander as a chess-player. Reporting information upwards to the senior echelons of command led to a degree of sluggishness. The French realized that. They also realized that it caused them to hand the initiative of the actions to the Germans, but they hoped to make up for this drawback by fighting an offensive battle in a defensive form. This meant a delaying action conducted by the advanced-guard, followed by a devastating counter-manœuvre directed against the decisive point.

Lieutenant-Colonel de Grandmaison fiercely attacked this defensive-offensive method when he gave his two lectures at the Centre for Advanced Military Studies in 1911. His first lecture, entitled *The crisis of the fronts and the concept of security,* took as its starting point the 'impression of anarchy in our tactical ideas'[111] – for that was the impression conveyed by the large-scale manœuvres. In his lecture, Grandmaison noted that the fear of being encircled by the Germans not only injected a high degree of caution into the advanced-guard combat, but also meant that the disposition-in-depth prescribed by the regulations – consisting of an advanced-guard, main body and reserve – was instinctively turned into a disposition that was as wide as possible. Similarly, he noted that manpower was being used inefficiently, with as much as half of the available strength being devoted to protection in the form of the advanced-guard, the flank-guards and also the outer security provided by the corps cavalry. To Grandmaison, the concept of the manœuvre-battle conducted like a chess game seemed unrealistic because it was too complicated:

> Reconnoitring by means of combat, securing one's flanks, establishing a base on the ground, supporting the attack, preparing a withdrawal – not to mention the reserves. ... We would need a checklist.[112]

In the context of the modern battle, where information circulated more slowly than before, 'no longer can one man single-handedly control a large, modern unit and lead it by directing the movements of each piece as if it were a pawn on a chessboard.'[113]

The entire edifice was at risk of falling apart in the face of the speed and extent of the German attacks. Grandmaison also thought that the concept of making a fighting retreat followed by a devastating counter-attack was fraught with danger. He pointed out that the retreat would undermine morale, making it even more difficult to mount an attack, especially as it was so tricky to ascertain the decisive point. But his ultimate argument was that this concept fostered a 'mindset totally at odds with the enthusiastic execution of the offensive'.[114] The method that Grandmaison advocated was to go even faster than the Germans and to gain the upper hand as soon as contact was made with the enemy.

The French would thereby obtain security automatically, by 'going for the enemy's throat' before he had managed to finish deploying. This required them to adopt dispositions, before the action began, that would enable them to strike hard and fast. The advanced-guards had to make contact aggressively. 'It is not a matter of tickling by lacy advanced-guards; these are attacks for real'.[115] The main body of the forces had to be pushed far forward. It was tempting, but not obligatory, to hurl the main body in an 'attack block' against the very heart of the over-extended enemy line.

It was, explained Lieutenant Laure,[116] the same stroke that had won the Battle of Austerlitz in 1805 – 'the finest model of the offensive manœuvre as it exists in the dreams of the French temperament'. Laure added: 'We will not go round this tide of men, this new and living Wall of China. We will break through it.'[117]

The final element in Grandmaison's system was that the French could move fast only if they did the same as the Germans: they had to give straightforward orders and then trust subordinates to implement them.

Hence the basis of combat consisted of every man acting aggressively. That required the French to prepare themselves 'by fostering anything connected in the slightest way with the offensive spirit – and doing so passionately and extravagantly, and going into the minute details of the training. Let's go to extremes, for it is possible even that may not be enough.'[118]

Grandmaison did not ignore the risks involved in seeking speed without taking the enemy's dispositions into consideration. He noted that, if 'taken to the absurd, this conception could become as dangerous as that of comprehensive security provided by the action of distant detachments'.[119] But he expected that his risk-taking approach would ultimately pay off, provided it was implemented intelligently.

When Grandmaison was setting out his ideas on how armies should manœuvre, he had yet to command anything more than a battalion. We can therefore detect the influence of the purely tactical ideas he had set out five years earlier in his *Infantry training for offensive combat*, which summarized what he had learned as a regimental officer. Here are some extracts from that book:

> The security of a unit in movement must be sought not in excessive security precautions, but rather in orders of march that ensure the unit is ready to fight at any moment. It is forgotten too often that what constitutes the real security of a column, particularly during an offensive march, is the ability to attack immediately.[120] ...
>
> The best way of getting out of trouble, at this difficult moment [an enemy surprise], is to switch to a determined offensive, without hesitation, without pause and without waiting for fuller information[121] ...
>
> The greatest initiative must be left to the men on the spot.[122] ...
>
> Trying to direct your units in an engagement like pawns on a chessboard is dangerous and foolish in equal measure. ... An engagement nowadays can be coordinated only by the existence of a shared aim, by all the officers being in the habit of considering a matter in the same light and of taking action on the desired lines without waiting to be pushed.[123]

This doctrine proved highly popular with young officers and even with some politicians. Many hoped to find in it a miraculous solution to all of the French army's flaws and a way of responding to any tactical situation:

> [If one of the two sides in a future war] strives – as the Russians did [in Manchuria] – to do too much digging and create impregnable positions, it will risk becoming another [General] Mack[124] ... A side that seeks to do what the Japanese did, in similar circumstances, namely extend its front and carry out a tactical envelopment, is in danger of racing to another Austerlitz [by weakening its centre and leaving it vulnerable to a breakthrough].[125]

### An operational doctrine that is lyrical but indecisive

By the eve of the war, and in the wake of years of political turmoil, a complete revision of the French operational doctrine had become imperative, for it was nearly twenty years-old. Joffre, the new commander-in-chief designate, chose the model of the new school to replace that of Bonnal, and gave it an objective character by making use of the *Kriegspiel* method. The result, in his view, was:

> an intense, general effort that involved the officers who were attending the Centre for Advanced Military Studies and the professors of the Staff College. Every idea, every concept, every daring approach and every timorous one, battled it out. Bit by bit, a doctrine emerged. The conditions under which an offensive might be conducted vigorously and yet wisely became clearer.[126]

The results of this work served as a basis for a new body of operational doctrine embodied in two manuals. The first of these manuals was the *Regulation on the handling of large units* of 28 October 1913, which dealt with the echelons of army and army corps. The second was the *Field service regulation* of 2 December 1913. These two manuals, and the new training regulations of the arms that were issued at the same period, were intended to form a single conceptual structure. The report to the Minister of War, which set out the principles of the *Regulation on the handling of large units*, drew heavily on three models – the Prussian army of 1870, Napoleon I, and the Japanese army in Manchuria – in order to claim that the French army had returned to its traditions and 'now recognizes no rule in the conduct of operations other than the offensive'.[127] No mention was made of the simulation exercises that according to Joffre were what inspired the offensive doctrine. The offensive was mentioned again and again. This voluntarism (the placing of the emphasis on willpower) was not new. It simply repeated, with an incantatory lyricism, the generally accepted idea that victory in war had always gone to generals who had desired and sought battle, whereas those generals who had had battle forced upon them had always been beaten.[128]

The *Regulation on the handling of large units* intervened openly in the doctrinal debate by siding against the theory of the 'impregnability of fronts' and against the possibility of using manœuvre to win decisively:

> We saw the reemergence of some theories that we might have thought had been abandoned for good ... we must always fear that a long period of peace will cause them to be reborn one day. [It is necessary] to prevent such a backward step ...[129]

Instead, the authors argued, 'the military operations seek to annihilate the enemy's organized forces'.[130] They set out clearly how to achieve this annihilation:

> The decisive battle, exploited to the full, is the only way of breaking the enemy's will, by means of destroying his armies. It constitutes the fundamental act of war.[131] ... [It is followed by] a relentless and merciless pursuit, using every last bit of energy, [a pursuit that] must ensure the complete destruction of the enemy's physical and moral strength.[132]

The paralysis of the country's economic life, caused by the scale of its mobilization, 'acts as a spur for seeking a decision as quickly as possible, with a view to bringing the struggle to a prompt end. ... [Hence] the first combats are very important, because of the predominant influence they can have over subsequent events.'[133]

In battle, it was a matter of using attacks by the main body of the forces:

> to seek a clear-cut and conclusive breakthrough of the enemy disposition.[134] ... This breakthrough requires attacks that are pressed to the limit, without any misgivings. It can be achieved only at the cost of bloody sacrifices. Any other conception must be rejected as being contrary to the very nature of war.[135] ... [However,] given the vast scale of the masses that are committed to action these days, the overall battle will consist of several battles of armies – battles that are more or less distinct from each other, but are all related to the same overall conception.[136]

At every level, much emphasis was placed on the overriding importance of willpower, or even obstinacy:

> Tenacity in pursuit of the same guiding principle is how the commander of a large unit manages to dominate events.[137] ... Battles are moral struggles above all else. Defeat is inevitable once there is no more hope of winning. Success therefore goes not to the side that has suffered fewer losses, but to the side whose willpower is steadier and whose morale is more strongly tempered.[138]

Command, therefore, was primarily an exercise of authority and voluntarism rather than 'skill in devising a manœuvre'.[139]

Yet it is interesting that the commission responsible for compiling the *Regulation on the handling of large units* did not take sides when it came to choosing an operational method. It distinguished between the 'battle by successive attacks' and the 'battle by simultaneous attacks'. The battle by successive attacks consisted of preparatory combats that might last several days, and then a decisive attack launched on the orders of the commander. In contrast, the battle by simultaneous attacks entailed secondary attacks to pin down the enemy on either the whole of the front or part of it, and a main attack against a wing. There was no question of breaking through the enemy's centre.

> After due consideration, the commission has concluded that there is no reason to set two systems against each other, when both of them have their merits, and

when the question of which one to use depends primarily on circumstances. It has wanted to leave the commander – who is the only person capable of assessing the whole range of information that contributes to his decision – with the unqualified right of making his choice in complete freedom.

This was hardly a doctrine based on inviolable principles. Nor could the French army be said to be completely in the grip of Grandmaison's ideas. The commission that produced the *Regulation on the handling of large units* provided not so much a definite guide for action as a supplementary element in the doctrinal mosaic.

\*

Hence the forty-three years that separated the wars of 1870 and 1914 saw four phases of intellectual output. The first, which lasted from 1871 to 1883, was a period of experimentation based on the lessons of the Franco-Prussian war, but it failed to impose a solid body of doctrine. This was followed in 1884-1902 by a period of certainties that were inspired by a glorious past. Then, in 1903-10, came a phase of turmoil in the wake of what had been observed in distant wars. Finally in 1911-14, with war looming on the horizon, an attempt was made to re-establish 'doctrinal unity'.

Each of these periods was dominated by either one or two poles of thought, which were linked to a particular tool of thought. Of crucial importance within each of these poles was the character of a handful of men: Maillard, Bonnal, Négrier, Langlois, Cardot, Foch and Grandmaison. The very notion of doctrine evolved. The positivist 'distilling apparatus' described by General Debeney gave way to the notion that 'doctrine is barely any more, at the top, than a state of mind and a way of thinking',[140] as Grandmaison put it in 1911.

But we still have to ascertain the influence that these ideas had on the way units acted. We have cited several manuals that, being regulations, were normally prescriptive and not open to discussion. Yet these manuals failed to weave themselves into the fabric of the regiments. The infantry regulations in particular were spurned, either for being contrary to the infantry's 'values' (1875 and 1904 *Infantry training regulations)*, or for failing to take enough account of the power of modern weaponry (the *Infantry training regulations* issued between 1884 and 1902). As for the April 1914 *Infantry training regulation,* it appeared too late to have the slightest influence. To what extent the infantry regiments really knew what to do in action is therefore uncertain. Thus we see the difference that can exist between theory and practice. On the one hand, there are ideas and the regulations that synthesize those ideas and represent a theoretical ideal. On the other hand is the actual 'practice', which is the sum of the skills that the units actually possess. The baptism of fire of August 1914 brutally revealed the gap that existed between these two concepts, and it is this gap that we are now going to analyse.

*Chapter 3*

# The Flaws in the Learning Process

Practice can be defined as all the procedures that units actually use and master. It is the sum of the habits they have picked up, their capital of experience, their knowledge of the regulations in force and the personal ideas of their members. Ideally, this practice should correspond to what the official manuals have prescribed – manuals that are themselves the formal expression of the dominant paradigm. Training is supposed to make possible this osmosis – this gradual absorption of the written word into actual practice. Yet as we have already seen, some regulations, especially in the infantry, were never really applied. This suggests the existence of problems in the process of assimilating doctrines. When Joffre was appointed commander-in-chief designate in 1911, he described his general impression of the troops:

> Tossed about for many years between the most extreme theories, supervised by officers who resisted any innovation, [they] nonetheless remained totally indifferent and lethargic. They undoubtedly knew that the offensive was fashionable up high, and they sought to act offensively, but under what conditions![1]

The problems varied depending on whether the level of application was operational or tactical, but in every case they could be traced back to a rigidity of outlook and a shortage of material means.

## Officer-Training
### Regulations
The first impediment to the application of the regulations was simply the fact that these regulations were far from being completely prescriptive in character. Manuals were nothing new, but until 1870 their usefulness was considered to be largely restricted to peacetime, as a way of 'automating' the troops so they acted like a machine. They were not deemed to be of much relevance in wartime, given the impossibility of predicting what would happen in war. The oldest officers tended to think their practical experience was not only sufficient, but also better than the thinking of young staff officers. For years, as we have seen, the directors of the annual, large-scale manœuvres often ridiculed the regulations when issuing preliminary instructions to the units taking part. Even though 'Captain Jibé' condemned this ridicule in *The new army*, published in 1905, he conceded that it was acceptable to question the written texts, since 'healthy criticism always produces an improvement'.[2] The notion of duty invariably proved stronger than the notion of sticking to the regulations.

What we then notice is that the regulations themselves had to evolve quickly in order to keep abreast of the many changes. These changes included technical advances, the switch to a two-year period of military service, the lessons of contemporary conflicts and the way in which France's potential enemy evolved. But in the absence of centralization, the regulations fluctuated in line with prevailing trends or even with passing fads. The result was that by 1888 there existed a total of 2,300 pages of regulations, compared with the German figure of just 900.[3]

The changes to the regulations were often radical in nature, but fell foul of the persistent slowness with which texts were assimilated. Thousands of copies had to be printed and issued. Everyone then had to make the effort of reading the often daunting document, understand it and above all accept the need for it. If this did not happen, the text might remain completely ignored. By the end of the nineteenth century, many officers were refusing to make this effort because it was so burdensome. Among them was Captain André Chalmandrey:

> Our officers are crushed by the ever increasing burden of your empty, hollow regulations teeming with contradictions and ambiguities. They barely have the time to become familiar with them, and have no time at all to put them into practice. Besides, your regulations are replaced so often that even a lifetime would not be enough to learn them all. We see them changing all the time, and we see the new ones are just as bad as their predecessors, so in the end we lose interest and regard them with indifference.[4]

Under these conditions, he thought that 'when you go off on manœuvres, you should know the training regulations, so you can stuff them in your pocket under your handkerchief! Yes, absolutely, the training regulations should teach that great process of muddle-your-way-through!'[5]

So strong was this trend that as late as 1909 Major Edmond Buat noted: 'Many claim that no principles exist at all, and that for any given situation there must be a suitable solution, found solely by weighing up the relative importance of the facts of the matter.'[6]

It was a return to the pragmatism of the Second Empire. In contrast, the five years leading up to the Great War saw an attempt to restore more prescriptive rigour. The operational doctrine and the training regulations were revised, but there was too little time to make up for almost twenty years of vagueness, especially as the revised texts failed to win universal approval.

### Regimental officers

Some officers were able to do two years of training at the Staff College if they passed its entrance examination. A few training courses were also run in military schools. But most of the 31,000 French officers – the figure for 1913 – had to make do with what they had picked up in the schools where they had done their initial and advanced training. They then did the rest of their tactical training within the succession of regiments in which they served, and in accordance with the numerous procedures set out in the texts. Officially, training was based on a knowledge of the regulations – a knowledge that was developed by means of applied training exercises and supplemented by lectures, studies and also courses undertaken in the other arms.[7]

Applied training exercises were conducted either with or without troops. Exercises with troops generally began in the spring, when the recruits had finished their individual training and when the state of the crops did not restrict units as they manœuvred across country. They finished with the autumn manœuvres. The exercises that the infantry preferred were competitive manœuvres, which pitted two sides against each other, each of which had a mission to fulfil. In garrisons where several arms were present, so-called garrison exercises were intended to enable the field officers to command combined-arms *groupements* on the ground. Training without troops, on the other hand, normally took place in the winter, with the help of map exercises, either in quarters or on the ground. The officers were also expected to attend lectures given at their gatherings and were urged to undertake written work.

What actually happened in practice? As is often the case, it varied widely. Much depended on the motivation of the colonels and captains. Some regiments, especially in eastern France, were tactical laboratories – such as the 35th Infantry Regiment at Belfort, commanded by Colonel Louis de Maud'huy. But routine seems to have been the dominant characteristic. Joseph Monteilhet, critical as ever of 'the barracks army', thought that 'officers, whatever their rank, did something completely different from tactics during the course of the year', being overwhelmed by garrison service and by the administrative or training tasks that the few committed NCOs were unable to carry out in full. Monteilhet reckoned that tactical training was limited to garrison lectures, many of which were very general and cautious since the young, qualified staff officers who delivered them were assessed on their performance. Monteilhet concluded that there was 'nothing more ludicrous or pointless'.[8]

Young, offensive-minded men took a more moderate and objective stance than Monteilhet. These young men, such as Lieutenant Emile Laure and Captain Marie Marcel André Billard, were concerned about the lack of interest shown in tactical training, which many officers 'cursed'[9] and deemed an 'extremely dull and boring'[10] part of their job. The system of taking actual examples of actions from military history and studying them either on a map or on the ground – 'a training system as prized by some as it was decried by others'[11] – was regarded as the work of a diligent schoolboy – undoubtedly a worthy bureaucrat, but someone totally unfamiliar with troops and ignorant of the role of senior officers.[12] Once again we find a generation gap within the officer corps: 'Nothing is more laughable than these battles dreamed up and cobbled together by scribblers who sheathed their swords so long ago, if they ever drew them at all!'[13]

Billard reckoned that the competitive exercises were unproductive: 'In general, a competitive command-post exercise is spent in endless palaver, with noses glued to the map.'[14] But Joffre believed in the importance of these tactical exercises. In 1908, while in command of an army corps, he ordered that each of his artillery *groupes* should do a weekly command-post exercise, on the map or on the ground. Major René Alexandre, newly allocated to the 17th Field Artillery Regiment at La Fère, noted the confusion of his fellow officers at that time, for nobody, not even the colonel, knew how to mount such an exercise.[15] After Joffre became chief of the General Staff, he tried to revive this officer-training. He ordered an increase in the number of command-post exercises and of garrison manœuvres, but during his visits he noted much inertia.[16]

### Generals

The training of generals for the operational command of large units also proved inadequate. In 1905, a member of the National Assembly called Auguste Gervais, a former officer who sat on the Army Commission, wrote on his return from the annual, large-scale manœuvres:

> The inadequate training of our command is most apparent. I do not want to mention names, but in practice, many leaders, taken aback by the demands of situations with which they are unfamiliar, lack coolness, judgement and common sense. I do not want to mention every mistake I saw, some of which are really beyond the absurd, but blunders occur that should not be made.[17]

Similarly, Joffre noted after the disastrous manœuvres of 1913 'that from army corps level, minds were not prepared for the conditions of modern warfare. ... In too many cases, minds were still paralysed by the habits of routine. Above all, knowledge about strategy was almost completely non-existent.'[18]

It must be pointed out that an officer who became a general might do so only twenty or twenty-five years after leaving the Staff College. These years often had a sterilizing effect. Officers during that time were practically left to educate themselves and keep abreast of technical changes or the lessons of recent wars. Furthermore, the most outstanding officers were allocated to staffs, where they had almost no contact with the troops. Once the Centre for Advanced Military Studies began its work in 1911, it was possible to alleviate these defects. But the officers who were trained at the Centre did not have enough time to rise to command large units by the time the war broke out. They did, however, prove to be excellent chiefs-of-staff.

The average age of the generals was higher than the life expectancy at that time: it ranged from fifty-nine years for the commanders of infantry brigades to sixty-seven years for the commanders of Territorial divisions.[19] These officers had been obliged to absorb a whole range of technical innovations during the forty-odd years of their military career, including a large number in the last few years before the Great War. They had had to do so by working on their own and with no particular supervision. Neither their standing nor their age motivated them to innovate or to take an interest in changes that could only undermine their authority, which was based on seniority and, in many cases, on political patronage.

Some divisional and army corps commanders took part in the large-scale manœuvres, but they never had any other chance to command units of a similar size to their war strength. The *généraux de division* would therefore find that they ended up commanding ten times as many men in wartime as they had ever commanded in peacetime. Furthermore, most of these *généraux de division* were infantrymen who remained ignorant of the use of other arms. They only really discovered their divisional artillery *groupes* when on manœuvres, and owing to this lack of familiarity they tended to monitor just their own arm: 'We therefore see an infantry general taking personal charge of a battalion or even a company.'[20]

The shortage of training grounds meant that many manœuvres were done only on maps, and as a general rule just one artillery officer was called to take part.[21] Target practice – firing exercises specific to artillerymen – almost always happened without any tactical context. General Alexandre Percin concluded in 1914: 'If we were to take the field tomorrow, our infantry divisions and divisional artillery would be commanded by leaders inadequately trained in the combined use of the two arms.'[22]

The general officer corps was ill-suited to modern warfare and was clearly in need of an overhaul. But it was difficult for the chief of the General Staff to withdraw a command that had been granted by a decision of the Minister of War. A law was therefore passed in 1912 to make it easier to remove generals whose incompetence became too blatant. Its impact was limited by the need, when removing a general, to request both the Minister of War's approval and the signature of a decree by the President of the Republic. The problem was how to prove incompetence in peacetime. Joffre and the Minister of War, Adolphe Messimy, decided to use the large-scale manœuvres for this purpose, since inability became blindingly obvious during manœuvres. Yet this purge was barely under way by the time the war broke out and did nothing to spare three future marshals – Ferdinand Foch, Emile Fayolle and Philippe Pétain – from experiencing slow peacetime promotion. It was October 1913 before Foch obtained command of an army corps. (He was sixty-three years-old in 1914.) Fayolle and Pétain both appeared to have reached the end of their careers by 1914, basically as a result of personal enmities.

## Training Insufficiencies

### Insufficient men

After a period of vacillation in the wake of 1871, the responsibility for training fell increasingly on the captains, the company commanders. This added responsibility went hand-in-hand with the new tactical role they had acquired. Yet at the same time, a regiment was seen less as a training school than as a nucleus that could be expanded to become a wartime formation. This meant that the number of regiments was deemed more important than their fullness. Company strengths were all the lower because of this desire to have a large number of regiments on mobilization. The fact that a unit was organized differently in wartime made its training all the more complicated.

An infantry company had a war strength of 250 men. This included the active personnel and also the reservists who rejoined the unit on mobilization. The Cadres Law of 1875 fixed the company's active strength at ninety soldiers, plus sixteen NCOs, corporals, drummers and buglers, making a total of 106 men. This was a significant improvement on the skeletal strengths of the aftermath of 1870. These 106 men increased to 125 after 1887 as a result of the disbandment of some units, but fell to 115 men by the turn of the century. In any case, these were just established strengths, since the captain in command of the company constantly had to put up with the regiment's support services removing however many of his officers, NCOs and corporals they reckoned they needed. The company was just 'a reservoir from which everyone drew'.[23] Absences for sickness, leave and all sorts of other reasons also had to be taken into account. They were all the more numerous in that the Two-Year Law of 1905 reduced the number of exemptions as much as possible and thereby brought recruits into the ranks who were in poor physical condition. Consequently, each company had no more than eighty men actually present during the exercises.[24]

The fact that up until 1914 companies were training with just one-third of their war strength produced many illusions. *Section* leaders could easily command the handful of men around them simply by shouting orders while standing up. They did not realize how difficult they would find it to control the fire of the fifty men that the regulation prescribed. Similarly, the captain, who might spend seven or eight years in his post, often acquired the habit of a highly centralized command style, especially as two of his four *section* leaders were young and inexperienced recruits. Everything militated in favour of tactical rigidity, and indeed a company almost invariably acted in a block under its commander's orders. By way of comparison, a German active company consisted of 140 men, with twice as many NCOs as a French company. The differences in strength might seem minor. Yet their importance was noted whenever French battalions spent several months stationed in fortresses with their strength temporarily topped-up, for these battalions proved far more proficient when they subsequently rejoined their regiments. The difference in quality was even clearer with the covering units that were guarding the frontiers of eastern France, namely thirty infantry regiments and all the battalions of foot *chasseurs*. Company strengths in these units were as high as 160 men.

It soon became clear that an established strength of 115 men per company was too low for first-rate tactical training. But it proved difficult to obtain more men, short of disbanding some of the regiments. As a result, the non-combatant posts were targeted. The politician Félix Chautemps protested against soldiers being used to fill the dozens of non-combatant employments within units whereas the Germans used civilians. He was particularly indignant about the 3,000 musicians who were trained every year in the regimental bands, and who received inadequate combat training even though they could not be used as bandsmen in wartime. Yet the proposal to abolish the bands sparked such an outcry among local politicians that the idea was quickly buried. As for employing civilians, that notion was soon dropped because of the costs involved and the fear that trade-unionism would be introduced into the barracks. As a result, Captain Billard could still describe a regiment in 1913 as being composed of an enormous musical band, machine-gun sections, detachments of telephonists, cyclists, a herd of motor-cars and some 'phantom companies'.[25] The solution that was adopted – just one year before the war – was the Three-Year Law, which increased company strength to 140 men.

Another of the French army's problems was its cadre ratio (the number of officers and NCOs, as a proportion of a unit's total strength). In 1905, a German company of 140 men had four officers and fourteen NCOs, or a cadre ratio of 13 per cent. A French company, if we ignore those units that were covering the frontiers, had three officers and seven NCOs, making a cadre ratio of 9.5 per cent, and the ratio was even lower if the men employed in non-combatant roles are excluded.[26] Yet the quality of training was often directly related to the cadre ratio. The ratio became all the more important in 1905 when the reduction in the length of military service made more efficient methods necessary. The shortage of professional NCOs was particularly critical. Professional NCOs were a prime target for the anti-militarism of the start of the twentieth century and they were badly paid. Many of them – and often they were the best – became officers as a result of passing the competitive examinations held by the schools of the various arms. The bulk of the NCOs within the cadres of units were therefore conscripts, willing but hardly any better trained than the men they commanded. This, combined with the absence of enough NCOs, meant that the officers had to deal with subordinate tasks,[27] and the training was often over-simplified. In the artillery, for example, the gunners handled just one type of gun, with one or two types of ammunition, and one or two models of fuses.

### Insufficient boldness

New recruits normally arrived at their regiments at the start of October. During their first year, they did recruit drill, followed by *section* and then company training. Towards the end of May, they had to pass a unit assessment before a panel of the regiment's field officers. The summer was generally devoted to battalion and regimental exercises, ahead of the autumn manœuvres. (The autumn manœuvres were held within the various army corps, and some of the army corps took part in large-scale manœuvres during the same season. On average, each army corps took part in the large-scale manœuvres once every three years.) The recruits' second year, which actually lasted just ten months, was devoted to internal duties and collective training. Yet there is no disputing that the training programme was constantly being undermined by a whole range of duties, including parades, the maintenance of barracks and equipment and the provision of guards of honour for dignitaries as well as sentries for the large number of military compounds. Another duty was intervening to maintain law and order, and there were many such interventions under the governments of Emile Combes (1902-5) and Georges Clemenceau (1906-9). Furthermore, there was the officer's social role (civic and patriotic training), which was growing in importance at this time, not to mention the educational and leisure activities (clubs and libraries for the soldiers).

All these duties and services frequently took priority over tactical training, which received little supervision and was less likely to advance an officer's career. In the cavalry, there remained an average of just twelve hours or so a month for horse-riding.[28] The limitation on the time devoted to tactical preparation on the ground was made even worse by a decline in the motivation of the cadres. Eugène Treignier, who was a member of the National Assembly and sat on the Army Commission, pointed out in 1912 that when an officer remained over twenty years in a company as a lieutenant or captain, it was impossible 'for such unvarying activities to sustain zeal and interest for so long'.[29] At a time when physical education was still a new concept, it was too much to expect the many lieutenants who were in their forties to be perpetually keen to repeat the same excursions to the training ground every year.

Military training was widely seen as being primarily a 'breaking-in'. Recruits often came from the rural population, and under the model inherited from the *Ancien régime* and from centuries of fighting in close order, training sought to instil in the new soldiers some of the noble qualities that the officer corps possessed by birth. Of all the methods used to instil those qualities, close order remained in favour. It entailed having a unit carry out movements like a machine. This process of automation by repetition and by the association of shouts with motions had parallels with the work of Ivan Pavlov, who won the Nobel Prize in 1904, or with John B. Watson's behaviourism. It fitted perfectly into the prevailing penchant at that time for the 'social sciences'. Such methods were useful for all the parades, guards of honour and other 'rendez-vous' I mentioned earlier, and had the additional advantage of not requiring specific training grounds. (Sites such as firing ranges or fields of manœuvre were few in number and often far away.) These methods were a great help for 'captains who were hard put to find something for their men to do'.[30]

Astonishingly, the formalism of the parade ground often gave way to a degree of laxity on the training ground, especially during the years of political turmoil. The German military attaché at Paris, Gerhard von Mutius, was surprised to see a French *section* playing football instead of training. He even witnessed an incident during the 1908 manœuvres that was incredible for a Prussian:

> I even came upon a skirmish line in which a newspaper vendor was successfully offering his wares. The newspaper-reading riflemen presented a bizarre picture. The officers looked on in acquiescence.[31]

Von Mutius had the impression that drill in particular was a compromise with the goodwill of the troops more than a serious school of obedience. The Italian military attaché returned from the 1908 manœuvres with the same impression of indiscipline: 'It was not rare to see troops in the firing line reclining in careless postures, just as it was not unusual to hear the officers repeat the same warning order, given in any case in a tone more of advice than of command.'[32]

Such habits remained strong just a few years before the war broke out. Lieutenant Emile Laure sought to bring about change in some of these attitudes, but in 1912 he noted the extent to which many of his comrades:

> regretted the evolution of our military institutions, and wanted to disown battalions that broke with the traditions of close order, disown soldiers who were taught to lie down under gusts of shrapnel instead of defying them by standing up to their full height, and disown young officers whose attraction to intellectual work seemed bound to wipe out for ever their taste for adventure.[33]

'Captain Jibé' noted that 'for some years now, the new ideas have been battering away at the sacrosanct citadel of the close order. But they find it difficult to enter a milieu whose members have almost all been inevitably conditioned by their initial training – a training based primarily on the correction of movements.'[34]

His remarks showed there was some validity to accusations from left-wing members of the National Assembly that the military caste had sabotaged the 'two-year army'. (The length of military service had been reduced in 1905 from three years to two.) Yet rather than regard it as a case of deliberate sabotage, we should see it as a conservatism that was reinforced by the inadequacy of the means allocated to the army. Monteilhet's verdict was not that far from the truth in regard to much of the home army:

> Three months of physical training for the soldiers, twenty days of drill in a camp for the regiments, fifteen days of large-scale manœuvres for the army corps. For the rest, internal duties.[35]

### Insufficient means

The shortage of means was particularly serious as regards the manœuvre training camps. The French army lacked the firing ranges and exercise grounds needed for first-rate training. To supplement the large camp at Châlons, numerous small camps were created after 1871, where infantry regiments could train and artillery batteries could do firing practice. (These artillery camps were just narrow strips of land, some 5 or 6 km long.) But this infrastructure soon proved inadequate as a result of the increase in the range of weapons and in the amount of artillery and the growing necessity for cooperation between the arms.

Two commissions, in 1897 and 1907, recommended imitating the Germans and creating no fewer than about ten camps for the three arms. But between 1908 and 1911, France assigned just 4 million *francs* a year for this purpose, compared with the German figure of 14.4 million.[36] In 1911, whereas the Germans had twenty-six camps larger than 5,000 hectares for the use of their army corps, the French army had available just eight. These eight camps were unfinished, and only four of them were at least 6,000 hectares in extent. Barely one-third of the active units and a quarter of the reserve units were able to spend time there. Some army corps were located too far away from the camps to be able to do combined-arms combat training.[37] An ambitious programme of 135 million *francs* over a seven-year period started to be implemented in 1911, but achieved little since the budgetary allocations failed to materialize. (Just 7.35 million *francs* were provided in 1913, instead of the anticipated 19 million.) A 15-million *franc* programme for laying out small training zones for reserve regiments received allocations of only 250,000 *francs* in 1913.[38] To aggravate the problem, all these camps were constructed at the same time. At each camp, the required tracts of land were bought not in one go, but in succession over a period lasting several years. As a result, land prices exploded in the vicinity of where the work was being carried out, which made the expansion of camps much slower.[39]

The manœuvre training camps were not the only thing in short supply. France had taken the gamble of having a mass army comparable to Germany's despite not having Germany's resources. This resulted in budgetary deficits, and so cuts were made to the training means. General Alexandre Percin condemned these deficiencies in his book, *Combat,* published in 1914:

> Our infantry will acquire greater skill in firing and in exploiting the terrain only when it has been given training means, which at the moment it completely lacks. It lacks cadres. It lacks shooting stands, fields of manœuvre, firing ranges and training camps.[40]

In 1912, a report from a member of the National Assembly, Eugène Treignier, confirmed these deficiencies: 'The training resources for our active regiments are totally inadequate. The musketry and gymnastics training, and even drill, are far from reaching the proficiency indicated by the regulations.'[41]

A series of practical problems also existed. The garrisons were scattered throughout France, and many battalions were accommodated inside towns in cramped barracks. In winter, during the period of individual training, horsemen found it difficult to use the grounds situated outside town. Spring was the time for company or battalion exercises, but these exercises required space, and the crops were strictly out of bounds. Training in the field was often limited, therefore, to marching along roads. General Charles-Arthur Maitrot reckoned: 'The infantryman had a fundamental weakness: he knew little or nothing. In particular, exploiting the terrain was almost unknown to him. He marched, but did not manœuvre.'[42]

The introduction of the Three-Year Law meant that two annual classes of conscripts started their military service in 1913 instead of the usual one. At a stroke, it increased the number of men to be trained, thereby aggravating the situation even further, while also creating other problems such as clothing and accommodation. The disorganization was all the greater in that the numbers of NCOs, which had been proportionately lower than in the German army even before 1913, failed to keep pace with the increased numbers of men. All these deficiencies had serious consequences that contributed to the infantry's unimpressive musketry, to the difficulties in coordinating the various arms and to the clumsy tactics that many units displayed whilst manœuvring.

## The example of musketry
The infantry's musketry policy came under the responsibility of the Musketry Training School. The School was based at Châlons camp, which is now Mourmelon camp in the *département* of the Marne. As well as testing new individual weapons, it ran five-month musketry courses for training the small-arms instructors of regiments or military schools. It also held weaponry courses lasting one month.

The Musketry Training School was complemented by two Applied Schools for Infantry Musketry, which were aimed at NCOs and were located at the camps of Le Ruchard (25 km south-west of Tours) and La Valbonne (25 km north-east of Lyon). Although the Musketry Training School was commanded by a mere colonel, it played a major role in the evolution of infantry combat. The philosophy that developed at the School was based on the assumption that the infantryman needed supervision if he was to be able to handle the complex steps involved in firing a rifle. If left to his own devices, a soldier would inevitably waste his ammunition without hitting anything. The notion that fire had to be centralized seemed to be confirmed by the initial lessons to be drawn from the actions at Plevna in 1877,[43] which highlighted the effectiveness of massed fires at long range. By the start of the twentieth century, therefore, the conception of tactical fire in the attack was as follows:

- at more than 800 metres from the enemy: fire was avoided as much as possible, as distances were difficult to judge;

- at medium distances, between 800 and 500 metres: these were suitable for the period of controlled or collective fires, which were regarded as the real firefight. The infantry *section* was therefore employed like an artillery battery to crush enemy resistance with 'gusts' and 'sprays' of bullets;
- at short distances: fire discipline progressively gave way to instinct, and there was less of a need to judge distances. Fire seemed less important than movement, and so individual fire at will was allowed.

*

In this context, it was largely pointless, or even harmful, to push individual musketry training too far. Overly accurate fire would result in too small a spray and would not cover the whole of the target. Most recruits seemed incapable of anything more than an average proficiency unless they had intense training, and even that level, which they had struggled to attain, fell when they were placed under the stress of combat. Experiments showed that fear caused the pupil – the opening of the iris of an eye – to dilate. This caused the soldier's fire to become less accurate, as he could no longer estimate distances correctly.

To demonstrate the limited importance of individual musketry training, the Musketry Training School even arranged for collective fires to be carried out on the ranges, first by an infantry unit and then, under the same conditions, by a unit of the train, which had, of course, received less advanced training. The results revealed no significant difference between the two units. Consequently, the emphasis was placed instead on training the cadres and on improving optics suitable for estimating distances accurately.

These notions had a major impact on subsequent events. As I have already highlighted, they led to closed-up dispositions, and this was all the more the case in that fire superiority – assessed by the difference in the amount of lead fired by either side – amounted to putting more rifles into line within a given zone than the enemy. Lieutenant-Colonel Jean-Baptiste Montaigne thought that this was similar to combat in the Renaissance era, but with 'pikes 2 km in length'. Such a concentration of men impeded both the tactical flexibility that the French extolled and the thinning-out of formations that was necessary under fire. The extension of combats in space and time raised fears about supply problems, so the supervision of ammunition consumption verged on becoming an obsession. Colonel Foch stressed in his course at the Staff College that:

> Fires that are controlled or at least directed, disciplined fires – either by volley or by bursts in short-lived periods of firing at will – are the only ones that good infantry will carry out when heavily engaged. In contrast, slow, continuous, undirected fires – wasteful firing – as well as disorderly firing at will ... must be strictly forbidden as being pointless squandering.[44]

The 1904 *Infantry training regulation* took up this idea several times, notably in Article 192: 'The *section* leader must put all his energy into preserving fire control for as long as possible. If the firing was left to the skirmisher, it would inevitably lead to excessive ammunition consumption without any significant result.'[45] None of this encouraged improvements to be made to rifle training. 'The tactical training of the rifleman is still virtually unknown to us ...', stated Major Louis Loyzeau de Grandmaison in 1908. 'You might almost think it was just an inessential extra.'[46]

Montaigne described his garrison at Castelnaudary (50 km south-east of Toulouse), where two battalions had to make do with a single firing range that had just a couple of firing positions at ranges of 400 and 200 metres.[47] This, too, did nothing to encourage the adoption of more modern weapons. It was decided to keep the Gras rifle of 1874, which was a single-shot weapon with no magazine and was a mere improvement of the Chassepot of 1866. This was done rather than adopt a more modern weapon such as the Kropatschek, an Austrian repeating rifle. (Using the bolt of the Kropatschek to eject a spent cartridge was enough to insert a new round into the barrel.) Hence French troops found themselves fighting on the frontier of Tonkin in the mid-1880s with single-shot weapons against Chinese forces equipped with the Winchester repeating rifle.[48]

The next step was a semi-automatic weapon, with the bullet being automatically loaded after each shot. But Lieutenant Emile Laure was one of the many who had serious reservations. 'Heaven forbid that this [semi-]automatic-rifle should ever be imposed on us ...', he wrote in 1912. 'How could quick-firing infantry not end up becoming enslaved to its ammunition?'[49]

As a matter of fact, there were no plans in 1914 to replace the old Lebel rifle. Yet, in this respect, too, the South African war had been a revelation. Some commentators, having noted the effectiveness of the widely spaced-out Boer fighters, began to think that riflemen were perfectly capably of managing by themselves, and they were strengthened in this line of thought by the example of wild-game hunting. They therefore argued that fire at will should become the core principle. Montaigne showed that a rifleman's average proficiency could quickly be raised by using appropriate methods. He described how a battalion commander spent three years devising one such method, which he then applied in 1900. The result was that the twelve worst shots in the battalion managed to hit the target with 100 per cent of their rounds when firing at a range of 400 metres. But the Musketry Training School refused to test his method.[50] Montaigne himself, in the initial sight adjustment of weapons in his own company, achieved an accuracy seven times better than that required by the regulation.[51] He also pointed out that allowing individual soldiers to control their own fire helped control their stress, and therefore limited the drop in effectiveness that occurred in combat.

Grandmaison went even further in criticizing the Musketry Training School's policy, which was based almost entirely on the weapon's technical aspect and not its psychological aspect. 'They seem', he wrote, 'to have lost sight of the fact that a unit is not a collection of rifles, but a collection of men armed with rifles.'[52] Grandmaison began by explaining how difficult it was for an officer to direct fire while being posted under cover himself. The officer had to assess the range and decide the right elevation and aiming point, and misjudging the range by just 200 metres would result in the effectiveness of the fire being non-existent. The soldiers themselves were subject to various psychological phenomena, such as inhibition or an adrenalin rush, a tendency to focus on the immediate threat and the instinctive imitation of what men nearby were doing. On the battlefield, these phenomena destroyed the uniformity of behaviour that was seen when a unit was on the firing range. On a firing range, the spray of fire against a large target was generally well distributed. But in combat: 'you note a vast, and completely uneven, dispersion ... It's a shower that covers a considerable extent of ground, and at some points turns for a while into a downpour.'[53]

A soldier fired a great number of shots, if only to relieve his stress. His priority targets were anything that posed a threat to him personally. Stray shots became common, whereas on the firing range they remained rare and did not vary much in frequency. Yet some riflemen were particularly effective in combat. This meant that centralized fire control was just an illusion:

> So no more firing ploys, no more sprays of bullets directed to their destination by means of skilfully indicated reference points, no more targets soundly chosen on the basis of their vulnerability and no more artificial concentration of fires. When a combatant finds himself in the difficult conditions with which we are familiar, he will fire without any malice at whatever he sees best, at whatever catches his attention. If he sees nothing, or has trouble seeing anything, he will fire at random.[54]

Priority had to be given, therefore, to advanced individual training, in an effort to increase the number of men who were good shots: 'Our entire training technique will therefore be directed towards the attainment of two results: flexibility of formations and effectiveness of fire.'[55]

Yet in 1914, only a minority of young officers supported these innovative theories. Some of these officers took the concept of the 'skirmisher of 1792' to its logical conclusion. Others were products of the 'fire culture' of the foot *chasseurs*. One former foot *chasseur*, Pétain, was attached to the Musketry Training School at Châlons in 1900, only to be transferred the following year after disagreeing with the prevailing ideas at the School. But such men were exceptional. The overwhelming majority of the infantry remained devotees of collective fire.

### The neglect of supplementary training

In 1905, the duration of military service in the French army was reduced from three years to two. The need to compensate for the lost year, combined with the adoption of more flexible and decentralized combat methods for the infantry, acted as a spur for making better use of the preparatory training that occurred before the start of military service and also better use of the periods that men spent on the reserve afterwards. Yet there existed a contradiction that proved impossible to resolve. On the one hand, restrictions were placed on costs and there was a disparagement of a professional (as opposed to conscript) army. On the other hand, it was hoped that young Frenchmen would volunteer to do military preparations or to be reservist NCOs and officers. Although the Law of 8 April 1903 tried to enhance the military preparation, the results were disappointing. This Law instituted a certificate of military aptitude that endorsed periods of training undertaken in an approved civilian society. This certificate made it possible to become a corporal after four months of service, and then in many cases a sergeant or even a reservist second lieutenant. Yet this option did not prove particularly popular. One reason was that not enough funds were made available: the annual budget for the military-service preparation societies was just 390,000 *francs,* compared with 1.5 million in Germany. Furthermore, the scheme had much in common with the school instruction battalions created in Paris from 1882, which themselves were too reminiscent of the National Guard of the end of the Second Empire that had provided the hard core of the participants in the *Commune,* the 1871 insurrection in Paris.[56] The military preparation only really got under way in 1911, when the certificate-holders were given the right to choose where they would be garrisoned.[57]

The reservists were a bone of contention. Some commentators saw them as a new National Guard, a useless or even dangerous force, but others regarded them as a manifestation of the army's Republican character. As a result, changes in the organization of reserve units reflected a high degree of uncertainty. An early arrangement, whereby a battalion of reservists was incorporated into each active regiment, was replaced with an entire army corps of reservists going into the line with the field corps. At the end of the nineteenth century, the organizational structure settled down, and was based on the concept of reserve divisions that were assembled in groups behind the field corps. In addition to these entire units of reservists, other reservists were used to bring the active units up to strength on mobilization, with the result that an active regiment's war strength was about one-and-a-half times its strength in peacetime. Hence the dissemination of tactical ideas within the military also had to take account of the reserve units and above all the networks formed by the reservist officers.

The first problem regarding the reservists was one of numbers. By 1905, the shortage of reservist officers was acute. This was notably so in the infantry, which lacked more than 6,000 of them – a shortfall of as much as half the required number.[58] The Two-Year Law of 21 March 1905 tried to improve the situation by taking pupils of the scientific *Grandes écoles* and making reservist second lieutenants out of them with the help of a sound military training. (The *Grandes écoles* are prestigious, specialized schools of higher education, separate from the university system.) Other young men who wished to become reservist second lieutenants could do an initial year of ordinary military service and then, if they were deemed suitable, take a six-month course at a training school of an arm, before spending the final six months of their military service as a second lieutenant. We should also note that, after 1900, a reservist staff officers' course provided excellent instruction every year for 600 reservist officers throughout the country. (In 1911, this course was placed under the direction of the commandant of the Staff College.)

The second problem was how to maintain the initial training. Reservists had to have done two training periods by the time they were 34 years-old. Initially, these two periods each lasted four weeks, but in 1908 their total duration was reduced to forty days. (Not included in these statistics are garrison lectures, which seem to have been poorly attended.) Men older than 34 still had military obligations in the Territorial army until they were 48. They were required to do a two-week training period, although in 1908 it was reduced to nine days.[59]

These periods of reservist training were not particularly beneficial. In 1906, more than one-third of those men summoned to take part failed to turn up.[60] The cadres did not exert much authority, and activities were restricted by the shortage of training means. General Henri Bonnal reckoned in 1908 that when reserve units took part in manœuvres, they usually did no more than march, occupy their quarters and cook.[61] Officers in general had a low opinion of the reserves. General Henri de Lacroix, a former vice-chairman of the Supreme War Council, stated: 'Since 1905, all the reserve regiments brought to the training camps have proved that, without regular cadres, they had only a very limited usefulness.'[62]

The German reserves were known to be composed of younger and better-trained men on the whole than their French counterparts. It was therefore strange that many Frenchmen remained optimistic. 'It is true that our reservists will probably be superior to the German reservists', argued a member of the National Assembly, Eugène Treignier. 'Our country is the only one that, on several past occasions, has managed to improvise formations capable of taking the field.'[63]

The radicals were firm supporters of the reserves. The paradox was that it was ultimately right-wing governments that would try to revitalize the reserve units by increasing their active cadres. Despite these efforts, reserve units felt the effects of the persistent shortage of training means even more heavily than the active corps.

## On the Eve of the War

### A *disparate body*

There were also big differences in terms of where units were posted geographically. As a result, we can actually identify three different armies. The first of these armies consisted of the five so-called covering corps that guarded the frontiers with Germany and Italy. Compared to the other corps, the covering corps had superior means of men and materiel, to enable them to protect the main body of the army. Above all, their personnel had a more exacting attitude than was found elsewhere. Captain Joseph Revol, an officer of the Alpine *chasseurs* (crack, mountain infantry), did two preliminary courses before entering the Staff College. These two courses were at Nîmes with the 38th Field Artillery Regiment and at Marseille with the 1st Hussars. He was surprised by the change in atmosphere from the *chasseurs*:

> No more at Nîmes than at Marseille did I find the will to work or the competitive team spirit that motivated us at Menton as a result of the closeness of the frontier. No secondary consideration or private convenience could distract the *chasseurs* from the overriding thought of their preparation for war. But cavalrymen and artillerymen alike considered war only in terms of a dubious contingency.[64]

The covering forces had the best-trained troops, and their staffs were generally better prepared than others for controlling large units.

The Colonial Corps, though not one of the covering corps, was a case apart. Its men were first-rate, for they were largely professional soldiers, under the supervision of a reliable corps of NCOs. On the other hand, the generals and staffs of the Colonial Corps were not accustomed to fighting at army corps level.

In overall terms, the rest of the active army was inferior. The dissemination of the operational doctrine frequently depended on the good will and ability of those responsible for its implementation, but many of these officers were simply not up to the task, even if their weakness was partly offset by the high quality of the staff personnel. On the whole, French large units were mobile, either by virtue of their own means or by using the railways, and had little to worry about in terms of logistical support. Training for carrying out a movement on foot or horseback was, of course, fairly straightforward to organize and did not require many resources. In contrast, anything that required complex work – such as coordinating the cavalry's intelligence-gathering, the artillery's fire and the infantry's movements – fell short of what the regulations prescribed. Such coordination required joint training, and that was difficult because of the shortage of manœuvre training camps and also because of the particularism of the various arms. Nor was defensive combat well known, basically owing to cultural reasons. The notion of fieldworks was beginning to be more widely accepted, but only in an offensive context.

The lower down the hierarchy we look, we find the weakness of the NCO corps inevitably resulting in a centralization of combat. In turn, this centralization, combined with a persistent lack of confidence in the troops, led to combat tactics being simplified. Lieutenant Laure thought that officers were making a mistake if their training programme required companies or battalions to carry out complicated operations with a tendency to cause them to deviate from the straight and narrow.[65] Elan, stimulated by the officers setting an example, served as a substitute for rigorous training.

All these problems could be found to an even greater extent in the reserve units. Each reserve regiment was fathered by an active regiment, which provided it with cadres as a skeleton. Steps taken immediately before the war had made it possible to address the most urgent failings, notably by doubling the cadres of active NCOs in the reserve units. But it was the same, old story: the Cadres Law was not enough to make up for years of neglect. The physical ability of the men declined as their years of military service receded further into the past. Their motivation, on the other hand, was actually stronger than suspected. This was just about the only asset that the twenty-five reserve divisions would take with them to war, although those units that were fathered by the covering forces in eastern France were often better prepared. The generals who commanded these reserve divisions were older officers recalled from retirement, and many of them had previously been assistants to army corps commanders. Along with their staffs, which were cobbled together at the last moment, they were as a group ill-suited to handling divisions. The subaltern officers were fairly well trained after 1905, but the NCO corps remained weak.[66] Everything suggested that the reserve units would prove fragile in modern combat.

### Revitalizing the training

The last few years before the war also saw an attempt to revitalize training within the army as a whole. In 1906, Grandmaison wondered: 'Are our training methods suitable for both the needs of modern combat on the one hand and the necessities of short-term service on the other? There is reason to doubt it.'[67]

By asking this question, Grandmaison showed that the problems of the training process did not go unnoticed at the time. The 'Young Turks' noted the high command's inertia in this area and tried, on their level and within the limits of the means at their disposal, to 'shake some garrisons out of their torpor'.[68] Publications about combat or education became more numerous and thoroughly reconsidered training and combat, particularly in the infantry. The aim was not to alter the actual training methods, which formed a comprehensive system of instruction, but rather to 'change the habits and traditions that shaped their spirit'.[69] Captain Billard and Lieutenant Laure therefore emphasized the training of the cadres:

> Instead of spending a sleepy afternoon in the rooms or their quarters, the officers will be more usefully assembled by the colonel or major for a map exercise. This will, of course, be less beneficial than an exercise with troops, but it will be much more so than a game of bridge.[70]

Officers, they argued, should be obliged to do individual study, based on reading both the regulations and above all certain authors. (Billard recommended Ardant du Picq, Bonnal, Maud'huy, Grandmaison and Langlois.)[71]

With the training of the cadres, the focus had to be on the soldier himself, since the conditions of modern combat meant he was increasingly out of his commander's sight. Grandmaison thought that the first step had to be to rethink and simplify the individual tactical training. This entailed having to abandon some of the formalism of close order, which not only wasted time but also instilled a misleading impression that an officer would have no difficulty in commanding his troops on the ground. It was necessary to train the recruits, starting from an almost Taylorian analysis of the infantryman's 'work' – what Grandmaison called 'the quest for the maximum useful return per man'.[72] At the same time, it was necessary to carry out a sort of indoctrination so the soldier absorbed a few simple precepts that he was to apply in any circumstances. This was close to the notion of an *homo offensivus*, an 'offensive man' who could be hurled against the enemy.

In 1914, with war apparently imminent, the pace of these efforts picked up. General Louis Franchet d'Espèrey had all his divisions spend time at Sissonne camp (35 km north of Reims).[73] Colonel de Maud'huy had been an outstanding trainer of his regiment, the 35th Infantry, and other excellent trainers were now commanding fine regiments, including Pétain of the 33rd Infantry and Grandmaison of the 153rd.

*

We have seen that it was possible to detect a gap, and even contradictions, between the various operational concepts on the one hand and the training regulations of the arms on the other. A chasm also separated what was demanded from corps and the reality of what they knew how to do. Units varied widely, but the practice – in other words, the sum total of the competencies that formed the foundation of tactics – was particularly poor when compared with the intellectual ferment of the officers' Forum. The choice that France made to have an army the same size as that of a wealthier adversary imposed severe material constraints. The Three-Year Law made it possible to fill the units out again at the last moment, but the problem of the manœuvre training camps remained unresolved when the war broke out. In 1914, a major effort was made in the 20th Infantry Division under General Elie Boë to organize a methodical combat and a sound use of fire. But, as Lieutenant-Colonel Maurice Larcher noted, 'its progress in this direction had been hindered by the shortage of training grounds and the dispersed nature of the garrisons. Despite energetic efforts, it displayed an inclination for doing it rather than having actually mastered the skill.'[74]

Resolving the problem of mindsets was yet more difficult. In many ways, France's Republican army proved even more aristocratic than the German imperial army. Although members of the old nobility were in a minority, their standards of behaviour were shared by the vast majority of officers, with the exception of the so-called 'hooligans' of the small, colonial army. The officer corps was compartmentalized into 'estates', where everyone was bound by duties and values – such as honour, courage, example and the sense of sacrifice – that considerably transcended the regulations. The rank and file were the victims of social prejudices that remained pronounced in these middle-class officers. They were therefore subjected to both patriotic indoctrination and the automation of their movements. The combat methods of fire and movement collided with a reluctance to place trust in men from the common classes. So acute was this deadlock that only after several years of war did it really disappear.

*Chapter 4*

# The Choice of Arms

The arms were intermediate organizations between the regiments and the high command. The three main ones were the infantry, the cavalry and the artillery. Each of these arms had four components: its technical and material assets, its organizational structures, its tactical methods and its culture. Culture is deemed to be the sum of the shared norms of thought and behaviour that people pick up through a learning process and by imitating each other.

Each of the four components of the arms evolved under the influence of numerous driving forces, such as technical innovation or psychological changes. These components also interacted with each other. For example, the invention of *Poudre B* – smokeless powder – led to the design of a new weapon, the Lebel 8mm rifle (technical innovation). The new rifle changed the combat methods (dispersion), which in turn led to new organizational structures (independence of the infantry *section*). Lastly, these changes collided with a cultural element (centralization of command), which reduced their impact (the captain in command of a company remained the tactical mastermind).

During the period that interests us, an abundant technical offer resulted in the material component of the arms being their centre of dynamism. A collective imagination enriched by several centuries of war made the cultural component a rather conservative centre. The other two components – the organizational structures and combat methods – fluctuated constantly between these two extremes, in accordance with various strategies, as the arms strove to meet three objectives. These objectives were to adapt to the enemy threat, to preserve internal cohesion and to avoid any loss of status in relation to the other arms. Many attempts at change were therefore made up until August 1914 within all the components, in the midst of real rivalries or constraints and within the context of efforts to imagine what a future war would be like.

## The 'Bayonet Men'
### The big battalions
The traditional infantry unit was the regiment. It normally contained three battalions and three machine-gun sections, but some exceptions existed, such as the reserve regiments, fortress regiments and overseas regiments. Each battalion had four companies, except for the *chasseurs,* whose battalions consisted of five or six companies. A company had four *sections*. Each *section* contained fifty men and was similar in size to a British platoon.

This organizational structure had changed as little since the Second Empire as had the uniforms or the variety of weaponry. (Ninety-eight per cent of the personnel carried the same type of rifle.) Hundreds of almost identical battalions existed, with a total strength of some 1.5 million men, or 70 per cent of the manpower of the field army that was mobilized in 1914.[1] The infantry's values still stemmed from centuries of fighting in close order. Bayonet fighting, man to man, remained the ultimate act of courage, even though statistics from conflicts since 1861 showed that the proportion of losses inflicted by cold steel amounted to no more than 1 or 2 per cent. Much talk was heard about 'seeking hand-to-hand fighting', which was reckoned to be enough to gain a moral ascendancy over the enemy. A convenient myth was therefore retained, which linked the imagery of the French Revolution with offensive fervour. Some attempts were made to adapt to the increase in firepower by using more cautious tactics, and by advocating – often through gritted teeth – artillery support. But the infantry officers lacked technical training and thought that technical problems had primarily moral solutions. They therefore preferred to accept the reality of greater firepower by idealizing sacrifice. Major Maurice Larcher, an infantryman serving in the 10th Army Corps in August 1914, described his arm's mindset and methods before the clash with the Germans at Charleroi:

> [In the offensive] any unit that came into the enemy's presence immediately thought of dashing forward, more as a reflex action than as a calculated decision. ... The attack troops gave priority to the speed and energy of their advance. They carried out the approach rapidly, in a fairly dense formation under the hostile artillery fire. ... The aim was to reach assaulting distance as soon as possible and in good order. Then the bugles and drums blew or beat the charge. The infantry dashed off against the enemy, with levelled bayonets. This was the way the manoeuvres invariably ended.[2]

Conversely:

> The mindset created by the repetition of attack exercises all but excluded the defensive. The defensive was deemed exceptional, and restricted to isolated cases. When you were not attacking, it was because you were awaiting the moment to attack. ... If units temporarily had to defend themselves, they willingly left their position at the last moment and rushed to meet the enemy assault. After an offensive failed, you did not cling to the ground. You preferred to fall back and then return to the charge with renewed vigour. Under these conditions, any work on defensive preparations was done in a cursory fashion.[3]

### The foot chasseurs

Although the infantry was a monolithic and uniform corps, it had created two small and specialized subdivisions using the foot *chasseurs*. The *chasseurs* were the infantry's élite and were formed into thirty-one autonomous battalions.[4] Each battalion contained six companies, with higher numbers of men compared with the 'line'. The *chasseurs* were stationed to cover the frontiers. The quality of these troops attracted the best officers, which had three, cumulative consequences. Firstly, there was intense competition among officers to enter the *chasseurs* and to gain the prestigious status that the *chasseurs* enjoyed. Secondly, the calibre of these officers maintained the quality of the troops. Thirdly, these élite officers often rose to the top jobs in the army, and while holding those posts tended to further the interests of the corps in which they had originally served.

The battalions of foot *chasseurs* had been created after the Napoleonic wars to act as light infantry, fighting as skirmishers ahead of the main body of the troops. Their culture was therefore based on the accurate use of fire, and also on mobility and the decentralization of combat. The bond between these dispersed men was a mixture of patriotism and *esprit de corps*. The quality of the battalions of foot *chasseurs*, combined with their autonomous character and their presence along the frontier, made them the natural choice for serving as the infantry's tactical laboratory. These were the battalions that were selected to give birth to two subdivisions: the Alpine *chasseurs* and the cyclist *chasseurs*.

The creation of the Alpine *chasseurs* was an innovation that was adopted as a precautionary and imitative measure. It followed the formation in 1872 of the Italian *Alpini*, a specialized, mountain warfare corps. When Italy joined the Triple Alliance in 1882, this corps became a potential foe. The men behind the creation of a French version were Ernest Cézanne – the representative of the *département* of the Hautes-Alpes in the National Assembly and one of the founders of the Alpine Club – and Lieutenant-Colonel Charles Zédé. In 1878, Zédé obtained permission from General Charles Bourbaki, the military governor of Lyon, to try out some manœuvres high up in the mountains with a battalion of foot *chasseurs*. The unit chosen was the 12th Battalion under Major Paul Arvers, who was an experienced mountaineer and a member of the French Alpine Club of Lyon. These trials soon involved the 13th and 14th Battalions of Foot *Chasseurs* as well, and continued until 1885. The following year, 1886, saw the creation of 'free squads', each composed of a sergeant, a corporal and fifteen *chasseurs*. These squads were the forerunners of the later skier-scout *sections*, and their purpose was to gather intelligence out in front of their battalion or on its flanks and to carry out raids or ambushes. Also in 1886, the possibility of using artillery in the mountains was explored.[5] In 1888, several laws prescribed the creation of one battalion of Alpine *chasseurs* for each valley, making a total of twelve. (A thirteenth battalion was added in 1912.) Each battalion was to have not only its six companies of *chasseurs*, but also a light artillery battery and a company of engineers. This was a highly innovative organizational structure. Since these battalions were not enough to cover the whole of the Alps, they were supplemented by three infantry regiments. One of these regiments, the 159th, launched the development of 'army skiing' at Briançon, at the instigation of Captain François Clerc and with the help of Norwegian instructors. In 1903, Clerc founded the first Ski Training School.[6]

The creation of the cyclist *chasseurs* followed a different path. Whereas the Alpine *chasseurs* had been created in order to adapt to an environment, the cyclists were a case of exploiting a technical innovation that was both cheap and widespread. The initiatives came from units that in the early 1890s were experimenting with using the bicycle for various missions, such as intelligence-gathering or the communication of orders. The trials were inconclusive, until Lieutenant Henri Gérard in collaboration with a French manufacturer called Charles Morel developed a folding, all-terrain bicycle.[7] On Gérard's instigation, the cavalry agreed to joint trials, for it had need of mobile infantrymen. In 1897, the first cyclist detachments appeared at the large-scale, annual manœuvres. The following year, one provisional cyclist company was attached to each cavalry division, with promising results. In the absence of any decision from the high command, a pressure group formed, which appealed to generals such as Henri de Lacroix, to parliamentary representatives and to the press. In 1899, this pressure group secured the creation of the first cyclist companies. But the group split when the cavalry's future was questioned in the wake of the South African war. Some cyclist advocates sided with the cavalrymen, in the belief that their fates were linked. Others, such as Gérard, called for the cavalry to be replaced by cyclist battalions. The battalion echelon was tried out at the 1905 manœuvres, as a mobile reserve for the army corps. In subsequent manœuvres, the cyclist battalions were again attached to the cavalry and undertook all its fire missions, such as the capture and defence of points, security, flank attacks and flank or rear protection.

In 1909, a cavalry division reinforced with cyclists totally outclassed another cavalry division that lacked them. This demonstration finally convinced the cavalrymen.[8] In 1912, an infantry cadres law formally approved the creation of ten cyclist *groupes,* each consisting of three platoons. Each *groupe* was formed by combining a couple of companies from one of ten battalions of foot *chasseurs.* These companies continued to belong to their battalions of foot *chasseurs,* partly for practical reasons but also to ensure that they remained focused on their proper role as supporting infantry and not play at being bicycle-mounted cavalry.[9] Shortly before the war, the adoption of motorized machine-gun carriers, or even motor-cycles, was considered as a way of enabling greater firepower to be carried. Captain Doumenjou, of the Musketry Training School, proposed that automatic-rifles should be used to equip the *sections* once these weapons were improved.[10]

## The Virtuosos

The artillery of 1914 was equipped with three generations of materiel. The oldest generation – de Bange's system – had been produced between 1878 and 1882. It consisted of field pieces with a calibre of either 80 or 90mm, and also a series of siege or fortress pieces, namely long or short-barrelled 120mm and 155mm guns and 220 and 270mm mortars.

In 1914, the fortresses and arsenals still contained 3,500 of the de Bange 80 and 90mm guns. To these must be added around 1,000 Lahitolle 95mm pieces – which had been ordered before the de Bange pieces. There were also 2,800 of the long or short-barrelled 120 and 155mm guns, and 230 of the 220 and 270mm mortars. The total amounted to 7,500 pieces with millions of shells.[11]

The de Bange guns and mortars were robust and accurate. But their range was limited – 9,000 metres even for the long-barrelled 155mm gun. Above all, they had a slow rate of fire. Whereas the most modern pieces in existence in 1914 could fire one round every thirty seconds, the rate of fire of the heavy pieces was one round every two minutes. Since the heavy pieces were intended to be used exclusively in siege warfare, they had only cumbersome, elevated carriages that enabled them to fire over a 2-metre high gabioned parapet. (A gabion is a cylinder, or other container, filled with stones, earth or sand.) The long-barrelled guns were incapable of high-angle or plunging fires. De Bange's system pre-dated the many technical innovations that appeared in the decade from 1884 to 1894, and was unable to benefit from all of them. Among the most noteworthy inventions of this period were:

- 1884: the combination fuse, which enabled the shrapnel shell to burst at any range, either after a set period of time as an air burst, or on impact with the ground;
- 1885: *Poudre B*, which increased the muzzle velocity without changing the pressure exerted on the gun. The fact that the powder gave off no smoke enabled batteries to be concealed and also made aiming easier, which resulted in a faster rate of fire;
- 1888: the Lemoine recoil brake with recuperators enabled rates of fire to be increased;
- 1888: the Robin shell considerably improved the effectiveness of shrapnel rounds;
- 1888-91: melinite and nitrate-based explosives resulted in increased ranges and more powerful, explosive shells;
- 1893: the invention of the Estienne goniometer allowed indirect fire.[12]

These innovations, combined with advances in metallurgy (nickel steel), allowed a new field gun to be designed – a second generation of artillery piece. Light but sturdy, it would have a hydro-pneumatic mechanism to absorb the shock of the recoil. Since the increase in muzzle velocities made it possible to reduce the calibre of the shell that was used, the gun could be made even lighter.

The result was the 75mm gun (1897 model), which was capable of firing fifteen to twenty shells a minute to a distance of more than 6 km. (Its practical range was 4 km.) It was a significant technical leap, which gave the French field artillery a marked superiority over its German counterpart for years to come. The 75mm gun progressively replaced the de Bange 80 and 90mm pieces. The field army of 1914 contained 4,000 of the 75mm guns. The shells, too, were of excellent quality. From 1911, half the ammunition with the batteries consisted of high-explosive shells, with the rest being shrapnel shells.[13] High-explosive shells would be the most commonly used type during the war. They could be made to ricochet and then burst a few metres above the ground, which made them deadly against infantrymen who were not under cover.

Apart from the actual guns, the technical environment consisted of just two telephones and 500 metres of cable for every staff of a *groupe* or battery. The telephone equipment was distrusted, and was not even mentioned in the 1910 *Artillery training regulation,* even though that regulation was extremely comprehensive. The same scepticism surrounded the use of aviation for adjusting fire.[14]

The third generation of artillery equipment was that of the heavy field artillery. It will be examined separately later in this chapter, since the problems that surrounded its creation were so complex and so typical of some of the challenges facing the French army.

*

The artillery's organizational structure was determined by the characteristics of the pieces. The 75mm, or so-called 'king gun', was the standard equipment for sixty-one out of the seventy-seven artillery regiments in the French home army (as distinct from the colonial army). Of these sixty-one regiments, twenty were army corps artillery units, each of which contained four *groupes* of three batteries, or twelve batteries in all. The other forty-one regiments were divisional artillery units, and each had three *groupes* of three batteries, or a total of nine batteries. Also stationed in France were three regiments of colonial artillery, which contained different numbers of batteries. The other branches of the artillery seemed entirely peripheral. Two regiments of mountain artillery were equipped with 120 pieces of 65mm calibre. Nine foot regiments served a wide range of siege, fortress or coastal equipment. Lastly, five regiments of heavy artillery were officially created on 15 April 1914 with 308 pieces.[15]

Besides these 'gun' subdivisions, the artillery contained several subdivisions that owed their origin to its technical supervision over anything that had an engine – namely the aviation (in competition with the engineers), the motor-transport service of the baggage train and the motorized machine-gun carriers. The partnership between the engine and the gun began in 1914 with the formation of a heavy artillery *groupe* with tractors to tow its guns.

The personnel to serve the equipment were sufficient in number. The artillery as a whole contained 11,000 officers and 428,000 men, or about 20 per cent of the French army's combat strength.[16] Their quality was high. The officers of the arm all had an excellent technical training, regardless of whether or not they were graduates of the *Ecole polytechnique*. On mobilization, they were reinforced by the civil engineers of the *corps de l'Etat* (the great, prestigious State bodies), by graduates of the *Ecole polytechnique* who had left the service and by pupils of the Central School of Arts and Manufacturing and the School of Mines. The rank and file were in many cases skilled workers (the gun layers), and they were trained in accordance with the 1910 *Artillery training regulation,* which was good enough to be used throughout the war. The regulation had little to say about tactics. Similarly, the officers had few tactical preconceptions. Even if the official preference was to use the 75mm gun in direct support, there was no reluctance to adopt other methods and carry out other missions.

The grandeur of the arm was serving the guns, for artillerymen were as attached to their guns as cavalrymen were to their horses. They had the same bravado in the face of fire as the infantry and cavalrymen, and this bravado delayed the installation of gun-shields on the 75mm pieces. They also had same penchant for duelling with the enemy, and in their case it took the form of counter-battery. General Alexandre Percin highlighted this tendency:

> It's natural enough for a cavalryman to compare himself with the enemy cavalryman, to claim to be better than him and to want to prove it by going up against him. It's also natural enough to reckon that the arm to which you belong plays a dominant role in the action, to think that the same is true on the enemy's side and consequently to believe that your equivalent arm is the most important of the targets you should consider destroying.[17]

Counter-battery, therefore, had a certain allure for artillerymen, particularly as they rightly regarded the enemy artillery as the main threat. But above all, artillerymen hated the notion that their arm was an auxiliary one and that its sole purpose was to assist the infantry, the 'queen of battles'. In 1906, the artillery's technical branch produced a Ministry of War circular about firing practice in preparation for war. The instruction was fifty-six pages long, but not once did it mention the word 'infantry'. Most artillerymen therefore regarded themselves as degraded when one of the articles in the 1910 *Artillery training regulation* gave the infantry commander responsibility for indicating to the artillery the point to be hit and the time to hit it.

Nevertheless, the artillery officers were technicians, and their approach to the coming war was broader and more flexible than that of the combat arms. The notion of how the artillery was to be used tactically was fairly simple. It fitted within the overall context of extreme offensive-mindedness. The field artillery had to be capable of hitting any enemy piece that appeared, and above all it had to provide support throughout the time the infantry was attacking. The paucity, or absence, of modern means of communication meant that the combat had to be decentralized. The basic tactical unit was the four-gun 75mm battery, served by about thirty men. The battery commander, a captain, was a virtuoso in firing from a concealed position, with the pieces hidden behind a ridge line, and in rapidly unlimbering or changing position. Yet, since a battery fired only at what its commander could see, its practical range was limited to the range of his vision, or 4 km at most. The captain had to convey his observations by word of mouth or visual signals. Hence his guns had to be near him, which meant they were also near the line of combat that they needed to support. But the men had no notion of protecting themselves and digging in, for it was not expected that a battery would remain in a single position. This was in contrast to the foot artillery, which thoroughly understood static combat, but was entirely ignorant of the tactics of the other arms.

The field artillery's combat depended to a large extent on cooperation between the arms. Even though this cooperation was much talked about at the time, it was far from being achieved in reality. This was partly because of the artillerymen's previously-mentioned reluctance to think of themselves as an auxiliary arm. Another problem was a contradiction that Lieutenant-Colonel Jean-Baptiste Montaigne summed up perfectly:

> The main service that the artillery requires from the infantry is to provide targets by obliging the enemy infantry to reveal itself. On the other hand, if the infantry is to advance it requires the artillery to force the enemy infantry to hide itself.[18]

Artillery support was designed as an attack against men rather than obstacles. It was, in fact, based on notions expressed by General Langlois at the start of the twentieth century – at a time when almost all shells were shrapnel rounds, which were ineffective against defensive works, and when the superficial nature of entrenchments obliged men to reveal themselves in order to fire. The fact that men could fire while remaining hidden was ignored, despite instances of it happening in Manchuria in 1904-5. Furthermore, artillerymen had difficulty ascertaining which of the available targets was the most profitable, so they often settled for the 'fine shots', meaning those targets they found it easiest to hit. This tendency was reinforced by the fact that the opposing artillery and infantry positions were not necessarily the same: whereas artillerymen favoured open spaces, the infantry preferred positions in close terrain. General Percin noted, while serving as artillery inspector, that during the 1910 manœuvres in Picardy:

> Out of fifty-nine attacks that needed the support of guns, there were only twenty-three in which the target of the artillery fire was the objective of the infantry attack. In the other thirty-six cases, the artillery fired on targets that the infantry was not attacking, and sometimes on friendly troops.[19]

Yet the manœuvres that Percin was describing did not include real threats and the batteries were extremely close to the infantrymen. It was not particularly difficult during the manœuvres to liaise either upwards by means of the command structure, or downwards by using signalling methods, liaison agents or artillerymen attached to other units.[20]

The German army could not rely on its 77mm gun to counter the effectiveness of the French 75mm, for the 77mm was inferior in capability. A four-gun 75mm battery was at least as effective as a six-gun 77mm battery. The superiority of a French army corps with its thirty field batteries over the eighteen batteries of a German corps was therefore significant, and was heightened even further by the more rudimentary methods of the Germans, who out of bravado still neglected fire from covered positions. In order to be able to outperform the French field artillery and enable their own pieces to support the infantry, the Germans had therefore developed an entire system of counter-battery based on howitzers. These howitzers were distributed so that each division had eighteen 105mm pieces with a range of 6,000 metres, and each active army corps had sixteen 150mm pieces with a range of 7,500 metres. Available at army level was a variable number of 210mm mortars and long-barrelled, long-range guns. The Germans had spent years experimenting with counter-battery, and its effectiveness was enhanced by both observation aircraft and highly refined methods.

When the French artillery went to war, it had some weaknesses but also great potential. The Directorate of Artillery had initiated the assessment and ordering of equipment that would prove vital in the second part of the war. A large artillery park existed in the fortresses, and although these pieces had been neglected, they could soon become useful if certain modifications were made. In the shorter term, the practical firing course at Mailly camp (140 km east of Paris) ensured that the artillery also had some 'prototypes of ideas'. Major Wisse had carried out experiments at the camp in spring 1914, using the telephone to direct and control the fire of several artillery *groupes*.[21] The French had also taken a lead from the Russians in the wake of the war in Manchuria, and had practised long-range counter-battery at Mailly, sometimes using aircraft to adjust the fire.[22] Many corps knew and remembered all of this: just a few months before the war, we find some of the colonels training artillerymen in aerial observation[23] or issuing instructions on the digging-in of batteries. The quality of the personnel, particularly the officers, held out the prospect of rapid evolution, as did the lack of any dogmatism in the officers' outlook.

## The Strange Case of the Heavy Artillery

During the German army's large-scale manœuvres in 1900, the Guard Foot Artillery Regiment appeared with its heavy pieces. Two years later, the Germans adopted the mobile, heavy 150mm howitzer[24] to accompany their field army. They brought the 105mm field howitzer into service in 1909. In the years that followed, all German active corps were provided with batteries capable of hitting targets 6 or 7 km away with powerful shells.

Yet in France, the first heavy artillery regiments were added to the order of battle only in April 1914, and the materiel with which they were equipped was rather old. In short, a technical gap had opened up within the space of just a few years. This gap would have dire consequences for the French army, which would be obliged to revert to outdated models of heavy artillery pieces. These old pieces, with their slow rate of fire, would rule out any French attempt during the first years of the war to take the enemy by surprise with an audacious offensive.

A key reason for the outcome in 1870 had been the technical superiority of the Prussian artillery. That makes the French deficiency in heavy artillery in 1914 all the more astonishing. The deficiency was also contrary to the usual practice of imitating an opponent by way of precaution – a practice exemplified by the adoption of machine-guns.

How could this 'failure' have occurred, given that it had such disastrous consequences? It was not as if the idea of creating a heavy artillery was a recent one. An initial scheme after the Russo-Turkish war of 1877-8 resulted in the Baquet system. (The short-barrelled Baquet 120mm howitzer, which had a maximum range of just 5,000 metres, would be brought back into field service in 1914.) At the turn of the twentieth century, Captain Emile Rimailho, the French artillery's most famous engineer, proposed a quick-firing 155mm piece, and manufacturers such as Schneider had other prototypes in existence. Generals Léon Lombard and Marie Félix Silvestre pressed for the adoption of powerful howitzers and long-range guns after returning from Manchuria. Yet the power to make decisions was so fragmented that barely any progress was made. The General Staff had the quick-firing, short-barrelled Rimailho 155mm piece adopted in 1904. In 1909, the Supreme War Council took a further step in the same direction by asking for a study to be undertaken for a mobile 120mm howitzer. On the other hand, there was greater reluctance within the Directorate of Artillery and its technical branch, in the course of tactics at the Staff College and in the practical firing course at Mailly.

Another problem was that since 1901 the artillery was at a disadvantage in that it no longer had directors of the calibre of such men as Generals Henri Berge, Charles Philippe Antoine Mathieu and Denis François Félix Deloye, who had possessed both strength of personality and a high degree of tactical competence. Their replacements were more politically-minded staff officers. In the view of General Louis Henry Auguste Banquet, who had seen the war in Manchuria as an observer with the Japanese army,[25] these new directors lacked firm ideas on either tactical or technical issues. They therefore found it difficult to assert their authority over scattered workshops. Each of these workshops had a research department, but was short of skilled personnel and lacked any links with large-scale industry.[26] General Frédéric Georges Herr reckoned:

No overall conception existed of a coherent artillery system, with the entire range of materiel included within it, that might direct men's minds towards a shared goal, connect fragmentary studies undertaken here and there, [or] coordinate individual endeavours ... Not since the 75mm gun had been perfected at the Puteaux workshops in 1897 had anything comprehensive emerged from the studies produced by the artillery workshops.[27]

The result of this compartmentalization and bureaucratic poisoning was that the development of innovations was very slow. In 1898, Captain René Alexandre discovered at Briançon that the Italians were able to pull large-calibre artillery pieces in the mountains by using *cingoli* – simple caterpillar tracks consisting of wide, articulated, wooden blocks fitted around the rims of the wheels. The governor of Briançon had a pair of *cingoli* made and tested, for a cost of between 600 and 800 *francs*. Alexandre drew up a full report, addressed to the Directorate of Artillery. Eight years later, he attended an artillery practice at Bourges in the company of the chairman of the Artillery Committee. When the firing was over, they were shown a 155mm piece with a new contraption for putting around the wheels, a contraption that had finally been rediscovered in storage at Briançon after the Austrians had carried out a stunning mountain manœuvre using a similar device.[28]

*

Another, more straightforward, cause of this inertia was a shortage of funds. Table 1 sets out the changes in military appropriations for the purchase of materiel.[29] These funds frequently eluded the operational commanders and the men in charge of doctrine, even after the 1911 reforms. In fact, they were often administered directly by the Minister of War in conjunction with the Financial Control Directorate, which specialized in technical matters relating to the budget but in many cases was out of touch with operational realities. The combination of 'technocratic' procedures (to use a modern-day term) and the transient, political nature of a Minister of War's decisions, which were often limited to a financial year, led to short-termist management. This was particularly disastrous for costly and complex projects. As a result of the organizational confusion and shortage of resources, the different currents of thought within the artillery arm tore each other apart in trying to impose their point of view in the doctrinal debate.

The main mission of a heavy field artillery was counter-battery and, as we have seen, it was a mission that suited many artillerymen. This conception was supported by the generals who had witnessed the war in Manchuria, and later by General Herr after he had observed the fighting in the Balkans in 1912. In 1909, just a year before the new *Artillery training regulation* was issued, Major Edmond Buat even stated: 'By the time the attack infantry has reached its first decisive fire position, the artillery must have wiped out the opposing batteries that are capable of acting either directly or indirectly against the attack zone.'[30] Buat was destined to command a vast heavy artillery during the Great War.

*Table 1: Changes in military appropriations for the purchase of materiel.*

| Year | Appropriations requested for the materiel (in millions of francs) | Appropriations voted by Parliament (in millions of francs) |
|---|---|---|
| 1901 | 95 | 60 |
| 1902 | 98 | 49 |
| 1903 | 59 | 31 |
| 1904 | 61 | 28 |
| 1905 | 44 | 26 |
| 1906 | 59 | 76 |
| 1907 | 33 | 23 |
| 1908 | 88 | 60 |
| 1909 | 98 | 66 |
| 1910 | 81 | 88 |
| 1911 | 113 | 86 |
| 1912 | 98 | 84 |
| 1913 | 115 | 119 |
| Total | 1,042 | 796 |

Yet the stance of these men was undermined by their perceived bias. Many of them belonged to the foot artillery – in other words, the heavy artillery used in fortresses or sieges, which was the least prestigious branch of the arm. Opponents of the heavy artillery put forward arguments of varying degrees of logic. The first problem, they pointed out, was logistical. A member of the Supreme War Council, General Alexis Auguste Raphaël Hagron, thought that 'to be constantly dragging [the heavy artillery] in the field would be difficult, and that the army corps' logistical chain is already 15 km long and could do without being extended even further'.[31]

Another complication was the increase in the number of different calibres. General Percin took the view that: 'We would end up having light guns, light howitzers, heavy guns, and mortars, just like them [the Germans]. Yet we have enough artillery as it is. If anything, we have rather too much.'[32]

A more serious point was that firing at ranges greater than 4 km was deemed impractical because the fire could only be observed if it was within sight. As for firing within the 4 km zone, the 75mm gun was highly effective. Some men suggested using forward observers, either on foot or in an airplane, who could communicate their observations to distant batteries, but their proposed solution was met with scepticism. The artillery aviation centre at Vincennes on the eastern side of Paris, run by Lieutenant-Colonel Jean Estienne, existed for just two years before being closed in 1912. The funds for a substantial allocation of telephone equipment were voted only in July 1914.[33]

In addition, the heavy shells were reckoned to lack enough accuracy or power to be effective against dug-outs. Percin expressed himself vehemently on this issue, just a few months before the war:

> I believe in neither the destructive effects of the large-calibre shells, nor the usefulness that these effects would offer if they could be achieved on the battlefield. The 1910 regulation does not seem to believe in them any more than I do.[34]

Above all, the heavy artillery seemed inconsistent with the operational doctrine, which emphasized mobility, the infantry's aggressiveness and the direct support of the infantrymen by the artillery. Hence the doctrinaires strove to wrench the artillerymen away from their natural, 'separatist' inclination that emphasised the countering of the opposing artillery and independence in choosing targets. The doctrinaires wanted as great a concentration of fires as possible to assist the infantry in its forward march. To achieve this concentration, they did not hesitate to cut every other mission. Major de Grandmaison summed this up perfectly:

> Artillery combat is impossible to consider in isolation from that of the infantry. There is just a single combat, in which each arm plays its role for the sake of the joint aim. To attack is to advance. The infantry should know that it needs the artillery's help if it is to advance. But the artillery should not ignore the fact that its task in combat boils down to this: using its fire to ease the forward movement of its infantry. When it works for its own account and not in the immediate and direct aim of assisting the infantry, its action is worthless.[35]

If this was so, then the heavy artillery was a pointless diversion of resources. Percin remarked that 'if the Germans want to increase the number of guns in their army corps even further, we must rejoice rather than imitate them'.[36] He argued that in a war of movement, faced with the need to find extensive fields of observation, the German 105 and 150mm batteries would lack enough time to pick suitable positions and would be easy targets for the 75mm guns.

*

After years of inertia, parliament reopened the issue during the debate on the 1910 budget. It concluded that artillery pieces similar to those of the enemy needed to be acquired as a matter of urgency. Owing to the Directorate of Artillery's slow response, the government in 1911 appointed a new Director, General Justin Mengin, and created a commission of new materiel under the chairmanship of General Léon Jean Benjamin de Lamothe. In October 1911, this commission presented a requirements specification for a field howitzer and for a long-barrelled gun with a range of 12 or 13 km. In view of the urgency of the situation, it recommended holding a competition for the production of these weapons, with private industry being allowed to take part in addition to the State-run establishments. In February 1912, the Puteaux state workshops presented two weapons. A month later, the Schneider company proposed a short-barrelled 105mm howitzer that had been made for Bulgaria, as well as a long-barrelled 106.7mm gun designed for Russia. Schneider's two weapons met the design brief. The Lamothe commission asked for them to be tested during the large-scale manœuvres in western France and, in the case of the 105mm howitzer, by the Commission of Practical Studies of Field Artillery Fire at Mailly.[37]

Schneider's weapons both proved satisfactory at the manœuvres. The 106.7mm was adopted in the form of a long-barrelled 105mm gun, and studies were undertaken for a 135mm and a very long-range, long-barrelled 155mm piece. On the other hand, the 105mm howitzer was delayed, since the Commission of Practical Studies of Field Artillery Fire dragged its feet. In February 1913, the process was accelerated by General Herr's report following his return from the Balkans war, and by General Lamothe's statements that the progress that had been made had removed all the technical obstacles to the formation of the heavy field artillery. But on 7 March 1913, the Mailly commission still criticized the extent of the dispersion of the time-fused shells of the Schneider 105mm gun. Joffre, supported by General Mengin and by the Minister of War, Alexandre Millerand, disregarded the criticism and placed an immediate order for 200 of these 105mm guns. Yet the Mailly commission managed to secure the adoption of the Malandrin disk to try and limit the dispersion of the shells. The disk, when fitted to the nose of a shell, slowed it down and made it fall at a steeper angle. It was cheap and immediately available, so it won over the parliamentary representatives,[38] but was completely ineffective.

As a result of administrative delays and the Schneider company's inflexibility, only a few of the long-barrelled 105mm guns were available by August 1914. Such was the urgency that the possibility was also examined of modifying the de Bange models that were used in the fortresses, in order to make them more mobile and easier to place in firing positions in the field. Fitting the old, long-barrelled de Bange 120mm on a Mourcet gun-carriage could have given a high degree of mobility to 1,000 guns that were still effective. But many technical experts bitterly opposed such a modification. Trying to extract some benefit from the old guns in this way was deemed a pointless expense, given that the modern, long-barrelled 105mm was expected to enter service shortly.[39]

Nevertheless, attempts were made to create units of heavy field artillery, using the available weapons and equipment. But the problem of materiel was simply followed by that of personnel. Joffre proposed taking the necessary men from the coastal batteries, which had become less important as a result of France's friendship with Great Britain. His proposal provoked an outcry from elected officials in the areas concerned, and consequently from parliamentary representatives, backed by certain retired generals who were former coastal inspectors or assistants at military ports. What finally resolved the problem of personnel was the rise in manpower that resulted from the increase in the duration of military service in 1913.[40]

Five regiments of heavy artillery were finally formed in April 1914. In all, they had around 120 of the long-barrelled de Bange 120mm guns, which although already outdated had a range of 9,000 metres. They also had a total of eighty-four of the short-barrelled Baquet 120mm howitzers made by the Creusot company, though these had a short range and too slow a rate of fire. Most importantly of all, they had 100 or so of the quick-firing, short-barrelled Rimailho 155mm howitzers, which were modern, powerful pieces, quite mobile even if they had a fairly limited range of 6 km. (Hitherto, the Rimailho had been distributed in such a way that six of them were with each army corps for the purposes of siege warfare, and they had taken no part in the large-scale manœuvres.)[41] In addition, many other heavy artillery pieces had been either designed or ordered, including improved versions of all the existing models of 155mm and a long-barrelled 155mm with a very long range. These various 155mm pieces would prove essential for the war effort.

In autumn 1914, Lieutenant-Colonel René Alexandre was serving as GHQ's liaison officer to the 5th Army. He met Colonel Besse, who had been a member of the Commission of Practical Studies of Field Artillery Fire and then a professor at the Staff College. Even though they were already several weeks into the war, their conversation ran as follows:

'Now do you believe in the heavy artillery?' asked Alexandre.

'Not yet!'[42]


## Twilight of the Cavalry

On 4 August 1870, shortly after the start of the Franco-Prussian war, the French order of battle included sixty-three cavalry regiments. A month later, just eleven of them remained. All the others had been destroyed in glorious but futile actions, such as the insane charges at Reichshoffen and Floing.

In the wake of that war, a complete rethink of the cavalry's role was needed. By 1914, this appeared to have been done, by means of the various *Field service regulations* issued between 1883 and 1913. The cavalry abandoned any idea of trying to break through the enemy with a charge. From now on, its main mission was to preserve the commander's freedom of action by keeping him constantly informed and protecting him from any surprise. The start of this mission involved covering the mobilization of the army's main body along the German frontier. The next stage was exploration, which meant searching for intelligence about the enemy and the terrain. Conversely, the cavalry had to conceal its own side's movements from the enemy's means of intelligence-gathering. Armed clashes were still not completely ruled out. They might take the form of delaying actions, or raids against the enemy rear, or an exploitation to turn an enemy defeat into a disaster.

This seemed a coherent doctrine governing the cavalry's use. The cavalrymen would take the approach of adapting to these missions and to the spectacular advances in weaponry, while at the same time preserving a culture that was based on fighting on horseback with cold steel. The main line they adopted was to consider combat against the opposing cavalry as an essential prerequisite to carrying out the mission. To chase away the screen of German reconnaissance detachments, the cavalrymen needed to have superior numbers available at each point of contact. They therefore demanded the formation of strong units: cavalry brigades for attachment to the various army corps, and then divisions of cavalry, or even cavalry corps.

This obsession with the German cavalry was all the stronger in that *Kaiser* Wilhelm II regarded his cavalry as a priority. Germany had twice the number of professional cavalry soldiers as the French, and also a superior horse stock. All the

French cavalry's other missions gradually took second place to that of 'counter-cavalry', which was akin to the 'counter-battery' of the artillerymen. Implementing the counter-cavalry mission could be done in one of two ways: dismounted action using fire, as seen during the US Civil War of 1861-5, or mounted action using shock. The second method soon prevailed, in the wake of some initial wavering immediately after the 1870 war. It was more in line with the dogma of the offensive and with the values of the cavalry arm. In fact, as General Percin pointed out, there was a widespread view that 'the use of the carbine amounted to the systematic defensive, based on the excessive confidence instilled by the advances made in firearms - a confidence that caused our disasters of 1870.'[43]

This conception had the additional advantage of satisfying the 'big brothers': the heavy cavalrymen, particularly the *cuirassiers*. Charges and mounted clashes seemed more noble than a discrete surveillance carried out for the infantry's benefit. The same attitude of mind would reappear in 1916 and 1917, among cavalrymen who had 'migrated' from their arm to serve in tanks or fighter aircraft. The outcome would be much the same as what General Charles Kessler had predicted in 1902:

> [If the enemy refuses combat], the cavalry will have difficulty encountering it and ... will manœuvre in a void, wearing itself out in vain searches, and will leave the army for whose sake it is operating completely ignorant of the foe's movements. ... [If the enemy accepts combat], there will probably be an alternating succession of partial successes and setbacks for either side [in numerous, decentralized actions, and nothing decisive will come of it].[44]

The means available to the cavalry matched this doctrine governing its use. An 8mm carbine was brought into service in 1890, but with an allocation of just forty-eight rounds of ammunition and no bayonet. Nor were there any entrenching tools. Also in 1890, lances were reissued to some regiments after an eighteen-year absence. They were made either from metal or from male bamboo from Tonkin. The regimental storehouses already contained *cuirasses* weighing some 6 or 8 kg. Mobility was emphasized, partly by reducing to a minimum the weight of the kit carried on the horses, although it was still more than 120 kg. Mobility was also enhanced by the adoption, beginning in 1901, of means of crossing cuttings: first the Veyry bridge, which was 50 metres long, and then in 1913 the 100-metre long Delacroix bridge. But it was difficult to take the adaptation of equipment any further, except by carrying out a major leap by replacing the horse with the internal combustion engine. That option did not really appear until just a few years before the Great War.

In terms of organizational structures, several cavalries can be identified. First of all there existed a 'noble' cavalry. Its structures had remained unchanged since the Napoleonic era, which was the main focus of its dreams. The basic unit was the troop of some thirty cavalrymen. Four troops formed a squadron, and four squadrons constituted a regiment of 650 men. Each cavalry division normally consisted of six regiments. From 1913, each of the five armies that were to be formed on mobilization was to have two cavalry divisions, and each army corps was assigned a cavalry regiment.

Alongside this active cavalry was a second-line cavalry, formed on mobilization with reservists, for missions that were less independent, and therefore less 'noble'. One squadron reconnoitred for each infantry division, and around 250 troops existed to escort the staff, to scout for infantry regiments, battalions of *chasseurs* or fortresses, or else to carry out policing missions in the rear.

The sum total of the cavalry came to 545 squadrons with 95,000 men and 100,000 horses, or barely 4 per cent of the numbers of men serving with the colours.[45] For missions other than scouting or mounted combat, attached elements could be used, and many of these elements came from the other arms. Thus, each cavalry division included an artillery *groupe* equipped with a light-weight model of 75mm gun, a *groupe* of around 400 cyclist *chasseurs*, a detachment of cyclist sappers and three machine-gun sections (with a combined total of six machine-guns). In addition, two of the cavalry divisions each had a squadron of airplanes. The airplanes were an innovation that overlapped with the mounted units, but no steps were taken to ensure their coordination.[46]

Mounted service required a long period of training. The cavalrymen were therefore appalled by the reduction in the length of military service to two years in 1905 and by the drop in the number of re-enlistments at that time. Prestige and training were also undermined by the cavalry's frequent use in enforcing law and order. But in 1911, a spectacular turnaround was seen, with a sharp rise in re-enlistments and a marked trend of joining the colours before the date on which a new conscript class was ordered to leave home. Unit strengths were able to be increased again as a result of the Law of 31 March 1913 concerning the cavalry's cadres and numerical strengths, and the Law of 7 August that reverted to the three-year period of military service. An inspector-general of cavalry was appointed that same year, 1913, to supervise the implementation of the doctrine. The cavalry's revival was accompanied by a new focusing of minds on mounted combat – despite the lessons of the South African and Russo-Japanese wars, and despite the fact that the other major armies were turning away from mounted combat. In 1914, out of the 157 publications devoted to the cavalry in Berger-Levrault's catalogue, just three were about fighting on foot, compared with thirty-seven about hippology (the study of horses). The introduction to the second volume of the 1912 *Cavalry training regulation* contained the statement:

> The cavalry acts by movement. Only an attack on horseback and with cold steel can achieve rapid and decisive results, and it is the cavalry's principal means of action. Combat on foot is employed when the tactical circumstances make the mounted attack temporarily impossible.

Even the charge was still deemed possible against a demoralized enemy, as a sort of thrust to finish him off. A general who directed the manœuvres of the 7th Army Corps shortly before the war had this to say about such a charge:

> The most sophisticated weapons become completely ineffective because the soldiers who either carry or serve them are prey to the whole range of human weaknesses. But against defeated troops, during the critical moments of the

action, the cavalry with drawn sabres is able to launch its squadrons unhindered by any hesitations: before them lies the prospect of an abundant harvest of success and glory.[47]

As General Percin emphasized, the cavalry 'preferred contest and sacrifice to [a] triumph devoid of any glory'.[48] In January 1912, two active officers took part in the reservist staff officer course:

[In the opinion of one of them], the cavalry had to remember that its main action, the one that justified its existence, occurred on horseback, with a sabre or lance. [The second officer thought that] the German cavalry would fight only on horseback, with cold steel, against the French cavalry. The Germans were right, for in a combat where it was possible to reach the objective by movement alone, without any fire support, it was pure madness to dismount even the smallest proportion of the men.

In June 1914, during a command-post exercise, General Louis Franchet d'Espèrey put a straightforward tactical problem to the colonel who commanded the cavalry of his army corps, and asked him for his solution.

'I charge!' replied the colonel.

'And your machine-guns. What do you do with them?'

'They charge with me!'[49]

Just weeks later, on 25 August, the same colonel would fall into a machine-gun ambush and would be trampled to death by his horse's hooves.

The cavalry's evolution was constrained by two inflexibilities. The first was the use of the horse as a means of conveyance, and the second was a culture that emphasized 'mounted' combat for scouting and in particular for clashes.

## Assaulting the Sky

When the war began, the aviation had its own directorate within the Ministry of War, but was not an arm. Instead, it was a subdivision that had the peculiarity of being shared by both the artillery and the engineers. This situation had its origin in the way that fortresses were organized, with the engineers supervising the 'containers' (the forts) and the artillery commanding the main armament (the park of guns and mortars).

The engineers were the first to take an interest in the possibilities of the third dimension. The initiative came from Captain Charles Renard, who ran the Central Establishment of Military Aerostation, which had been set up in 1877 at Chalais-Meudon in the south-western outskirts of Paris. This body built on the experience of the balloon observation companies that had been active since the eighteenth century and had proved useful during the sieges of Paris and Belfort in 1870. Hence the sappers focused on opportunities for communicating between besieged fortresses and the outside world, but above all on opportunities for obtaining intelligence about the enemy from vantage points that commanded views extending up to some 10 km. Gradually, the idea was considered of 'lighter-than-air' craft that could carry out controlled flights for the purpose of reconnaissance in depth. It was with this in mind that Renard supervised the construction of *La France,* which in 1884 became the first dirigible to make a fully controlled flight.

Balloons came to be of interest to the artillery, since they could be used in combination with the telephone, photography and wireless telegraphy to adjust the fire of long-range guns. The artillerymen had a pioneering figure of their own who deserves to be mentioned, namely Captain Ferdinand Ferber, who also took an interest in gliders.

At the start of the twentieth century, the artillery had *de facto* control over the use of the spherical balloons of the fortresses, and left the dirigibles to the sappers. But the paths of both the spherical balloons and the dirigibles ended in failure. The first generation of dirigibles, each of which had a capacity of up to 9,000 cubic metres, proved unsatisfactory. Dirigibles regained favour just a few years before the war, basically in order to challenge the prestige enjoyed by the German Zeppelins and to undertake reconnaissances as far as the Rhine. Three large airships, each with a capacity of 23,000 cubic metres, were in the pipeline in 1914.

Meanwhile, captive balloons were more or less abandoned since they did not fit into the notion of the highly mobile combat that was contemplated. Only the balloonist companies of the four great fortresses of eastern France – Verdun, Toul, Epinal and Belfort – were retained. They used mediocre, spherical balloons that were small in volume and slow in movement and altogether inferior to the elongated German kite balloons.

A sort of technical Darwinism would result in the airplane, which had the advantage of mobility, replacing the balloon to take over the reconnaissance missions of the engineers and the fire-adjustment missions for the artillerymen. The airplane's addition to the tactical fabric owed much to the passion shown by public opinion and hence by parliamentary representatives. Starting in 1892, the Ministry of War under Charles de Freycinet provided financial support for Clément Ader's experiments in powered flight. Following the failure of those experiments in 1897, the Ministry took a close interest in the work of the Wright brothers, who made their first flight in 1903. France bought some prototypes from the brothers, and on 31 October 1908 the Army Commission (with Georges Clemenceau, Paul Doumer, Louis Barthou and Adolphe Messimy) went to Auvours camp near Le Mans to witness the flight of a Wright machine.[50]

The year 1909 was a turning point for military aeronautics, partly because of Louis Blériot's exploit in flying across the English Channel, but above all because of the big aviation week held on 22 to 29 August at Bétheny outside Reims. As a result of this aviation week, General Pierre Auguste Roques, the Director of Engineers, managed to secure the support of the Minister of War at that time, General Jean Jules Brun, for the purchase of five airplanes. But Brun was an artilleryman, and he was sensitive to the arguments of the modernists of his arm, such as Major Jean Estienne, who saw the airplane as an excellent means for observing and adjusting fire. Brun therefore authorized the Directorate of Artillery to create its own aviation service – the Military Aviation Establishment at Vincennes on the eastern side of Paris – as a rival to the engineers' establishment at Chalais-Meudon. This new body was placed under

Estienne, who was promoted to lieutenant-colonel. The engineers immediately strove to absorb it, but were thwarted by a record-breaking long-distance flight that Estienne organized for 9 June 1910 between Mourmelon (at Châlons camp) and Vincennes. This expedition outdid the engineers in their own favoured field. It sparked such popular acclaim that the engineers abandoned their scheme, and Estienne was then able to carry out more and more experiments.

The first adjustment of artillery fire by air occurred on 10 August 1910. The following year, Captain Georges Bellenger and a cavalryman, Lieutenant Charles de Tricornot de Rose, assisted by the professional engineer Raymond Saulnier, began experimenting with using a machine-gun mounted on an airplane. But in October 1910, Vincennes was absorbed into the newly-created permanent inspectorate of military aeronautics. General Roques, a sapper, was placed in charge of the inspectorate. The engineers therefore retained their dominance, helped by a large influx of staff officers whom the engineers had requested because of their own shortage of officers, and who were attracted by the prestige of having pilot status.

Following the turning point of 1909, a second important year was 1912. The Law of 29 March 1912 set out the organization of the aeronautics. Flight logs and roundels were instituted, and uniforms agreed. The aviation became a fully-fledged military institution and on 14 July 1914 it even received a flag. In May 1912, Colonel Auguste Edouard Hirschauer replaced Roques and gave the aviation even more of an 'engineer' orientation. He had aeronautics centres established in the fortresses of eastern France, and the military establishment at Vincennes was disbanded in September 1912.

A year later, the artillery secured Hirschauer's replacement by Colonel Bernard, who separated aerostation and aviation. The artillery also secured the creation of an aeronautics directorate under its guardianship.[51] Yet Bernard was not a specialist, and the aeronautics did not evolve much under his command. This was even the case with the elements that were dedicated to working with the artillery, although admittedly the artillery was entirely focused on its 75mm guns firing over open sights. On the outbreak of the war, Bernard, expecting the conflict to be short, assigned most of the aviation's support personnel, including mechanics and instructors, to the other corps.

A tactical structure for the aviation soon emerged as a result of the large-scale manœuvres, and it was in line with the focus on reconnaissance that the engineers had established. Eight two-seaters carrying observers appeared at the 1910 manœuvres in Picardy. A sapper commanded the airplanes of one side and an artilleryman those of the other. In the 1911 manœuvres, the different types of airplanes were grouped into mixed squadrons. In 1912 and 1913, each side had available a dirigible and a *groupe* of three or four squadrons. Each of these squadrons had six airplanes of the same type and adequate numbers of trained observers. Each squadron was allocated all the materiel it needed to be autonomous, such as hangars and repair lorries.

At the start of the war, France had twenty-one squadrons, each containing six machines, as well as two squadrons for the cavalry with four airplanes each. There was also an artillery aviation section belonging to Colonel Estienne's 22nd Field Artillery Regiment and consisting of two airplanes that could be readily dismantled. The total number of machines was about 160, and they could be reinforced by about half as many again within the first weeks of fighting. The squadrons were distributed in such a way that four or five of them were assigned to each French army. In peacetime, the armies existed as mere administrative organizations under the Second Departments (Intelligence) of the army staffs, and the chief of each of those staffs was advised by a director of the aviation service.

The use of airplanes was still based on trial and error. Even though eleven different models existed, none of the machines were specialized in particular sorts of mission. Some were 'pusher' biplanes, with the propeller located behind the engine. Others were 'tractor' biplanes, with the propeller in front. Some had a fuselage, and others did not. Machines could even be found with flexible wings (Breguet). Monoplanes also existed, such as the Morane-Saulnier 'parasols' or the Nieuports. The performances of these aircraft varied widely, but were always limited. The service ceiling was no more than 3,000 metres. Reaching that altitude took between 25 and 60 minutes, depending on the model. Engines ranged from 70 to 140 horse power, and speeds between 85 and 150 km-per-hour. Turning these aircraft into effective combat machines seemed difficult.

The Germans had a definite superiority with their nine Zeppelins and their *Drachen*. In the *Kaiser*'s army, the 'heavier-than-air' machines formed thirty-four squadrons, each with six airplanes, as well as seven fortress squadrons. These made a total of around 235 airplanes of similar quality to the French models. The methods of adjusting artillery fire were more advanced than in France, even if the artillery lacked its own airplanes.[52]

French military aeronautics seemed in 1914 to have sprung suddenly into existence. But the creation of the aeronautics should actually be seen as a continuation of the plan for the military conquest of the sky, a plan that had begun several decades earlier. Although this allowed the airplane to insert itself easily into the tactical fabric, it also kept the airplane tied to the missions that were inherited from lighter-than-air craft.

*

Between 1870 and 1914, there had been a strong desire to modernize the French army. Yet when the army corps were observed in the large-scale manœuvres, they remained strangely similar to those of the Second Empire in how they were uniformed and equipped and in how they acted. If there was so little sign of change, what had become of the impetus of the many technical innovations we mentioned earlier? The answer is that it had been absorbed at the level of the arms, partly by the creation of specialized sub-divisions and partly by certain values such as sacrifice being taken to extremes, but above all by an underestimation – conscious or otherwise – of the threat. By paying the price of this loss of impetus, the arms had been able to maintain an overall coherence that preserved their own cultures. But they had thereby created a mismatch and had left themselves vulnerable.

*Chapter 5*

# The Test of Fire

In the morning of 14 August 1914, the 13th Infantry Division underwent its baptism of fire. It was taking part in the 1st Army's offensive in Lorraine, when it came under fire in front of the German-held village of Plaine. It launched a succession of head-on bayonet charges, but these charges foundered in the face of the machine-guns and howitzers posted either in the village or on the heights to the north-east. But then, at 4.00 pm, the French established two *groupes* of 75mm guns opposite the enemy stronghold to prepare another attack. This time, the attack was made in a new style. Disregarding the regulations, it pinned the Germans down with a frontal action while also turning their flank. The Germans had to fall back.

Between August and December 1914, the performance of the French army as a whole evolved in an equally spectacular way as that of the 13th Infantry Division. The bloody month of August – the month of the Battle of the Frontiers – gave way to the turnaround on the Marne in September. During the ensuing race to the sea, from October to mid-November, the French beat off the final large-scale offensives that the Germans would launch before 1916.

The French owed their initial failures to the many flaws in their combat units' preparation for war. But their subsequent victories were all the more surprising in view of the apparent scale of the German tactical superiority. Such a reversal of the situation was eased by circumstantial factors that are well known today. For example, the Germans withdrew two of their army corps and sent them to East Prussia to counter the Russian offensive. The fact that the French managed to turn the situation around also suggests that they might not have been so absurd after all in staking everything on the use of masses of men infused by an unshakeable morale. Despite their disasters, their appalling losses and a gruelling retreat, the 'red trousers' held on (along with the blue trousers of units such as the foot *chasseurs)*. France's mobilization effort helped offset her significantly smaller population, even if it did send men to the front who were older or worse trained than the German soldiers. The Germans opted for quality rather than quantity of men, and that indisputably deprived them of victory. But what I am going to focus on here is another aspect of the human factor: the capacity to change.

## The Cost of Confusion
*The face of combat is as expected, but is accompanied by unforeseen disasters*
The features of the general battles fought in 1914 were more or less in line with what the 1913 *Field service regulation* had described. The operations

were highly mobile, with the French army's centre of gravity shifting in just three months from Lorraine to Champagne-Ardennes, to the Marne and then Picardy. The French high command excelled in these large-scale movements of forces. Both sides used turning manœuvres: the German Schlieffen Plan, the French double-envelopment on the Marne and the race to the sea.[1] The first phase of the operations only narrowly fell short of producing the decisive battle that had been envisaged. (The outcome of such a battle, however, would have favoured the Germans, which was something that the French had not envisaged.)

At this level of warfare, it was the Germans who sprung the only surprises, by using reserve corps alongside their active corps and by unveiling a powerful siege artillery that enabled them to smash the defences of fortified towns. The French failed completely as a result of taking the concepts of the new school – breaking through the enemy centre, attacking him wherever he was found and favouring speed over security – and extending these concepts to the strategic level. The French then reverted to the offensive battle in defensive form. Even though the defensive-offensive had been fiercely criticized before the war, it ended up succeeding on a gigantic scale, when the Battle of the Marne was fought between Paris and Verdun at the start of September.

At the operational level, every one of the French armies that saw action in the opening weeks of the war suffered a clear-cut reverse. As an example, let's see what happened to the 4th Army in the Ardennes.[2] At 7.00 am on 21 August, GHQ issued an order to the army commander, General Fernand de Langle de Cary, to take up position north of the Semois, a tributary of the Meuse, and then on the 22nd to attack the flanks of the German 4th Army in the Belgian Ardennes. In order to do this, it would first have to cross a long, forested barrier several kilometres deep. In terrain this enclosed, the former doctrine would have required light advanced-guards, composed of cavalry and battalions of *chasseurs,* to hold the exits. These light forces would then have been reinforced by the advanced-guards of the large units, and any necessary defensive preparations would have been made in order to protect the movements of the army corps.

Instead, priority was given to speed and surprise. This was done in the spirit of the new school, and in the belief that the intelligence was right when it indicated only a weak enemy presence. Scouting was limited to the advanced-guards of the leading divisions. The 4th Army placed its two cavalry divisions in covering positions on the far left of its disposition. It launched the five army corps straight ahead, between Montmédy and Mézières, each within a zone some 8 to 10 km wide, into a difficult region unfamiliar to everyone and with only a few copies of the detailed maps that had been produced by the French staff. The disposition as a whole lay along the line of the Belgian frontier and therefore at an oblique angle to the axis along which the Germans were assumed to be moving.

The various army corps moved off on 22 August. They were successively staggered from south-east to north-west, in a sort of rising 'staircase'. The 2nd Corps was on the right, next came the Colonial Army Corps and then the 12th, 17th and 11th Corps. But at the same time, beyond the screen of

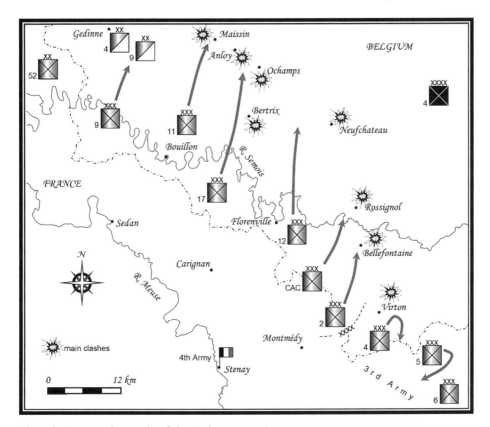

The 4th Army at the Battle of the Ardennes, 22 August 1914.

the forest, three army corps of the German 4th Army under Albrecht, Duke of Würtemberg were in the process of wheeling round towards France. On Langle de Cary's right flank, the two divisions of his 2nd Army Corps were moving forward in column along a single route. A single German brigade checked the leading division for the whole day just outside the village of Bellefontaine. Meanwhile, the rear division, which had neglected to take any precautionary measures to cover its eastern flank, came under a fierce attack from that direction by a strengthened enemy brigade. Hence the 2nd Army Corps was completely pinned down for the whole of the 22nd, despite having the advantage of numbers.

Consequently, the neighbouring Colonial Army Corps was left uncovered on the right as it continued on its way northwards. Its two divisions of colonial infantry were likewise in column on a single axis. The corps commander and the commander of the leading division – the 3rd Colonial Infantry Division – were convinced that the 2nd Army Corps was covering them to the east, and their only security measure was an advanced-guard composed of a colonial infantry regiment strengthened with a cavalry squadron and some 75mm guns. Quartermasters were actually present with this regiment to find cantonments for the night, as if they were taking part in the annual, large-scale manœuvres.

Out in front of the Colonial Army Corps, the two German divisions of the Silesian 6th Army Corps were coming southwards. The opposing advanced-guards met in the wood north of Rossignol. But whereas the Germans immediately established themselves on the defensive there, taking advantage of the favourable ground, the French advanced-guard charged furiously and gradually sucked in the rest of its division. Some hours later, in accordance with the method prescribed in the German regulations, the German division followed up the checking blow it had made frontally by attacking the exposed left flank of the colonial troops. Further east, meanwhile, another Silesian division attacked the right flank of the 3rd Colonial Infantry Division. That colonial division was surrounded and, although its men fought courageously, two-thirds of it were destroyed. The 2nd Colonial Infantry Division was some kilometres to the rear, but failed to intervene because it was in army reserve and the corps commander reacted too slowly, being too far away from what was happening.

On the same day, even further to the west, a similar scenario occurred. The French 12th Army Corps under General Pierre Auguste Roques – a future Minister of War – was checked by a single brigade. On its left, the 17th Army Corps continued moving forward. Its two divisions were abreast, but 5 km apart. On the right, the 33rd Infantry Division passed the village of Bertrix and made enemy contact after crossing the wood. The corps commander ordered the 18th Field Artillery Regiment to send observers to the edge of the wood, in order for it to be possible to support the attack on the German-held village of Ochamps. But the order was misunderstood. The entire regiment entered the wood and did so on a single axis. It was surprised, as was the main body of the 33rd Infantry Division, when attacked in the flank by a German infantry division. Here, too, no security measure had been taken, so the result was total confusion. Panic spread. The leading brigade of the 33rd Infantry Division was entirely destroyed. So was the 18th Field Artillery Regiment, and part of it even came under fire, as it tried to fall back, from the artillery regiment belonging to the neighbouring French division.

Since the commander of the 17th Army Corps was utterly paralysed with shock, the corps artillery commander tried to restore some order. The other division of the corps – the 34th Infantry Division – likewise passed the wood and it, too, then found itself facing a strong German force established in the village of Anloy. This time, the artillery remained to the rear of the wood, but nobody seems to have thought of sending observers to the edge of the wood to adjust the supporting fires. Hence the division failed to seize Anloy, despite having the advantage of numbers, although admittedly this advantage was offset by two German artillery *groupes* skilfully sited facing the axis of attack.

To the left of the 17th Army Corps, the 11th in its turn came up against a German brigade that was holding the village of Maissin. The corps commander had to commit all his regiments in succession before he finally seized the village at the end of the day. His corps, exhausted and completely disordered, was unable to pursue. Hence the overall result in this sector of the front was that three French army corps – the 11th, 12th and 17th – had found themselves checked by the German 18th Army Corps.

On the far left of the French 4th Army's disposition were the 9th Army Corps, a cavalry corps (consisting of two divisions) and an infantry division. These units failed to make enemy contact and were of little use. In the evening of the 22nd, the whole of the French 4th Army fell back some 15 km. During the course of that day, it had demonstrated the French deficiencies in a concentrated form: it had combined the dangerous recklessness of the 'ultra-offensive' theories with the slowness of timid 'chess players'. Above all, the weaknesses in the training of many generals and field officers had been laid bare. This stinging defeat had much in common with that suffered by the 3rd Army – which had received the same mission further to the east – and was also similar to the defeats in Alsace, Lorraine and Belgium. The Belgian historian Emile Wanty summed up all these shortcomings:

> On this same day [22 August], on different terrains and at different times, all the French divisions made the very same mistakes: no intelligence-gathering, scorn for long-range security, poor short-range security, no cooperation with neighbouring units, flawed communications between commanders and units, and absurdly reckless attacks without fire support.[3]

## Origins of the Shortcomings

The similarity of these defeats, and the fact that they occurred all along the front at the same time, point to the existence of deep-rooted causes. Yet if we ponder these causes, we simply find ourselves identifying all over again the French army's pre-war weaknesses. As could have been foreseen, many generals had proved inadequate – and indeed the speed with which they were dismissed suggests that their deficiencies had come as no surprise.

During the Battle of Charleroi, the commander of the 3rd Army Corps (part of the 5th Army) could not be found at the most critical moment of the day. Instead, the corps artillery commander, General Gabriel Rouquerol, had to stand in for him. 'Same notable incompetence in the 14th Corps, in the 5th Corps', noted General Joffre laconically.[4] The consequences were immediate. By 31 December 1914, 162 generals, or colonels acting as *généraux de brigade,* had been removed from their command or duties. They included three army commanders, twenty-four commanders of either army corps or units of similar size and seventy-one divisional commanders.[5] In all, more than 40 per cent of the commanders of large units had shown that they were incompetent and ineffective. In particular, almost 70 per cent of the army corps commanders were removed, and yet they were the very men who had long been in charge of supervising the preparation of units for war.

Many of those who were dismissed blamed GHQ's desire to shift responsibility for the initial setbacks on to scapegoats. They also blamed the malignant influence of the staff officers who composed GHQ. The historian Pierre Rocolle, in his book *The mass sacrifice of the generals,* has drawn up a comprehensive list of these cases of incompetence. He himself has stressed the numerous appointments that had been made for political reasons during General Louis André's time as Minister of War and also the fact that many generals were too old to have attended even the earliest courses of the Staff College. But the fact that such a high proportion of generals proved incompetent suggests that the causes of the problem were deep-rooted. These causes have already been mentioned: inadequate training for commanding large units, along with a failure to keep up with recent advances in weaponry – a failure that explains why many commanders were too stunned to be effective.

Yet these command failures do not explain everything. Many generals had demonstrated a high degree of tactical competence whatever their doctrinal inclination. The 40th and 42nd Infantry Divisions in the Ardennes, for example, had been commanded in outstanding fashion, as had the 1st Army Corps under General Louis Franchet d'Espèrey and also General Philippe Pétain's 6th Infantry Division.

## The Turnaround
### The high command's role
Such a drastic turnaround of the situation was indisputably the result of the steps taken by the high command, which directed its forces capably. But if the high command had tried to achieve this turnaround by using the same military instrument as before, it would have risked a repeat, at the tactical level, of the same bloody defeats. Within just a few weeks therefore, a profound transformation had taken place – a transformation that had been impossible to carry out in the three years leading up to the war. This transformation seems to have had three causes: corrections imposed by the staff, the purge and revitalization of the army's generals, and spontaneous adaptations made by the units themselves.

GHQ disseminated two notes to the army commanders on 16 and 24 August, just a couple of weeks after the fighting had begun. These notes summarized the key mistakes that had been made and provided guidance on the necessary remedies. The soundness with which these notes analysed the situation shows that information was being properly circulated by means of the numerous liaison officers and the systematic reports that were sent after each action. The most serious flaw that was noted concerned the infantry's tendency to dash impetuously into the attack in dense masses, usually without allowing the artillery enough time to be ready to lend support. As a result, the infantry suffered sickening losses through its own fault and found itself vulnerable to counter-attacks – all the more so in that it failed after conquering ground to prepare it for defence. The remedies were mostly reminders of the regulations that were in force:

- at no time were the generals to lose control of the action;
- attacks prepared more carefully would be all the less costly in lives;
- before an assault was launched, the action was to be opened using lines of skirmishers supported by artillery;
- officers had to learn to wait for artillery support and prevent the troops from exposing themselves too soon to enemy fire;
- the infantry had to exploit the terrain, rather than simply making a head-on attack against the enemy's front;
- units were to prepare conquered ground for defence, by digging in with artillery to prevent any enemy counter-offensive.[6]

In short, the existing doctrine was not called into question. The one exception concerned the role of the artillery, which was now considered capable of preparing the infantry's attacks instead of merely supporting them during the course of the action.

On 3 September 1914, a new instruction was issued that served thereafter as the charter for positional warfare. It addressed such matters as an advanced line, a second line with deep trenches, concealed reserves, tours of duty and breastworks to protect guns.

Information also circulated horizontally, between units. The paradox was that the traditional scepticism concerning written regulations actually furthered this horizontal movement of information. Ideas circulated freely between neighbouring units, or between officers who happened to meet former classmates from military schools in the small world of the combat zone. The 10th Army Corps, for example, received a note from the 1st Corps that described how the Germans used machine-guns during the fighting at Dinant on 15 August, as well as the danger of adopting excessively dense formations or overly inflexible dispositions.

Constantly living together, and having to confront problems that required urgent solutions, broke down the barriers of compartmentalization and made interactions more common. Yet it would be unrealistic to assume that these orders and notes, or the information circulated by word of mouth, could produce immediate results. Two notes – dated 12 and 15 August and signed by General Edouard de Curières de Castelnau, the commander of the 2nd Army – emphasized 'a methodical organization of the forward push' and 'the thorough preparation of artillery fire' before launching the infantry. Castelnau also emphasized the need for the troops to establish themselves solidly on the ground they gained.[7] Yet, at this same time, three divisions of his army made senseless attacks without any support whatsoever. The worst case occurred when the 26th Infantry Division tried to seize the village of Cirey-sur-Vezouze on 14 August: it launched a charge from as far away as 2 km and completely neglected its artillery, which lost half its guns the next day in a hurried withdrawal.[8]

Major Maurice Larcher reckoned that the 10th Army Corps was unable to digest quickly enough the note of advice it had received from the 1st Corps. 'It was too late to benefit from these observations', he wrote. 'The necessary evolution would emerge in the course of the battle and would become clearer in the even more distant future.'[9] As for GHQ's note of 16 August, it reached the 10th Army Corps on the 19th and was unable to prevent the defeat at Charleroi.

The dismissal of whole swathes of generals allowed the officer cadres to be renewed and enabled men who had proved their worth to come to the fore. Note that this revitalization favoured the pre-war intellectuals, and it did so regardless of their tactical views since the newly promoted men included not only Grandmaison, but also Pétain, Maud'huy and Fayolle. The dismissals also meant that GHQ could excuse itself from any blame by pinning responsibility for the initial defeats on subordinates who were on the spot. Conversely, generals were spurred into trying to outdo each other in energy and willpower, lest they suffered the consequences.

## The awakening of the infantry

The most important adaptation occurred within the actual units. It happened almost instinctively under the pressure of events. As Joffre admitted:

> if the success that I desired occurred on the Marne, it was to a very great extent because by the start of September our armies were no longer the same as in the first days of the war. The infantry had learnt from the hard experience of the battles fought on the frontier. Despite having lost many of its cadres, it made better use of the terrain, it was more willing to use its entrenching tools – whose value it now understood – and it no longer went into action without artillery support.[10]

The Germans were excellent teachers. During the fighting at Dinant on 23 August, Colonel Jacques Elie de Riols de Fonclare, the commander of the 127th Infantry Regiment, was able to see clearly the way in which the Germans attacked a neighbouring unit. Preliminary reconnaissance from the air and an intensive artillery preparation paved the way for an infiltration supported by machine-guns. 'A wonderful lesson for us', he concluded.[11]

The French often did enough if they simply avoided repeating their initial blunders. General Emile Fayolle noted on 25 August:

> In the 70th [Reserve Division], disaster between 7.00 and 9.00 am during the attack of Hoéville: there were far too many men in line ... There was no reconnaissance, no fire preparation ... In the 237th [Infantry Regiment], Colonel Clerc received three wounds. In the 279th, Colonel d'Hérouville was killed, as were the two battalion commanders. In the 360th, Colonel Chenot was wounded ... [The division lost 4,000 men.] How could this have happened? No combat patrols, no scouts, the pointless masses of men! No preparation. It's insane.[12]

On the next day:

> The order is to go forward once more. We are beginning again, but this time very cautiously, very slowly. It has been a good lesson. I have been able to bring only four battalions back from Lenoncourt ... The rest are recovering ... I advance by bounds under the protection of all the artillery and after reconnaissances have been carried out.[13]

As for the 13th Infantry Division, it continued its advance after the action at Plaine, but in an inflexible manner. Over-extended along a 20-km long front, it became heavily engaged in the valleys without ensuring that it had bases of fire in place on the mountain passes. Practically the only initiative taken by the colonels in command of the regiments was to go forward – and, in the case of two of them, to get themselves killed. One battalion commander, located in the middle of his foremost lines of skirmishers, saw the Germans outflank him. He felt the immediate instinct to shout: 'Forwards, with the bayonet!' But his voice failed him. Pulling himself together, he instead gave the order to lie down and open fire. He thereby managed to check the Germans and organize a withdrawal.[14]

Despite being sorely tried by the enemy counter-attack, the 13th Infantry Division always carried out its retreat in an orderly manner, as part of the more general withdrawal of the 1st Army. It did so by successive echelons under pressure from the Germans, whose infiltration methods inspired admiration. Here, too, the French learned quickly:

> They sensed the enemy's superiority of means, and wanted to bring everything into play to make up for it. This explained their splendid aptitude for sticking to the fire, for even longer than their officers would sometimes have wanted. It explained their astonishing skill in the counter-offensives that were becoming one of the most effective methods of manœuvre for all our armies.[15]

It was at this time that artillery *groupes* started to go right forward to the first lines so they could provide moral support and improve the coordination of their supporting fire. Despite the half-heartedness of the French when it came to defensive training, the 13th Infantry Division turned the village of Celles into a strongpoint on 22 August with the help of its engineer company and some artillery barrages. By the 28th, the division had managed to re-establish itself in position on the pass of La Chipotte. It had lost 6,000 men, of whom 98 per cent were infantrymen.

The division was brought back up to a strength of 200 men per company by replacements from the depots, and was transported by railway to take part in the Battle of the Marne. The division detrained and was attached to the 4th Army. On 8 September, as it was marching to the battlefield, it sent its artillery on ahead to take up position in the first line and hold on until the slower-moving infantry could arrive. This was a completely new role for the artillery. The actions from the 8th to the 10th were more cautious than those of a month earlier, as was the subsequent pursuit towards Souain, 20 km north of Châlons. The densities of fire per kilometre of front were four times greater than in the Lorraine offensive, and the advance was slowed down, if only because one-third of the men in the ranks were new recruits.

When the division once again made enemy contact, on 13 September, it came up against German entrenchments that had already been skilfully organized with obstacles and effective fires. Since the orders that were given remained as offensive as before, and just as few material means were available, a gap started to open between the troops, who evolved quickly, and a less flexible command. One of the division's officers reckoned:

> for us, this was the first stage in a new awareness. Even as we obeyed the orders we received, we used to consider it a duty to implement those orders in a way that matched what was possible. We went ahead, at the set hour, with the attacks we were ordered to make. But we had them carried out by chains of skirmishers that were widely spaced and not particularly vulnerable, and which flattened themselves on the ground if their appearance was greeted by bursts of fire from machine-guns opening up from behind intact wire.[16]

The losses in these actions amounted to another 2,900 men, or 29 per cent of the troops committed to action. On 6 October, the 13th Infantry Division was again moved by railway, this time as far as Lille, and it then took up position north of Lens. Two of its battalions were transported in motor-vehicles. On the 9th, General Louis Henry Auguste Baquet was relieved of command of the division, just some weeks after his predecessor. By 13 October, the front had been 'closed', and the division dug in. Digging in was what all units were now doing and, following the start that had been made on the Grand Couronné heights outside Nancy in August 1914, their earthworks had progressed far beyond the infantryman's simple 'scrape' as described in the 1906 *Practical instruction on fieldworks* ('the excavated earth, dumped on the side facing the enemy, will form a parapet protecting at least the head of each rifleman').

The troops instinctively grasped that digging in was the only immediate and possible answer to the effectiveness of the artillery and automatic weapons. They dug rifle-pits at first, but then continuous trenches to make communications easier. To prevent surprises, barbed-wire and other obstacles were set up and machine-guns were established. (Hence machine-guns were both a cause and a consequence of the development of entrenchments.) Even if it was the commanders who gave the order to fortify captured points and then quiet sectors, the development of continuous trenches along the entire front was a largely spontaneous phenomenon, made necessary by the revelation of the firepower of modern weapons. Everyone regarded it as a temporary situation until more ammunition could be supplied and units could be brought back up to strength. It was not realized that this solidification of the front, which was completed in November 1914, indicated a radical change in the art of war.

### The rediscovery of the artillery

According to initial thinking, the artillery was to be used to support the infantry and neutralize just those German batteries that were visible. But as soon became clear, this notion was both hard to put into effect and too restrictive. The artillery found it difficult to support attacks. It was harassed by the German heavy pieces, which had a longer range. It was often late in providing fire support, as a result of the infantrymen's excessive haste and the limited means of communication. In many cases, the enemy was concealed. When artillerymen were left to their own devices, therefore, they often preferred to fire at the targets they could see, and sometimes they did so at the expense of the manœuvre as a whole. To resolve these problems, the artillery strove to improve coordination with the infantry and to find a way of countering German batteries that were hardly ever visible.

The evolution that was required of the artillery basically amounted to an improvement of its existing tactical methods. It did not challenge the values of the arm. It was made easier by the artillery's new links with the infantrymen, for gunners and footsoldiers now lived and died together. It benefitted from the artillery's outstanding level of professional and technical knowledge, and from its relatively low losses, which meant that a collective tactical memory could be formed and passed on, whereas the infantry was constantly having to train new replacements. The artillery possessed resources that were unused, for it was accorded too little importance in the French army's operational doctrine owing to the control exerted over that doctrine by infantry officers who had trained at Saint-Cyr.

The artillerymen began by forgetting the 1910 *Artillery training regulation* and the 1913 *Field service regulation,* and diversified their missions. No longer did field batteries merely support assaults, they also prepared them. In the 13th Infantry Division, as we have seen, the 1913 *Field service regulation* became obsolete after just half-a-day. Two weeks later, on 27 August, General de Castelnau instructed his 2nd Army that 'the main bodies of infantry must put in an appearance only after the whole of the artillery (protected by minimal numbers of well-disposed infantry under good cover) has softened up the enemy infantry.'[17]

To improve coordination, artillery liaison officers were attached to the infantry. The colonel in command of the regiment of divisional artillery became the divisional general's adviser, and left his second-in-command to organize the fire of the batteries. To make command and control easier, and interventions quicker, the artillery was often grouped in mass. A *groupement* of thirty batteries was sometimes formed, as was favoured by General Joseph Bro, who commanded the artillery of the 1st Army Corps. Following the German example, these *groupements* were placed as far forward as possible. The old method of directing fire from a position close to the artillery pieces increasingly gave way to direction from a distance. That required telephone lines, so men searched every post office and even private houses. One army corps commander sent an officer to Paris to buy all the telephone equipment he could find.[18] Some such quests even went to Switzerland.

Zone fire, or firing against unseen targets, was also tried out. Long-range fire to counter the German howitzers was improvised by digging in the trails of the guns – a method for which no training had ever been given. On 7 August 1914, a battery of the 2nd Army Corps devastated a German cavalry regiment at a range of 5,000 metres, much further than the fire practised on target ranges.[19] At the Battle of the Mortagne at the end of August, General Firmin Emile Gascouin had fire directed at large assemblies of enemy troops at a range of 9,500 metres. For this purpose, he used shrapnel shells that were meant to be fired against aircraft, since they were fitted with special noses with long time-fuses.[20] The fire was adjusted by means of three tethered balloons that had been removed from fortresses.[21] Such long ranges meant that the fire had to be adjusted from the air, but only a few airplanes were available for the necessary observation. In some army corps, the artillery commander managed to obtain the loan of airplanes for the use of hurriedly-trained observers. (In a few cases, these observers had been trained as a precaution before the outbreak of hostilities.) At the height of the Battle of the Marne, General Frédéric Georges Herr, who commanded the artillery of the 6th Army Corps, described some guns 'camouflaged with sheaves of wheat, others firing against airplanes by using pits dug in the ground. [The gun trail could be placed in a pit so the barrel pointed at the sky.] One of our aircraft was trying to adjust fire against the 210mm mortars.'[22] Such a sight would have been unthinkable just a few weeks earlier. Elsewhere during the Battle of the Marne, at the village of Montceaux-lès-Provins on 6 September, Colonel Jean Estienne, who commanded the 22nd Field Artillery Regiment in Pétain's division, managed to silence a German artillery grouping. He did so with the help of two aircraft, designed to be readily dismantled, whose construction he had ordered when he had been in command of the Aviation School at Vincennes.

The artillery had initially expected to be constantly manœuvring, but found increasingly often that its *groupes* had to remain in position for days on end. This meant not only that it had to have its firing positions fortified and constantly occupied both night and day, but also that it had to coordinate arrangements with completely separate supply units. None of these things were described in the 1910 *Artillery training regulation*. Instead, the artillery took a lead from the personal instructions issued by some of its more far-sighted commanders.[23]

\*

The high command formalized all these adaptations, which soon became widespread. As early as the middle of August, it authorized the removal of heavy artillery pieces, along with gunners, from the fortresses. In the second week of August, the 3rd Army received six batteries of 120mm pieces that had been withdrawn from the fortress of Verdun. Three heavy batteries from Epinal reinforced the 1st Army in the night of 27 August and opened fire the next day to the Germans' surprise. Their fire was directed by three artillery-spotting airplanes and by Major Jacques Saconney's observation balloon, which was deployed in the Charmes forest.[24] In September, the 2nd Army defended the Grand Couronné heights outside Nancy with ten heavy batteries and some forty de Bange 80 and 90mm guns.[25] This allocation of heavy artillery did something to make up for the 75mm gun's limitations, and it also helped spare the field artillery batteries, whose ammunition was starting to run short.

To compensate for the limited range of the 75mm, the Directorate of Artillery ordered a series of technical improvements to be examined, including modifications to the carriages and an enhancement of the aerodynamics of the projectiles. These improvements eventually allowed the range to be increased by between 25 and 37 per cent, with the figure varying from gun to gun. But in the meantime, the first French heavy artillery wasted away as it moved repeatedly all along the front and as it frequently fired with the maximum charge – a practice that increased the range but quickly wore away the gun tubes. The long-barrelled 120mm *groupe* towed by tractors – the first artillery *groupe* not drawn by horses – covered 700 km on 20 September. It moved another 300 km on 16 October and on the 20th opened fire on the Yser front near the Channel coast.[26]

The rapid, improvised adaptation of the artillery enabled its capacities to be exploited to the full. The artillery was reinforced by 600 guns (75mm calibre) from the depots, and its action increasingly took the place of an infantry that commanders had been using too lavishly. On 25 August, four *groupes* of 75mm guns, posted in over-watch on the Borville plateau, broke the advanced-guard of the 6th (or Bavarian) Army as it marched on the Charmes Gap.[27] On 10 September, a fierce attack by the German 5th Army under Crown Prince Wilhelm was pinned down at La Vaux-Marie by a massed action of the entire artillery of the French 6th Army Corps.[28] Just a few days earlier, on the 6th during the Battle of the Marne, the 15th Field Artillery Regiment single-handedly checked a German assault on General Charles Mangin's heavily-depleted division, and did so by firing at times at point-blank range.[29] This incident revealed the psychological steadiness of the gun crews. Serving a gun involved several roles – for example, the role of the gunner who aimed the piece or that of the man who served the ammunition – and the inter-dependence of these roles created powerful, mutual, moral obligations that made the crew more resistant to stress. The resilience of the crews, and the performance of their arm, were further strengthened by the protection provided by the gun-shields (despite earlier disputes about the usefulness of such shields), by the profession's technical knowledge (the effectiveness of which was recognized), and by the artilleryman's attachment to 'his' gun. Few cases of panic are known to have occurred within 75mm *groupes* in firing positions. In contrast, an infantry skirmisher was under tremendous psychological strain when in a situation of extreme danger, facing the emptiness of the battlefield and the *marmites,* or large shells, of the German heavy artillery. He felt defenceless against these dangers, and this psychological strain is one reason why the effectiveness of infantry units fluctuated so greatly.

*

On 7 September, the Germans began to rely on night attacks in an effort to avoid the French artillery fire. But nocturnal barrages became commonly used by the French corps, following the example set by the 1st Army, which had ordered night fires to be carried out as early as 24 August. The Germans abandoned their massive night attacks at the end of September.[30] The SOS barrage (emergency fire support) came into widespread use, as did zone fires of various extents on unseen targets.

Colonel Emile Alléhaut described an assault that a battalion of the 20th Infantry Regiment – part of the 33rd Division – delivered on 26 September in the wake of the victory of the Marne:

> Our infantry had made a rush forwards. Part of the Bavarian line fell back. Another gust [of shrapnel] from our 75mm guns, this time a bit longer in range than the first. Another, almost simultaneous, rush by our infantrymen. Sticking to their artillery's projectiles, they advanced with wonderful eagerness and reached the Bavarian infantry at almost the same time as our shells. It continued like that, with rushes following gusts until at last the Bavarians ... flowed back in disorder.[31]

This method was strikingly similar to that of the rolling barrage, yet the rolling barrage would not enter the regulations until 1916. The method was born spontaneously, under the pressure of circumstances, and as a result of the bonds that existed between an infantry colonel and a captain commanding a battery after they had spent months working actively together.

The artillery had adapted rapidly to the new conditions of combat. This was partly due to a battery drill that itself was already suitable for the war and would subsequently undergo little change. It can also be attributed to the circulation of ideas and to the excellent technical training of the officers, practically all of whom had an engineering background. The artillery's relatively low losses enabled it to build on this firm foundation. When the war of movement resumed in 1918, some men would still retain this know-how, which would prove useful for adapting the arm once more.

Nevertheless, by the end of 1914, the limits had been reached of a weapons system that had been widely and mistakenly regarded before the war as the answer to everything. The 75mm gun lacked enough range for counter-battery, and enough power against the defensive works that were beginning to appear along the front. In addition, the allocations of high-explosive shells, which were by far the most effective type of ammunition, had been heavily reduced as a result of consumption having been so much greater than expected. The artillery's adaptation had been remarkable, but had happened in a rather anarchic manner and in the absence of any centralizing body apart from GHQ, which was stretched to the limit by the day-to-day running of the war. The artillery regiments therefore tended to develop their own, divergent methods. Until 1916, the artillerymen lacked a place behind the lines for carrying out experiments, and so they remained largely ignorant of certain phenomena such as the maximum range of the high-explosive shell fired by the 75mm gun, or the ways of using this shell in high-angled fire – an issue that had been overlooked before the war.[32]

### The exhaustion of the cavalry

The cavalry fulfilled its initial mission in 1914 – covering the mobilization – with no particular difficulty, and the clashes with the German cavalry that had been expected during this period were in fact rare. But difficulties began once the fighting started. On 11 August, in Alsace, a *général de division* of the cavalry was dismissed for 'total apathy',[33] and shortly afterwards the three provisional cavalry corps each suffered a setback in Lorraine, the Ardennes or Belgium. On 14 August, General Louis Conneau's corps was given the mission of carrying out a raid against the enemy rear through the Sarrebourg corridor, but was unable to pass that town. General Adalbert Abonneau's corps was ordered on 17 August to explore Belgian Luxembourg. But after covering 200 km in four days, it was driven back following a fierce encounter action on foot. General Jean François André Sordet's corps rode 250 km in Belgium between 5 and 15 August, before withdrawing behind the Marne, having lost the equivalent of one regiment in each of its divisions, with little to show for it. The Minister of War, Adolphe Messimy, wrote to Joffre on the 26th: 'Sordet, who has done little fighting, is asleep.'[34]

By the start of September, the cavalry was exhausted. Thereafter, it played only a minor role. On the 7th, early in the Battle of the Marne, General Michel-Joseph Maunoury ordered Sordet's corps to carry out a turning manœuvre intended to cause disorder in the rear of the German 1st Army under General Alexander von Kluck. Sordet said he was incapable of carrying out the mission, and was relieved of his command. His replacement, General Marie Joseph Eugène Bridoux, managed with difficulty to form a *groupement* of 1,800 cavalrymen,[35] which sowed confusion in the rear of von Kluck's army.[36] Yet the cavalry was unable to play an effective role in exploiting the victory of the Marne, failing in particular to seize the bridges over the Aisne river. It should be noted that the absence of the German cavalry during these clashes was equally conspicuous. Major Emile Laure, of the 13th Infantry Division, reckoned:

> The German cavalry may have been just as worn out as ours was at this time, for it did nothing to hinder or delay our advance. A sort of collusion in weariness

kept victors and vanquished about one day's march apart. It induced both sides if not to desire, then at least to accept, this tactical pause, which gave them a chance to relax.[37]

During the race to the sea, the cavalry once again found itself carrying out its strategic covering mission, to enable the armies to take up position on the battlefront one after the other. In the process, the cavalry expended the last of its forces by being used in a way contrary to what the regulation had envisaged. Its men had to cling to the ground like the infantry, a role for which they had neither the training nor the equipment.

On balance, the cavalry during the war of movement in 1914 had been a failure, despite occasional moments of usefulness. Its failure can not be ascribed to unsuitable missions, for its missions had in fact been appropriate for this type of war. The failure stemmed instead from the means that were used – and the first and foremost of them was the horse. By the end of the race to the sea, 180,000 of the 780,000 horses who had taken the field were dead. Ten per cent of them had been killed by fire, and 90 per cent by exhaustion, accidents or illness.[38] Replacing these losses took a long time, for horses can not be hurriedly trained for war service. There were many causes for the rapid attrition, including the excessive weight of the kit that the horses carried and the necessity for keeping a large proportion of them mounted for night watches owing to the cavalry's shortage of numbers. Above all, units were regarded as reserves to be given all manner of tasks and were therefore over-loaded with missions.[39] Sordet's corps received as many as four missions between 24 and 25 August.[40]

It is also true that the provisional corps were in dire need of modern means. They had skeletal staffs and inadequate means of communication. It was 13 August before Sordet's corps received an order that had been sent on the 8th. An infantry brigade had been assigned to support Sordet, but the lorries provided for its transport proved insufficient to move more than a battalion. Nor did the provisional cavalry corps have any organic artillery. Two cavalry divisions were each assigned a squadron of six aircraft, but these airplanes were difficult to coordinate with the mounted units and had an effective range of no more than about 50 km. The cavalry made little effort to try and keep these air squadrons when they were disbanded in the first half of 1915.

The fetishism for certain ideas also played a role – such as 'marching to the utmost limit of your strength'. So, too, did the teaching at the Cavalry School at Saumur. The exaltation of 'drive' had distracted attention from the issue of the endurance of the horses and also perhaps that of the men, who had to spend much of their day caring for their mounts even if they did not march on foot like the infantry.[41] The problem of supplying animals with fodder likewise contributed to the cavalry's attrition. The 1913 *Regulation on the handling of large units* had already pointed out: 'The duration of the cavalry corps' operations is limited by the difficulties of feeding a substantial number of horses in a restricted area.'[42] Supplies collected locally were insufficient in practice, especially for large units. The ration was commonly less than two-thirds of the 1,500 kg of oats and forage needed every day to feed a squadron. Horses had to be shod as well as fed. On 10 August, for example, Sordet's corps urgently demanded 10,000 horseshoes.[43] Thereafter, the presence of the horse continued to hinder the evolution of the arm. The need to care for the horses and do riding training left no option but to rotate units between the trenches and cantonments in the interior of the country.[44] At the same time as keeping up their riding skills, cavalrymen had to absorb a mass of new equipment and train to fight on foot.[45]

The cavalry's methods were no longer suitable for modern warfare. It was loathe to fight on foot, for quite apart from being burdened with lances and *cuirasses,* it was steeped in the doctrine of shock and of mounted combat.[46] Yet it never really managed to confront the German cavalry in the way it wished, and had to fight actions on foot that grew progressively tougher as the front became static. In a cavalry division, the role of dismounted combat was normally assigned to the cyclist *groupe,* but its 400 men soon proved insufficient. As for the squadrons, they had limited combat capabilities, since each of them could dismount only around 100 men while the others held the horses. The men had an ordinary carbine with forty-eight rounds of ammunition, and were burdened with their bladed weapons. At Courcelles, and later at Staden, regiments were even seen attacking on foot, while carrying their lances.[47] When the cavalrymen had to cling to the ground, as happened during the race to the sea, they felt their lack of entrenching tools.

If the cavalry was to deal with this situation, it had to increase its firepower and its ability to hold ground and yet still retain a high degree of mobility. The first adaptations appeared fairly soon, but as isolated initiatives. The 2nd Cavalry Corps managed to distribute entrenching tools without the knowledge of the high command, which was set against them. The cavalry divisions used dismounted cavalrymen to create foot battalions, which were known as light *groupes.* Each cavalry corps obtained lorries to transport its cyclists and acquired some *groupes* of motorized machine-gun carriers – civilian vehicles on which a machine-gun was installed. Yet these transformations remained limited. Real adaptation would have required a technical break with the past, with the horse being replaced with the internal combustion engine. This evolution would in fact have been possible with the motor-vehicle equipment – or even the airplanes – that were available at the time. The main stumbling block was psychological. Men who had spent years learning mounted combat, and who knew nothing of the mechanics of motor-vehicles, were hardly going to be able to separate themselves from the horse, which automatically featured in all their dreams. Such a psychological leap was further impeded by the officers' lack of a technical background, the artillery's monopoly on motorized vehicles and the belief that the war would be short.

### The revelation of the air service

Just two months after the start of the conflict, the aviation had already demonstrated its indispensability in long-range reconnaissance. Every day, in both the morning and the evening, the four or five squadrons of each army in the field carried out reconnaissances that might extend around 50 km behind the foremost enemy forces. The morning reconnaissance ascertained the size of the enemy columns and the direction in which they were heading. The evening reconnaissance established the line they had reached.[48]

The information supplied by the aviation often proved decisive. It made possible the 2nd Army's counter-attack on the Mortagne river on 2 September. To take a more famous example, it led to the detection of the swerve in the advance of General von Kluck's army and to the realization that Kluck was exposing his flank to the French 6th Army. The aviation's intelligence-gathering role increased all the more quickly as a result of the cavalry having blatantly failed in its mission and also owing to the progressive entrenchment of the front, which prevented probes from being made on the ground. Furthermore, the dirigibles proved a disappointment, even though much store had been placed on them. The few dirigibles that the French possessed were too slow, fragile and dependent on the weather. They were therefore withdrawn from land operations to help the fight against submarines. In contrast, tethered balloons, which had been eschewed since they had been deemed pointless in the war of movement, became useful again as soon as the front stabilized. Thus the airplane emerged pre-eminent, both because of its own strengths and because of the failure of its rivals.

At the same time as the airplane became established in the role that had been assigned to it, it was used more and more frequently for adjusting artillery fire, which had to hit targets at a much greater range than had been foreseen. The use of the airplane for artillery observation became predominant once any part of the front stabilized. A good deal of spontaneous experimentation also occurred. Each aircrew acquired the habit of using reconnaissance missions to hit troop concentrations with a few bombs or boxes of *fléchettes* (small, steel arrows). On 14 and 18 August 1914, two French airplanes bombed the Zeppelin hangars near Metz. Secret agents were flown behind enemy lines. In the autumn, experiments became more numerous. They included dropping various projectiles, taking aerial photographs, firing pistols and then machine-guns and also executing a night flight, which Jean Laurens carried out on 31 October. The crews, which had carried arms from the start so they could defend themselves in the event of a forced landing, now sought to fight aerial duels. Sergeant Roland Garros and Captain Charles de Tricornot de Rose resumed the experiments of firing through propellers that they had begun before the war. Meanwhile, Captain André Faure of Squadron V24 asked the manufacturer Gabriel Voisin to fit a light, Hotchkiss machine-gun on the front of his airplanes (the propeller was mounted at the rear). On 5 October, two members of this squadron, Sergeant Joseph Frantz and Air Mechanic Louis Quénault, gained the first confirmed aerial victory in history.

*

The bloody defeats of August 1914 established the flaws in the process of preparation for war. Every arm experienced the shock of rediscovering war after several decades of peace. This initial trial gives us the opportunity to ascertain just how big a gap could exist between the way in which men imagined the future war would be like and the complexity of actual events. We also have the opportunity to note the French army's capacity to adapt: it had suffered some bloody defeats at the start of the campaign, but had then managed to snatch a decisive victory on the Marne, before imposing the 'stalemate' of November 1914. Although a few technical improvements were made to existing materiel, the French army's adaptation was primarily tactical. During the first months of the conflict, its organizational structures underwent little change and its mindsets even less so. The infantry's fervour remained the same, despite its losses. Its assaults may have been slightly less suicidal, but it now defended every metre of ground step by step, even if that ground was untenable. As for the cavalrymen, they refused to think the unthinkable, namely replacing the horse with the internal combustion engine.

In an increasingly technical and industrial setting, the combat arms were at a disadvantage compared with the arms of the third dimension, namely the artillery and the aviation, for which the deadlock of the front promised a glittering future. There can be no doubt that what drove the evolution was the pressure exerted by the front on the first-line units. The micro-innovations and ideas that transformed the arms were born on the front. They were disseminated either horizontally through good ideas being imitated, or vertically by means of reports, enquiries or suggestions. Just as the 'demand' of the front guided the industrial and technical 'offer', the changes adopted at the front rose up the hierarchy of command and put pressure on the doctrinal paradigms.

*Chapter 6*

# The Pressure of the Front

The situation of deadlock that came into existence towards the end of 1914 had much in common with the notion of economic crisis. An economic crisis is a disruption in the balance between resources used and results obtained. We know from the writings of the economists Joseph Schumpeter and Nikolai Dmitrievich Kondratiev in the early twentieth century that this balance becomes highly unstable when technical and social innovations are introduced on a permanent basis. Since the French army at the start of the twentieth century was itself exposed to the powerful effect of technical and social changes, its 'performance' likewise varied with time. Yet a key difference existed. Whereas an economic system experiences continual adjustments, an army is subjected to a sharp division between peacetime and wartime. Hence the way it evolves is more drastic and can lead to a tactical impasse, as indeed happened in November 1914.

Ending this impasse required either the bringing of new resources into play so as to obtain a crushing superiority, or the reassignment of the old resources to new methods and means. Numerical superiority, resulting from the industrial mobilization of France or from the addition of new Allied armies, took a long time to materialize. For the immediate future, the only sure option was tactical innovation. This meant seeking and exploiting new opportunities that would enable the demands and needs of the French arms to be met more satisfactorily. The pre-war process of evolution, which was shaped like a pyramid and began with doctrinal thought at the top of the hierarchy, was no longer suitable. Tactical evolution now originated instead inside units subject to the dialectic of the front.

## Micro-Transformations

To deal with a tactical situation, a unit has a 'repertory of responses' at its disposal that come from training or experience. This repertory is sufficient so long as the situation conforms with what has been expected, but it has to be changed urgently if any surprises occur. Neither the murderous effectiveness of modern weaponry nor the defensive strength of trenches had been anticipated. They largely overturned the models that had been learned and obliged the units at the front to make an immediate effort to innovate. This process deserves to be described in detail since, although it was not new, it became particularly significant because of the duration of the war and because of France's unprecedented industrial effort.

### Strategies and sources of inspiration

Tactical innovations were the 'raw material' of the French army's adaptation. Many of them occurred during the Great War. They came in varied forms, but can be classified by either their purpose or their method. In terms of purpose, the distinction is between technical and procedural innovations. These can be defined as follows:

- technical innovation: a new combat unit combining new equipment and men trained to use it. One example was the *grenadier* and his Viven-Bessières grenade-launcher. Another was the fighter airplanes and the pilots who flew them;
- procedural innovation: a new way of utilizing the means. This might be a new organization, another manner of using equipment or an innovative combat method.[1] Examples include the Air Division, the rolling barrage, indirect machine-gun fire or the use of parachutes for resupply from the air.

In terms of method, the distinction is between radical innovations – those making a clean break with the past – and incremental innovations:

- radical innovation: a break with what was done before. The creation of the infantry half-*section* as the autonomous combat unit was a radical procedural innovation, since it profoundly transformed the structure of the infantry units;
- incremental innovation: improvement of an existing method or existing unit. The standardization of the half-*sections'* composition was incremental, since it amounted to an improvement of that structure.

In every case, the innovation was a rational step that met a precise aim and proceeded by analysis and investigations. The main sources of inspiration for French units were:

- the past: they rediscovered helmets, liquid fire, grenades and the old siege techniques;[2]
- similarities: the organization of the motor-transport service was based on that of the railways. (A notable example was the *Voie sacrée,* the road used to help supply Verdun.) Artillery barrages were the direct inspiration for the use of *groupements* of machine-guns firing barrages of bullets;
- imitation of Allies: French and British invited each other to attend their tactical experiments.[3] The British attack at Cambrai on 20 November 1917, which made a deep impression on the French GHQ, was the subject of a detailed and widely-disseminated study;[4]
- imitation of the enemy. As early as September 1914, for example, Joffre issued a note about German field entrenchments so his armies could draw inspiration from them.[5] The writer Joseph Bédier reckoned that: 'the clearest law in this constant stream [of tactical evolution] was that the French army both suffered and benefitted at the same time from the ideas of the German army, and vice versa, and that the basic concept of each discovery by one army came from a discovery made by the other'.[6] By the end of the war, Bédier noted, the French army was closer in appearance to the German army than to its own self of 1914.

- exploitation of an unexpected success: owing to the growing shortage of horses, the artillery began in September 1917 to turn to motorization in order to transport the guns of the *groupes* belonging to army corps. The resulting increase in strategic mobility was so great that it was decided to create forty, completely autonomous, regiments of lorry-borne guns. What had initially been seen as an expedient to deal with a shortage had soon become a major step forward and a vital component of the artillery;
- a different way of looking at things: in 1917, the acceptance of the idea that young NCOs were capable of directing an action by themselves opened the way to the creation of new tactical units. In the same year, the artillery abandoned the systematic quest to destroy its targets in favour of simply neutralizing them. This change of approach transformed offensive combat as a whole;
- diversion: equipment might be used for purposes other than those initially intended. The parachute began as just a straightforward means of emergency back-up, but soon became an instrument of resupply or even a means of transporting combatants behind enemy lines. Cavalry carbines were shorter than the Lebel rifle and became much in demand as soon as trenches were dug, since they were better suited to that setting. They were issued to the machine-gun companies, and at one stage there was even talk of them replacing all the Lebel rifles.[7]

### Organization and innovations

In *The fatal conceit* (1989), the Austrian-born economist Friedrich von Hayek explained how, in a complex society, the spontaneous order of millions of individual decisions produces a more stable equilibrium than exists in a centralized system, which simply can not handle all the information in real time.[8] Similarly, the tactical problems of the Great War, starting with the very first clashes, were so new, so urgent and evolved so quickly that only the units directly in contact with the front were able to deal with them promptly. As Captain Georges Kimpflin emphasized:

> the combatant has a limited field of vision ... He marches with blinkers, and the lower a rung he occupies on the ladder of the hierarchy, the more closed his blinkers become. Yet the narrowness of his view makes it accurate, and its restricted extent makes it distinct. He does not see much, but what he does see he sees well. He sees what actually is, because he is receiving information through his own eyes and not through those of other people.[9]

As we have seen, regiments began spontaneously at the end of August 1914 to try and rid themselves of their most deadly flaws and to come up with new and more effective methods. Innovations were tried out within regiments with the use of makeshift means, and since such innovations were small in scale, the necessary adjustments could be made rapidly. These micro-transformations continued to occur for as long as mistakes were punished by hostile fire, in other words throughout the war.

Yet some projects were impossible for units to develop using their own means, since in many cases the necessary financial, industrial and technological investments were so great that they formed a barrier to the creation. Only a larger organizational structure could initiate such projects. At a 'macroscopic' level, the French army, eight times larger in size than at the start of 1914, had the benefit of extensive resources. The high command was able to invest in projects – such as the tanks – that would have been deemed too expensive before 1914. It also seemed easier at the macroscopic level to 'seize the technological opportunities', or exploit the 'technical fields' that had been brought into being by scientific developments.[10] Furthermore, the various components of a large organizational structure could benefit from interacting with each other. The many innovations in fire direction and control that were made by the heavy artillery helped all the subdivisions of the artillery arm.

The pressure exerted by the challenges of the conflict produced a multitude of responses. Within this somewhat anarchic environment, we can see a division of tasks rapidly taking shape in the way that innovations were managed. The units soon became the main source of ideas, and GHQ inclined towards the role of selecting, supporting and disseminating those ideas. The high command also grasped that it had to rationalize on a regular basis the methods that were used. Otherwise, units would evolve separately and would tend to generate a confused profusion of procedures.

In between the units and GHQ, we can identify three categories of individuals who played a vital role in disseminating innovations. The first category was that of the experts. Combat is a complex job, carried out under extreme psychological pressure, and individuals vary widely in how skilled they are at it. Aerial combat is a particularly striking case in point, since the 182 French 'aces' – in other words, those fighter pilots credited with at least five victories in the air – accounted for a total of 1,756 confirmed victories out of a total of 3,950 claimed by the French fighter force as a whole.[11] If we compare this number of 182 'aces' with the 16,500 pilots who were present on the front at the end of the war, we grasp the importance of this handful of men in the conflict. These men were real professionals who, by flair, hard work and often by inclination, acquired a perfect mastery of the practical skills they needed for operating in so tough a setting. The case of the fighter force is well known because it is relatively straightforward to demonstrate, even though as time passed the aerial combats seemed more and more like confused mêlées. Yet professionals as clinical as Lieutenant René Fonck – the 'ace of aces' – could be found in every arm. Major Louis Bouchacourt wrote in 1927:

> If good attack troops existed during the 1914-18 war, it was because their infantry (partly as a result of the right personnel being selected) contained an élite – élite troops and élite cadres. It was because this infantry was fired up by *esprit de corps* and by the prestige it was accorded. It was because every good regiment had some renowned officers, some 'aces', victory-grabbers.[12]

Sometimes the know-how of these men could be communicated verbally. This can be seen in the case of the German pilot Captain Oswald Boelcke, some of whose rules of aerial combat remain valid today. But in many cases it was all about the men's motions, the equivalent of the 'personal touch' of good workers and craftsmen, and the only way these motions could spread was a slow process of imitation.

Devising and disseminating tricks of the trade was one thing. But the larger innovative projects were on a more advanced level and had to be driven by true 'entrepreneurs'. These entrepreneurs were not necessarily creators themselves, nor even combatants, but they had the ability to see a project through to completion despite all sorts of obstacles, such as rivalries or administrative hassle. GHQ was assailed by numerous proposals. Some were hardly practical, such as Second-Lieutenant Malassenet's proposal for a new telegraphic alphabet to replace Morse code, or the idea put forward by Private Raffray of the 103rd Infantry Regiment for a rather fanciful apparatus intended as a substitute for liaison personnel. These suggestions were turned down, yet they – in common with all the others – had been carefully considered.[13] Other submitted papers were more serious and important. In November 1914, Major Duchêne of the engineers proposed a trench-mortar, a proposal that led in January 1915 to the 58mm trench-mortar.[14]

In May-June 1915, Captain André Laffargue wrote an *Examination of the attack during the present period of the war*, in which he made some proposals about infantry combat. He was summoned to the Third Department of GHQ, and his pamphlet was widely disseminated within the armies as a model to be followed.[15] Captain Jacques Saconney's numerous proposals resulted in French ballooning being almost completely reorganized. But the most famous entrepreneurs were the big organizers of aeronautics (Major Edouard Barès and Colonel Maurice Duval), of wireless communications (Colonel Gustave Ferrié) and of the Assault Artillery (Colonel Jean Estienne). They had the direct support of the commander-in-chief and became his direct advisers. They were the successors to the pre-war figures of Captain Charles Renard (ballooning), Lieutenant Henri Gérard (military cycling) and Captain Ferdinand Ferber (aviation).

The third and final category of individuals who were vital in disseminating innovations were the generals. They had a special role as intermediaries. In common with the officers at GHQ, they had to conduct operations and manage change at the same time. But since they were closer to the troops and the front, they grasped this second role of the management of change sooner than did GHQ. On 11 September 1914, General Auguste Dubail, the commander of the 1st Army, had an instruction written that drew on reports from subordinates and notes from GHQ to provide an initial synthesis of the tactical changes that needed to be made. He recommended, for example, negating the superior range of the enemy artillery by favouring night approaches or wooded zones, and he recognized the need for an artillery duel even though this was frowned upon by the regulations. Each captured position was to be fortified with the help of trenches that were hidden from enemy sight and protected by obstacles set up in front.[16] Dubail, too, received many proposals. On 16 October 1914, he attended demonstrations of an 'armoured wheelbarrow', of case-shot rounds, of machines for the instant generation of smoke and rods fitted with a string of high-explosive petards for blasting gaps through barbed-wire.[17] On 30 October, Dubail met Colonel Marie Hippolyte Alfred Fetter, who told him about his idea for a flame-thrower.[18] On 10 November, he visited the workshop and testing ground where the 8th Corps made and tried out bombs, rifle-grenades and small mortars.[19]

The high reputation of some generals made their patronage important in disseminating ideas. Colonel Estienne's tank project, for example, benefitted from the support of Estienne's superior officer, General Pétain, who was known throughout the army by the end of 1915.

### Laboratories and migrants

Many innovators, regardless of whether they were civil or military, did not work alone. Instead, they belonged to small groups, or 'schools', which acted as 'laboratories' in which men could listen to, and inspire, each other.[20] The French army had many such tactical laboratories during the Great War. One example was Squadron MS3 and its development of fighter techniques in 1915: this was the squadron of Sergeant Georges Guynemer, Paul Tarascon and Captains Albert Deullin and Antonin Brocard. Other tactical laboratories included Champlieu camp for the tanks, or the 4th Army's training centres in the field of infantry tactics in 1917.

Let's take the example of Major Charles de Tricornot de Rose's *groupement* at Verdun. When the Germans launched their offensive against Verdun in February 1916, they managed to concentrate large numbers of fighter aircraft above the combat zone: 180 of their Pfalz E and Fokker E airplanes, which were fitted with synchronization gear to enable a machine-gun to fire directly in front between the propeller blades. The German intention was to neutralize the French artillery's means of aerial observation. The few French airplanes were flying individually and were soon swept from the sky, leaving the artillery almost blind. To counter this threat, the French were obliged to fight an air battle – the first air battle of history.[21] On 28 February, Major de Rose, the head of the 5th Army's aeronautics, was placed in charge of the combat aviation at Verdun. He formed a specially-constituted *groupement* of fifteen squadrons using the best of the fighter aviation's personnel and machines (Nieuport XI airplanes). The experiment, which continued until the French conclusively gained air superiority, was highly productive. The concentration of talent in the *groupement* gradually developed most of the techniques of air superiority. These techniques included permanent patrols by squadrons within clearly-defined limits of space and time, large patrols of between ten and twenty-five airplanes with the 'aces' in top cover, and solitary patrols of 'aces'. Other techniques were air-ground coordination, air sectors that matched the army corps sectors and the integration of technical innovations for attacking balloons (Le Prieur rockets fired electrically and incendiary bullets). There were also procedures for group flight: wing-wagging to give alarm signals, actions 'by imitation' and the control of formations by the group leader and file-closers.

Men whom we may call 'migrants' played a leading role in making units fruitful. According to a study by Albert Shapero, people who have migrated away from their country of birth are more likely to produce innovations than people who are still living there.[22] It is therefore significant that the vast majority of the French troops in the Great War were mobilized civilians who retained their civilian know-how when they put on their uniforms and had few preconceptions on tactical matters. For example, Lieutenant Cailloux, a reservist officer who would later invent the stroboscope, was serving with an artillery regiment in the Vosges in spring 1915 when he managed to retrieve two tractors with caterpillar tracks that he owned on his farm in Tunisia. These two tractors were then used for a variety of tasks, not least to bring a couple of 370mm mortars up to their firing positions in the mountains so they could prepare the attack on the Hartmannswillerkopf.[23]

The engineer graduates of the *Ecole centrale*, who were all assigned to the artillery as reservist officers, made a major contribution to developing the technical and scientific character of that arm.[24] The mistrust they frequently encountered from the active officers drove them towards the pioneering organizations – the heavy artillery, tanks, aviation and trench-mortars. An officer of the trench-mortars described the reservists:

> Their habitual exclusion meant that too many of them were still confined to being commanders of ammunition columns or leaders of fatigue parties. They came flocking at the first summons, keen to swop these duties for a real command, or simply out of desire to see the infantryman's life in the trenches at closer quarters. Most were engineers, managers of farms or directors of industrial and commercial businesses. They were used to being in charge of mature men, rather than 20 year-old recruits, and were accustomed to acting on their own initiative and taking responsibility. In short, they knew how the world worked and they, more than anyone else, were qualified to take command of new units that were generally left to their own devices. ... In a wholly new speciality, where everyone was starting off on the same footing, the professional soldiers could claim no superiority over them from a technical point of view ... and so the stereotype quickly emerged of the *crapouillot* [trench-mortar] officer, a man of practical accomplishments, very unmilitary in appearance, who went directly to the point with complete disregard for any trivialities.[25]

A second major stream of 'internal migrations' was provided by the cavalrymen, who had nothing to do behind the trenches. More than 4,800 of their officers left for the other arms. Among them were many personalities, such as Captain Jean de Lattre (the future Marshal de Lattre de Tassigny), who joined the infantry, Lieutenant Charles de Tricornot de Rose, who went to aviation, and Major Louis Bossut, who opted for the tanks.[26] The cavalry also exported to the other arms its spirit and some of its methods. The movement of personnel meant that the new organizations could be assigned high-quality human resources, consisting as they did of motivated volunteers. The movement did not necessarily undermine the arms that the men left, such as the infantry or the cavalry, since those arms were obliged to innovate in order to economize on manpower. The cavalry, for example, had to take an interest in motorization as a way of addressing the shortage not only of men but also of horses. (Many of its horses were turned over to the artillery.) Migrations were therefore a driving force for improving the whole army.

## The Model of Scrabble
### The game board
The acceleration of the industrial revolution at the end of the nineteenth century had turned the military assimilation of the technical offer into a crucial issue. The process of assimilation is worth describing in detail. It was actually similar to a game of Scrabble. Industrialists combined resources (the letters) to propose technical innovations (the words). These innovations then had to be inserted into the existing doctrinal fabric (the game board). This required enough space and a link

with something that already existed. Only a few designs for tanks were put forward before the war, and they were rejected because they could not be linked to anything. Airplanes excited slightly more interest since they answered a need. Using the third dimension became attractive since modern firepower made reconnaissance missions dangerous or slow if they were carried out on horseback or on foot. It was therefore possible to place the airplane on the 'game board'. Once an innovation had been placed, it altered the tactical fabric and in turn made new links possible. The presence of airplanes introduced the need to counter them. Some industrialists had prototypes in existence of motorized machine-gun carriers, and these carriers were tried out during the large-scale manœuvres in an anti-aircraft defence role. Various cavalrymen who took part in the manœuvres then noticed these vehicles and thought of possible alternative uses for them that were put into practice in 1914.

Other factors intervened in the 'game'. The opponents – the French and Germans – had similar resources available and spied on each other. The creation or insertion of a 'word' on one side was often known by the other and frequently led to a 'precautionary imitation'. Sometimes, it was prestige that took a hand in the game, as was the case with the impressive dirigibles that were so popular with the public. Once a technical innovation had been inserted, it normally took several years to be assimilated tactically. That required the innovation to pass through various stages: experiments had to be carried out, the innovation had to be distributed, habits had to be formed and all the possibilities of the innovation had to be explored. The compartmentalized nature of the French system meant that the dissemination of an innovation was hindered by the need to interest enough members of the Forum to influence decisions. Only two options really existed: either the impact of an innovation was obvious to the Forum's long-standing members, or else those men who had actually used the new means gained access to the Forum.

In 1886, the Lebel rifle entered service. Its ammunition used a powerful, smokeless powder that made the infantryman a more efficient killer. At the same time, infantry regulations were issued that prescribed a return to closed ranks, volley-firing and attacks carried out to the beating of drums. In the end, it took the South African war of 1899-1902 to show up this contradiction, by revealing the murderous effects of the new ammunition. All the regulations in force then appeared obsolete and were hurriedly replaced. Yet in 1906, Major Louis de Grandmaison noted in his *Infantry training for offensive combat* that musketry training was still not entirely appropriate for smokeless powder ammunition. He himself totally ignored machine-guns, which in all likelihood he had rarely encountered in his regiment. Similarly, the effects of the new artillery were under-estimated, largely because few officers had seen 75mm guns firing. Even if they had, the firing was carried out at a safe distance and with training shells that had a feeble bursting charge. The effects of the fire of heavy field howitzers were wholly unknown, for the few existing models almost never left the depots. They did not even appear at the manœuvres.

### Machine-guns

Machine-guns exemplified the difficulties of developing a technical innovation. Although used in 1870 – they had been known at the time as 'bullet-firing cannon' – they had been a disappointment. Manned by artillerymen with little training in their use, they were employed in batteries, like cannon. Their limited range, and the curtain of smoke given off by the black powder, meant they had only a minor influence on the fighting. Yet they remained on the 'game board' as ditch-flanking pieces in fortresses. (When the French army mobilized in 1914, most of its machine-guns were still located in fortresses. Since many officers had seen these weapons in fortresses, they thought of them in terms of defensive tasks.)[27]

After the 'bullet-firing cannon' were withdrawn from field service, a space opened on the 'game board' for the new models of machine-gun. In 1902, some Hotchkiss machine-guns were tried out by battalions of foot *chasseurs* as a precautionary and imitative measure in response to the South African war and in the wake of the German manœuvres of 1899 to 1901. The Russo-Japanese war accelerated the process of insertion. The Second Department (Intelligence) of the General Staff reported:

> The war in Manchuria has shown the unquestionable value of machine-guns. Opinion is unanimous regarding their great physical and moral impact. It is above all on the defensive that these weapons demonstrate their fearsome effectiveness.[28]

Nobody, stated a Russian officer, should 'be astonished that nowadays our infantrymen are more concerned about machine-guns than artillery pieces'.[29] Although the Russians and Japanese had few machine-guns at the start of the campaign, they rapidly increased their allocations until by the end of the fighting each regiment had two or three machine-guns. French observers also noticed that the ammunition consumption of these weapons was not as high as expected, which undermined the main argument against their introduction. What followed was a phenomenon of precautionary imitation. In 1905, General Jean Brun noted that the Germans had increased their allocation of machine-guns. 'Unless we give our infantry comparable weapons', he informed the Supreme War Council, 'it seems difficult for us to avoid being inferior to our potential enemies in terms of morale and equipment, even if we have equal numbers of men.'[30]

Consequently, the machine-gun units in both French and German armies were similar in number and were organized in much the same way, with each infantry regiment having six machine-guns. It was at this time that the process was slowed down by the refusal of the artillery service to be reliant on the private company of Hotchkiss, even though Hotchkiss had equipped the Japanese army with machine-guns. The artillery therefore developed its own model, the Saint-Etienne. The weapon was designed by engineers who were free from any constraints of time and profitability. Sergeant Charles-Maurice Chenu described the Saint-Etienne when he was doing a training course in 1915:

> It is a complicated weapon and when dismantled has an unimaginable number of parts. It is the pride and joy of the authorities. Think of it! Only the Saint-Etienne has a change in speed. It can slow down or speed up its rate of fire when desired. Yes, but for what? For nothing – and that's the problem. The Saint-Etienne has, on the other hand, some drawbacks. It becomes hot and can not fire more than a strip of twenty-five rounds without jamming. In the final days as the training comes to a close, we are casually shown another machine-gun, the Hotchkiss. Simple design, with six or seven components in all and no over-heating. A marvel that does not let you down – and the future will justify this opinion twenty times over.[31]

By 1908, every large army in Europe was equipped with machine-guns. But the French doctrine for using these weapons remained vague. The only example on which to draw was the war in Manchuria, where the Russians and Japanese had used the weapon to defend positions.[32] That, of course, contradicted the offensive paradigm. Hence the machine-gun would continue to be neglected until it was embellished with offensive virtues. It also had the disadvantage of being simultaneously under the control of both the artillery, which was interested only in guns, and the infantry, which was interested only in rifles. In 1904, General Henri Bonnal reckoned that 'the future face of battle is not going to be changed significantly by the handful of 'Maxim' machine-gun batteries that have only recently come into service in the German army.'[33] Similarly, when Colonel Louis de Maud'huy's *The infantry* was published in 1911, it did not mention machine-guns. (At this time, Maud'huy commanded the 35th Infantry Regiment.) Lieutenant-Colonel Jean-Baptiste Montaigne thought in 1913 that 'the current weapon of the infantryman is the rifle'.[34] In 1911, nine years after the first machine-gun trials, General Hubert Lyautey noted while commanding the 10th Army Corps that 'ideas about the tactical use of machine-guns were most fluctuating and indecisive and it was therefore vital to set a doctrine.'[35]

In fact, it was only in the three years leading up to the outbreak of the war that ideas about machine-gun tactics really began to be developed. A regulation for the use of machine-guns appeared in July 1912. The following year, Colonel Eugène Debeney, the head of the infantry course at the Staff College, devoted an entire lecture to the subject. It was now universally accepted that machine-guns were effective in defence. Recognition of their effectiveness also began to find its way into offensive combat. Debeney reckoned:

Machine-guns are an excellent infantry tool. The speed and accuracy of their fire make them an unusually powerful fire element. Ample use must be made of this addition. ... As with any fire element, their function is to support movement and their vital role is in the offensive.[36]

The machine-gun was initially earmarked for use in the most 'static' missions of offensive combat, such as protecting a flank or consolidating conquered positions. It then came to be seen to have a role in supporting attacks. Although confined within these limits, the machine-gun became a respectable weapon and was able to make a coy appearance in the 1914 *Infantry training regulation*. This is how the regulation described its main use:

The machine-guns represent a powerful fire reinforcement for the chain [of skirmishers]. ... They are brought into line at those points where the intensity of fire needs to be increased in order to support the movement. From then on, the machine-guns follow the movements of the chain as closely as possible, by going to those points from where they will be able to support it with their fire to the best effect, usually on the flanks, in front of gaps or on commanding positions. They accompany the skirmishers to the assault, and try to reach the opposing position at the same time as them in order to secure its occupation and pursue the enemy with their fire.[37]

Yet this endeavour to adapt the use of machine-guns to the dominant mode of thought – the offensive – came too late to do more than scratch the surface. By 1914, the machine-gun remained of little interest, and men did not really know how to use it. Chenu, who at the time was a young conscript, recalled a machine-gun training exercise just before the war:

> Two machine-guns – which jammed after every ten rounds – had opened fire in front of us. Their commander was slightly shame-faced as he explained their role, as though he was apologizing. At the command of 'Break ranks', our officers had a great laugh at the expense of the machine-guns. 'Those things?' exclaimed a major, to everyone's approval. 'Come now! They'll never be able to match a squad of good shots!'[38]

During manœuvres, the infantry movements were so quick – and unrealistic – that the machine-gun sections had trouble following them. This raised fears that the machine-guns might slow down the troops and, according to Major Henri Bouvard, 'demand constant resupplies of ammunition, of which they get through large amounts'.[39] Long-range fires were forbidden, in order to limit ammunition consumption.[40] Significantly, although the Berger-Levrault catalogue contained eighty-four publications and articles devoted to the infantry, only three of them dealt with machine-guns, and these three were written by young lieutenants.

The final stage in the insertion of machine-guns on the 'game board' was the coercion exerted by enemy fire. During the Battle of the Frontiers in August 1914, the German machine-guns were used in superior fashion and caused devastation everywhere. Thereafter, the French Saint-Etienne machine-guns soon appeared in the first line in both attack and defence. The machine-gun was now fully inserted into the tactical fabric, to the extent of becoming the central weapon of infantry combat. This was the moment at which it began the upward phase of an S-shaped lifecycle.

## Dynamic of the Tactical Innovations

Tactical innovations evolved in the circumstances described above and in accordance with a lifecycle that was essentially the same in every case. But that lifecycle did vary in intensity as a result of being affected by a certain number of stimulants. The most important of these stimulants were the enemy, the technical offer and the shortage of men.

### The lifecycle

In order to be born, an innovation needed fertile soil, a ripe context.[41] The origin of an idea was often complicated, or even impossible to identify. But the idea surfaced at the moment when it could be heard or, to put that another way, at the moment when it could constitute a response to a precise need. Its effectiveness then followed an S-shaped curve. A slow start generally gave way to rapid development, followed by a slowing down. Then the idea was either relaunched using new methods, or made obsolete by an enemy counter-measure.

Take, for example, the adjustment of artillery fire in positional warfare. It initially went through a degree of trial and error. Several methods of adjustment from the air were tested: wagging of wings, messages dropped in weighted bags, flares and the wireless. Meanwhile, the heavy artillery studied indirect fire and did so in a scientific manner by addressing such subjects as ballistics and aerology (the study of the atmosphere up above the ground). Similarly, the fighter force experimented with the best way of protecting the artillery observation aircraft. All this took nearly two years, but the system of fire adjustment worked well during the period between the Battle of the Somme in July 1916 and the Aisne offensive in April 1917. Thereafter, its efficiency decreased, owing to a fall in the effectiveness of aerial observation, the diversion of means to the fighter force and the fact that the time needed to adjust the artillery fire was too long. But the adjustment of fire was then radically transformed by the quicker methods of the 'scientific preparation of fires' (see Chapter 8).

It was possible to extend an innovation's life. This could be done by protecting its secret, for example by forbidding a new fighter aircraft to fly beyond its own lines. Alternatively, the life of an innovation might be prolonged if one side had a big technical head start over the other, as was the case with the Germans and their chemical weapons, or the Allies and tanks. An innovation was also likely to last longer if the cost of putting it into effect was much lower than it was for the enemy. In 1918, for instance, the French were able to create an Air Division because they had numerical superiority in the air.

Conversely, counter-measures could be developed if the enemy's machines were captured, and even more so if his methods were analysed. This meant that some weapons became tactical objectives. On 8 April 1916, the French finally captured a Fokker E.I aircraft equipped with synchronization gear that allowed a machine-gun to be fired between the propeller blades. Similarly, when the Germans got their hands on three Renault FT tanks at Chaudun on 31 May 1918, they immediately took the machines to the rear for detailed examination.

### The stimulants

It takes two sides to fight a war. This results in an experimental process, which is kept in a dynamic state by the confrontation between the adversaries and their interaction with each other. The prolonged war of 1914-18 was a phenomenon unseen since the Napoleonic era, with the exception of the US Civil War. As the war dragged on, the struggle between the opponents followed a dialectic of innovation and counter-measure on a hitherto inconceivable level. It was now vital, when formulating doctrine, to take into account the enemy's ability to evolve. If a new method was applied, it produced a response in the weeks or months that followed. This made it necessary to put into effect a tactical innovation that was so stunning it might provoke a decisive collapse. Alternatively, it was vital to know how to ensure an innovation evolved quickly.

The method that the Allies used on the Somme was to try and break through the front with a succession of very methodical attacks. But this method failed, because it gave the Germans time to adapt and to thwart the firepower of the Allied artillery, which had initially been devastating. What the Germans in effect did was to try and avoid providing the Allied heavy artillery with any targets. They stopped concentrating their means of defence in lines that were easy to locate and shell. They established automatic weapons in a chequered pattern in shell-holes out in front, and so these weapons became impossible to spot. They vacated the bombarded zones and took the method of defence-in-depth a step further by adopting an 'elastic defence'. This entailed yielding ground to the attacker, but forcing him to repeat his attacks endlessly and to consume vast amounts of ammunition. The Germans thereby managed to avert a breakthrough of their front, despite the power of the Allied attack.

The tactical innovations of the Great War were also stimulated and shaped by the scientific and industrial environment. This environment was so productive that we might easily assume it helped drive the innovations of the front in their earliest stages, or even produced them. But in fact the scientific and industrial environment was only tenuously linked to the army's needs, since the slow tempo of the research laboratories' work seemed incompatible with the front's rapid changes of state. If technical innovations had stemmed simply from research, equipment would have been produced without there being any clear idea of how it might be used, but this was never the case. Instead, research was actually driven by the front, for the 'demand' exerted stronger pressure than the technical 'offer'. Furthermore, only a limited amount of research was carried out, since the French offset the time needed to develop heavy materiel by resorting almost exclusively to prototypes that – with the exception of tanks – had already existed before the war. Even so, it was 1916 before most of this heavy equipment started to be brought into service.

The 'demand' from the units could vary in strength. An historian of the war, General Marius Daille, pointed out the problem that initially existed. 'Each arm did undoubtedly have some experts on whom it could rely', he wrote. But the weakness of the French army's technical culture meant that 'you could enumerate those experts who had given any thought to orchestrating the many existing types of equipment and above all those types that were worth producing and bringing into service. On the whole, the French army's weaknesses could be said to be the inadequacy of its technical training and the shortcomings of its weaponry.'[42]

We have already seen the officers' attitudes, and the troops themselves were undoubtedly less receptive to technical innovations than were the men in the British or German armies, a higher proportion of whom came from urban, working-class backgrounds. When Colonel Bernard Serrigny visited units that were in training in the Central Army Group in 1916, he noted that 'the technical knowledge of both [officers and men] was generally very poor'.[43] Moreover, many officers were convinced that the war would be over long before new types of equipment appeared. Since they realized that time would be needed to develop the equipment, they obviously lacked the motivation to take an interest.

Nor was the need for that new equipment necessarily felt. In 1932, the British economist John R. Hicks showed that the increase in the cost of one of the factors of production – capital or labour – was an inducement to favour the other. If the cost of labour is high, for example, it is preferable to invest in machines. When the historian Marc Bloch wrote his article about mediaeval inventions, he described the water mill being developed at the end of Antiquity for this same reason, namely the disappearance of slave labour and the need to find other ways of generating energy.[44] At the start of 1915, the French army found itself in a similar situation, and this was particularly true in the case of its infantry. Shells were in shorter supply than infantrymen at that time, and so the offensives of 1914 and 1915 were akin to experiments in 'throwing' men at the enemy. It was only towards the end of 1915 that a concern to 'spare the infantry' really arose, and that was also the stage at which modern equipment started to be adopted on a huge scale. Similarly, the most serious manpower crisis would see the launch at the end of 1917 of the largest industrial programmes of the war.

## The Restraints on Change

The play of the dialectic of the front exerted a constant pressure for change. But many psychological restraints also existed. These restraints stemmed from the need for organizational structures to be stable and permanent.[45] Some of the restraints can be compared to a person's immune system reacting to a transplant, and they disappeared with time. But others stemmed from pre-war habits and remained inflexibilities during the entire conflict.

### Scepticism, rivalries and prejudices

Scepticism was the first restraint on innovation. The installation of wireless sets on airplanes proved instantly effective, yet it provoked resistance from those 'men who had settled into the war, men who did not want to complicate their lives with innovations, or who remained sceptical when confronted with an achievement that seemed to them impossible.'[46]

Similarly, many officers opposed even the notion of air battle. On 21 March 1916, they managed to have Major de Rose's *groupement* disbanded, despite its achievements.[47] After just several days it became clear that the disbandment had been a mistake, and the *groupement* was reformed. In this case, innovation served to uncover hidden resistance.[48]

Internal rivalries could act as a restraint and not just a source of emulation. This happened with the development of the tanks. After the approval of Colonel Estienne's project, which was entrusted to the Schneider company, the technical branch of the motor-transport service decided that it wanted its own tank and collaborated with Saint-Chamond, the firm that was Schneider's competitor. Each of these two projects, which were pursued in parallel and without coordination, made the other wholly redundant. They thereby delayed the overall development of the Assault Artillery.

Rivalries between the arms, or within them, were also important. Each arm tended to favour its 'noble' part and to neglect those branches that were dedicated to assisting the other arms. The aviation, for example, soon gave priority to fighters over the observation service, and delayed the creation of a specialist, ground-support aviation.

Prejudices – especially national prejudices – could be another obstruction. The most fruitful source of tactical innovation was imitation of allies and the enemy. Yet this mimicry did not occur automatically:

[General Oskar] von Hutier's tactics [rapid infiltration methods] had been known since January 1918, but had not been taken as seriously as they deserved. This was because they were carried out first against Russians and then against Italians. Even after 21 March, the [French] staff was inclined to think that, if these tactics had succeeded, it was because they were being used against British troops who were said to be of poor quality.[49]

It was also difficult to adopt methods that had previously been disparaged. Once the French high command had described the German assault units as 'divisions of gladiators' and as an indication of the overall weakening of the German infantry, it was difficult to imitate them, even after the defeats inflicted in 1918 by those same 'gladiators'.

### Inherited inflexibilities

More difficult to overcome were inflexibilities inherited from habits that had been formed before the war.[50] Three of them in particular had a profound effect: the distaste for digging in, the fervour for the offensive, and its defensive counterpart, namely the phobia for losing ground.

The need to entrench the front had not been foreseen, and the men had not been trained for it. Even though orders were issued for the ground to be prepared for defence, the work was done reluctantly. From the very start of the fighting, infantrymen proved instinctively reluctant to dig. Digging was regarded as a task for the engineers and, 'as soon as it was a matter of making a defensive work of the slightest importance, even of laying barbed-wire, the help of sappers was requested'.[51] Nor did the men understand the point of these labours, convinced as they were that the offensive would be resumed. On 23 January 1915, General Emile Fayolle wrote: 'I have all the trouble in the world to organize [the works] in a rational manner ... Many lose interest in them. As for the men, they prefer to get themselves killed rather than work ...'[52]

On 20 August 1915, a note from GHQ stipulated: 'Some units consider earthworks as tasks that are beneath them. Good infantry should wield the entrenching tool as well as the rifle.'[53] But on 6 December, Fayolle was still noting:

> How is it that I am unable to have my ideas translated into practice? ... The truth is that nobody was prepared for this [positional] warfare. Quite the opposite was the case: saps and earthworks were regarded with the greatest disdain. Nobody knows what a trace is, or a rational framework. There is a huge amount of education to do, and it can't be done in a day. Nothing can be improvised in war.[54]

Since the infantry came largely from the rural population, its distaste for digging is astonishing. Only gradually did this reluctance disappear, starting in 1916 when a reduction was finally made in the number of days each unit spent at the front, thus alleviating the burden of the *poilus'* troubles.

On the other hand, faith in the intrinsic value of the offensive persisted throughout the war. Major Emile Laure described the state of mind of the 13th Infantry Division in Artois in 1915:

> In terms of tactics, we received instructions from GHQ that sought to inject some prudence into our attitude to fire and in particular to ensure that the infantry cooperated better with the artillery ... But deep within ourselves, we remained loyal to the fervently offensive impulses of our pre-war education.[55]

Two years later, after Laure had been transferred to GHQ, he admitted:

> I am one of those who previously went overboard in expressing my generation's offensive fervour. I am not unaware that the tendency of our training should be to curb this fervour for a while, in the spirit of *Directives numbers 1* and *3*. It is true that almost three years spent with the troops have made me much more mellow and that, along with my companions-in-arms in the infantry, I foresee this new spirit having the most positive outcome.[56]

Yet there remained many officers who criticized the 'defensive-minded' Pétain, the 'temporizer', and who remained convinced that the Nivelle offensive in 1917 could have succeeded had it not been for a series of unfortunate circumstances.

Once the front had become fortified, the fervour for the offensive was frustrated and turned into a fierce determination to defend every inch of ground whatever the cost, and to defend it with all the more energy in that 'each lost corner of ground is a strip of flesh torn from the land of our fathers'.[57] This mindset had serious tactical consequences. For a start, it occasionally made it necessary for units to establish themselves on lines that were dangerous. Fayolle noted on 8 March 1915:

> Never has [the command] agreed to a correction of the line. We have dug in where we were, however precarious or difficult the situation. Sometimes falling back 40 metres would have been enough for us to have a secure hold on the ground and to be out of danger.[58]

Losing ground was forbidden. Any small-unit leader who lost his trenches was obliged to retake them whatever the cost. Furthermore, the density of troops occupying the first (and most exposed) line remained high for a long time, despite GHQ's instructions to the contrary.[59] 'It seemed', Joffre later wrote, 'that [the commanders of large units] could defend the trenches only by filling them with men elbow-to-elbow behind the parapets.'[60]

In the 8th Army on 4 December 1914, seventy-eight out of the 153 battalions were in the first line.[61] In these circumstances, the infantry suffered severe attrition, without being able to train or even to organize the defensive front in a rational manner. Losses were all the higher in that the first line almost invariably fell to any major offensive. Mindsets changed as the adoption of numerous, powerful, automatic weapons made it possible to defend the lines more economically. But the reluctance to yield the least ground, even if that meant heavy losses, lasted until the end of the war. This was clearly demonstrated by the argument about the new system of defence-in-depth that was set out in *Directive number 4* on 22 December 1917.

### The controversy about the 'army battlefield'

This controversy is a good example of how a disciplined organization might resist changes that collided with its core values. The new German attack methods were well known, having been used spectacularly against the Russians at Riga in September 1917 and against the Italians at Caporetto in October. Since the French had several years' experience of fighting on the offensive, they also knew the effectiveness of the deep defensive dispositions used by the Germans. Everything seemed to indicate, therefore, that it would be easy for sound defensive methods to be defined and learned. The first position needed to be transformed into a mere outpost line, with the real resistance being made further back in the second position. Yet implementing this system of defence-in-depth (Pétain called it 'the army battlefield') did not prove easy at all. In fact, GHQ had the greatest difficulty imposing these methods. The resistance it encountered stemmed from a whole range of reasons. In the first place, it was the usual case of men being unwilling to make the effort to learn something new:

> Let's not be too astonished by the resistance that was put up against us, for it's inherent in human nature. Someone risking his life every day has enough on his plate without bothering about any other concern, not even about learning how to risk his life to better effect. You can understand why a regimental officer would fail to show much enthusiasm if, after returning from a sector, with all his dangers left behind and with the prospect of a well-earned rest ahead of him, he suddenly found himself confronted with having to learn new regulations, or with having to do or direct exercises.[62]

Naturally, an even greater effort was required if there was a sharp break with the methods that had been learned up to that moment. The effort increased as weariness grew. Pétain complained of this once he became commander-in-chief:

> The length of the war tends to foster 'incuriosity' and laziness of thought. The new weapons are familiar only to those who use them. The lessons drawn from operations are poorly disseminated among those who did not take part in them. ... The staffs must therefore get out of their offices and be put in touch with reality.[63]

After several years of war, each regiment had built up a capital of experience. The combatant therefore felt he knew 'everything in this field [of defensive combat], simply because he was defending himself every day on the small corner of ground that he was responsible for holding'.[64] In a way, what was seen was a rigidification, or simply an inertia that grew as the war progressed, increasing at the same rate as the weariness and amount of accumulated know-how. In many cases, this inertia was fostered by a rising scepticism towards doctrinaires, since the mistakes they made could be seen repeatedly.

When the doctrine changed from holding ground 'whatever the cost' to defensive manœuvre, what were the soldiers to believe? Why would the bitter defence of Verdun, step by step, not be more effective? The German victories were regarded with the same scepticism: had these victories not been won against Russians whose morale was flawed and against Italians who were deemed indifferent soldiers? Above all, how could anyone readily think of giving up ground that had been won at so high a price? 'Had it not cost much blood and much trouble to conquer and hold these 4 or 5 km of ground that were being voluntarily abandoned to the enemy?'[65] Hence the phenomenon of habitual inertia was combined with a defence of core values.

The same unease clearly affected the generals. The 'opposition' included most of those generals who had formerly advocated the offensive at any cost, with the moral primacy once held by the offensive now switching to the bitter defence of the first line. General Denis Auguste Duchêne, the commander of the 6th Army on the exposed sector of the Aisne, was typical of this resistance. His strategy initially consisted of temporizing. He argued that working on the second position was incompatible with the need for in-depth training, and then argued about the unique nature of the terrain he had to defend. He also benefitted from the protection of General Ferdinand Foch, having been his chief-of-staff in the 20th Corps back in August 1914. Foch did not share Pétain's ideas. At this time, he was the chief of the General Staff of the French army and regarded Pétain as his most dangerous rival for the new post that was taking shape for an Allied supreme commander.[66] Duchêne's last resort, after the Germans had begun their string of offensives in spring 1918, was to use one of Foch's directives (it forbade the abandonment of ground in Flanders) as an excuse to do the opposite to Pétain's orders. But on 27 May, Duchêne's front was attacked and his first line, on which he had concentrated his defensive efforts, was overrun. Not until 4 June was the situation restored by emergency measures. By then, the French army had suffered its greatest reverse in the war. Yet it took this disaster to impose the new defensive concepts. 'After 27 May, eyes began to open in the subordinate staffs and even in the regiments.'[67]

Nevertheless, as late as 9 June, the main body of the forces had still not been completely withdrawn to the assigned main line of resistance. Some units still fought on the advanced-posts.[68] As the historian Guy Pedroncini has stressed:

> It was very difficult for General Pétain to impose a doctrine that was not only new but also complex, in the place of a doctrine that was simple and therefore easily understood, that had become anchored by three years of habit in men's minds and by three years of practice on the ground. We must recognize that General Pétain had to wage a crusade for his ideas.[69]

Permanent adaptation entails overcoming restraints and inflexibilities. It also involves adapting to new tempos.

## Unsettled Time

> This war often seemed to slow down and march on the spot, but in contrast everything in it changed. Even during those periods that seemed the most stagnant, everything – weapons, doctrines and techniques – was evolving, and everything was happening with the most disconcerting speed.[70]

This apparent contradiction, as highlighted by the writer Joseph Bédier, was a new phenomenon. War 'time' had changed the tempo of the process of evolution. Compared to the pre-war period, the process of evolution was characterized by a sharp acceleration and deep discontinuities that could not fail to disturb the participants psychologically. An idea of the acceleration can be gained from the rate at which the training regulations were updated. From 1875 to 1914, the main training regulations (infantry or large units) were renewed roughly every nine or ten years (1875, 1885, 1894-5, 1904 and 1913-14). From August 1914, the tempo increased to one major regulation a year. We can therefore estimate empirically that in wartime the changes were ten times faster than in peacetime.

Furthermore, time in war was not continuous. It consisted of periods that were crammed full of events, but also others that were far calmer. Some of these variations were seasonal, but more commonly they were linked to operational activities. The August to October operations in 1914, the 1915 offensives, the Battles of Verdun and the Somme in 1916, the Aisne offensive in 1917 and so on were all peaks of activity during which the changes abruptly sped up owing to the strength of the dialectic of 'innovation-response' between the opponents. Each of these peaks of activity generally contained surprises. The surprises might stem from either the emergence of an innovation or the unexpected character of an action – such as the Allied attack of 18 July 1918 at Villers-Cotterêts – and in many cases these two elements were combined to heighten the surprise effect.

But starting in 1915, the surprises tended to become more spaced out. As well as being separated by longer intervals of time, they tended to stem from the exploitation of a temporary technical superiority, such as tanks, mustard gas or new fighter airplanes.[71] Technical surprise tended to replace tactical surprise, which was particularly difficult to achieve, especially for the French who lacked quick-firing heavy artillery and had to 'pound' the enemy for several days before launching an offensive.

Technical surprise was not a new notion. Earlier examples included the bullet-firing cannon of 1870 and the 75mm gun of the turn of the century. But the phenomenon became particularly important during the Great War owing to the conflict's duration and above all owing to the scale of the resources that were used in it. The US sociologist Alvin Toffler has shown in *Future shock*[72] that an individual or group of individuals has a unavoidably limited capacity to adapt to multiple, rapid changes, and that psychological disorders ensue if this limit is exceeded. Some particularly violent surprises can therefore amount to shocks. The start of the Great War naturally included some of these shocks. But many shocks also occurred during the period of positional warfare, despite its apparent immobility. They included the first use of poisonous gas (near Ypres in April 1915). This is how Major Henri Bouvard reacted when faced with mustard gas two years later:

> We were left behind. Not until April 1918 would we respond really effectively by using a product of the same nature. The Germans' head-start was a source of real concern at any given time, for the attacked units lost many of their men, and nothing was more demoralizing than fighting against mustard gas.[73]

Another example of shock was the confusion of many infantrymen when faced with the flexibility of the German assault troops' manœuvres during the early actions of 1918. Confidence could fall if it seemed to be the enemy who was invariably springing the surprises. Even a side that held the operational initiative could find itself affected by this phenomenon. Between November 1914 and April 1917, the French army was almost constantly in an offensive posture, but had to endure a mounting number of tactical setbacks and nasty surprises, such as well-organized German defensive lines, trench-mortars *(Minenwerfer)*, poisonous gas and fighter airplanes fitted with an axially-mounted machine-gun. When the French were defending Verdun, the Germans surprised them again with their air superiority and massive use of quick-firing artillery. The feeling crept in that the French army was always lagging behind the Germans, and this frustration revealed itself in the infantry's loss of confidence in its own abilities and in those of its leaders. One undoubted reason why General Robert Nivelle and his methods sparked such enthusiasm was that he was able to surprise the Germans in the final actions of 1916 at Verdun – an ability that had not been seen before.

Sometimes, the unease felt in the face of the rapid changes had other origins. In 1916, the infantry started to receive a host of new types of equipment. But the cadres, who were the natural instructors of the men, failed to master this equipment. This made it necessary to create a special training structure that took the men away from their leaders in order to train them in specialized centres. Many officers thought their authority would be weakened as a result. That was the main reason why General Pétain's *Directive number 2*, which rationalized and developed the training infrastructure, provoked a degree of resistance.

This unsettled time was also a source of tension between the armies on the one hand, subjected as they were to intense pressure, and on the other the rear services, which retained many of their peacetime characteristics. Since war 'time' was no longer the same for everyone, the result was a growing divergence. The most obvious example concerned the birth of the tanks. 'To accomplish anything entails consciously resigning yourself to doing less-than-perfect work.' That was Colonel Estienne's motto. In keeping with it, he preferred to have prototype tanks built rapidly, so they were at his disposal and could be tried out under the actual conditions of the front to enable improvements to be made. In contrast, many of the departments of the interior of the country still adhered to bureaucratic procedures that focused on the quest for the perfect product at the expense of practicability. The attempt to achieve 100 per cent effectiveness tended to cause delays to increase in an exponential manner.[74] Whereas just seventeen months elapsed between Estienne's proposal and the appearance of the first tanks, eighteen years separated the development of the 75mm gun in 1896 and the start of the war – a period in which the artillery workshops produced not one new system.[75]

\*

Within a short space of time, thousands of tactical innovations had emerged from the combat units. This constant generation of innovations had shaped the face of the modern French army – sometimes by small steps and sometimes in a more radical manner. Yet this rather anarchic profusion of innovations had to be exploited more effectively. The increasingly complex organizational structures also had to be managed, and units had to be prevented from growing more and more dissimilar. It was therefore necessary to regulate the tactical innovations not only with a rational training structure but also with a modern command organization that could conduct both operations and change at one and the same time.

*Chapter 7*

# GHQ and Tactical Change

The onset of positional warfare marked the end of the pre-war process of evolution. The starting point within that process had been a 'Forum' of qualified staff officers with privileged access to the lessons of a 'virtual front' constituted by history, recent wars and war games. The information from the 'virtual front' had been used to establish both a dominant paradigm and methods of applying that paradigm, and these had then been communicated to the units in a top-down manner.

But now the front was very real, and the units were the first to have access to its lessons. Hence the process of evolution reversed direction, and the generals and GHQ found their roles altered as a result. Tensions arose from this restructuring, since most of the figures in the Forum were involved in conducting operations, either at GHQ or at the head of large units. Even as they put their pre-war thinking into practice, they were also responsible for carrying out adaptations to the military machine. If they introduced any changes, they would in effect be calling into question what they themselves had devised. Furthermore, they would have to consider such changes in depth, and that was difficult for them to do when at the same time they were conducting operations on a daily basis. Gradually it became clear that a reshaping of roles was required. Two structures needed to be set up: one for developing innovations and another for disseminating them by means of a rational organization for training the troops.

## The Reshaping of Roles
*A growing gulf*
During the opening weeks, the conduct of the war took precedence over doctrinal thought. The situation was one of rapid operations with the country's safety at stake, and the war was expected to last for no longer than a few months. In any case, the high command felt no need to question the existing doctrine. In September 1914, with the assistance of the army commanders, it managed to turn a tricky situation around in a remarkable manner and in doing so emerged from the ordeal with increased stature.

In contrast, the units had failed in August, even if they had done so as a result of poor tactics rather than any lack of courage. Their failure made it tempting to pin full responsibility on them for the initial defeats. One of GHQ's officers, Lieutenant-Colonel René Alexandre, did precisely that when he noted: 'The real causes of our defeats are the training and leadership [of the units], which almost universally leave something to be desired. What can you do if your tool is bad and buckles in your hand?'[1]

Adapting to the conditions of the conflict therefore amounted, during its early stages, simply to correcting the many faults that had emerged in practice. To make that possible, a good reporting mechanism was needed. This mechanism consisted of liaison officers and unit reports. The liaison officers were young field officers responsible for ensuring that GHQ and the large units worked smoothly together. In particular, they were used to supervise the performance of large units. They were widely feared while Joffre was in command, for if they formed a bad impression of a senior officer, it might lead to a dismissal.[2] Lieutenant-Colonel Alexandre, who was one of these liaison officers, described their role during the difficult days of 1914. Before a liaison officer left GHQ, he would visit its departments to bring himself up-to-date regarding issues that affected his particular army. He also received personal instructions from the commander-in-chief and his assistants.

> On reaching the headquarters of [his] army, he did the rounds in reverse order, starting with the general in command and then going to the staff departments. He brought good news, provided the needed and impatiently-awaited information on the overall situation, and explained what solutions the high command had given for outstanding issues. He then personally found out what events or local incidents had recently happened ... [and] in short ensured he was able to bring back an accurate picture of the army's situation.

If time allowed, the liaison officer would spend the next day visiting the command posts and the lines to 'take the pulse of the men on the spot, [and] listen to their complaints, which in many cases were justified'. During days of battle, the officer was constantly in touch with GHQ by telephone.[3]

The high command could also draw on the reports that were systematically made at every echelon after any operation. Major Bernard Serrigny, who was serving under General Philippe Pétain, described the stages involved in writing the 2nd Army's report after the Champagne offensive of September 1915:

> This work took me a long time, for every officer was determined to put himself in a good light by telling me each and every one of his deeds. I continually had to bring my interviewees back to the precise points in which I was interested. I then had to check the statements of the most senior officers by those of their subordinates. My modest rank of major, which inspired confidence in 'the little ones', proved very useful to me in these circumstances. Around 20 October, after the enquiry was finished, I drew up the well-known report about the 2nd Army's operations in Champagne. General Pétain discussed the content with me at length. Every word and every sentence was dissected. He himself rewrote the conclusions. I then amended his, before it was deemed 'ready to sign'.[4]

GHQ was therefore informed about the situation on the front both rapidly and accurately. This is shown by the notes it issued as early as 16 and 24 August 1914 to correct the key mistakes that had been made during operations. The principle of systematic reporting existed at every echelon. On 8 November 1914, for example, the 8th Corps carried out a local attack. Two days later, the relevant army commander, General Auguste Dubail, examined its report and immediately sent his comments back. Most of these reports seem to have been objective and open in tone, and this allowed the command to have a fairly accurate picture of the tactical situation, if not of the real conditions of the men's existence.

With the passage of time and the onset of a new form of warfare, a gulf opened up between GHQ on one side and the generals and troops on the other. The 'little, young men' at GHQ, and more specifically the 'aristocracy' of qualified staff officers in its Third Department, were now detested more widely and not simply by men who had been dismissed:

> They were accused of being tightly in thrall to official doctrine, of bothering to visit just the staffs and not the troops, and of combining their limited experience with an intransigence that was based more on theory than on practice. The endless conflict between men behind desks and those who had to implement orders was never more acute than in connection with them.[5]

These GHQ officers were still full of pre-war ideas, and the gulf between them and the realities of the front was growing:

> For the first three years of the war, GHQ's Third Department displayed in a marked way all the characteristics of a coterie. Filled with the same admirations and driven by the same antipathies, they thought the same way and had difficulty accepting that it was possible in military matters to come up with an opinion different from theirs. This doctrinaire intransigence, the harshness they used to make their authority felt and the jealous watch they kept around the commander-in-chief earned them the nickname of 'Young Turks'.[6]

General Firmin Emile Gascouin thought that:

> In this war, those at GHQ very quickly came to fear new ideas. This was completely natural at the start of the war, when not enough bodies existed to absorb those ideas. At one time, in 1915, front-line officers were even forbidden to concern themselves with anything other than professional matters, in other words anything other than their routine, day-to-day duty.[7]

An increasingly stark contradiction appeared between GHQ's role of the conduct of operations, which remained highly authoritarian, and its role of adaptation, which entailed asking the generals to act as intermediaries.

Only by calling the existing doctrine into question was it possible to adapt, but GHQ's self-assured officers found it hard to take criticism, especially if it inferred that they were responsible for futile bloodbaths. Since the generals were closer to the front, they perceived changes more readily and thereby gained a growing advantage over the high command. At the end of 1914, the scepticism felt by General Edouard de Curières de Castelnau and some of the other army commanders could not prevent the policy of the offensive-at-any-price from being followed. But 1915 saw rising protests from the generals.[8] The army group commanders began to criticize GHQ for being authoritarian and out of touch with the realities of the war. Others complained of being directed 'by theoreticians and professors'. Pétain was already making it known that the May 1915 offensive had failed 'because of its deplorable method' and that this would have been avoided if the unit commanders had been consulted beforehand. General Emile Fayolle, who was at the head of an army corps, wrote on 6 January 1916: 'I do not think that the senior commanders, and the little, young men who revolve around them, are up to scratch. They are too far from the front and do not know how things are really going.'[9]

The growing tension showed that a reorganization was needed. But it was only after Pétain had replaced General Robert Nivelle as commander-in-chief in May 1917 that the reorganization really occurred. It turned GHQ into 'an instrument capable of adapting to the way in which the conditions of warfare were likely to evolve'.[10]

## The reorganization of GHQ

In order to manage change, the new commander-in-chief relied on closer and more flexible relations with the generals and units, on the help of experts and also on the training section, a new and specialized body compatible with the changed conditions of warfare. The training section made it possible to transform the army profoundly, in accordance with a set of general directives that constituted the new body of doctrine. This transformation was accomplished, even if with some difficulty, by a constant process of interaction between the know-how acquired at the front and the authority of the commander-in-chief.

Pétain's assumption of the supreme command marked a change in how the commander-in-chief's role was perceived. Joffre's war diary during his time at GHQ was concerned only with the conduct of operations. At no point did it make any remarks about profound transformations to be made to the military machine. Joffre was not opposed to change. He was even active in supporting the promoters of new weapons, such as Major Edouard Barès or Colonel Jean Estienne. But he clearly considered his prime role to be the strategic conduct of operations. He left training and the changing of methods and organizational structures to the Third Department. His frame of mind was particularly clear from an entry he made in his war diary on 14 July 1916 castigating Pétain, who at this time commanded the Central Army Group. Joffre, who had received a note from Pétain about 'the organization of anti-aircraft fire', condemned his tendency 'to didactic concerns at the expense of command concerns'.[11] Nor did Joffre see any need for direct contact with the men in order to ascertain their state of moral or win them over. His GHQ relied on receiving objective reports and issued written communications that, since they amounted to orders, seemed to give the recipients no scope for any leeway in how they were applied.

In contrast, Pétain personally involved himself in change and was more pragmatic and realistic in his outlook. He reckoned that a whole range of variations existed between absolute obedience and blatant disobedience. In three years he had held all the successive levels of large unit commands, and he therefore realized that GHQ simply had to take account of the experience of the front in making its decisions. He relied in the first place on the general officer corps – and principally on the army group commanders, whose role and powers he increased. This gave him the time to visit the units, so he could 'know the frame of mind of his generals, as though he wanted to ensure they took part in what he deemed to be everyone's duty, namely to ponder the war, not in the light of momentary, fleeting events, but by taking broad perspectives.'[12]

Representatives from the armies came to GHQ 'to report what was being prepared in their sector, what observations had been made and what experiments had been tried out, whilst delegates from the various departments took notes'. It is true that Joffre had likewise received liaison officers every week, 'but even so you sensed a more effective ferment of activity here [under Pétain] and a more flexible critical evaluation'.[13] Pétain also promoted greater freedom of speech amongst officers, for he believed the absence of that freedom of speech had contributed to the mutinies of May-June 1917. He required staff officers to spend periods at the front. In his view, orders were liable not to be carried out properly if they ran counter to the deeply-held convictions of the men. Hence the liaison officers, and the officers of the Third Department, had an educational mission and had to explain to units why the instructions and regulations were appropriate. If that proved insufficient, the commander-in-chief himself paid a visit and used personal persuasion. A notable example of this happened in January 1918, when Pétain sought to enforce his *Directive number 4* concerning defensive preparations. Such visits had the added effect of restoring trust between the troops and GHQ, and that in turn made it easier to ensure instructions were carried out.

Pétain surrounded himself with advisers who were 'the foremost brains in how to use the arms when the scientific and judicious utilization of equipment was paramount.'[14] These key technical experts were General Frédéric Georges Herr for the artillery, General Jean Estienne for the tanks and Colonel (later General) Maurice Duval for the aviation. In order to improve cooperation between the armies and the support services – which had been a constant problem during the first years of the war – these specialist advisers of the commander-in-chief were accredited to the Minister of War and approved by him. They could therefore influence every aspect of the development of the most technical arms.

The new commander-in-chief formally broke with the pre-war doctrine by issuing a set of directives that amounted to a real charter. In the view of Colonel Pascal-Marie-Henri Lucas:

> From now on, the French army was organized specifically for the situation in which it found itself, and would be able to deal with the various eventualities that might arise without having to resort to improvisations that were bound to be haphazard. In this particular respect, an undeniable improvement had been made over everything that had been done before.[15]

Pétain's directives – there were five of them – were issued between May 1917 and July 1918. They addressed every aspect of modern warfare in turn.

### The training section

On 23 May 1917, Pétain ordered the creation of a 'training section' within the Third Department. It was to have the mission 'of providing and making use of documentation with a view to refining the regulations and instructions and the improvements to be made to some organizational details'.[16] The creation of this section made it possible to separate once and for all the role of conducting operations (except during critical periods) from that of defining combat methods. Hence a specialist group of officers with front-line experience now handled the information that went back up to GHQ, and synthesized and regulated it. General Eugène Debeney, assistant chief-of-staff at GHQ, summarized the spirit and methods of this group of officers:

> We need a new team to undertake work that will be down-to-earth, meticulous and largely – if not wholly – devoid of any flights of fancy. It will be dull but practical, governed by an awareness of, and concern for, what is possible. The team will be called the training section, because its role will be to monitor issues pertaining to the tactical preparation of the combat arms. It will visit the front, the units and the schools. It will gather the opinions and the wants of the men on the ground, before drawing up the manuals that are to guide them.[17]

The training section was commanded not by a qualified staff officer, but by Lieutenant-Colonel Paillé, an experienced 'man from the ranks'. This in itself was proof of the change in attitudes. Each arm was represented by a field officer, except for the new subdivisions – tanks and aeronautics – whose use was analysed by Estienne and Duval, the experts who were at the commander-in-chief's side. Hence the tanks and aeronautics were better represented than the infantry or artillery, and that showed how important they had become in Pétain's mind. The cavalry, which was going through much internal debate about its role, was the last to establish a cell. Communications, which were becoming increasingly important, were also represented.[18]

Various methods were used, but what they all had in common was that they were consensual, they stemmed from views expressed by the troops, and they were tried out before being applied:

> This is what the commander-in-chief wants. Whenever we have anything to write, we first obtain the views of the men on the ground. We show our drafts to those men and discuss them. Finally, we issue the documents only after we are sure they can be implemented.[19]

For work that was beyond the capabilities of staff officers, such as redefining the use of large units, Pétain set up commissions. On 1 August 1917, a 'review commission' was created, with the mission of revising the current manuals concerning the use of large units and synthesizing them into a single instruction.[20] The commission was chaired by an army corps commander and included four colonels from the various arms, the head of GHQ's Third Department, and representatives of the aeronautics and of GHQ's telegraph and liaison branches. An officer of the training section was the editorial secretary.[21] Towards the end of August 1917, the commission produced an initial draft instruction[22] that was then tried out during the Battle of La Malmaison on 23 October. The finalized *Instruction on the offensive action of large units in battle* was dated 31 October.

For issues concerning small units, GHQ created study groups under the training section's supervision. In August 1917, one such group was given the task of studying the use of long-range, indirect fire from machine-guns. Its chairman was a colonel in command of an infantry brigade, and its members consisted of several captains who ran machine-gunner schools, as well as a major who was an assistant to the inspector-general of artillery equipment for the field armies. This study group had at its disposal four companies of machine-guns and a training battalion from the 3rd Army. The machine-gun companies were drawn from four different regiments. Two of the companies were equipped with the Hotchkiss machine-gun and the other two with the Saint-Etienne. GHQ also provided the group with German documents, prisoner interrogations and reports on the methods that the British used in this field. The Directorate of Infantry and the Paris Commission of Ancillary Experiments issued tables of fire and barrel wear.[23]

The training section's final and most frequent activity was to carry out enquiries and surveys. It did so, for example, when considering how best to organize the infantry company in order to make the most of the increased number of automatic-rifles.[24] On 20 May 1917, the section drew up an initial plan for the organization of the infantry company, with several options proposed. This plan was sent to an army group – the Northern Army Group – which disseminated it within several divisions and within its training centre for automatic-riflemen. The note went down to the level of infantry regiments and then back up towards GHQ, annotated at each echelon with the opinion – very freely expressed – of the generals and colonels who commanded the infantry within the divisions. All these various movements of the note were completed in under ten days. Meanwhile, the training section had obtained some British documents on the matter. On 18 July, the section published a new plan for reorganizing the infantry company. The plan concluded: 'Before adopting this organization, it should be tested in one company of each army corps.'[25] Hence the plan went back to the corps to be tried out. The reports on the trials were all returned during August, and the commander-in-chief adopted the final organization on 10 September 1917.[26]

The training section was also directed to work closely with the Second Department (Intelligence) in order to analyse the main British and German successes, as well as the enemy's tactical methods. (The Second and Third Departments were grouped together under a single head, General Maurice de Barescut, in order to overcome the compartmentalization that had existed before Pétain's arrival.)[27] These analyses began to be issued in June 1917, and included a translation of a German document about defence-in-depth and a detailed examination of the methods the Germans used on the Aisne.[28] There followed evaluations of the successful German attack against the Russians at Riga (September 1917) and of the fighting at Cambrai (November 1917), the findings of which were widely disseminated in February 1918 in the wake of a series of notes about German offensive and defensive methods.[29]

The training section would continue its work after the Armistice. It would be given the task of compiling *The Organization of the army on a war footing*, a vast work of synthesis that it would carry out using the same pragmatic methods and would complete in February 1919.

## The Assimilation Through Training

In order to adapt to the conditions of the war, it was not enough simply to define new methods. There also had to exist an ability to disseminate those methods within the units and to assimilate them. This meant establishing a training structure that was not only on an unprecedented scale but also had the capacity to evolve at the same rate as the rest of the French army. Yet up until 1916, the organization of training remained largely the result of local initiatives. Only after the notion of a long war took root did GHQ help organize training, and only after Pétain became commander-in-chief did it consider the issue in a rational manner.

The adaptation of the French forces initially took the form of self-training. It consisted of learning through experience, which meant accumulating know-how within the basic tactical units. This led to the emergence of the 'soldier of the trenches', and the fact that he adapted to his setting explains the apparent paradox of why the war saw a steady fall in the monthly loss rate even as the enemy's firepower increased. Yet there were drawbacks to this form of adaptation. Free time was needed to make possible the osmosis, or gradual sharing of know-how, between the old and new *poilus*. Yet the French infantrymen were constantly on the go until spring 1915. Self-training could only really come into play when proper rest periods were introduced. Until then, 'almost the only way our soldiers could train themselves was a tragic process of trial-and-error in the trenches or in action'.[30]

Even more importantly, building a 'tactical memory' would have been difficult if losses were too heavy and units had a constant turnover of men. This phenomenon affected the arms in different ways, as can be seen from the statistics of the 13th Infantry Division. During the initial war of movement of 1914, an artillery battery of the division took an average of five days of combat to lose one man, whereas an infantry company took just three hours. During the years of positional warfare, the corresponding figures were fifty days for an artillery battery and twelve hours for an infantry company.[31] Building up a capital of solid experience would have been difficult for units such as the 64th Infantry Regiment, which had forty-four of its fifty-five officers out of action as early as 20 September 1914, or the 19th Battalion of Foot *Chasseurs,* which in the course of the war lost sixteen times its established strength.[32] Conversely, the other arms could adapt more easily to the growing complexity, particularly in the case of the artillery.

The final drawback of self-training was that the longer it continued, the greater was the extent to which units became different from each other and developed methods that did not conform with the regulations. The adoption of different concepts by particular units could lead to friction, both amongst the units themselves and with the high command. This became blatantly obvious during the initial actions at Verdun in 1916, when the artillery units that remained in place while the infantry was relieved did not always work harmoniously with the new divisions to which they were attached.

### The academy of mud
The first phase in the organization of training at the front began in autumn 1914. The temporary lull in the fighting allowed an initial system to be improvised, although it had no real infrastructure and was in immediate contact with the front. This system applied in the first instance to the units of reservists, whose technical and tactical proficiency was deemed a cause for concern. In October, General Dubail, the 1st Army commander, imposed a 'cascading' training system on the 2nd Group of Reserve Divisions. General Maurice Joppé, the commander

of that Group, was to train his generals, who in turn would train their field officers, and so on. 'Within each unit, the officers and NCOs will be taught practical theories, so that the training of the troops for combat is run reliably.'[33]

Other problems arose once the 1914 conscript class – the annual intake of conscripts – was incorporated (received into the regiments) in December. The training given to the young recruits, it was noted, did not match the new realities of combat. When Joffre was informed of these shortcomings, he prescribed an initial series of measures. In particular, he required instructors in 'cushy' posts behind the lines to be replaced with wounded or convalescent men who had actually been under fire.

On 26 November, General Dubail gave an order 'to improve target practice, by having each man – especially young soldiers – fire, in the trenches, six bullets every day at a selected target (an embrasure or loophole in the opposing line) under the supervision of an NCO or qualified senior soldier.'[34]

The army corps created training units to enable the young conscript classes to learn the know-how of positional warfare. The Third Department of the 1st Army's staff distributed an instruction to the army corps about infantry tactics, which was to serve as a guide for setting up training programmes. On GHQ's order, this note was disseminated to the schools outside the theatre of operations.[35]

In short, the traditional training structure could not meet the new demands of combat. As for the field armies, they were unable to maintain a proper level of training, owing to their manpower problems, the length of the front they had to hold, the construction tasks they had to carry out and the fact that too many of their troops were in the front line, not to mention the absence of suitable training facilities, which had been inadequate even in peacetime. Hence the armies were unable to prevent both men and units from becoming increasingly disparate in their tactical and technical proficiencies. Furthermore, peacetime habits took time to change and so soldiers often found their periods of rest and relaxation a disappointing experience. Many officers protested about this. Lieutenant Roger Campana of the 42nd Infantry Division wrote:

> When the men return from the trenches, they need to be able to forget a bit that they are at war ... so they no longer see the haunting vision of death, which has brushed past them and will brush past them again. So why are they made to do drill morning and evening? The manual of arms, *section* drill, bayonet practice: are these really all that useful in the war we are waging? ... In my opinion, these drills do nothing except irritate the men.[36]

The careful preparation that was required for the string of offensives in 1915 added yet another training need. Several weeks of preparation were now needed before each breakthrough attack, instead of the handful of days, or even hours, that had been necessary during the war of movement. Intermittent periods of training were therefore organized behind the lines, with the aim not only of assimilating the lessons of previous actions but also of preparing the next ones. After the actions of May 1915 in Artois, for example, the 13th Infantry Division spent three weeks at Saint-Riquier camp, north of Abbeville, to 'fine-tune the lessons of the fighting'.[37]

In an effort to rationalize this training, the armies on their own initiative created infantry schools. These schools involved units, or categories of officers, being withdrawn from action, in turn and for a few weeks at a time, in order to be taught new techniques at training centres not far from the firing line.[38] Starting in June 1915, the armies also set up induction and training courses for NCOs and subaltern officers. GHQ supported this trend by creating divisional training centres.[39] Even more importantly, it organized the front in depth, beginning in October 1915 when Joffre ordered the number of men left in the first line to be reduced to the bare minimum so the training of the troops could be improved.[40] From now on, there was a line of armies, army group reserves and general reserves. This new organization, combined with the shortening of that part of the front held solely by the French army, finally permitted a real training network to be set up immediately behind the lines.

Training needs became even more extensive in 1916 as new equipment came into service, especially in the infantry. In response, a training battalion was formed in each division, using the divisional depot and the fourth company in every infantry battalion. (This training battalion became the divisional training centre in 1917.) As well as being a focal point for training, it served as a 'flywheel' of manpower. Located close to the units, it received replacements from garrison depots in the interior of the country and constituted an immediate reserve of trained reinforcements who were ready to be sent forward.[41] The training battalion was where the teaching of methods and new weapons was worked out. Yet it proved to be an inadequate solution. The reason was a new phenomenon: the cadres, who were regarded as the natural instructors of their men, failed to master the new equipment.

It was therefore necessary to set up specialized training centres. Courses, schools and training centres proliferated at the end of 1916,[42] often as a result of decisions taken by the army group commanders. Pétain, for example, increased the number of initiatives in the Central Army Group soon after taking command of it in May 1916. That August, he created an engineers' research centre, which was 'endowed with a complete museum of the engineer equipment in use at that time'. The research centre was a place for trying out innovations, and within it Pétain then formed an engineers' training school for subaltern officers.

Among other training centres that were set up was one at Matougues in Champagne for airplane observers. In each army within the Central Army Group, following the establishment of schools for subaltern officers, a school was created for majors and training centres for the rank-and-file (schools for machine-gunners, automatic-riflemen, *grenadiers* and liaison agents). The staff officers of the 4th and 5th Armies were sent on training courses held by the large units that were fighting in front of Verdun. Numerous information bulletins were disseminated within units: they might concern aviation, for example, or be issued by the Intelligence Department, or be *aide-mémoires*.[43] An entire training infrastructure was established in camps, including grounds laid out to replicate conditions at the front, trenches, telephone networks and the necessary documentation for exercises. In particular, each army had a large manœuvre training camp. Mailly camp was enlarged in such a way that a French army corps composed of three divisions could train there.[44] Within the Central Army Group, General Henri Gouraud's 4th Army played a pioneering role in studying, testing and sharing methods of manœuvre that the high command had either recommended or prescribed.[45] 'A certain zest for raids'[46] was always prevalent in the 4th Army, but was different in nature from that of the winter of 1914.

## GHQ's intervention

The organization of training gradually became rationalized as GHQ took it increasingly into consideration. The first step saw inspectorates created once more to monitor doctrinal developments and the training of the arms. (The inspectorates had fallen into disuse following the outbreak of the war.) Thus in 1916, inspectorates-general were set up for the heavy artillery, for the super-heavy artillery and for the mounted and mountain artillery, as well as a technical inspectorate of tanks and an inspectorate-general of the aviation schools and depots. In 1917, Pétain created the inspectorate-general of artillery training and then that of anti-aircraft defence.[47]

In summer 1916, GHQ began issuing regulations to put the training organization on a formal footing. On 18 August, it produced a *Note on the training of large units in the camps,* whose principles endured until the end of the war. On 4 September, two years after the start of the war, there appeared a *Note on the organization of training in the armies.*[48] This note, which was largely inspired by the example set by the Central Army Group, established three types of training centres:

- training centres for specialists and junior cadres;
- training centres for cadres and rank-and-file who were to be sent as replacements to combat units;
- training centres for instructors.

The training of the various specialisms was shared between the different echelons of command. The divisional depot took responsibility for the training of the range of infantry specialisms and for the training of *section* and company commanders. The army corps taught anything pertaining to air-ground coordination. The army concerned itself with the engineers and trench-mortars. During active operations, some schools might be temporarily disbanded. A field officer post with responsibility for training was created at the army and army corps echelons. The holder of the post at army echelon was an officer who had commanded an infantry unit in action, and he had two assistants (one for the artillery and the other for the engineers).

In June 1917, Pétain as the newly appointed commander-in-chief made training one of his priorities, and he rationalized the training structure, which had developed in a somewhat anarchic manner.[49] To do so, he took the ideas he had used as an army group commander and extended them to the level of the French army as a whole.[50] He set out these ideas in his comprehensive *Directive number 2*. The directive considered training to be the core component of the French army's efficiency, and understood it in a broad sense, encompassing moral education, the instilling of discipline and training for operations. The main innovations of the directive were:

- training for operations: this required the command to consider 'the characteristics of the operations to be carried out' and to set aside time to train the troops for a particular mission;

- the combination of special-to-arm training with combined-arms training, by means of infantry exercises in conjunction with the aeronautics, artillery and tanks;
- the setting up of advanced training courses for unit commanders and general officers.[51]

Although most officers endorsed this approach, a few were quick to resent such a degree of centralized control, and the result was a degree of discord. Pétain, who paid close attention to these matters, therefore instructed the officers of the training section to take any opportunity they could to explain the spirit of the directive. Consequently, Major Emile Laure visited the army commanders, but found that his reception varied. He was greeted enthusiastically by General Gouraud, the 4th Army commander, who was passionate about training, but more coldly by General Adolphe Guillaumat, the head of the 2nd Army. General de Castelnau, the commander of the Eastern Army Group, told Laure:

> Be careful, for you are on the verge of going too far at GHQ ... The fact that our eagerness for the offensive has been curbed is excellent. So too is the desire to equip our troops with everything they need to win, as is the insistence on the troops and their commanders having a better technical induction. But don't turn the army into a pedagogical domain. Don't produce too many teachers for us, nor too many pupils. Leave the unit commanders with more to do, for they're the real instructors of their cadres and men. Don't disorganize the battalions and regiments by continually removing too many men from them.[52]

These misgivings, combined with the lessons drawn from the latest operations, made it necessary to revise the directive, and so it became *Directive number 2b*. It appeared on 30 December 1917 after much time had been spent in explaining it to the generals. The new directive reaffirmed the priority given to combined-arms training and the need to unify the methods of positional warfare and those of the war of movement. It then tried to resolve the problems that had surfaced when its predecessor was being enforced. It reaffirmed the principle that the unit commander was the permanent trainer of his troops. (This principle had hitherto been compromised by the arrival of new weapons that the cadres had been slow to master.) Steps were taken to ensure that the sending of men and instructors on training courses did not overly disturb the units, for example by limiting the number of personnel who were detached and the duration of the courses, and also by making it compulsory for instructors to be returned to their original units, as well as by permitting courses to be temporarily suspended for corps that had to do exercises. The directive also specified the various methods of collective training:

- training in the camps: the organization was identical to that described in the note of August 1916, but it was stipulated that the periods spent in the camps should not 'overwork the troops and cadres' and should preferably occur after a rest period;
- training in the rest zones: the emphasis was on the teaching of discipline and basic and small-unit skills, if possible up to battalion level. Training

at and above regimental level took the form of map exercises. Each rest zone was to have permanent installations, including firing ranges and small manœuvre grounds, and also spacious cantonments at the centre of the zone for whichever divisional training centre was temporarily in residence;

- training combined with labour tasks: the proportion of personnel doing training was to be kept at one-third. In other words, a soldier would do one week of training during every cycle of around three weeks;
- training while in a sector: units that were at rest would do training. The divisional training centre was to be established in permanent cantonments that would be handed over from one division to another.

The French army took advantage of the relative lull at the end of 1917 to undergo instruction in the vast training network that now filled the immediate rear of the front.

In short, a complete organizational structure for managing change was progressively set up. It gave the command a growing capacity to gather the lessons of the front, support the many unit initiatives and take on board the constant introduction of new equipment. Conversely, the command also acquired an increasing ability to organize the standardization, dissemination and teaching of innovations. Yet this was not a continuous development. It involved a fundamental break at the time that Pétain became commander-in-chief. Before May 1917, it was simply assisted by GHQ with a series of improvised adjustments. After that date, in contrast, it amounted to a rational approach by a command that was fitted for industrial warfare. The new training organization embraced change as being the normal occurrence in modern warfare, rather than regarding it as a series of accidents. It thereby enabled a greater quantity of equipment and associated methods to be assimilated in the final eighteen months of the war than the French army had seen in the first years of the war, or even in a large span of its recent history. But although this constant, intellectual ferment enabled the military machine to become ever more efficient, it did not set out the best way of using that efficiency to gain victory. Hence there was still a need for doctrinal thought.

## The Lost Paradigms
### A discontinuous process
Doctrine did not evolve gradually, by incremental improvements. Instead, over the course of four years a succession of comprehensive, structured doctrines appeared, with each doctrine being implemented until a final crisis caused it to be replaced. These doctrines were theoretical crystallizations of a whole range of tactical, psychological and technical innovations. Groups of men through a process of discussion made sense of scattered data and gave it a structure. The process was similar to both political debate and the model described by Thomas Kuhn in *The structure of scientific revolutions*. In many cases, the replacement of one paradigm with another saw a new set of men take over, just as a changeover occurs when a political party loses its majority in parliament. The process was barely any different from the pre-war process that I described earlier. It was simply faster,

since actual events provided an impartial sanction whenever a major operation was launched. We even find again, in a modernized form, the two poles in the debate about the relative virtues of fire and shock. The dialectic of these poles produced four successive models:

- the 'breakthrough by rapid, direct attack' in 1915;
- the 'scientific conduct of the battle', applied at the Somme in 1916;
- the 'Verdun school', which attempted a decisive offensive on the Aisne in 1917 by applying on a greater scale the attack tactics that had driven the Germans back from Verdun;
- Pétain's 'combined-arms battlefield' in 1917 and 1918, which I will examine in Chapter 11.

It is clear that the 1915 'breakthrough by rapid, direct attack' was in keeping with the *offensive à outrance,* the old notion of the 'all-out offensive'. So too was Nivelle's 'Verdun school'. Both these models sought to gain a decisive success by the rapidity of the action and the élan of the troops. In contrast, the emphasis in the other two doctrines was on using materiel in a rational way in order to win a series of limited victories, the combined effect of which would prove decisive.

The distinctions between the two sides in this debate were not clear-cut. In general, graduates of the *Ecole polytechnique* – especially artillerymen such as General Fayolle – were to be found amongst the advocates of the methodical approach. Supporters of 'élan' tended to be graduates of Saint-Cyr, infantrymen keen on the 'social sciences'. But some personalities did not fit into this pattern. Pétain was an infantryman and had studied at Saint-Cyr, yet he was the most prominent figure in the methodical school. Nivelle was an artilleryman, a graduate of the *Ecole polytechnique,* who nevertheless advocated a decisive breakthrough by brute force. Foch was a hybrid case.

In this doctrinal debate, the army commanders – or even the army corps commanders – became increasingly important. In 1914, the generals had been stifled by the urgency of the actions, which had required decisions to be carried out with no time for any argument, and they had been broken by the wholesale dismissals, the *limogeages.* But from 1915 onwards, they came to be at the forefront of the doctrinal debate. Their status as intermediaries between the realities of the front and GHQ worked to their advantage, since GHQ found it increasingly difficult to remain in touch with those realities and to direct the operations single-handedly.

### The final flickers of the all-out offensive

The emergence of a continuous line of trenches from the North Sea to Switzerland came as an unpleasant surprise. It was a reminder of the theories that had been developed at the very start of the twentieth century, about the 'impregnability of fronts' – theories against which the supporters of the 'all-out offensive' had rebelled. The fortified front had imposed itself on a high command that had not wanted it, and was proof that the front was not under the control of the decision-makers. Back in 1913, General de Castelnau had informed the Governor of Lille, General Albert Lebas: 'If the Germans extend their fighting front as far as

Lille, they'll get themselves cut into two. There's nothing we would like more.' Yet in August 1914, it was de Castelnau's army that was the first to start entrenching: it did so in order to defend the Grand-Couronné, the hills that protected the city of Nancy.

The combatants on the Grand-Couronné began by digging shallow shelters, and then small trenches that thereafter became ever deeper and more sophisticated. In eastern France, the armies of both sides did the same, for they were on the defensive during the race to the sea. The armies in the north followed suit, and continuous lines of trenches now stretched from the sea to Switzerland.

The strength of these trench lines was all the more astonishing in that the fortresses in Belgium and northern France had fallen. In October 1914, General Fayolle's diary revealed his surprise and concern:

> Is not a single region on this entire front suitable for a massive deployment of artillery that would enable us to open a way through for an army corps? If the line is broken at one point, it might put an end to it all. ... Contrary to my expectations, it is extremely difficult to attack.[53] ... We really must break the line somewhere, or else remain face to face indefinitely.[54]

The French high command had doubts about which method it should follow. It recognized the wisdom of resuming the offensive only when its British allies were able to take part, but in the meantime it had to help the Russians, who were in difficulties. Faith in the virtues of the offensive remained strong. Even now, the French did not expect the war to last long and were astounded that the British were making contracts and hiring areas of land for three years.[55]

Yet this unforeseen form of warfare posed a problem, for few written procedures existed for it. They were limited to the *General instruction on siege warfare* (30 July 1909, updated on 9 August 1913), the *Instruction on artillery service duties in siege warfare* (19 June 1913) and some manuals of a specialist nature whose existence was barely known. These regulations suggested that a mass of powerful equipment was needed, that artillery action was predominant, with the artillery being directed in a 'scientific' manner, and above all that the infantryman's role would have much in common with that of the sapper during slow and methodical operations. These were 'all reasons why we do not favour this type of warfare'.[56]

Many examples of sieges were known, including Paris and Belfort in 1870, Plevna in 1877 and Port Arthur in 1904. Manœuvres designed to study the attack and defence of fortresses had been held at Langres in eastern France in 1906. But in the view of Colonel Lucas, 'we thought of all this as being just very specific cases of no possible interest to anyone except certain specialists'.[57] Hence the French army mastered none of the know-how required for this new form of warfare. Nor was it willing to think deeply about it, for that would have seemed too akin to a fundamental reconsideration. Instead, it addressed the challenge by a process of trial and error. Problems were dealt with one after the other, following a simple method of 'actions-and-corrections', for action always took precedence over theoretical thought. Each operation was the subject of reports and specific analyses that resulted in instructions being issued. 'Experiments conducted by throwing in men' were progressively expanded in scope by mounting larger and larger offensives. The high-level staffs, and the Third Department of GHQ in particular, were especially 'productive'. Jean de Pierrefeu, who spent three years at GHQ, was highly critical of the staffs, but recognized that:

> The command had to resolve a never-ending stream of difficulties. Every day of action added to its experience and brought it new information. We must do the staff the justice of saying that it spared itself no effort. How many combat regulations were changed the day after they were issued! It was a never-ending search for improvement in every field.[58]

Yet, deluded by the faith in willpower, which was held up as the supreme quality, the officers at GHQ believed that they simply needed to give vigorous instructions and the units would immediately digest all these documents. The initial expectation was that the men's ardour, and their leaders' energy, would make up for the shortage of means,[59] or at least take the place of doctrine. The troops were therefore ordered to show the greatest activity and to endeavour to progress step by step. It was important to keep the enemy under constant threat and to prove to him 'our vigour and our resolve to close with and fight him'.[60]

Activity quickly turned into mere bustle. Sometimes, as Fayolle noted on 28 December 1914, ulterior motives lay behind the bustle:

> I grasped in the course of the conversation that the senior commanders' biggest concern was the desire to do something to distinguish themselves. As soon as an army commander achieves anything – and it might be no more than capturing a poorly-fortified post, a 50-metre long trench or the corner of a wood – the information bulletin exaggerates the achievement and then the newspapers do the same. Immediately, the neighbouring commanders want an achievement of their own and launch stupid or pointless attacks regardless of losses ... Not one of them is willing to take responsibility for a general engagement that might tarnish his reputation or cost him his command.[61]

The French were also convinced that if they did nothing while waiting for the pivotal event of the war to arrive, they would kill off the offensive spirit, as had happened in 1870. General Dubail took the view:

> We are too much inclined to believe that we will spend the winter in the same situation as now, namely in trenches that are almost comfortable. If we're not careful, we will lose the taste for boldness and rifle-fire. It's a bad thing to leave the troops of the first-line trenches inactive. We must demand a forward bound, and a new trench, every night.[62]

These minor operations were not just substitutes for serious thought. They were also intended as one of the only means of improving practical training. Hence the winter of the first year of the war was characterized by constant activity, with soldiers clinging to the enemy 'in a horrific guerrilla war of listening posts, in which they spent nights and days killing each other at point-blank range.'[63]

Faith in willpower not only caused these final flickers of the 'all-out offensive', but also provided a convenient justification following setbacks. General de Langle de Cary, commander of the 4th Army, commented on the meagre gains:

> These painful sacrifices were offset by the advantage of keeping the troops on their toes, of giving them confidence and of worrying the enemy. By upholding morale and preserving our offensive superiority, our raids prevented the wavering that could have resulted from prolonged inaction in the mud of the trenches in harsh temperatures.[64]

GHQ strove to codify the lessons of these actions systematically. The *Instructions* of 2 and 3 January 1915 were an initial attempt to address attack methods (meticulous preparation, cooperation with the artillery) and they also stipulated how defensive systems were to be designed. But the *Instruction* of 2 January remained short and incomplete. Just two-and-a-half pages long, it said nothing about surprise, the disposition of troops or the way to lay out a sector ready for an offensive. Above all, it took the view that trench warfare 'has in no way invalidated the principles on which our offensive doctrine is based'.[65] It was no more than a modification.

Fayolle noted on 16 January 1915:

> Character, character! The more stupid bloodletting someone inflicts on magnificent troops, who should be carefully kept in being for days of pivotal importance, the more character he has. I believe that even an epileptic who went everywhere shouting 'Attack! Attack!' would be acclaimed a great man.[66]

In much the same vein, General Charles de Lardemelle wondered ironically in a report whether it was necessary to gain the moral ascendancy over barbed-wire.[67]

More ambitious operations were then organized: Perthes in the Champagne region (February-March 1915), Les Eparges 19 km south-east of Verdun (February-April) and the Hartmannswillerkopf in the Vosges (January-May). These operations were entrusted to commanders who never hesitated to resume the attacks when ordered to do so, 'however difficult it might be to carry them out'.[68] In many cases, the operations were clumsy and amounted to no more than direct assaults without any coordinated fire support. Gains were meager. After a month of fierce fighting at Perthes, the 4th Army conquered just 3 square km of ground. Yet its commander was satisfied, since this offensive 'has been a great help in boosting morale, at a time when [it] would have been in danger of becoming depressed had the monotony of life in the trenches continued'.[69] The methods used were often starkly at odds with the notes that had been issued in January. This showed that inflexibilities were hindering the circulation and assimilation of lessons, and that incessant activity was making it difficult to carry out in-depth training.[70] Nevertheless, coordination between the arms did see gradual improvement. Some airplanes were equipped with radios. Several methods of visual communication were devised, and in Champagne a divisional commander, General Géraud François Gustave Réveilhac, had artillery observers follow his companies.

\*

The appearance of a new written instruction on 16 April 1915 marked a significant evolution. The *Instruction on the aim and conditions of a general offensive action* set out the need to seize the whole of the enemy position in a single blow, and to break through immediately afterwards. The artillery had a vital role to play. Before the attack, it was to destroy the defences by covering the entire enemy position with zone fire. During the actual attack, it had to counter the enemy artillery while at the same time supporting the infantry with barrages. These missions illustrated the process of trial-and-error that governed the use of the artillery. Counter-battery fire had been frowned upon before the war and was still regarded with a degree of lingering prejudice. Yet the quest to destroy the enemy position required an artillery preparation lasting for days on end, and the destruction was illusory. As for the infantry attacks, they were to be carefully organized and had to strive to maintain surprise and rapidity. Reserves were to be held in readiness to intervene and exploit success. But the infantry skirmish line retained the same density that had been prescribed in the *Infantry training regulation* of 20 April 1914, namely one man for every metre of front.[71] In terms of the defensive, the French were moving away from the old, linear disposition to the establishment of a 'position', meaning a collection of trenches and dugouts connected by communication trenches and protected by barbed-wire and other obstacles. Work also began on a second position, which was a step the Germans had taken long before.

The Artois offensive (9 May – 18 June 1915) provided an opportunity to try out the measures prescribed by the *Instruction* of 16 April. The means assembled for this offensive were substantial: three army corps and 350 heavy artillery pieces on a front of 15 km. Three weeks of meticulous preparation went into the operation. The ground was particularly well laid out, with jumping-off trenches at a distance of 150 metres from the enemy, assembly trenches for reserves and supports, along with dressing stations and ammunition, tool or ration dumps, all linked by a network of communication trenches, some of which were designated for the evacuation of the wounded. For the first time, the artillery preparation was conducted in a rational and methodical manner, with a fire plan and permanent fire control. The results were encouraging: the ground gained on 9 May was 3 km deep and 6 km wide. The 33rd Army Corps under Pétain was particularly successful. Two of its divisions seemed to be advancing against no opposition, and signs of panic were detected in the enemy rear. But the breach was too narrow for the reserves to be able to pass through. When the offensive resumed on 18 June, it lacked any advantage of surprise and failed completely.

The partial success of 9 May made a lasting impression and was regarded thereafter as the model of the breakthrough battle. A breakthrough was possible, it was concluded, so long as more powerful resources of heavy artillery were available, and so long as the exploitation was better organized.[72] A phase of assimilation followed these actions. GHQ's Third Department issued more notes. While this indicated a degree of uncertainty, it also demonstrated that GHQ was gradually taking over the role of adapting to change. On 20 May, a note appeared about the *Initial lessons to be drawn from the recent engagements*. The *Instruction* of 16 April 1915 was amended on 26 May and then again on 10 July. An appendix issued on 18 June specified the cavalry's action during the exploitation phase. Fighting on the defensive was the

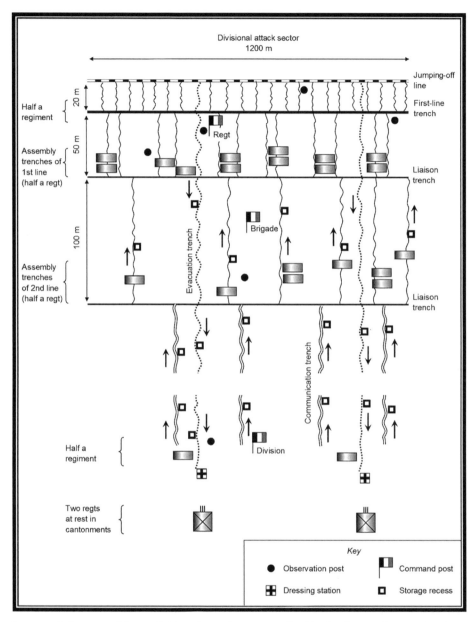

Layout of the ground for a divisional attack, as prescribed in the *Instruction on the aim and conditions of a general offensive action* (16 April 1915).

subject of a note dated 8 July. It prescribed that each position was to be organized into strongpoints and centres of resistance, no more than 1,200 metres apart. The gaps in between were defended by the artillery and by counter-attacks launched by reserves.[73]

As the fear induced by the wholesale dismissals of 1914 subsided, the generals began to voice criticisms. Some of those who had an infantry background, such as General Paul Maistre, were loath to subordinate the infantry's action to the artillery fire plans, which they regarded as a renouncement of manœuvre. Other generals had doubts about the very idea of the breakthrough. Foch, in particular, was sceptical:

> It seems unwise to base all our hopes – and risk all our available forces – on the possibility of breaking through, on the concept of using weight of numbers to make a breach and gain a decisive victory. ... A breakthrough is unlikely to materialize until we provide the offensive with many new means, such as asphyxiating gases.[74]

But Joffre stuck to the concept of breakthrough. He could point to the German example of Görlitz in Galicia on 2 May, as well as the unexpected – and possibly exaggerated – success of the Moroccan Division on 9 May.

Supporters of the 'surprise battle' demanded, and obtained, another rapid, direct attack. The offensive of 25 September marked a further increase in effort. For the first time, two attacks took place simultaneously, in Champagne and in Artois. The means assigned to these attacks were unprecedented: fifty-three infantry divisions, 1,200 pieces of heavy artillery and 3,000 of the 75mm guns. The length of the attack front in Champagne was 35 km, and the total length of both attack fronts was 44 km. But no possibility existed of surprise. The preliminary tasks of physical labour needed to mount the offensive had begun in August. Six days were required to register the guns, and the artillery preparation lasted three days in Champagne and five days in Artois. In the two attacks, the troops as ordered dashed in a frenzied race that gained several km and took the first German position. (In Champagne, they did so on a breadth of 25 km.) But so great was the disorder beyond this position that the units – which in many cases had become entangled with the reserves – broke on a second position. The Germans had established this second position on a reverse slope, and so it had suffered little from the French artillery fire. The French artillery failed to go forward in the wake of the infantry, except for the 75mm batteries and some batteries of short-barrelled Rimailho 155mm pieces. The German barrages and counter-attacks then wreaked havoc. The offensive was halted. When it was relaunched on 6 October, the results were even more disappointing. In Champagne, the French had lost 138,000 men, for a gain of 40 square km.

The failure triggered a crisis. In Joffre's view, the outcome could be blamed on the incomplete training of the troops and on the shortcomings of their commanders. In fact, it would have been impossible for the training to be anything but poor, owing to the absence of suitable facilities and the months that the troops had spent at the front.[75] Besides, the means of coordination with the artillery were still in an embryonic state. It was realized that the problems of organizing and moving the artillery inevitably made the attack on the enemy's second position less powerful than the attack against the first position. The failure of the September offensive put GHQ in an awkward position, and marked the end of the concept of the rapid, direct and decisive attack:

> This time, it was the end of a phase. The superb French infantry had smashed itself against uncut barbed-wire entanglements. The senior officers on the ground demanded modern combat methods and weapons.[76]

'What's happening up above?' noted Fayolle on 12 November. 'Nobody seems to know what should be done.'[77] He added on 31 December: 'My opinion is that we will not succeed as things stand, without the addition of new means.'[78]

### The scientific conduct of the battle

The failure of September 1915 marked the end of the paradigm of the 'all-out offensive'. The 'impregnability of fronts' – a notion that had been so disparaged before the war – now emerged as a self-evident reality and led to a doctrinal crisis. The winter of 1915-16 therefore saw much intellectual activity.[79] The outcome was the triumph of a new school of thought called 'the scientific conduct of the war'.

The 'methodical men' – Generals Foch, Pétain, Fayolle and Victor d'Urbal – based their approach on the Artois offensive of 9 May, where a combination of method and power had sometimes produced excellent results. Pétain's success in Artois and in Champagne gave weight to his ideas. His report of 1 November 1915 on the September offensive served as the basis for the new doctrine. He noted that, in the absence of a change in weaponry, in the method of preparation or in the forces opposed to him, it was impossible 'to take the enemy's successive positions in a single rush'.[80] A decisive breakthrough would not succeed until the enemy had been worn down along the entire front by successive, but slow, attacks in which the artillery played the dominant role.

As for Fayolle, he stated:

> For every position there has to be a battle, with these battles following one another as quickly as possible. Each of them requires a new organization, a preparation. If we go too fast, we risk a failure. If we go too slowly, the enemy has time to create successive positions again. That's the problem, and it's acute.[81]

This was a reaction against the infantry's 'crazy ventures' during the 1915 battles: 'mathematical certainty gained the upper hand over psychological considerations'.[82] These ideas were taken up in a spate of regulatory papers, including the *Instruction* on the heavy artillery (20 November 1915) and the *Note on the lessons of the September battles* (27 December 1915) – a note that was permeated with the first-hand experience of the combatants. Coordination between the infantry and artillery became a priority, and all possible means were to be used to achieve it.[83] Even more importantly, the *Instruction on the offensive combat of small units* was issued on 8 January 1916. It introduced a new conception of the infantry:

> You do not fight with men against materiel ... The infantry rapidly becomes worn out ... Care must therefore be taken, both at the start and during the course of an offensive action, not to make the fighting line too dense. When gaps occur, the line must be reinforced discreetly, while guarding against the overcrowding that adds to the disorder and losses.[84]

The French sought, in a gradual and limited way, to replace men with machines such as automatic-rifles and machine-guns.[85]

Two other important instructions appeared in January 1916. The first, on the 16th, was the *Instruction on the aim and conditions of a general offensive action,* which was intended to supercede the similar note of 16 April 1915. The second, issued on the 26th, was the *Instruction on the offensive combat of large units.* Together, these two instructions marked a crucial stage in the evolution of the combat doctrine. They constituted a clean break with the flaws of the 1913 *Field service regulation,* which had continued to influence the operations of 1915. The aim remained the same: to break through the enemy's defensive positions. But the breakthrough was now to take the form of a drawn-out operation consisting of a series of methodical attacks on successive positions. Once the breakthrough had been achieved, the success was to be exploited, and the leading role in this phase would fall to the cavalry.

This new concept was intended to be put into effect at the Battle of the Somme. The Northern Army Group, which spent four months of preparation, became the focus of thought about the 'scientific conduct of the war'. The artillerymen took centre stage: Foch (commander of the Northern Army Group) and Fayolle (at the head of the 6th Army) established the general doctrine. Colonel Carence, who was the chief-of-staff of the 6th Army's artillery commander, organized and conducted in a scientific way the search for technical solutions and the dissemination of those solutions. In Carence's view, an army's offensive power lay in its heavy artillery. In an analysis written in October 1915, he stated: 'Artillery first, then the infantry! In the preparation and execution of attacks, everything must be subordinated to the artillery.'[86] Foch added that the infantry had to take the utmost care never to hinder the artillery's freedom of fire.[87] The Northern Army Group made great efforts to train and organize the forces. Particular attention was paid to using aviation to coordinate the arms.

This radical change in outlook made many infantry officers feel uneasy. It meant they had to 'unlearn' the idea that the élan and promptness of attacks could be a substitute for effective fire.[88] They also feared that their arm would become inhibited and would lose its skills and pre-eminence. The command came to realize, therefore, that a radical change of method, especially one that threatened core values, also required a transformation of men. Hence the Northern Army Group embarked on an educational mission. It issued notes to explain that 'in reality what shatters the infantry's élan is the presence of intact barbed-wire entanglements, or enemy machine-guns opening fire from a flank. This is why the aim to be pursued is to destroy them before every attack.'[89]

The appearance of new weapons – such as automatic-rifles, grenade-launchers and 37mm guns – seemed an opportunity to ensure that the infantry once again had an effective role in offensives. The intention was that these support weapons would allow the infantry to continue its action for as long as possible by giving it the ability to reduce nests of resistance, particularly machine-guns. The infantry's new weapons enabled it to begin to catch up in technological terms with the artillery, which had been the first to transform itself.

Yet it proved difficult to define the new infantry procedures. The fighting at Verdun, which began on 21 February, showed that the January 1916 instructions were not fully satisfactory. A note from GHQ, dated 9 June, deemed the infantry attack formations to be still too dense, and strictly forbade assault waves consisting of men arranged elbow-to-elbow. Furthermore, during the course of the Battle of Verdun the infantry continued to have as many problems as before in preparing ground for defence:

> Everyone works for himself, without any direction. They shift a lot of earth, but in a disjointed manner. They have no trenches and no real dugouts.[90]

A note of 2 July found it necessary to specify: 'Preparing ground for defence during the battle is a military operation that, as with any other, can succeed only when there is leadership.'[91]

*

The Somme offensive of summer 1916 was intended to break through on a 40-km front. The hope was that it would reach open country towards Cambrai and towards the main line of communication that supplied the entire German northern front. On the French part of the front, the artillery preparation lasted six days and, in contrast to the British bombardment, proved highly effective. The rest of the battle consisted, as anticipated, of a series of pushes, notably on 1, 14-20 and 30 July and on 3 September. These pushes were powerfully prepared and supported by the artillery. Air supremacy was gained, and coordination between the aviation, infantry and artillery was outstanding. Yet the breakthrough never materialized, and after six months of fighting the Allies had still failed to reach Péronne, even though it lay less than 10 km from their jumping-off line. Hence the Somme fell short of being the desired battle of annihilation, even if it shook the German army more badly than the Allies suspected at the time. Disappointment and a new crisis were the result.

Over-centralization and a clinical deliberateness certainly prevented some opportunities from being exploited during the Battle of the Somme, as did the inescapable restrictions imposed by the limits to what the artillery could achieve. On 3 July, the 1st Colonial Army Corps conquered the Flaucourt plateau, but when it reported that the terrain was free of the enemy and proposed an exploitation, it was ordered to stick strictly to the plan.[92] The artillery's methods proved too slow. It persisted in seeking destruction instead of being content with neutralization, which meant that the preparation took significantly longer. Enough heavy artillery pieces were now available, but they still had a slow rate of fire, and this was another reason why artillery preparations took a long time. Surprise was out of the question. The terrain pounded by the artillery preparation was so torn up that it hindered the advance of the troops and guns, or even created excellent shelter for the defenders. The duration of the pause between two attacks was dictated solely by how quickly the artillery could reorganize, and this pause was longer than the time the enemy needed to recover.

Infantry combat, in contrast, had grown more flexible. The automatic-rifle became the core of small, offensive *groupes* that were more difficult to spot on the ground. The density of ordinary riflemen on the Somme was just half that in Artois: 1,600 men for every kilometre of front, compared with 3,500. Losses were lower than ever before. During the seventy-seven days on which the 13th Infantry Division was engaged on the Somme, each of its infantry companies lost an average of one man for every day of action, compared with seven men in 1914 and five in 1915.[93] Yet the rate of loss during the Battle of the Somme tended to rise as time passed. This can be seen from the cumulative total of French soldiers who had been either killed or evacuated to the rear. By the end of July it stood at 68,000, but by the end of August it had climbed more steeply to reach 215,000. (By the end of November, it was 319,000.)[94] In short, persisting in the offensive was more costly than the initial attack. This made it tempting to try and revert to a decisive attack, but the infantry's ability to fight that sort of engagement seemed to be declining. On 6 August, with the battle still in progress, Fayolle was obliged to record:

> Some infantry officers have recently shown signs of a deplorable mindset. If this mindset persisted, it would tend to deprive the infantry of all its offensive power and reduce it to just a passive tool for occupying ground that the artillery has already cleared of any obstacles and even of any enemy.[95]

The reason for the infantry's loss of dynamism was clear to supporters of shock (or 'surprise battle' as it was now known). The supporters of shock constituted the 'opposition' to the existing paradigm. They reckoned that the infantry lacked dynamism because it now ran relatively little risk in actions where every difficulty was solved by a profusion of artillery. The failure on the Somme led to the establishment of another paradigm intended to bring the war to a victorious end. Foch was removed from command of the Northern Army Group. 'Adventurers' such as Generals Charles Mangin and Joseph Alfred Micheler were now in favour, rather than cautious men such as Fayolle. Most importantly of all, the government intervened directly in military matters and took the opportunity to ditch Joffre.

### The 'Verdun school'

Late in 1916, as the rigid offensives on the Somme were coming to an end, attention shifted back to Verdun. In two attacks at Verdun, Nivelle made gains that were smaller in scale than those of the Somme but far more spectacular. The initial attack on 24 October, whose results included the recapture of Fort Douaumont, was notable for the excellent coordination between the arms. The artillery was able to continue its action during the actual assault by using the rolling barrage, a technique that had now been mastered. Rehearsals had thoroughly prepared the infantry for what it had to do. It gained all its objectives within an hour, except for Fort Vaux which fell a few days later. The subsequent attack on 15 December pushed the German lines back even further, and took 11,000 prisoners and 115 guns.

The techniques used at Verdun meant that any future attack was regarded as certain to capture the first German position. But Nivelle and the proponents of the 'Verdun school' then had the idea of expanding this method to the operational level. They thought it would enable them to seize the first two German defensive positions, on a broad front and in a single rush, and then to exploit their success in open country. This alluring formula was combined with what would nowadays be called skilful 'messaging' targeted at politicians – including attack demonstrations and displays of the most modern equipment. Nivelle's formula enabled the advocates of shock to modernize their outlook, using the slogan of 'the new spirit', and to regain the upper hand. On 17 December 1916, Nivelle was appointed to command the French armies.

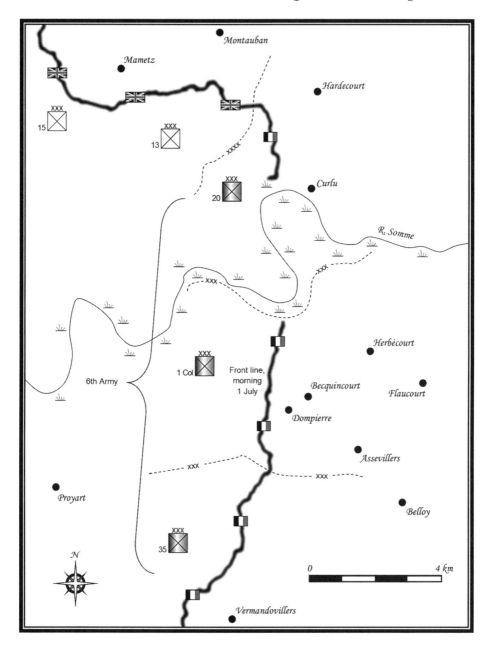

The French sector at the Battle of the Somme, 1 July 1916.

Meanwhile, a series of documents had shaped the new doctrine in the light of the lessons of that year's great battles. On 27 September, an *Interim note appended to the instruction of 8 January 1916 on the offensive combat of small units*[96] reorganized the infantry around its new weapons. This marked the birth of modern French infantry. The *Instruction on the use of cavalry in battle* (8 December) did the same for that arm, which was reorganized on the model of the infantry and given greater firepower for the purpose of exploiting successes.

Most importantly of all, the new methods were enshrined in the *Instruction concerning the aim and conditions of a general offensive action* (16 December).[97] The *Instruction* was a return to the concept of attacks made on as broad a front as possible, with these attacks seeking to take the enemy's artillery line, following one after the other with the shortest possible pause, and having the potential to exploit a complete success. The speed of the offensive remained restricted by the artillery's mobility. Hence the time needed to shift the artillery pieces forward had to be reduced to a minimum, partly by detailed planning and partly by modern guns being brought into service. But the artillery's role was still directed towards destruction, and artillery preparations continued to last for several days on end.

The infantry's attack had to be 'fervent and rapid'. It was to be carried out in successive stages, but the only constraint on these stages would be the resistance that was encountered. (Points of resistance were only ever to be attacked after a violent preparation.) No longer were there any limited objectives. What existed instead were just lines that had to be reached as a minimum requirement.[98] Much scope for initiative was left to the colonels with a view to exploiting success 'boldly and energetically'. The exploitation phase, using units designated for that purpose, was carefully planned.

Nivelle decided to apply these principles in April 1917. Multiple attacks would be launched on wide fronts – an initial series to absorb and wear down the enemy reserves, and the subsequent ones to break the front in twenty-four or forty-eight hours by means of a rapid, direct attack. The heavy artillery was to pound the entire depth of the enemy's defensive zone.[99]

The first attack was launched by the British in Artois on 9 April, on a front of 24 km. Six days of fighting resulted in an advance of 8 km. Then the French Northern Army Group attacked on 14 April, but was unable to break into the Hindenburg Line. Next to attack was the Reserve Army Group. It did so on 16 April, after a nine-day preparation by 4,000 guns on a 40-km front. The attack took the first German line, but was immediately blocked by the *Eingreif,* or 'intervention', divisions that had been held in readiness further to the rear. On 17 April, the Central Army Group attacked on a 16-km front, but with limited success. After the 21st, the French abandoned the quest for a breakthrough, and until 15 May merely sought to wear down the enemy reserves.

Public opinion was deeply disappointed as a result, and the infantry's morale collapsed. On 15 May, Nivelle was replaced by Pétain. The failure of the Nivelle offensive was partly due to a whole raft of conjunctural causes – specific, unpredictable circumstances that happened to come together at the same time. They included the delay in launching the offensive, the need to revise the plan in the wake of *Operation Alberich* (the deliberate German withdrawal to a shorter line), the security lapses that gave the Germans prior warning of the attack plan, and the difficult terrain and weather that hindered coordination between the arms. The role played by these conjunctural causes allowed supporters of the 'school of élan' to retain a degree of hope that their favoured method might yet work. Not enough modern equipment had been available for the Nivelle offensive. There had been only 428 short-barrelled Schneider 155mm pieces, instead of the required 800 or 900.[100] Some modern equipment had fallen short of expectations: the French tanks had foundered on 16 April when used for the first time. Nor had it been possible to gain control of the skies.

*

Hence the French army adapted to industrial warfare, but did so on two distinct levels and in accordance with different processes. One process was the evolution of doctrine – in other words, evolution in the thinking about how the military machine should be used. This process remained largely unchanged from before the war. It was based on the same debate between two poles: the pole of the supporters of élan and the pole of the supporters of fire. These poles simply adapted to the conditions of modern warfare. It was still not a smooth and continuous evolution resulting from constant adjustments. Rather, it consisted of a succession of crises and of solutions that were in the form of comprehensive models. Yet the process did differ in some respects from before the war. No longer was the debate conducted by military intellectuals who used the vigour or logic of their arguments to gain the upper hand. Now the debaters were actual practitioners of the art of war. The merit of their ideas had a real impact on the lives of millions of men, and was made obvious by the outcome of events. Furthermore, the succession of models happened more rapidly than during the pre-war period: practically every year saw a different paradigm become established.

The second process was the evolution of tactics. But it no longer amounted solely to the implementation of regulations derived from doctrine. Instead, the adaptation occurred primarily in a spontaneous way within each unit. But the units were unable on their own to assimilate the mass of innovations properly. A training structure was therefore necessary to try and rationalize this constant stream of changes. The training structure was initially established at the level of large units, and then moved up through the hierarchy to the higher echelons.

GHQ tried to coordinate these two processes through trial and error. Its efforts to do so can be split into three phases. Initially, when the war was expected to last just a few months, centralization of command contributed to rapid decision-making and made possible such victories as the Marne. At that time, the role of managing change was a limited one. The second phase arose from the new situation that was created by the continuous front. Joffre and GHQ now increasingly took second place to the generals as far as doctrinal thought was concerned, and to the units as regards the evolution of practice. This was, to a certain extent, an involuntary development and it caused many tensions. Pétain's appointment ushered in the third phase, and was an opportunity to forge a truly effective relationship between GHQ, the generals and the units. It not only made possible a less jerky evolution at the doctrinal level, but also allowed the units to assimilate a vast amount of modern equipment and new procedures within just a few months. From then on, the process was a modern and coherent one.

## Chapter 8

# Confronting the Trenches

We have seen how difficult it was to formulate a doctrine that was capable of adapting to a siege war on a continental scale. Now let's go down a notch and examine the tactical problem as it appeared to the French combat units on the front. Although they sometimes had to defend their own lines, they more frequently had to 'bite' into the strip of terrain, just a few kilometres wide, that ran across the country like a scar.

Each of the two opposing defensive systems was divided into several positions, and each position consisted of two or three trench-lines. The first position, which was in contact with the enemy, generally had three trenches that were roughly parallel. The fire trench, about 2 metres deep and slightly over 1 metre wide, included a parapet at the top – a sort of rampart made from sandbags and pierced with wooden loopholes facing the enemy. This foremost trench was protected to the front by belts of barbed-wire and was extended towards the enemy by listening posts, in which look-outs spent uncomfortable nights. The trench itself was interrupted by traverses and chicanes – in other words, contractions that not only prevented fire from being poured right along the trench but also made it possible to seal off any parts that fell into enemy hands during an attack. A fire-step at the foot of the forward wall of the trench made it possible to fire over the parapet. Recesses were dug into the rear wall for ammunition, grenades and also signal flares for calling down SOS fire (an emergency artillery barrage in the event of an enemy attack). This rear wall of the trench also included some first-aid dug-outs, which ended up some 6 or 7 metres deep under layers of earth, rails, cement or stones.

Some tens of metres behind the fire trench was a second, similar trench. Known as the supervision trench, its main purpose was to shelter the troops when the first trench was heavily bombarded. This was where the foremost reserves were placed. Around 100 to 200 metres further back was the support trench, with the company command post and some means of support (mainly trench-mortars). Machine-gun nests were established in small, sheltered bastions hidden throughout this trench network. The second and third trench-lines contained the reserves of the first echelon, and often took the brunt of an artillery bombardment. All these parallel lines and trenches were linked by communication trenches, which either zig-zagged or twisted in curves as a precaution against enfilade fire from machine-guns.

In 1915, a second position appeared several kilometres behind the first. It had much the same layout, but made better use of the terrain, particularly any reverse slopes. This second position accommodated reinforcements in vast, sheltered assembly points, which in many cases were made of concrete. The second position also shielded the array of artillery pieces. A third position appeared towards the end of 1915. Communication trenches linked all these parallel trenches by joining them at right angles. The lines of the telephone network ran along the communication trenches.

This was the new setting in which millions of men would fight for several years. Let us examine how the various arms responded to this new challenge.

## The Industrialization of the Infantry

In 1917, the writer Joseph Bédier attended infantry combat exercises on the firing range at Bouy in Champagne:

> We were given a startling object lesson. One company was armed just with rifles as at the start of the war and was given, by a generous arrangement, the support of a machine-gun section. It deployed in skirmish lines and for ten minutes fired in the same way as in 1914. Then, for the next ten minutes, another company exercised in its turn, but in the manner of 1917. Having formed its four *sections* in two assault waves, it unleashed all at once the rifle-shots of its *voltigeurs,* the grenades of its *grenadiers,* the fire of its automatic-riflemen, as well as bursts from the machine-guns and shelling from the supporting howitzers. To eye and ear alike, the contrast seemed tremendous.[1]

Within just a few years, the French infantry's small units had undergone a profound transformation. The masses of 'bayonet-men' gave way to fire units that integrated modern, complementary weapons. On the other hand, the infantry regiments did not become specialized: they all belonged more or less to the same type. Hence the infantry evolved in the opposite way to the artillery. The artillery's tactical units – the firing batteries (the elements that batteries used to carry out fire missions) and the *groupes* of batteries – underwent barely any change, but became enormously diversified into heavy artillery, field artillery, trench-mortars and so on.

Another peculiarity of the infantry compared with the other arms was the appalling scale of its losses. As a result, it was seriously short of men during the last two-thirds of the war, and was obliged to adopt a radically new organization. Furthermore, since almost all the fighting was concentrated on French soil, the infantry shaped itself around the answer to a specific problem: how to break through the German front. It therefore became more and more adapted to positional warfare, but gradually lost its manœuvring skills.

### *Underground soldiers*

Basic beliefs about how the infantry should be used were slow to evolve when confronted with the fortified front. Offensive determination continued to seem the surest guarantee of victory, especially in a war that was still expected to be short. The decisive battle advocated by the writer Carl von Clausewitz lived on in the form of 'breakthrough'. The infantry retained its offensive-minded aggressiveness, only this aggressiveness was no longer manifested in vast, Napoleonic manœuvres but instead in assaults against narrow, entrenched positions. The hitherto neglected notion of terrain, of key positions, became crucial. Success was now measured in terms of how many metres of ground had been either won or preserved.

Achieving a breakthrough entailed seizing an area of fortified zone several tens of square kilometres in extent. It required the mastery of an art of war that was not only completely new but also particularly complex. How could the attacker go fast enough to achieve and exploit a breakthrough before divisions of enemy reinforcements arrived? How could the attacker achieve speed in the absence of surprise? How could the attacker coordinate the actions of thousands of men in the confusion of trench fighting? Those were just some of the problems that surfaced as engagements progressed. They were resolved in a sort of organized chaos by the combined effect of three phenomena: firstly, the micro-innovations of the front, which circulated or climbed up the hierarchy by capillary action; secondly, the synthesizing work done by GHQ's Third Department; and thirdly, the generals' own, personal objectives.

At the lowest level, the main difficulty lay in crossing the dense entanglements of barbed-wire, in order to reach and destroy the machine-gun nests that formed the basic framework of the defence. The only technical solutions – apart from some dangerous do-it-yourself devices, such as armoured wheelbarrows or improvised mortars – were developments of equipment that already existed and that could be taken 'off the shelf'.

To neutralize the enemy machine-guns, the French initially relied on their own machine-guns, which had already been issued and whose production simply needed to be increased. Hence the number of machine-guns allocated to the units rose from 5,000 in August 1914 to 11,000 by 1 January 1916.[2] This meant that each regiment now had twenty-four machine-guns at its disposal, compared with just six at the start of the war. The Hotchkiss (1914 model) gradually replaced the less robust Saint-Etienne (1907 model). Yet the problem was that machine-guns were heavy, slow to bring into action and tricky to use, making them more effective in defence than in attack.

Hand-grenades were also reintroduced in enormous quantities. They were more practical than the Lebel rifle for trench warfare, since trenches were no wider than 1.60 metres, whereas the rifle with its fixed bayonet was as long as 1.80 metres. Even so, the Lebel remained the infantryman's basic weapon (along with a bayonet that inflicted a negligible proportion of enemy deaths), until the arrival of the automatic-rifle, which was a sort of machine-gun light enough to be carried during assaults.

Similarly, little change was seen in organizational structures, with two exceptions: firstly the disappearance in February 1915 of the distinction between reserve and active units, and secondly the creation of machine-gun companies. Since the infantry lacked suitable means of its own, it relied on the artillery to tear up the barbed-wire entanglements and neutralize the defenders long enough for the assaulting troops to close in. But 75mm guns were ill-fitted for this mission, and in any case the early stages of trench warfare saw a shortage of shells.[3]

The difficulty of manœuvring on the ground made it necessary for the time being to use the third dimension. Artillery and aircraft rained fire from the sky. As for the infantry, it dug in. For the first time, human action actually changed the terrain of the battlefield, by means of entrenching tools and large-calibre shells. In 1915, a 500-metre dash across no man's land against a German company established on the defensive meant struggling with barbed-wire under an intense fire consisting of some 20,000 bullets – those '2-km long pikes' as Lieutenant-Colonel Jean-Baptiste Montaigne had referred to them. To have any hope of survival, therefore, the men had to organize the terrain offensively. They dug a jumping-off trench no more than 200 metres from the enemy, with communication trenches leading back to link it to the first line. All trenches running parallel to the front were provided with steps and wooden footbridges to make them easier to pass for those waves of attackers who were sent from parallels further behind.

Recesses and bombproof dumps were created in the first line, not only for ammunition, but also for the supplies that were needed to hold whatever ground was gained: barbed-wire, stakes, sandbags, tools, rations and telephone equipment. First-aid posts, too, were set up there. Further back, an entire network of communication, liaison and evacuation trenches was created, as well as parallels and assembly trenches for the second, third and fourth assault waves. The positions of the final wave included storage recesses, dressing stations and supply dumps. To prevent men from becoming lost in this underground labyrinth – hardly any of which could be seen from ground level – a complete circulation system was organized, including signs, guides, direction arrows, and the naming of places and lines, along with personnel to maintain order. All the work involved in organizing the ground in this way took weeks. General Fernand de Langle de Cary described the preparation for the offensive against Perthes during the winter of 1914-15:

The whole of the work had to be done at night, in the muddy ground of Champagne that made men slip or flounder, and under fire from an enemy who had plenty of searchlights and illuminating flares. Add to these difficulties the rain and snow of a cold, wet winter. Bear in mind, too, all the supplies that were needed for the men doing the work: logs to shore up communication trenches and parallels, sandbags, hurdles and stakes for revetments, ammunition, rations and everything else down to the very last flask of water. All these supplies had to be carried on men's backs, in complete darkness and – initially at any rate – without the slightest cover.[4]

\*

By the time of the Artois offensive in May 1915, the art of organizing the terrain for an offensive had been more or less mastered. What still posed many problems were the imperatives of planning, coordinating and conducting operations. As an example, let us see what happened during the Artois offensive to a brigade of the 34th Infantry Division, which formed part of the 10th Army. On 9 May, the brigade had the mission of seizing the south-eastern spur of Vimy ridge, which meant that it had to cover a distance of 3 km after going over the top. Its attack front was just 900 metres wide. The 88th Infantry Regiment was in the first echelon with two battalions up front and one in reserve. (The 59th Infantry Regiment was in the second echelon in the assembly trenches.) Each of the two foremost battalions had two companies in the jumping-off trench that had been specially dug for the attack, and the other two behind in what had formerly been the front-line trench. These companies faced a couple of German bastions infested with machine-guns and linked by four lines of trenches. The entire defensive system was protected by dense entanglements of barbed-wire.

The means available for supporting the attack were limited to nine heavy batteries for the entire army corps. Seven of them were allocated for pounding the German second echelon. That left just two heavy batteries and seven 75mm batteries for short-range support. The heavy pieces had a slow rate of fire, and the 75mm guns were ineffective against underground defences. The artillery preparation during the days leading up to the attack proved inadequate against the first position and also destroyed any hope of surprise. The so-called 'immediate' preparation, just before the assault, consisted of five periods of fire for effect, lasting several minutes each and separated by intervals of different lengths. But no provision was made for laying down machine-gun fire either during the immediate preparation or in support of the actual attack.

At the end of the artillery preparation, the 75mm guns lengthened their fire by 100 metres and then moved it forward in lifts of 25 metres at a time, to ensure it always remained 250 metres in front of the infantrymen. The men of the first echelon hauled themselves out of their trench with the help of steps and assault ladders, to the sound of the *Marseillaise* and of drums and bugles playing the charge. But the men were instantly cut down by machine-gun fire coming from the two bastions. The survivors formed vulnerable clumps as they dashed towards the gaps in the barbed-wire, but managed to seize the first trench. They then came up against another barbed-wire entanglement. Their colonel was killed. The second wave was cut to pieces by artillery fire, and the reserve battalion was unable even to go over the top. Any artillery support was now impossible, owing to the uncertainty about the locations of the troops. The 59th Infantry Regiment tried to renew the assault, but in vain. Three hours later, a German counter-attack regained the lost trench. The 34th Infantry Division had lost 1,500 men, with nothing to show for it.[5]

These problems were still unresolved by the time of the offensive of 25 September 1915. The artillery preparation lasted three days, but this proved insufficient either to open gaps right through the barbed-wire or to neutralize the defences. During the actual attack, the artillery was supposed to support the infantrymen by lifting its fire by 200 or 400 metres at a time, in response to their requests. But the deeper the attackers drove into the enemy lines, the more difficult communications became between the troops on the move and the batteries. Commanders had too weak a grip on the conduct of the infantry action. The generals, down to brigade level, now commanded by telephone, but the lines were often cut as the battles raged, especially those lines that were unrolled behind the assault troops. Hours might pass before what happened in the first echelon came to the knowledge of the divisional commander. At this stage of the war, the lines of infantrymen were still too dense and close to each other, and they came up against the German second position, which had suffered barely any damage from artillery fire. Too great a mismatch existed between the complexity of the operation that the infantry was required to carry out and

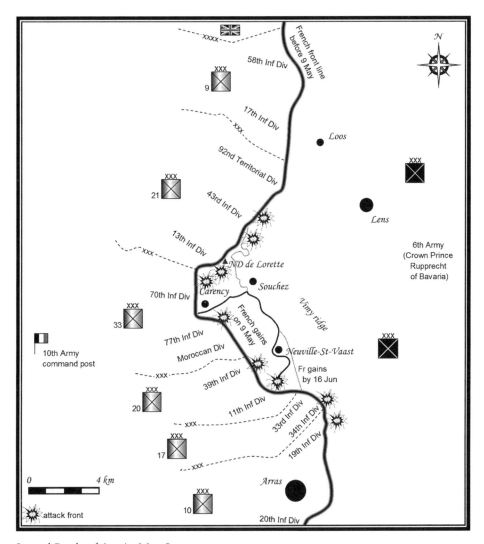

Second Battle of Artois, May-June 1915.

the difficulties of directing that operation. Most importantly of all, the cost had been 138,000 men. With losses on such a scale, it was impossible to see how the same approach could be pursued.

Out of the 1 million French infantrymen who were killed during the First World War, more than half fell between August 1914 and November 1915. The 70th Infantry Division, which had an average strength of 8,000 infantrymen, lost nearly 17,000 men during the first seventeen months and another 10,000 during the rest of the war. In short, by the end of 1915 the division had already lost twice its total number of infantrymen – and it was not even one of the most engaged units.[6] In the 13th Infantry Division, each infantry company had an average strength of 200 men and lost an average of 700 during the fighting of 1915 alone.[7] The survivors were worn out. For months they had been fighting or carrying out preparatory work without either rest or leave, since the war had still been expected to be short. The first signs of despondency, or even discontent, were obvious. The situation resulted in an important psychological change: it was finally accepted that courage and a disregard of losses could not solve every tactical problem. The new *Instruction on the offensive combat of small units*, issued on 8 January 1916, recognized that 'you do not fight with men against materiel'.

### In the wake of the shells

Another consequence of the infantry's losses, and the repeated failures of what were meant to have been decisive offensives, was an intense frustration. This feeling manifested itself in a fairly common hatred of staff officers, and in a distrust of the instructions, notes and directives that came from 'up high'. The underlying frustration was aggravated by the often miserable conditions of life, and by the professionalization of the combatants who, after several years of war, were in a position to pass expert judgements on what they were being asked to do. From a psychological point of view, it was therefore astonishing that generals imbued with social sciences should have made the mistake of launching further attacks at the beginning of May 1917, after the supposedly decisive Aisne offensive had been checked the previous month. This chasm between the commanders and the lower echelons made it even more difficult to impose new methods.

The infantry lost confidence not only in itself but also in the arrival of new weaponry. It felt powerless without constant protection from the artillery, not least because the current doctrine encouraged that mindset. In the opinion of Colonel Pascal Lucas:

> The infantry was already tried by its losses and frustrating attacks. It learned that it could no longer do anything without the artillery, and this lesson was repeated in the instructions. It was enough to sap the self-confidence, the élan, the drive – in short, the offensive spirit – of this arm that had already been through so much. Yet these were such vital qualities in combat.[8]

The result was that for two years, 1916 and 1917, the infantry tended 'to march only in the wake of artillery shells'.[9]

The infantry had to have new weapons to increase its firepower. The Chauchat automatic-rifles were eagerly awaited, along with the Viven-Bessières rifle-grenades, which had an arched trajectory and a range of 200 metres. So, too, were the support weapons, such as the Brandt and Stokes mortars, which lobbed a 81mm shell between 1,000 and 2,000 metres, and the 37mm guns, which were capable of hitting a machine-gun nest 2,000 metres away using a shell with a high muzzle velocity.

But these weapons had been conceived belatedly, and not until the autumn of 1916 would they actually reach the units. Until then, the infantry's action had to remain subordinated to that of the artillery, and the artillery's methods were made more flexible. Two major innovations began to be developed in summer 1916: the rolling barrage and the divisional aviation. The rolling barrage was an actual wall of shells that fell in front of the infantrymen and shifted in accordance with a precise timetable. The divisional aircraft were two-seaters that used flares, the wireless or messages dropped in weighted containers to provide a link between the assault troops, the artillery and the commanders. Also tried out were support sections of 75mm artillery (sometimes towed by tanks). But these sections were easy targets, and there was not enough time to design motorized limbers that had armoured plates and caterpillar tracks.[10]

This was the first phase in the process of providing the French infantry with modern equipment, and it tailed off in mid-1917. The second phase began in May 1918, when the light tanks, which were true infantry-support vehicles, became commonplace. In the four years from 1914 to 1918, the density of materiel surrounding the infantryman as he moved and fought increased by a factor of around sixty. When the army mobilized in 1914, an infantry regiment had just two types of weapon. By the time of the Armistice, it had been equipped with nine different models.

The shortage of men also spurred innovation in the infantry's organizational structures. The brigade echelon was abolished, and the division was reduced to three regiments. Although this reform provoked strong reservations, some officers, such as Major Emile Laure, saw it as an opportunity for change:

Some of us rejoiced at the decision that had been made, because ever since the start of the war we had been struck by the losses incurred by an over-abundance of infantry. How many engagements had been fought and pursued by throwing in men, when materiel alone should have been used! How many cases had occurred of assault dispositions being stubbornly and pointlessly reinforced – and yet this stubbornness would have been discarded if excessive numbers of battalions had not been available in reserve on so many occasions. We therefore gained the impression that we would be forced to adopt a tactic of sparing the infantrymen and that (in line with what had been seen both at Verdun and on the Somme) we would be

*Table 2: Materiel as a proportion of men armed with rifles.*[11]

|  | 1914 | 1917 | 1918 |
|---|---|---|---|
| Infantry support weapons | 1/400 | 1/7 | 1/5 |
| 75mm guns | 1/200 | 1/70 | 1/55 |
| Heavy guns | 1/5,000 | 1/116 | 1/70 |
| Airplanes | 1/5,000 | 1/280 | 1/90 |
| Tanks | n/a | n/a | 1/233 |
| Labourers | 1/25 | 1/2 | 1/1.5 |

For example, '75mm guns: 1/200' means one 75mm gun for every 200 men armed with rifles. Infantry support weapons: machine-guns and automatic-rifles.

obliged to fight the battle by coordinating the various arms to best effect, according to their own capabilities. That is what would be called manœuvring.[12]

The lightening of the infantry structure caused tactics to become more frugal and flexible. Each regiment could be coupled with a *groupe* of field artillery and could thereby forge close bonds. To replace the two brigade commanders, a commander of the divisional infantry was created – on the model of the divisional artillery commander – and the various missions he might be given included commanding an echelon of the division or coordinating the first-line units with the divisional artillery. One of the infantry companies in each battalion was abolished and replaced with a machine-gun company. Men were replaced by machines. But despite every division being reduced by one regiment, and every battalion by one company, the theoretical strength of the infantry units continued to decline relentlessly. The company strength, which was initially 250 men, fell to 200 in 1915, to 194 in 1916 and to 175 by the end of the war.[13] The deficit made collective training difficult, and the figures take no account of the number of men who were absent because they were either convalescing, on training courses or on leave – a number that became higher and higher at the end of 1917. Individual training was more or less sound, but collective tactics rarely surpassed the mediocre.

## Prisoners of Glory

The French cavalry's engagement in the war was a failure. Within a month of the start of fighting, it had worn out its horses to such an extent that it could no longer carry out its missions properly. Since the German cavalry suffered a similar fate, the underlying cause of this premature 'consumption' was to be found, it seemed, in the unsuitability of the horse to the conditions of modern warfare. This mismatch grew even more pronounced when the front became fortified. The cavalry, finding its very existence under threat, was forced to embark on a transformation, and yet that transformation remained incomplete since there was no intention of giving up the horse altogether.

### 'Desert of the Tartars'

The cavalry was faced not only with the general problem of a shortage of men, but also with the reduced usefulness of mounted units in positional warfare. Initially, it had to compromise by agreeing to provide personnel to those arms that were either below strength or undergoing expansion. The cavalry supplied the other arms with a total of 4,800 officers – as many as had been at its disposal at the start of the war – along with 45,000 men.[14] By May 1915, half the NCOs of the cavalry regiments had transferred to the infantry, where they commanded *sections*. Officers who left the cavalry were particularly attracted by the new, motorized arms – tanks and aviation – where they rediscovered a bit of the lost dynamism of their arm of origin. Their tendency to favour these arms can be seen as a further indication of the need to replace the horse with the internal combustion engine.

The cavalry had to surrender horses as well as men. In 1916, it supplied 4,000 horses to the artillery. Then, in March-April 1917, the heavy artillery received the mounts of eight disbanded squadrons.[15] By 1918, the cavalry had been bled dry. Its depots had nothing left, since no young conscript class had been inducted in those depots, apart from some volunteers. An attempt to call back former cavalrymen who had transferred into other arms produced just 350 men, which showed just how much the cavalry had lost its allure.[16] Under these conditions, it was impossible to preserve every unit. Seventy-three squadrons were abolished as early as the end of 1915, followed by four divisions between 1916 and 1918.[17]

The cavalry continued to be whittled down throughout the war. If it was not to disappear altogether, it had to find ways of adapting to the conditions of the Western Front. The first way was to agree for some of its men to be temporarily dismounted. This answered one of the cavalry's needs: the ability to fulfil missions where it had to gain or hold specific points of ground. Starting with the war's opening engagements, the cavalry regiments had improvised foot units with assorted weapons and some requisitioned bicycles.[18] A note from GHQ dated 14 January 1915 formalized these units by ordering them to be combined into light *groupes,* so that every cavalry division had one of these identical *groupes.* The cavalry divisions were also required to occupy sectors of the front. Hence provisional, composite squadrons were assigned to serve in the trenches on a rotational basis.

On 8 August 1915, a note issued by GHQ obliged each cavalry division to equip a foot regiment – a 'light regiment' – composed of six temporarily-dismounted squadrons, the light *groupe* and the cyclist *groupe.* (Each cavalry corps was to be able to form a light division by grouping together these foot regiments.) Then, on 1 June 1916, six regiments of foot *cuirassiers* were formed. They lost their horses to the artillery and were organized in the same way as infantry regiments. (The need to bring them up to the required strength meant that the light regiments had to be disbanded.) Finally, in January 1918, they formed two divisions of foot *cuirassiers.* These divisions properly formed part of the cavalry corps, but were almost immediately withdrawn from them. As a result, the cavalry corps found themselves back in the same situation as in 1914, reduced to just their mounted elements. The only infantry support that the cavalry divisions now possessed was the cyclist *groupe.* This *groupe* was a powerful fire element, highly mobile and of proven worth, but its strength had been reduced in 1916 from 400 to 200 rifles.

Even the organizational structure of the mounted units gradually conformed with that of the infantry. When the cavalry units were dismounted with fighting in mind, they were systematically fused by pairs and had to adopt the terminology of the infantrymen. For example, two troops became a *section,* while two squadrons became a company. This arrangement was retained, even though it was not welcomed by the cavalrymen.

Hence the cavalry managed to transform units of horsemen into units of 'trench cavalrymen'. Their fine bearing under fire enabled them to preserve the symbolic devices identifying them as cavalrymen and to avoid being simply absorbed into the infantry. Yet it was universally regarded as a provisional solution stemming from the exceptional character that the war had acquired. All this imposed a double constraint of training on the arm. Not only did it have to adopt new equipment and learn how to fight on foot – something to which it was completely unaccustomed – it simultaneously had to maintain its equestrian know-how. Since these two tasks were so demanding, the cavalry in reality ended up becoming split. The mounted part remained largely isolated from the fighting and also, therefore, from the evolution of the arm.

By paying this price, the cavalry managed to preserve a number of mounted squadrons. Just as the characters of a subsequent novel, the *Desert of the Tartars,* wait endlessly for a conflict to give meaning to their existence, the cavalrymen waited in vain until the end of the war for the 'breakthrough', the essential prelude to the great, destructive mounted rides of which they dreamed. This hypothetical outcome perpetuated their conservatism. Until the very end, they remained in a dream world. The cavalry had no justification for assuming that the same limitations on its effectiveness would fail to produce the same results in 1918 as they had done in 1914. Yet each of the great and supposedly decisive offensives – the Champagne in 1915, the Somme in 1916 and the Aisne in 1917 – brought disappointment and caused the cavalry to postpone its hopes to the next offensive.

With the resumption of the war of movement, General François-René Boullaire believed that the cavalry's time had finally come.[19] The cavalry was unable to debouch at Villers-Cotterêts in July 1918, nor in Flanders that October. Yet it still pinned its hopes on the Lorraine offensive which, had it not been for the Armistice, would have enabled 'their arm to drive the Germans back to the Rhine'.[20] Admittedly, such hopes were bolstered by some outstanding cavalry actions on the peripheral fronts, namely those of General Eberhard *Graf* von Schmettow's corps in Romania in 1916 and the Commonwealth cavalry in Palestine in 1917-18, but even more importantly the raid by General François Jouinot-Gambetta's brigade to take Uskub in Macedonia in September 1918.

### An incomplete transformation

The successive French commanders-in-chief did not have set opinions about the cavalry's future. Joffre retained the cavalry divisions with a view to exploiting possible breakthroughs, and pressed for the cavalry's transformation into a powerful and highly mobile 'mounted infantry'. As for Pétain, he hesitated to 'destroy completely an arm that could not be created again',[21] not least as it had remained loyal during the 'mutinies' and as it could perform useful police service if trouble arose in the interior of the country. He therefore remained cautious and followed Joffre's lead in encouraging the cavalry's transformation.

Gradually, therefore, the mobile shock force became a force of mobile firepower. The men's personal weaponry was improved. The musketoon of the start of the war was replaced by three successive models of carbines between 1914 and 1917. The cavalryman's equipment was superceded by that of the infantry, including a personal entrenching tool, hand-grenade pouch, gas masks and location panel. The crew-served weaponry saw similar advances. The allocation of automatic weapons increased from one machine-gun section for every brigade to two sections for every regiment, in addition to six automatic-rifles and nine rifle-grenade launchers for every squadron. By the end of the war, a cavalry division – including its two *groupes* of armoured machine-gun carriers – had the same firepower as an infantry division, but could move twice as fast and had just half the infantry division's numbers of men.[22]

The other way for the cavalry to adapt to the conditions of the front was motorization. By 1914, machine-gun carriers had already existed for around fifteen years, and some had been used either on the Moroccan frontier or in the large-scale manœuvres. At that time, they seemed bound to undergo a similar path of development as the airplane. They were a means of long-range reconnaissance that also had armoured protection and much firepower. This made them seem particularly suitable vehicles for cavalry missions. Yet the cavalry showed barely any interest in them. Machine-gun carriers, it was widely thought, would simply duplicate the mounted units, while being more difficult to keep supplied.

In August 1914, General Jean François André Sordet was one of the first to realize the usefulness of these vehicles for supporting reconnaissances, escorting columns of lorry-borne infantry, or providing a means of liaison. At Mézières near the Belgian border, he improvised a small *groupement* of six requisitioned motor-cars, armed with machine-guns borrowed from an infantry regiment's depot.[23] On 6 August, these motor-cars set off on campaign with his cavalry corps, performed important services as it rode through Belgium and then disappeared during the retreat.

Then, at the end of September 1914, General Louis Conneau's cavalry corps was equipped with two sections of armoured cars, which were served by sailors. Most of these cars had machine-guns, but some were instead armed with guns. The usefulness of such vehicles was recognized: this was obvious from the haste with which the ones that Sordet had lost were replaced and with which the size of the *groupe* belonging to Conneau was increased. Each cavalry division was allocated a mixed *groupe* of gun-carriers and machine-gun carriers in 1915, followed by a second *groupe* in June 1916.

## The Transformations of the Artillery

At the end of August 1914, the French artillery had 400,000 men serving eight models of guns, including three modern models. By 1917, it had doubled the amount of materiel that it was allocated, and its men served twenty-four different types of pieces. The artillery included a dozen specialities, including the tanks, while half of the aviation was used to assist it. It had almost as many men as the infantry, and absorbed most of the country's financial, industrial, technical and logistical resources. The artillery was poised to become the 'great power' of the French army, yet its spectacular growth did not stem from a steady development. It resulted instead from several 'leaps', each of which was a response to a major challenge.

### Adapting to trench warfare

As a first step, the French had to acquire a powerful heavy artillery that would be able to counter the enemy artillery and smash even the strongest defensive works. They had started the war with just 300 modern heavy pieces, compared with the German figure of 2,000, and had practically none of those 300 pieces left by October 1914. That same month, GHQ decreed a programme that made it possible to improvise a heavy artillery with two components. The first component was the heavy railway artillery, which used naval weapons, and the second was the heavy artillery in the narrower sense, which consisted of weapons withdrawn from the fortresses. As a result, 272 batteries were available by August 1915, and were split between the various armies and a reserve at GHQ's disposal. A ministerial decision of July 1915 diversified the heavy artillery by creating twenty regiments of horse-drawn heavy artillery and ten regiments of tractor-towed heavy artillery. Finally, on 30 May 1916, a major programme set the organizational structure of the artillery of the large units for the rest of the war, along with the additional materiel that was required.

From then on, the heavy artillery regiments developed relentlessly. By January 1917, 469 batteries were available. A year later, there were 900, in eighty-seven regiments.[24] The artillery's greatest undertaking during the war was the creation of a heavy component. In August 1914, there were thirteen field pieces for every heavy piece. But by the end of the war, the ratio was practically equal, with about 5,000 pieces in each of the two categories. By then, the heavy artillery, with the General Artillery Reserve under the direct command of the inspector of the arm, had become the new core of the artillery.

Yet the heavy artillery laboured under the disadvantage of being an improvisation. All the materiel that was developed had already existed as prototypes before the war. Even though this saved at least one year, not until 1918 did masses of modern materiel arrive that were a match for the German equipment. The technical inferiority of the French heavy artillery had several consequences. Firstly, it was a powerful stimulus for innovation, since the heavy artillery was a subdivision that had to impose itself in the face of a superior enemy and even within its own arm – it was accused of getting the best officers. As a result, the heavy artillery's fire management ended up becoming superior in many respects to that of the enemy, and the methods that were developed spread throughout the artillery arm as a whole. On the other hand, until 1918 the French heavy pieces had a slow rate of fire.[25] Preparations for attacks lasted several days, whereas the German artillery was able to produce the same effects in a matter of hours.[26] Such differences radically transformed tactical approaches. Since the German army had the benefit of surprise in all its offensives, it was able to develop bolder and more flexible tactics for its infantry. In contrast, artillery preparations that lasted for several days precluded any surprise. Hence the French infantry had a more difficult task when they attacked, and highly centralized and methodical operational methods were developed by way of compensation.

The need for greater diversification was clear as early as 1915. The artillery had to adapt urgently to the use of chemical weapons, and did so with a lag of one year behind the Germans and on a smaller scale.[27] But it was not until the final year of the war that the use of chemical weapons had a meaningful impact on the fighting. The French also had to improvise a 'trench artillery', which was the term they gave to trench-mortars. They knew that the Germans had possessed a cohesive trench-mortar weapons system even before the war.[28] Whereas the Germans could hurl enormous 'torpedoes' weighing some 40 or 50 kg, the French had to use outdated mortars that had been stored in fortresses, and cobble together mortars and bombs using assorted materials. They then brought into service the 58mm *crapouillot* ('little toad'). The first trench-mortar units were created at the start of 1915, but it was the end of 1916 before the organization settled down. When the war of movement resumed in 1918, the

Soldiers of the 11th Infantry Division advancing during the Battle of the Somme, 1916. Tactics had become more sophisticated than the massed charges of August 1914.

Schneider tank.

French infantryman, 1914.

French infantryman, 1915.

Alpine *chasseurs*.

A French infantry sergeant, 1916. The man is a veteran. On his chest is the *Croix de guerre*. The chevrons on his upper left sleeve show that he has done more than two years of front-line service. Note the entrenching tool (upside down, with the handle next to his left fist).

By November 1918, the French had five regiments of railway artillery.

An artillery staff in 1916. Reports arrive by telephone or liaison officers. The locations of German batteries are marked on the map on the wall. The artillery underwent a massive expansion during the war, and became the 'great power' of the French army.

Lorries transporting troops along the *Voie sacrée*, the supply route to Verdun, in 1916.

General Auguste Dubail commanded the 1st Army in 1914 and then the Eastern Army Group until 1916.

*Left*: General Emile Fayolle. An artilleryman by background, he commanded the 6th Army during the Battle of the Somme.

*Right*: General Henri Gouraud, the commander of the 4th Army. He was passionate about training.

The ridge of Les Eparges, 19 km south-east of Verdun. It was one of the most notorious points of friction on the Western Front.

A water-logged trench.

Voisin aircraft bombing Ludwigshafen on the Rhine river, 27 May 1915.

*Left*: The air ace Georges Guynemer (left), with his squadron commander, Captain Antonin Brocard.

*Right*: Colonel Maurice Duval. In August 1917 he became assistant chief-of-staff in charge of aeronautics in the theatre of operations. It was he who ensured that the Air Division was created in 1918.

trench-mortars lost much of their relevance. Only one 58mm battery was kept for every army corps. The surplus was grouped into five regiments attached to the General Artillery Reserve.

In 1914, the anti-aircraft artillery had just a handful of weapons and had carried out some studies and tests for a motorized 75mm gun.[29] It expanded during the war to keep pace with the developing threat from the air, and ended up with more than 400 pieces (motorized 75mm guns, 75mm guns on trailers, 75mm and 105mm guns on platforms) along with means of listening and illumination. The whole force was organized into six regiments. In 1917, when the first tanks came into service, a start was also made on creating an anti-tank artillery, but its development suffered from a lack of urgency in the absence of an enemy tank threat.

*

The artillery's firing sequence consisted of putting means of fire in place, acquiring targets, adjusting fire for accuracy, actually delivering the fire and then verifying the results. The first problem was target acquisition: to a greater and greater degree, targets were hidden and distant. To resolve this difficulty, artillery intelligence departments were created in November 1915 at army corps level and subsequently at army level. Their role was to sort, centralize and disseminate the information that was collected. At their disposal were specialized air assets (balloons and photographic-reconnaissance airplanes), as well as sound-ranging sections and ground-based observation sections. Their paramount mission was counter-battery.

The next challenge was ensuring that the fire was accurate. Hence field survey groups belonging to the Army Geographical Branch began to map the theatre of operations. They produced large-scale maps showing all the known enemy trenches, batteries and other useful details. Published by topographical sections, these maps soon became indispensable to artillery and assault units alike. By 1917, two special trains for printing maps were available to the field survey groups and could follow armies during their operations. By the end of the war, the survey groups had specially-equipped, motorized lorries that made it possible to supply more than 4 million maps a year.

Counter-battery, which was the prime mission of the heavy artillery, required accurate, long-range fire. The heavy artillery therefore carried out pioneering work in two fields. The first was the scientific preparation of fires, including the application of topographical methods, the identification of ammunition lots and the use of aerological and ballistic calculations. The second field was the employment of aircraft for adjusting artillery fire. Following the experiments made in 1914, the adjustment of fire by aerial observers soon became indispensable. But finding effective communication methods was a matter of trial-and-error until wireless sets were installed on board airplanes – something that was first tried on 13 December 1914. Aerial adjustment of fire improved significantly and by the end of 1916 reached a peak of effectiveness. Alongside the improvement in means of air-ground liaison, advances were made in communication between the artillery and infantry. These advances involved the setting up of dense wireless networks and, starting in 1915, the assignment of 'liaison and observation detachments' to any unit that was given artillery support.

Yet a degree of confusion within the artillery was revealed by the initial setbacks during the Battle of Verdun in February 1916. The constant development, the diversification and the profusion of innovations within the artillery regiments had resulted in increasingly divergent methods being used. Hence the rapid replacement of one artillery unit with another posed serious problems of coordination. Furthermore, whereas before the war the artillery had been decentralized and oriented towards supporting an infantry assault that it could actually see, from the start of 1915 it focused exclusively on preparing and supporting offensives. It was therefore disconcerted when faced with having to improvise defensive actions. Thus the artillery had a new challenge: having developed its means and methods, it now had to master the complexity of its missions. The first step was to set up an appropriate command structure and also, alongside it, a structure for managing change.

## Managing complexity

From the end of 1914, several changes were made that were driven by necessity. Firstly, the colonel of the divisional artillery regiment became his divisional general's adviser. Secondly, an army corps artillery command was created. In August 1915, a heavy artillery commander was added at army corps level. But not until 9 December 1916 was a note issued that put appropriate staffs in place at each level of command. The belatedness of this step was despite the fact that vast amounts of firepower were now being assembled, with concentrations of more than twenty batteries for every kilometre of attacked front.[30]

On 14 February 1917, Nivelle grouped together the components of the heavy artillery into the General Heavy Artillery Reserve. Its commander was General Edmond Buat, who had advocated this initiative. The means at Buat's disposal gave him the ability to carry out an 'artillery manœuvre'. He had a staff, liaison officers, a motor-transport service, a centre at Mailly for maintenance, training and transport, and also a branch specifically for railways, including track-construction batteries, supply dumps and a school for training locomotive mechanics and drivers.

On 26 January 1918, the General Heavy Artillery Reserve became the General Artillery Reserve, a real 'state within a state' that grouped together all units not permanently assigned to divisions or army corps. In particular, it absorbed the foot artillery and the trench-mortars. The General Artillery Reserve was now able to produce powerful concentrations of fire. Artillery organization centres were also created – one for each speciality – in order to organize newly-created regiments and modernize the weaponry of old ones.[31]

On 27 May 1917, Pétain created a Directorate-General of Artillery Training. This was a response to the need to manage the evolution of the artillery's methods and means, disseminate new ideas and develop closer ties with the rear-area services. General Frédéric Georges Herr was entrusted with this directorate-general. At the same time, the Minister of War created a Central Artillery Commission – an instrument of liaison, coordination and technical research – which likewise came under Herr's chairmanship. An *Instruction* of 26 January 1918 replaced the Directorate-General of Artillery Training with an Inspectorate-General of Artillery that had more extensive powers.

The huge expansion of the artillery arm, combined with its innovations and new equipment, created a need to complement and unify the training of all the artillery officers. Between December 1915 and February 1916, three heavy artillery training centres were opened at Châlons, Amiens and Toul.[32] Every officer of the arm was summoned to these centres to study the lessons of the Battle of Champagne, the *Instruction* of 20 November 1915, the heavy artillery's regulations and the scientific rationalization of fire. These training centres were reopened after the Battle of Verdun, in order to amalgamate the methods used by the field and heavy artillery, which had shown a tendency to drift apart. The Applied School of Artillery at Fontainebleau continued to train *aspirants* and second lieutenants for the arm (10,000 of them in 1917). In addition, a 'field artillery course' was set up within each of the French armies to prepare young officers for commanding a battery.

On 27 June 1916, the artillery research centre was created at Châlons. It was responsible for creating a centralized resource of written information, defining the drill, improving technical training and ensuring the commanders of large units had the benefit of every innovation concerning the use of artillery. The centre was also to scrutinize the implementation procedures that various units had hatched under the pressure of circumstances. This meant that it had to carry out the methodical experimentation that was not possible on the actual battlefield. It had to retain those procedures that proved their worth, and ensure they became commonplace. In August 1917, the decision was taken to publish a monthly artillery bulletin to disseminate the new ideas about technical and tactical matters.[33]

Another means of managing the new complexity of methods was planning. It existed in an embryonic form by 1915, but underwent extensive development in 1916 as a result of the influence of the artillery research centre. The centre codified and promoted the use of artillery plans that enabled the stages of the firing sequence to be controlled.

The artillery was the ultimate technical arm. Anything with an internal combustion engine fell within its remit. Hence the traffic-control units, the motorized machine-gun carriers, the tanks and even the aviation all came under its wing. In reality, the artillery was so vast that it was unable to retain the supervision of these branches, which were too much on the fringe compared with its 'noble' element, which consisted of the field artillery and now also the heavy artillery. Faced with a choice between the internal combustion engine and the service of the guns, the artillery opted to remain focused on its 'profession' and to let the peripheral subdivisions either gain their independence or be absorbed by other arms.

The separation was all the easier in that the personnel of these subdivisions had a whole range of origins and did not necessarily have an artillery background. The Assault Artillery, for example, was created on 1 October 1916 and was also known as the Special Artillery. It came under the Directorate of Artillery, partly because tanks were regarded as guns on caterpillar tracks, but primarily because Colonel Jean Estienne, the proponent of the Assault Artillery, was himself an artilleryman. But the tanks acted solely for the benefit of the infantrymen and in close cooperation with them. In fact, they even threatened the pre-eminence of the guns by becoming a substitute for the artillery preparation. The tank 'batteries' of 1917 were renamed 'companies' in 1918, and on 1 March 1919 the tanks were permanently attached to the infantry.

Similarly, from 1916 onwards the *groupes* of motorized machine-gun carriers were attached to the cavalry.[34] At that time, half of the airplanes were still devoted to working directly with the artillery, but the development of the fighter aviation saw the artillerymen's control over aeronautics disappear almost completely.

## Cavalry of the Skies

Aircraft were the eyes of the heavy artillery, and the development of the aviation was closely linked to that of the heavy artillery. Since the war involved the combat arms fighting for a strip of ground just a few hundred metres wide, it was tempting to exploit the airplanes' range in order to pass 'over the wall' and strike even further than the heavy guns. This was GHQ's new vision of how aircraft should be used. The man whose influence lay behind that vision was Major Edouard Barès. A fortnight after becoming head of the air service on 25 September 1914, he had the first aeronautics plan drawn up. The plan rationalized the organizational structure by reducing the number of different types of aircraft, and by turning the squadrons into specialized units: bomber squadrons at the level of GHQ, reconnaissance and fighter squadrons at army level, observation and artillery-spotting squadrons at army corps level, and cavalry squadrons. The number of squadrons reached sixty-five, half of which were for observation and artillery spotting. The plan considered all of the aviation's future missions:

> The aviation is not merely a tool of reconnaissance, as might have been assumed earlier. It has made itself, if not indispensable, then at least extremely useful for adjusting artillery fire. It has also shown that it is capable of acting as an offensive arm by dropping high-explosive projectiles, either in long-range missions or in cooperation with the other troops. Finally, it still has the duty to pursue and destroy the enemy airplanes.[35]

### The artillery's eyes

The training structure was re-established on 25 October 1914, with the reopening of the aviation schools at Pau in the south-west and Avord in central France. (The aviation schools had been closed at the start of the war.) Thereafter, the training structure expanded continuously. By March 1915, the aviation schools were starting to produce results and their output grew without a break until they were supplying the armies with 600 pilots every month. Similarly, the training centre at Vadenay in Champagne produced balloonists.[36] By 1916 there were also schools at the front, as well as a *groupe* of training divisions, training centres for fighters, bombers and artillery observation, and a depot school for technical personnel.[37] A battalion of hangar constructors was created, as well as an aeronautics command at army group level, with a park, ammunition columns, searchlight sections and units of labourers.[38]

Specialization therefore became official policy, and it enabled the various aviation branches to develop rapidly. Priority was given to the observation service, which the historian Major Jean Orthlieb has called the 'real aerial miracle of the war'. It had three main missions: gathering intelligence, adjusting artillery fire, and communicating with the infantry or commanders. (Only by installing wireless sets on board aircraft was the problem of adjusting artillery fire solved.) The growing importance of the observation aviation reflected that of the artillery itself, to which it was closely attached. The observation aviation always amounted to half the size of the aeronautics.[39] It was distributed between the army corps. Each corps had one squadron of airplanes (two squadrons from 1917), as well as a squadron of balloons. Each tractor-towed regiment of heavy artillery also had a squadron of its own. In 1918, squadrons even began to be assigned to divisions.

Aerial observation reached a peak of effectiveness during the Battle of the Somme in the second half of 1916. For example, when the 13th Infantry Division was attacking on the Somme, it constantly had a heavy-artillery squadron flying overhead to adjust counter-battery fire, and another a squadron to coordinate the divisional artillery for the immediate benefit of the attack units. Plentiful means of communication, ranging from wireless sets to flares and location panels, made genuine conversations possible between the ground and the air, with 'the airmen becoming the "guides" of the shells towards their targets.'[40] An infantry aviation was also set up: its low-flying aircraft kept track of the infantry's advance and the general progress of the action, monitored the enemy and reported any impending counter-attacks. But the development of this intelligence-gathering aviation then tailed off, as the growth of the fighter aviation monopolized the best men and equipment.

### Striking in depth

The concept of the airplane as a fighting machine appeared early on. But everyone thought of this fighting machine as primarily a bomber. It was also reckoned from an early stage that airplanes could be effective only if used in mass. On 27 September 1914, the first bomber *groupe* (GB1) was created at Malzéville near Nancy on the urging of Major Louis de Goÿs. It consisted of three squadrons of Voisin LA.S – a mediocre, 'pusher' machine with the propeller mounted at the rear. Another three bomber *groupes* were added between June and August 1915, along with two squadrons of Maurice Farman airplanes, including the pioneering squadron of 'the red devil', Captain Maurice Happe.

On 27 May 1915, GB1 launched its first major raid, eight months after it had been created. The raid targeted the factories at Ludwigshafen on the Rhine river, but was carried out with just eighteen Voisin aircraft and had no more than a psychological impact. From June onwards, a raid was organized roughly every ten days, against Zeppelin and weapon factories and railway marshalling yards, and this was done at the same time as the bomber airplanes were taking part in all the battles. Some of the first fighters were used to try and protect the slow and heavy bombers, but with disappointing results. The problem was that the aircraft had different characteristics, as became clear from the mixed *groupe* of fighters and bombers formed as an experiment in the Saint-Pol area in Artois in May 1915.

The Germans responded by positioning anti-aircraft batteries and armed airplanes near sensitive locations. Once the latter became effective, losses among the bombers rose quickly. The counter-measures that were thought up, such as flying in a V-shaped formation, as was done by Captain Happe's Squadron MF29, proved inadequate. Hence the four bomber *groupes* had to switch to bombing either by night or no deeper than the enemy's immediate rear, until aircraft could be developed with greater technical capabilities. The evolution of the bomber branch was practically brought to a halt by technical shortcomings, until the arrival in late 1917 of the Breguet XIV, which for several months remained fast enough to evade the German fighters.

### The return of knights
Official recognition of the fighter aviation came with the launch of an equipment programme in October 1914. The plan included the creation of the first squadrons to specialize in both reconnaissance and aerial combat. Some squadrons acted as research laboratories for fighter tactics. One example was MS3, the squadron of Second-Lieutenant Georges Guynemer and Antonin Brocard. Another was MS12 under Captain Raymond de Bernis.

MS12 had pre-war origins, but was reborn as a specialized fighter squadron in February 1915 on the initiative of Major Charles de Tricornot de Rose, a cavalryman and aviation pioneer (the number on his military pilot's licence was 1). Even before the war, de Rose had experimented with using a machine-gun mounted on an airplane. In order to win support for the concept of a fighter squadron, and to insert it into the tactical fabric, he emphasized its potential for destroying the enemy's means of observation. He had the support of his superior, General Louis Franchet d'Espèrey, the commander of the 5th Army. He also took advantage of the low cost involved in gathering together six Morane-Saulnier machines – the fastest and most manœuvrable airplane at that time – along with twelve pilots and observer-gunners. Nine of these men had come from the cavalry, and this was a deliberate choice on Major de Rose's part, for he saw close parallels between fighting on horseback and flying the first airplanes.

Yet there was no question of fighting aerial duels. Combat amounted simply to flying at high altitude, spotting an observation airplane, swooping down to take position some 10 metres behind it, and then shooting the crew members with a rifle.[41] The fighters' tally remained modest. Not until 1 April 1915 did MS12 gain its first victory, and by the end of that summer its total was just four. The fighters seemed condemned to escorting observation airplanes. Yet the cavalrymen of the skies did not find this mission congenial, and so they sought a remedy in the development of the weaponry carried on their aircraft.

Roland Garros had resumed his pre-war experiments. He managed to solve the problem of how to fly his airplane and at the same time use a forward-mounted machine-gun. By firing the machine-gun between his propeller blades, which had armour to deflect any bullets that hit them, he managed to shoot down an enemy airplane at the beginning of April 1915. This led to the single-seater aircraft, which was more manœuvrable than the two-seater, becoming the favoured tool of the fighter aviation. As a result of the invention of the armoured propeller, Garros was able to win fame for his success in the air, but his career came to an end on 18 April when he was forced to land behind enemy lines. The industrialist Anthony Fokker then produced for the Germans a mechanism that went a step further than Garros' device, by solving the problem of how to synchronize the fire of the machine-gun and the passage of the propeller blades. His synchronization gear may have been a rudimentary invention, but it had far-reaching consequences. The German airplane that was made incorporating this mechanism, the Fokker E.I, enjoyed a crushing superiority over its opponents, and enabled the German fighters to dominate the skies for almost a year in a period known as the 'Fokker scourge'. In France, a mechanism similar to Fokker's was designed by Sergeant-Mechanic Robert Alkan, but for some reason it was used only from the summer of 1916. Until then, another device was adopted instead. Proposed by Private-Mechanic Martin and Captain de Bernis, it enabled a Lewis Gun to be mounted above the upper wing of a Nieuport XI *Bébé* in order to fire over, rather than through, the propeller.

These technical developments signalled the start of successive generations of airplanes being supplanted one after the other. The introduction of new machines enabled each side in turn to acquire a decisive technological superiority for a certain time. But the technological superiority conferred by new aircraft became progressively smaller in duration and magnitude, owing to the expansion of the belligerents' industrial and technical infrastructures. Four periods can be detected:

- summer 1915 to spring 1916: German superiority with the Fokker E.I;
- spring to summer 1916: French superiority (Nieuport XI and XVII);
- autumn 1916 to summer 1917: German superiority with the Halberstadt and Albatros series of aircraft (the Albatros were fitted with twin machine-guns);
- summer 1917 onwards: the Allies once more gained the upper hand, and held it until spring 1918. A rapid succession of aircraft models came into service on each side (including the French Spad VII, XIII and XVII, Nieuport XVII and XXVIII, and various British fighters, against the Fokker D.I, D.VI, D.VII, D.VIII and triplane). In summer 1918, the Fokker D.VII gave the Germans a degree of superiority again for a few weeks before it was outclassed in its turn. Each side had to bring out a new type of machine every six months or risk being left behind.

Yet from autumn 1915, other factors were involved besides technical ones. At that time, the increased number of fighter aircraft made it possible to consider using them collectively. The Germans were the first to implement the notion of air superiority at a specific point of the front, namely the skies over Verdun in February 1916. Their domination of the air enabled them to deprive the French artillery of its main means of observation – namely balloons and artillery airplanes – and thus interrupt its firing sequence. The French needed to counter this threat and protect their reconnaissance airplanes, and so they were obliged to accept an air battle, despite a widespread reluctance to do so. The result was the specially-created *Groupement* de Rose, the first French fighter *groupement*. The same innovation was adopted later that year for the Battle of the Somme with the creation of *Groupement* Cachy, consisting of eight Spad squadrons. *Groupement* Cachy secured mastery of the skies during July and August.

The concept of the fighter *groupe* was then officially endorsed in an instruction dated 10 October 1916. But the tactic tipped into excess and became the 'all-out air offensive'. A 'cavalier' and 'particularist' inclination within the aviation reached its apogee with Major Paul du Peuty, who briefly served as the head of the aeronautics under Nivelle. In his order of the day of 15 April 1917, du Peuty gave a straightforward mission to the fighter *groupes:* 'the destruction of the Boche aviation'. This was to be achieved by seeking out the opposing aircraft over the German side of the front: 'from now on, no airplane of the fighter *groupes* should be encountered inside the French lines'.[42] The protection of the observation aircraft – a less noble mission – had become 'indirect' protection.

The result of this approach was similar to what happened in 1914 when the French cavalry sought out a confrontation with the German cavalry and ended up simply bustling around without achieving anything. During the Aisne offensive in April-May 1917, the air battle was a bitter failure. The German fighter aviation not only remained intact, but also inflicted substantial losses on the French observers, who could no longer count on close protection.

*

The Italian intellectual, Antonio Gramsci, stated that a 'crisis lies precisely in the fact that the old is dying and the new can not be born.' According to his definition, it was the combat arms (the cavalry and infantry) that were the first to go through a crisis when confronted by trench warfare. The cavalry, which was brought to a halt by even the most basic barbed-wire entanglement, was out of play as early as 1914. A year later, the infantry recognized that it would remain powerless until it received its new equipment. Thus the artillery, a combat-support arm, seemed dominant. With its long-range fire adjusted by aircraft using the wireless, it pushed the war into the third dimension. Yet in 1917, the artillery's sheer abundance and rapid growth ended up generating difficulties of command and control. The same period of the war also saw the dashing of the hopes that had been placed in two new branches: the fighter aviation and the Assault Artillery. Every arm was therefore in crisis following the failure of the Nivelle offensive.

*Chapter 9*

# In the Death Zone

Discussing tactics requires us to descend yet another echelon, as far as 'the coalface'. Down here, at the very lowest echelon, we must see how the men – and the infantrymen in particular – wrestled with the life-or-death problems that confronted them.

In the night of 5 April 1918, Corporal Georges Gaudy and his squad were in Picardy, waiting to assault the Château du Mont-Renaud:

> Can it be that we'll be over there in just a few minutes? We might even be lying dead in the middle of the courtyard.
>
> It's 4.56 am.
>
> 'Are you ready, pals?'
>
> They don't reply. They're holding their rifles and choosing the spot where they'll find it easiest to climb out of the trench. So long as everything goes well, so long as the various *groupes* entrusted with the assault all go over the top at the set time! Three minutes left. I find they're really dragging by now. I wish I had already set off. We don't talk any more. We continue to wait. A few more seconds until the fire is unleashed. From the direction of Carlepont come the deep voices of some heavy guns. I listen to them, with one knee resting on the parapet. ...
>
> Oh! Our trench is lit up to the right. Intense small-arms fire rolls all around us. Rifle-grenades rain down on the outbuildings, the garden wall, everywhere. Amid the flashes of their explosions, the entire house rises up, more sinister than ever. Two automatic-rifles riddle the windows and door with bullets, producing a shower of sparks. This series of little blasts ceases abruptly. All of us lift our heads at the same time. The green star [a flare to signal the start of the assault] has just burst open in the sky.[1]

Corporal Gaudy and his squad then entered the bubble of violence that had just sprung into being. It was a strange world governed by its own laws. It was the death zone. Men who entered and fought inside it were transformed by the fear of death. When they left, they awoke from a nightmare.

## Surviving in a Nightmare
### *A tortured landscape*
When an infantryman entered the death zone, he knew for a start that he would be moving about in a surreal and sinister landscape. A German soldier, Lieutenant Ernst Jünger, wrote of a:

burnt-out wasteland, where the bombardment has stamped the landscape level ... and where the shell explosions spurt up in tall, dense sprays like geysers in one of the volcanic zones of Iceland ... a blackened and torn-up earth from which the clammy gas fumes of our shells are still rising. ... At first glance, all this seems as strange and weird as a dreamlike landscape, which, with its details and improbabilities, seizes the senses in a flash, holding them spellbound and blotting them out at the same time.[2]

A French infantryman, Jean Galtier-Boissière, described a village that had vanished in this no man's land:

It's a vision of an infernal nightmare, the gloomy setting of some fantastic tale by Edgar Poe. These aren't ruins, for there are no longer any houses, walls, streets or even shapes. Everything has been pulverized and levelled by the pestle. [The village of] Souchez is no more than a revolting pulp of wood, rubble and bones, crushed and kneaded into the mud.[3]

The actual combat zone had clearly defined limits. In general, when an assault took place, an infantryman in the front line remained within a space just a few hundred metres in extent, between two belts of entrenchments that combined barbed-wire entanglements, advanced posts, machine-gun nests and two or three trenches with connecting links. When fighting was in progress, this zone was covered by a vault of artillery projectiles. Jünger described the 'complex, venomous hissings from the trajectories that are weaving a fine mesh closely over our heads, forming a burning surf that surrounds us like Greek Fire, as if it's a single, unbroken element'.[4]

From 1916, artillery barrages made the battlefield even more compartmentalized. This was particularly true of the rolling barrage, whose dust and explosions formed a sort of impenetrable wall in front of the infantrymen as they made their way forward. By hiding the attackers, the rolling barrage filled the defenders with dread. The attackers themselves were spellbound, and felt drawn along by this wall of shells that lifted 100 metres every two minutes.

The smoke- and dust-filled landscape was regularly punctuated with flares of various colours, which gave a surreal appearance to the overall scene.[5] The air itself was filled with the stench from corpses, mixed with poisonous gases, the exhaust fumes of tanks, smoke from various explosives and soil thrown up by the shelling.

An experienced infantryman knew that he would not actually encounter many enemies in this dreamlike world. The defenders were crouched, or even curled up, in holes to withstand the artillery fire. As for the attackers, they bounded from shell-hole to shell-hole, hunched forward with heads down, ready to fling themselves to the ground at a moment's notice. Both sides could see what was happening only from ground level and through the dust. Furthermore, fear tended to result in actions being fought at long range, with automatic weapons playing the leading role. This meant that the landscape of the death zone appeared empty. An officer described his arrival at Verdun in 1916:

The impression is one of an immense desert. ... Where are they? Where are our men? Nothing. We can see nothing that is alive. Could they all have been killed, swept away by the hurricane that has been raging around them for four months? ... In this dead and barren region, the only signs of life come from the guns.[6]

Sergeant Charles-Maurice Chenu, who was preparing to set off for an attack, noted:

The enemy? As usual, we won't be able to see him. It will just be shells and bullets. The most we'll see of the enemy will be silhouettes in the distance, rising and merging into the ground.[7]

On the other hand, an infantryman knew he was almost bound to encounter terrible sights. He overcame the shock of seeing dead or badly wounded men for the first time by suppressing his sensitivity in the heat of the action. Later, he became used to such scenes. During an attack in 1918, Jünger, who was a battle-hardened soldier, found a corpse in his way: 'I step over the body, and by the time I've taken another three paces, the incident has already slipped from my mind.'[8]

Yet even veterans found themselves upset by particularly dreadful sights. Jünger, during the same offensive as he described above, saw his company struck by a large-calibre shell:

From my little niche – from this alcove [of an old shell-hole] – I look down on the gaping crater as if on a gruesome amphitheatre. What I see pierces my heart like a blade of ice. At a stroke it renders me completely helpless and paralysed, as if it's a garish apparition in a nightmare. ... My heart wants to ward off this image, and yet registers it in every detail.[9]

Jünger fled.

Horrific sights were not as common as might be thought from reading certain books. Yet men often found old, suppressed memories resurfacing in their minds, especially if they were waiting for an action to begin. They remembered hearing the screams of suffocating soldiers, or seeing corpses in grotesque postures or entire units mown down.

### The infernal orchestra

Even if the battlefield often seemed empty, it was noisy. These noises spanned the range from shell explosions to wounded men's screams, and included the varied sounds of bullets and the din of engines and caterpillar tracks. A combatant had to rely mostly on his ears to detect any threats, for he saw few enemies and practically never caught sight of them actually firing shots. With time, he learned to pick out the different noises from the pandemonium.

The most frequent sounds came from bullets fired by rifles and, even more so, by machine-guns. They were much more complex sounds than they seemed. Since a bullet initially travelled faster than the speed of sound, it caused a shock wave in the air. The whip-like crack produced by this shock wave was distinct from both the report of the shot being fired and the hissing as the projectile whizzed along its trajectory. This crack was the loudest sound, and it was what filled most of the backdrop to infantry combat. During the preparation for a raid in 1918, Lieutenant-Colonel Jean Armengaud was supported by indirect fire from a *groupement* of eighty-four machine-guns, and found that the cracks from the bullets passing over his head made such a noise that he could no longer hear the artillery barrages.[10]

These supersonic bangs also had a psychological impact, for the sound oppressed the soldiers by being projected down on them from above. Ignorance of this phenomenon could have serious consequences. The crack, which was heard first, might be confused with the report of the shot being fired. Inexperienced soldiers then located the enemy in the wrong direction and nearer than he actually was. Some units had even been known to panic, under the impression that they were under attack from the rear. Such confusions gave rise to many myths, including twin-shot rifles, machine-guns established in trees and above all explosive bullets. An officer in the brigade of *Fusiliers-marins* explained how difficult it was to make his men understand what was really happening:

> They fear the crack from the Mach wave. I have never managed to get them to grasp this phenomenon. Instead, they cling to a simplistic explanation. If the unpleasant crack occurs near trees or houses, it comes from the bullet hitting an obstacle, a tree or a wall. If it happens in the air ... there can be no further doubt that it is an explosive bullet.[11]

Ascertaining the origin of machine-gun fire was even more difficult, since the succession of cracks completely drowned the faint reports of the shots being fired. If the din of battle permitted, a trained ear might sometimes detect the very faint reports of the last bullets to be fired. They alone indicated the true direction of the weapon. Machine-guns usually fired at their target from an angle, so the most common mistake of a soldier who was under fire was to think the machine-gun was in front of him, in line with the cracks. A machine-gun, with its regular and rhythmical clatter, made more of an impression than rifle bullets, which were just the 'humming of insects'. The machine-gun seemed to be an insensitive mechanism, 'like an automatic reaper of human lives, ideal for sowing death with extreme accuracy'.[12]

The crack might be followed by a hissing. The hissing was less of a surprise, but produced an unpleasant sensation. Men instinctively ducked when they heard it – they 'bowed' – but did so pointlessly since the bullet had already passed far beyond them. Old soldiers learned not to 'bow', but knew that this hissing, which was audible only within a short radius of the bullet, was a sure sign that they were being shot at. It was also useful to know that the hissing could be heard only beyond a certain range, which in the case of the German Spitzer bullet was 800 metres.

Nor must we forget the ricochets and echoes that occurred, especially in an urban environment or inside woods. The sound of the crack bouncing off walls or trees threw the men off balance even more. A far more gruesome sound was caused when bodies were struck. Bullets and shell splinters produced quite a dull thud, but the sound might become high-pitched if they were deflected by a bone.

From 1916, a footsoldier also had to get used to hearing infantry-support guns and, above all, grenades. The infantry-support guns were direct-fire weapons that discharged small shells – high explosive or armour-piercing – with a high muzzle velocity. Grenades were thrown by hand, or else launched from a rifle or light mortar. They gave little warning, for they often arrived silently or (if launched from a mortar) were preceded by a faint noise. To avoid them, men had to watch the sky constantly, and as a general rule they were thereby able to take cover in time. So-called offensive grenades, which had just a shock effect, made barely any impression on hardened soldiers, who quickly recognized them from the dry sound they made when they burst and from the absence of hissing fragments.

The sound environment was filled with shells as well as bullets. Shells produced the same phenomena as bullets, but more loudly, and they also exploded when they arrived. An infantryman did not always hear the report when they were fired, for the guns were distant and sheltered by the terrain. The crack of a sonic boom occurred only if the muzzle velocity of the shell was greater than the speed of sound. The crack was fairly far away from the infantry, and its loudness was lessened by distance. The most noticeable sounds were therefore the hissing of the shell and its explosion. The hissing that warned of the shell's arrival was much louder than the hissing of a bullet:

> While the shell is in flight, before it bursts, it squeaks or hurls into the air a sort of long, shrill scream. Depending on whether the shell has a time-fuse or bursts on impact, depending also on its calibre, its speed and the flatness of its trajectory, its din varies from the wail of a siren to the metallic rattle of a speeding train. All the soldiers have learned to distinguish each calibre of shell, from the German 77mm to the 420mm, just from the rumbling, caterwauling or other singular sound that sets it apart.
>
> Yet the sound of the shell burst – the thunder of the explosion – is what produces an intense response from those who are listening. The shaking of the ground, shock waves passing through the air, and violent suctions have psychological effects. These are added to the countless auditory reactions produced at the same instant by the shell splinters and by the noise of earth and stones thrown into the air or falling back to the ground. Concentrated gusts of artillery fire multiply these disquieting effects into a sensation of catastrophe, as if a wall of iron is collapsing.[13]

The effects of fear were heightened by the unexpected crash of the explosion and by respiratory or circulatory problems caused by the blast.

Three types of shell existed:

- shrapnel shells: their explosion was not as powerful as that of high-explosive shells, and their radius of effect was more restricted. Although much used at the start of the war, they soon fell out of favour because of their ineffectiveness unless set to burst at exactly the right height;
- high-explosive shells with a time fuse: they exploded very loudly, with all the sound energy being passed into the air. Calculating the right time-length for the fuse was difficult;
- high-explosive shells with a percussion fuse: these were the most effective because of the splinters they sent flying through the air, and the powerful moral effect produced simultaneously on the eyes (geysers of earth, plumes

of smoke and dust), the ears (crash of the explosions) and the nervous system (shaken by the blast and the ground tremors). These were the most frequently used shells. They were also the only ones that could cause major physical damage to entrenchments, but they were more or less neutralized when they buried themselves into the ground before exploding. Furthermore, their spray of splinters contained many dead angles.

Large-calibre shells could be recognized by the 'soft hissing' of their fairly slow flight. These 'heavies' could often be seen in the air near their point of impact, falling to the ground like large stones. Men in dugouts may not have had to worry about the splinters or blast effect of the shells, but they took the full force of the shaking of the ground. Men inside concrete dugouts found their nerves acutely strained by the continuous hammering of the concrete slab by large-calibre shells, which they could not hear coming. The German garrison abandoned Fort Douaumont on 23 October 1916, after being terrorized by 400mm shells landing every ten minutes.

For an infantryman in the trenches, shells were the main threat. He was petrified by the mutilations inflicted by the explosions, and petrified also by the sense of powerlessness he felt when being shelled:

Under the shower of iron and fire, we feel just as impotent as in the presence of a dreadful natural disaster. What use are our grenades and our little rifles against this avalanche of earth and machine-gun bullets? What use is our courage? Does a man defend himself against an earthquake that is about to swallow him up? Does he fire rifle-shots against a volcano spewing out burning lava?[14]

Jean Galtier-Boissière described his baptism of fire:

Suddenly, shrill hisses ending in furious sniggers make us dive in terror face down against the earth. The *rafale* [an abrupt, violent gust of fire] has just burst above us. ... The men, on their knees, hunched, covering their heads with their knapsacks, arching their backs, knit themselves together. ... From under the cover of my knapsack, I cast a glance at my neighbours. Breathing heavily, they are racked with nervous trembling. Their mouths are contorted into hideous grimaces, and all of them have chattering teeth. Their faces, deformed by terror, remind me of the grotesque gargoyles on Notre-Dame cathedral. Lying in this bizarre posture, with lowered heads and arms crossed over their chests, they look like tortured victims offering the nape of their necks to the executioner's axe. ... It is terrible to await death like this. How long will the torture last? Why do we not move? Are we going to remain motionless there, and get ourselves massacred for no purpose at all?[15]

An exploding shell produced not just splinters, but also a 'blast'. This was actually an aerial wave, condensed in front where the air was compressed, and expanded behind where it was thinned out. The speed of propagation of this wave was greater than the speed of sound. Blast caused multiple shocks, particularly to the brain – the effects included deafness, dumbness, anaesthesia, trembling and paralysis – and could damage internal organs without leaving visible wounds on the outside of the body. If the blast was contained, its effects were intensified. Whereas some men might escape unhurt when whisked off the ground, examples were noted of machine-gunners being found dead at their weapon, killed by a blast effect coming directly down on them from above, with no room to allow the energy to be transformed into movement.

The projectiles that made the greatest impression were the enormous ones fired by the trench-mortars:

> A mortar bomb, which was swinging through the air, lands some metres away with a mighty explosion. We feel our lungs bursting, our heads emptying and the 'blow to the back of the neck' that is typical of the blast. Red, green and yellow lights pass before our eyes.[16]

When the bombardment continued for several hours, or even days, it had dreadful effects on the nervous system. One combatant, Jacques d'Arnoux, described:

> an inordinately long time [during which] we listen to the masses of iron falling on our trench. Shells that burst in the air or on impact, 105mm shells, 150mm, 210mm, shells of every calibre. Amidst this storm of falling projectiles, we immediately detect the one that is intent on burying us. As soon as our ears make out its dismal hooting, we look at each other in fear. Completely tensed, we are all huddled up, and we bend under the pressure of the blast. Our helmets collide, and we sway like drunkards.[17]

Yet losses were often lower than might be assumed from seeing these terrible bouts of drumfire, these 'hurricanes of fire'. It took an estimated 1,400 shells to kill just one man during the Great War.[18] Even so, artillery inflicted almost three-quarters of the losses.

'Friendly fire' was even worse to bear. It was hardly a negligible phenomenon. General Alexandre Percin estimated that the French artillery killed as many as 75,000 *poilus* by mistake. There was more acceptance of the risk of friendly fire during offensives, for attacking infantry stuck close behind the rolling barrage in order to give enemy machine-gunners less time to recover their wits after the shelling had lengthened.

In 1918, infantrymen also had to contend increasingly with the threat from the air. Bombs dropped from aircraft may have been inaccurate, but they were daunting because of their 'rustling murmur' that grew suddenly louder, the crash of their explosion and the sense that nothing could protect you from this sword of Damocles constantly hanging overhead. When an airplane attacked at low altitude with machine-gun fire, this 'aerial meteor diving at you with a great roar from the engine and the hammering cracks of the bullets'[19] had a great moral effect, but the bullets were scattered and the moral effect ended as soon as the attacking airplane climbed again.

Soldiers found themselves endangered by more than just projectiles. An artillery shelling, especially in 1918, might include mustard-gas shells – 'this gas with a bland, inoffensive smell, mustard gas that burns the eyes and lungs, mustard gas that kills after inflicting agonizing pain'. This threat terrified the *poilus*, who:

put on their snout [gas mask], pulling the straps so tight as to cause bruises, and running a finger all round the edge to check it is a close fit. ... They focus their whole attention on the click-clack of the valve, and to force it to work they breathe deeply, with a tightness in their chest.[20]

This was easier said than done if a soldier was breathless from fear or physical exertion, as was often the case. Wearing protective equipment not only increased his sense of isolation, but also undermined his self-confidence by reducing his ability to deal with threats.

Danger could also come from below, in the form of mines, saps and traps of every sort. Furthermore, from June 1918 in particular, the 'big clashes' saw tanks crossing the battlefield, crushing obstacles and moving forward with a din from their engine and caterpillar tracks, scornful of any fire from opposing infantrymen.

During major engagements, the multiplicity of sounds that dominated the battlefield acted as an anaesthetic, making men numb to the numerous dangers they faced. According to Lieutenant-Colonel Armengaud:

This continuous thunder drowns the hissing, softens the cracks and explosions, and makes it difficult to pick out the projectile that poses a threat from amidst all the others. In an attack with a full orchestra, men barely 'bow' at all to bullets or shell splinters, nor do they fling themselves to the ground under the shells that are raining down around them. If they march boldly towards the objective, one reason why they do so is that they are temporarily deafened.[21]

No one could enter an environment like this without feeling intense fear. The writer Jean Norton Cru, who was a *poilu* for two years, argued:

Every soldier without exception is afraid. The vast majority demonstrate an admirable courage by doing what has to be done despite their fear. We are afraid because we are men, and fear is what has kept all of us survivors alive. Without fear, we would not have lasted twenty-four hours in the front line. We would have committed so many rash blunders through carelessness that we would soon have caught the bullet that lies in wait for a reckless man.[22]

The courage needed to overcome this fear had several aspects.

## Courage
### The myth of hand-to-hand, bayonet fighting
Even today, the bayonet charge is still often associated with the Great War. Yet the first clashes of August 1914 were enough for combatants such as Captain Charles Delvert to realize that it was a myth:

So wrong were our notions of combat at that time that we all thought we would soon be fencing with sabres against the German bayonets. Most men had had their blades sharpened. I had imitated them. ... The Battle of Ethe on 22 August cured us once and for all of any thought of bothering about either the sabre or the bayonet.[23]

The reality was that hand-to-hand combat was rare. In March 1918, a British infantry officer, Second-Lieutenant H. Jones, shot some Germans with his revolver: 'That was the only occasion on which I shot any Germans in two-and-a-half years of front-line soldiering.'[24] Lieutenant Erwin Rommel, in two years of war as either a platoon or a company commander, experienced forty-eight actions of greater or lesser importance:

- twenty-four ended in one side withdrawing before contact was made;
- six ended with troops surrendering at the moment their position was overrun;
- eighteen degenerated into indecisive exchanges of fire.

Rommel recounted only one case of actual physical contact between two opponents: during a night-time raid, a French soldier leaped at the throat of a German sergeant and was shot with a revolver.[25] Even though Rommel described himself as 'an enthusiastic bayonet fighter', he recorded just one occasion on which he used the bayonet. It happened when he came upon several Frenchmen inside a wood. Since the magazine of his rifle ran out of ammunition, he made a bayonet charge, only to be shot and wounded almost immediately.[26]

Sergeant Chenu reckoned:

Nobody wants any more of the *déjeuner à la fourchette* (the bayonet). [A *déjeuner à la fourchette* is a 'luncheon' eaten with a fork, as distinct from a breakfast of soups or other liquids]. This luncheon is just a basic, set menu, and is not very satisfying. The bullet, machine-gun and grenade have triumphed over the bayonet, which is little more than a symbol of attack. Projectiles have killed off cold steel.[27]

Courage, in this industrial war, was more about stoicism than bravery. In Jean Norton Cru's view:

There was no fighting [between small units], except in very exceptional cases. Almost invariably, one side struck the blows and the other could do nothing but arch his back and take them. ... The soldiers were either torturers or victims, hunters or prey, and in the infantry it seemed that for most of the time we played the role of victim, prey and target.[28] ... Every type of bayonet assault ultimately boiled down to two scenarios. The assault failed, and the wave collapsed a good distance from its objective under the crossfire of machine-guns. ... [Or else] the assault succeeded, and the wave instantly overran the enemy position, where the enemy surrendered if he had not had enough time to withdraw. If any pockets of resistance appeared, it was definitely not the bayonet that might help to reduce them.[29]

Lieutenant Pierre Chaine thought that 'courage today amounts to not flinching in the face of a death that can be neither seen nor avoided.'[30]

A modern infantryman, argued Major Charles Coste, felt that he was pitting himself against things rather than men:

> Hence his personal skill no longer guaranteed survival. His own protection had to be entrusted to others, since for most of the time he was powerless to answer the shots he received. As a result, he seemed to be struggling with himself even more than with the enemy. In order to conquer, he first had to conquer himself.[31]

Fear and courage varied greatly between individuals and the phases of the action.

### Awaiting the assault

No greater test existed in an attack than the wait beforehand in the trench. The cruelty of this wait lay in the soldier's inability to do anything even though his nervous tension was practically at its height. He had to suppress his fear in silence and inaction, even as his imagination ran riot. In Galtier-Boissière's opinion:

> Before going into action, you are like a gentleman in the dentist's waiting room, trembling as you hear the screams of the patient ahead of you. Fortunately, once you are actually in the storm, you no longer have time to think of anything.[32]

Chenu wrote of 'the impatience that gnaws away at a soldier's guts, the rage that makes him bitter about what is stopping him, the frenzied need to move and do something, the horror of finding death without being able to budge or fight against it.'[33] Tics and gesticulations increased among the men in the assault trench, as a way of alleviating their fear. Some units were unable to refrain from firing – an 'emotional safety valve' – or even from going over the top earlier than planned. As the hour of the attack approached:

> A hubbub of calls, not so much heard as surmised, rises from the packed throngs of men … The second hand [on a watch], this tiniest slither of steel within a whole sea of steel, makes its final lap. We go up the steps to emerge, and for as far as our eyes can penetrate the dense fog, we see grey masses with weapons carrying out the same movement as ourselves.[34]

### The diverse reactions of the troops

Going over the top came as a relief for an infantryman. 'His existence feels as if it has been freed from any apprehension and fear. He no longer has time to think of danger.'[35]

As soon as an action began, two different 'survival reactions' appeared amongst the troops. Some men were stimulated: in the face of danger their bodies drew on every reserve they had. Others were inhibited: they were stopped by fear as they came closer to danger. Those who did give way to their fear remained frozen inside the trenches, or else they fled – and in some cases they got themselves killed as a result of fleeing towards the enemy. But the vast majority did not give way to fear. These men were divided into two unequal and fluctuating groups:

'immortals' and 'followers'. The 'immortals', paradoxically enough, were in a state of euphoria that verged on recklessness. Adrenaline temporarily boosted their strength. Their senses were sharpened and focused on the direction of danger. The perilous nature of the situation was ignored. Lieutenant Rommel described some soldiers in September 1914 who 'were so glad to have a Frenchman in their sights that they fired standing. ... Our own zeal was responsible for the large gaps in our own ranks. This morning's fight was more expensive than the [earlier] night attack.'[36]

Ernst Jünger reckoned that 'battle is like an opiate'.[37] Corporal Gaudy, near Mont-Renaud in 1918, was in the same state:

During the minute I have taken to empty the magazine of my Lebel rifle, I could not have been more supremely in control of myself. In those moments you are never afraid. You almost offer your forehead to the bullet that is going to kill you. I have seen, with absolute indifference, a soldier fall near me with his eye punctured and a hole through his head.[38]

The 'followers' were more numerous than the 'immortals'. They took action only when ordered to do so, or when given an example. Fear had undermined not only their initiative, but also their ability to think and act. 'Followers' were subjected to two major, contradictory forces: a strong inhibition that restricted their ability to think, and an intense need to do something. This meant they would imitate the first example of action they happened to see.

It was the 'immortals' who led the action. They were the aces and victory-grabbers that Major Louis Bouchacourt mentioned.[39] Jünger reckoned that 'any success can be traced back to the actions of enterprising individuals. The mass of those who follow just supply the shock and firepower.'[40]

Captain Rimbault wrote:

You instinctively turn to them for reassurance when your body quails in sticky situations. Regardless of whether they hold positions of command or are just private soldiers, at the right moment you can always count on finding them where they are needed and as they are needed. Those are the men who win battles.

The 'immortals' were therefore a spearhead, and the officer and NCO cadres naturally had a key role within this spearhead. An officer fell all the more easily into the 'immortals' category owing to the strength of his cultural imagination – which included such components as honour, loyalty and traditions – and also owing to 'the influence of the notion that he has a role to play, a professional duty to fulfil, an example to set'.[41] The thought of having to persuade others led him into autosuggestion. He benefitted from the docility of the men, who felt in a confused way that their personal safety was bound up with the safety of the unit, and who were released from the effort of having to think. 'One of the good fortunes of the soldier is that he just has to follow a lead. He relies on his leader, who does the thinking for him.'[42] Lieutenant

Maurice Genevoix described how, on 24 September 1914, he organized the withdrawal of his *section:*

> Every command can be clearly heard. That makes a *section* docile and quick on the uptake, a fine, fighting *section.* My pulse is strong and regular. For the moment I am sure of myself, calm and cheerful.[43]

But let us set aside the élite 'immortals'. Most of the men – even if they were good soldiers – were merely 'carried along':

> A bayonet charge is a band of frightened men who dash forward with their eyes closed and their rifles clutched to their chests. This lasts for as long as it lasts, until a volley makes them duck to the ground, or a shell disperses them, or until the enemy has been reached. Real hand-to-hand fighting is extremely rare. Of the two sides, the one that is less sure of its strength either surrenders or flees seconds before impact. Soldiers have been given trench knives, and are still given them. The only use they have ever made of them is to cut their meat or sharpen a pencil. Our rustic men will never think of stabbing with that implement. So, no bayonet, no knife! Surely the men use at least their rifles? No, almost not at all ...[44]

Yet these 'followers' were not useless. Even if in many cases their direct action did not amount to much, they played a vital, psychological role. What a combatant could see was restricted and was focused on his own situation. He had difficulty knowing what his neighbours were really doing, but was reassured or stimulated simply by knowing they were nearby. The burden of fear tended to make the troops close up – without being aware they were doing so – in order to suppress the anxiety they individually felt. The closer they were to the objective, the more they tended to close up. Attackers were completely consumed by the sense of being a powerful being, an unwavering mass, an invulnerable force. Therefore a soldier always did the same as his comrades, namely fire, advance and close with the enemy:

> A man is afraid in case he ceases to remain this person embodied in the mass that is being carried along by collective action. ... He turns his head to the right and to the left, to check the alignment of the troops and reassure himself that he is not on his own. He wants to be bound to his neighbours, and they likewise bind themselves to him by a sort of reciprocal magnetic attraction.[45]

Experienced soldiers were less prone to close up, for they knew the drawbacks of offering a large target and – even more importantly – they trusted their comrades enough for the bond between them to be more distant. In actions within woods, in towns or at night, where it was possible to see only a short distance, a combatant was tormented by fear of being outflanked or cut off. The same gregariousness was also evident between units. Troops liked to be flanked and supported on all sides. Just as an individual felt strong only because of the body of men around him – because of his own *groupe* that would base its opinion of him on how he acted – the *groupe* itself felt powerful only because of the endeavours of the units that were either alongside it or in support.

Although soldiers reacted to combat in different ways, these psychological divisions might fluctuate with time:

> You are not brave or cowardly by definition. You are not born into one of these classes, unable to leave it. Many subtle distinctions exist between individuals, and also between different moments in the same person ... You are not constantly in the same state. You oscillate from one extremity to the other fairly easily and often very quickly. ... People behind the lines have made enough stupid remarks about fear for them to need a reminder that the dauntless *poilu* is a myth.[46]

Simple 'followers' might turn into lions if they were affected by a sort of combat intoxication. Jünger recalled a rifleman who, 'seized with wild eagerness at our advance, bounded on to a barricade right in the middle of the action. He fired as he stood in the open, and was immediately thrown back, riddled with bullets, into the bottom of the trench. Instead of learning a lesson from this, I myself repeated the same idiocy a few minutes later, but escaped lightly with just a graze on my head.'[47]

Corporal Gaudy personally experienced a similar intoxication:

> I have become frenzied. I am drunk with victory. I scream, I shout unrepeatable things and I fire the rifles that Lhoumeau hands to me. Filled with elation, we stand up on the parapet. Suddenly, Barinet gives a shout and starts shaking with gusts of laughter. He holds out his arm and shows us a hole that a bullet has just made in his helmet.[48]

Soldiers rarely saw the enemy nearby, but when they did, it could have the same elating effect:

> The defenders have to take the consequences if they continue to fire bullets into an attacking force until the two of them are just five paces apart. A man who sees red can not suddenly overrule his emotions as he closes with his foe. He is driven to kill, not take prisoners ... Only after blood has flowed do the mists befogging his brain dissipate and he then looks around him as if waking from the bondage of a dream.[49]

At the end of July 1918, elements of the 52nd Infantry Regiment hurled lumps of chalk after running out of grenades whilst fighting the Germans at Mont Sans-Nom in Champagne.

### The theatre of the mind
Paradoxically, even though each combatant tried to blend in with the *groupe* as a whole, his world remained confined to just a short radius around him. During one attack, Chenu, who was serving as a liaison agent, thought that:

> the battlefield had shrunk. The three of us, the captain, the bugler and myself, saw ourselves on a sort of mound. I had the impression that the earth was a tiny sphere, too short to allow my body to lie down flat on it, and that my head was jutting out beyond the edge and hanging over a void. The regiment had vanished.

There was no longer anything in the real world except this islet, this ball that emerged with its three men, its three castaways.[50]

This isolation was the result of the compartmentalization of the battlefield, dissected as it was by the trenches and shell-holes and shrouded by the dust that was kicked up. It was also the result of the din that in many cases prevented soldiers from hearing anything more than a few metres away. It was also explained by an unconscious refusal of men to see dangers that they could do nothing to ward off. In this reduction of the field of awareness, their minds focused on a single idea or a single concrete image, namely their leader, their flag or the objective that they had to reach:

We were advancing straight ahead, timidly and without any shouts. We would have been afraid of letting all our courage escape if we had so much as opened our mouth, for we were holding on to that courage with clenched teeth. Body and mind alike were striving towards a single aim: reach the wood.[51]

This focusing on a single, guiding idea explains how troops who were fighting bravely might suddenly crack when something unexpected happened. A unit advancing victoriously into the enemy positions could offer only weak resistance to a counter-attack, for mentally it was unprepared to fight a defensive action. Captain Paul-Henri Maisonneuve concluded: 'The most that the ordinary, front-line combatant can be expected to do is carry out a single concept: go forward, follow a leader, fire without stopping, carry out a straightforward order.'[52]

A soldier had another automatic, psychological defence, besides a narrowing of the scope of his awareness. He became temporarily insensitive to the horror:

Your mind is shielded from the horror, in the way your body is from infection. Endure – you could do nothing else – but don't react, don't think. Don't let sensation develop into images, don't let it awaken emotions. Bottle it up, so to speak, within yourself. Drop it like a stone.[53]

This insensitivity should not be confused with selfishness. Altruistic behaviour was common in situations of extreme danger, and might even go as far as self-sacrifice. Nor was this insensitivity a 'hardness of heart, since the loss of comrades, of close friends, is painfully felt on the day after an attack. Even at the front, their loss is the toughest test of war, all things considered. But when you are under fire, you have little time for emotions.'[54]

During these harrowing hours, a combatant thought of his family only at the rare intervals when there was a lull. He lived wholly in the present moment and within the narrow confines of his *groupe*. At times of turmoil, his brain no longer worked 'normally'. He acted as though he was having hallucinations or a nightmare:

Our senses are already starting to grow confused from the strain of the stimuli placed on them. It has already become impossible for anyone to scrutinize what he feels, thinks or does. It's as if an outside will is intervening between us and our actions. ... We are all drunk despite having had nothing to drink. We are all living in another, fabulous world. All the usual laws seem to have been suspended. We find ourselves deep within a feverish dream of an extreme reality, in another sphere of humanity and even in another sphere of nature. Clusters of ghost-like trajectories cut through the air. Blasts from explosions shake the atmosphere, making solid things tremble and dance like the flickering images of a silent film ... I have lost the ability to be astonished. I perceive things as if they are dreamlike.

A soldier who sensed his life was at stake was prompted by inner exhortations – like demonic shouts or flashing, red alarm signals – to exploit every possibility of time and space.[55]

Such conditions distorted a man's assessment of what was happening around him: 'Nobody retains his sanity. Nobody is capable of thinking any more. Every act is decided by another mind, decided from the outside.'[56]

Reports were often exaggerated, and orders sometimes incoherent. Nobody managed to keep track of time. When Jünger was wounded by a ricochet, he remained in shock for a time that seemed to him to drag on forever, 'and after this interminable pause that has lasted for barely a few seconds in terms of clock time, I turn back towards the trench'. Some hours later, he noticed that 'one man has attached himself to us and yet we do know how long he has been there'.[57] A little later, Jünger was injured more seriously, but being awash with endorphins, he experienced his wound as a dream:

I cease to take any part in the killing that is going on around me. I notice how my thoughts become blurred, until I am left with just a single, cheerful notion: 'So long as this is as bad as it gets! This does not hurt at all!' ... It's strange how at such moments your own body seems to be a foreign object. It's as if you leave yourself, you leave with your innermost life force and feel the desire to turn away from yourself as if from a picture that lacks any meaning.[58]

### From the defenders' perspective
The psychological situation of the defenders differed somewhat from that of the attackers. Attackers benefitted from their sense of having greater freedom and a choice of means, and possibly also surprise. As the defending side was well aware, an opponent attacked only if he felt strong. Furthermore, 'fire that walks' – the rolling barrage, for example, or the fire from *groupes* of light machine-guns – made a greater impression than fire from a fixed position. On the other hand, the defender had the benefit of heavy automatic weapons, which the attacker was unable to carry. In psychological terms, these heavy automatic weapons, and the crews serving them, were the toughest components in the whole of the infantry. However heavy the artillery preparation may have been, these sub-units always formed pockets of resistance that held up the attack troops. The defender was also protected by entrenchments. Yet entrenchments that were underground could prove to be psychological traps. Men particularly dreaded finding themselves suddenly caught inside and then gassed or buried or burned alive. They were even more fearful of this prospect when they were crammed inside dugouts, and many cases are known of entire companies surrendering after becoming trapped inside strongholds.

## Panics

Most men simply followed an example of action set by others. Although this might result in heroic advances, it could also lead to panics, which entailed the disintegration of any organized structure. The combat unit became a mere crowd or herd. The process of disintegration required both a favourable situation and a trigger. Conditions that favoured panic included overcrowding, long waits, misunderstandings, mass hallucinations, the surprise produced by a new enemy tactic or piece of equipment, leaders being wounded or going missing, and a feeling of being outflanked. Panics were also more likely to occur in areas where shelter was readily available, such as in a wood, and this was known as 'the lure of the shelter'.[59]

The severity of an onslaught was a highly subjective issue, but if it was close to the limit of the amount of terror a man could bear, a single event would be enough to trigger everything off. It might be a mere misunderstanding, a misinterpretation of orders or a mistaken assessment of the situation. Friendly fire was another common cause of panic, even when it did not kill anyone. So, too, was the fall of a leader. An event such as these caused a unit to act – sometimes in a completely rational and justified way – and its action was then misunderstood by the neighbouring units and snowballed into a mass panic.

Excuses for a flight were always found in retrospect. During the Battle of the Marne in September 1914, Lieutenant Genevoix witnessed the death of a comrade who was commanding a *section*:

> A shell has just exploded amidst the *section* commanded by the second-lieutenant who has come from the infantry school of Saint-Maixent. I saw the second-lieutenant himself take a direct hit from the shell. I saw it distinctly. ... On the ground lies a shapeless mass of white and red, an almost naked, crushed body. The men, left without a leader, scatter.[60]

A few weeks later, near the Tranchée de Calonne, Genevoix tried to stop some fleeing troops:

> 'But we're not legging it, lieutenant, we're falling back. It's an order.' ... The sergeant explains to me that his entire battalion has been ordered to fall back because the ammunition has run out. ... These men reek of contagious fear. All of them gasp out bits of sentences, mumbled shreds of words... 'The *Boches* ... *Boches* ... turning ... lost ... .'[61]

Flight was not the only manifestation of panic. Bouts of panic-stricken firing also occurred. Lieutenant André Pézard watched helplessly as one such case unfolded:

> The *Boches* are here! The *Boches* are here! The small-arms fire starts to crackle wildly. The men jostle each other in the hollow and shout mutual encouragement. Those in the first rank fire over the earth of the northern lip. Those who cram behind, on the crumbled slope where they can barely remain standing, fire over the heads of the ones in front, fire without being able to see anything, fire into the air.[62]

In circumstances such as these, Genevoix reckoned, soldiers no longer knew where they were. They were simply aware that everyone around them was firing, and they automatically did what they saw others doing.[63]

### The end of the fighting

When a soldier advanced under fire, he continually cheated death by a fraction of a second. He had to fire, dive to the ground and get back up at the right moment, and do all this without losing sight of his objective. An advance under fire was extremely stressful psychologically and hence used up an immense amount of energy. When the danger ended, a reaction set in, causing weakness. A soldier might feel revulsion at having killed someone, or he might fall asleep or even give way to laughter. Lieutenant Rommel described how, after the capture of a French position and with the situation still unclear, one of his riflemen provoked mirth by finding some items of female underwear in an abandoned dugout.[64]

This lowering of tension could make soldiers vulnerable if the fighting had merely paused. There were many cases of troops being caught by surprise after having fought outstandingly for several days. By the evening of a battle, men were knocked out by the efforts they had made. After the First Battle of the Marne, most combat units were so worn out that they simply stopped and faced each other in their opposing positions.

The end of the fighting came as a relief. But the combatants found it difficult to recall the full sequence of events, in the same way that a man does when he awakes from a nightmare:

> On the evening of an action, how comforting it is to find familiar faces once more around a blazing fire of vine shoots! How comforting to chat with pals who have been conscripted in the same year as you, to swop impressions, to recall, as you are lying down at rest, the dangers that you are still amazed you have escaped. Everyone tells in a straightforward way his own adventure in the great fight. The accounts complement each other and gradually an overall picture emerges of the battle, of which each man notices only a tiny corner.[65]

Chenu admired his 'comrades who talk about the battle as if they have understood it'.[66] An infantry sergeant, Marc Bloch, recalled the fighting as 'a discontinuous series of images, vivid in themselves but badly arranged like a reel of movie film that showed here and there large gaps and the unintended reversal of several scenes.'[67] Often, an outsider was needed – an historian years later – to examine and arrange events that for the time being were just elements of chaos. Otherwise, the men remembered events in their own way and might even have a sense of failure whereas their unit had actually been remarkable.

## Holding on

What could possibly have enabled an infantryman to 'hold on'? In other words, what allowed him to preserve a degree of mental stability? It is a reasonable question to ask when we consider the environment in which he lived and fought. We must start by noting that some men, such as Jünger, genuinely enjoyed the thrill of combat: the 'charm of ... the bold game of life and death seems far superior to anything else that existence can offer'.[68]

Yet by 1918, Jünger felt that he had had his fill of adventures and bloodshed. Men began to grow accustomed to fighting as they added to the number of times on which they had seen action. But becoming used to fighting did not necessarily mean the same thing as becoming psychologically stronger. Captain Delvert wrote:

> During this dreadful war, the firing does not stop for a single moment. So badly does the war strain the soldiers' nerves that their fear does not lessen but instead rises all the time. It's like that for everyone. They do, of course, reach a point where they no longer pay attention to a passing shell or hissing bullet. But every time we set out again for the trenches, I see the men's faces a bit more tensed up.[69]

As a new action drew near, suppressed memories came back to the surface and heightened the tension. 'It's a mistake', Jünger reckoned, 'to think that soldiers become tougher and braver as a war progresses. Whatever progress they might make in terms of skill, in the art of attacking the enemy, is offset by a sapping of their nerves.'[70]

Patriotism, and other key values, need not detain us for long:

> Pick 100 men from the common classes. Talk to them about their country. Half will laugh in your face, out of amazement and incomprehension. Another twenty-five will tells us that they couldn't care less whether they were German or French.[71]

Yet the same men would become angry with people who posed as patriots without sharing the dangers of the front. It was not so much patriotism that men felt, but more 'a tacit and fairly deep conviction that we were on the right side and that the war, once we were in it, was necessary'.[72]

Nor do we need to dwell on rewards such as the *Médaille militaire,* or the fear of court-martial or other punishments. 'Who thinks about that when they are in an assault wave? What do the trinkets of earthly justice matter when someone is walking into danger or death?'[73] Soldiers already had a more substantial underpinning available to them in the form of *esprit de corps.* The regiment was a miniature nation, with its own history, culture, values and continuity:

> If you've never been on campaign, you'll never grasp the emotion with which an old sweat says: *my* regiment, *my* company, *my* squad. We all think in terms of *images d'Epinal* [the romanticized, popular prints produced at the town of Epinal]. The regiment consists of all the men who have the same number on the identification patches of their uniform. These 3,000 soldiers ... have taken part in the same actions, endured the same sufferings, shared the same enthusiasms. The company, as the captain says, 'is a big family, and he's its father'. Its 200-odd lads know their commander, and their commander knows them by name. The squad is composed of close friends and is a small, joint venture.[74]

The better that soldiers knew each other, the more they felt a moral obligation. A soldier was not under much compulsion if he had strangers beside him. He was not particularly concerned if they formed a bad opinion of him. But the opinion of comrades whom he had known for a long time was more important. Soldiers may have been afraid, but they preferred to endure physical suffering than incur the shame of being regarded as a coward. Hence cohesion within a small group developed around a handful of long-serving men. They thought the same way as each other, just as players do if they have spent years developing together within the same sports team.

This 'comradeship principle' became even stronger when the introduction of new weapons made men more interdependent. A grenade-thrower or two, for example, needed men around them to provide close protection, to act as extra eyes and ears or to supply more grenades. All these tasks were as important as honour in binding men to each other. Gun-crews were particularly strong sub-units, since their men acted so closely together around a powerful and prestigious weapon. In 1916, infantry combat became centred on machine-guns and automatic-rifles, whereas many *voltigeurs* – ordinary riflemen – never actually pulled the trigger on their firearms except perhaps to steady their nerves. Jünger described his company before the German offensive of 21 March 1918:

> It's a unit with which you can really get stuck in: men armed with rifles, machine-guns and an abundance of other weapons, men who have proven themselves in difficult undertakings and who, in recent weeks, have been thoroughly trained and well rested. Above all, we have come to know each other. We have had enough time to fuse together and incorporate the young recruits, so that we form not a mere armed crowd but a solid and self-contained unit that moves with a common spirit in the danger zone and is far superior to most. We have reason to hope that this spirit will also embolden the weak in the fearful times ahead and will make all act for one, and one for all.[75]

Captain Delvert's company, badly depleted by losses, was disbanded when it returned from its spell at Verdun. The men were distributed within the rest of the battalion:

> When news of this step reached my poor lads, the chow was being brought. Nobody could eat. Many were crying. In units, the bonds that existed between combatants were very strong.[76]

When men were in the death zone, it was honour, comradeship and *esprit de corps* that enabled them to hold on.

*Chapter 10*

# The Steel Fist

On 2 October 1918, Major Erich von dem Bussche-Ippenburg, representing the German GHQ, admitted to the *Reichstag* that any possibility of defeating the enemy had now vanished. The enemy's tanks, he claimed, were a prime reason for this helplessness:

> The enemy has committed tanks in unexpectedly large numbers. ... Tanks broke through our foremost lines, opening a way for their infantry, appearing in our rear and causing local panics that dislocated our control of the action.[1]

Tanks were one of the essential contributors to the victory. Their development had obliged France to create two generations of completely innovative machines, produce them in their thousands and refine specific methods for using them. This had required a complex, modern organization of over 20,000 men to be created from scratch in under three years. It was a remarkable achievement, occurring as it did within an institution that is perceived as having been rather conservative. As such, it deserves a special study.

## Why did Estienne's Project Succeed?
### *The tanks: a difficult birth*
At the start of the twentieth century, as men considered the potential of the internal combustion engine, they developed schemes for using it for military purposes. In France, a prototype of a motorized machine-gun carrier existed as early as 1902, and in 1908 motor-vehicles equipped with weapons were used not only in the large-scale manœuvres but also in Morocco.

The first military motor-vehicle with caterpillar tracks was proposed in 1904 by the Englishman, David Roberts. But only in 1912 did a couple of designs appear for what were true tanks. One of them came from an Australian, Lancelot de Mole, but was spurned by the British War Office. The other was produced by an Austrian officer, Gunther Burstyn, but was turned down by the Austrian and German staffs.[2]

Motorized machine-gun carriers – and indeed airplanes – were quickly adopted by the French military, although only for a few, specific uses. In contrast, tracked motor-vehicles aroused little interest. The main reason for this wariness was the need to weave such inventions into the doctrinal fabric. A tracked vehicle, slow and not particularly self-sufficient, had no place in the mobile warfare that was foreseen at that time. Only when the front as a whole became fixed during autumn 1914 did the possible uses of such a vehicle begin to become clear: as a way of neutralizing enemy machine-gun nests that were solidly entrenched and protected by barbed-wire entanglements.

The technical offer was now considerable, stimulated as it was by the urgency of the new situation. Some of the many projects deserved serious consideration and included a proposal from a member of the National Assembly, Jules-Louis Breton, for a motorized, armoured vehicle equipped with a spur that would cut barbed-wire. For its part, the Schneider company, with the engineer Eugène Brillié, sought to add caterpillar tracks to motorized machine-gun carriers. At the end of 1915, Breton combined these two projects – his own and that of Schneider. The engineer arm, which had become interested, placed an order for ten Schneider tractors. But the problem with the various projects that had been submitted was that they ignored the realities of the front. Nor did they make use of caterpillar tracks, until the Schneider company started work.

On the demand side, GHQ's Third Department (Operations) waited until it had tried every option that fitted the paradigm in force. It was the failure of the September 1915 offensive that changed the high command's outlook. The tactical problem had become a dead-end and the only way forward was to explore novel options. This was the background when Colonel Jean Estienne wrote to the commander-in-chief on 1 December 1915:

> I regard it as within the bounds of possibility to create motor-vehicles that enable infantry (with weapons and baggage) and artillery pieces to be transported across every obstacle, and under fire, at a speed above 6 km an hour.[3]

Estienne had all the skills needed to champion an innovative project. As a graduate of the *Ecole polytechnique,* he had received a sound, scientific training, and his creative mind made the best use of it. He had won fame for his many inventions during his career as an artilleryman, and was therefore given the mission in 1909 of organizing an aviation centre at Vincennes on the eastern side of Paris. It was there that he developed his ideas on the aerial adjustment of artillery fire. He put these ideas into effect on 6 September 1914 at the village of Montceaux-lès-Provins, during the Battle of the Marne, using for this purpose the two special airplanes that had been built on his initiative. He was serving at the time of the battle in the 6th Infantry Division, whose commander was General Philippe Pétain.

In December 1915, Estienne received permission to seek the industrial assistance that was needed to construct a prototype of the vehicles he had proposed in his letter to the commander-in-chief. From Major Léonce Ferrus of the Directorate of Motor-Transport Services, he found out about the Schneider company's project. Brillié and Estienne agreed to abandon their initial concepts and to combine their ideas in a project whose design might be ready for January 1916. To win GHQ's approval, Estienne relied on a line of argument that emphasized that the cost would be low even if the venture ended in failure. He stressed that a sound project already existed, which meant that production could immediately go ahead. Furthermore, if these machines did not prove satisfactory, they could easily be transformed into tractors for towing artillery. He likewise highlighted the psychological boost that the 'landships' would give an infantry frustrated by the failures of 1915. Nor, he pointed out, could the technological initiative be left to the Germans. Estienne managed to persuade Joffre, who on 31 January 1916 requested the rapid production of 400 Schneider landships.[4]

It was not one man alone who imposed the idea of the tank, but an entire network of men centred on Estienne. This network included not only Major Ferrus and the Schneider executives, but also Pétain, whom Estienne went to consult on 26 December 1915. Buoyed up by his successes, Pétain was a 'star' among the generals. (A star can be defined as someone who, in his field, has an outstanding professional reputation, certainly within his own organization and often outside it as well.)[5] The godfather of the network was Joffre, who (like Estienne) was a graduate of the *Ecole polytechnique*.

The strength of this informal group, which had enabled it to come up with a project so quickly, also allowed it to contend with a rival network, that of the French interior.[6] The rival network included both Albert Thomas (the Minister of Armaments) and General Léon-Augustin Mourret (the Director of Motor-Transport Services). This network managed to take control of the Schneider tanks project, which was entrusted to a commission that excluded Estienne. In addition, the network ordered its own, different type of tank from the Saint-Chamond company,[7] whose technical director was another famous artilleryman, Lieutenant-Colonel Emile Rimailho.

But Estienne used his contacts to try and keep in touch even while he was carrying out his duties at the front. He was kept up to date by *Monsieur* Deloule, the head of construction at Schneider, on the ditherings of the Directorate of Motor-Transport Services' commission. He was permitted to attend trials held at Vincennes on 17 March 1916. In June, he visited the British tank centre at Lincoln. On his return, thanks to Joffre and Breton, he was entrusted with organizing a tank force as a new subdivision of the artillery arm, although he was placed under the orders of the Directorate of Motor-Transport Services, which he did not exactly find agreeable. Then, on 30 September, he was finally appointed commander of the Assault Artillery as it was known, and was attached to GHQ. (The Assault Artillery was also called the Special Artillery.)

Using the above evidence, we can draw up the equation:

Military innovation =
a tactical problem that defies solution by familiar means
+ resources that already exist and are obvious
+ limited cost of a failure
+ willingness to believe it possible
+ an entrepreneur capable of leading the project.

Both the French and the British satisfied all the terms of the equation, and they came up with the idea of the tank at almost the same time. The Germans were in a different situation. They were not in a tactical dead-end. Their quick-firing, heavy artillery and other available resources meant they were still able to win offensive victories, and so they explored few radically new paths apart from gas warfare. They had no civilian tracked vehicles. Nor was there any sign in Germany of a 'man of imagination and faith as was found in England and France' to shake people out of their inertia.[8]

## A delicate childhood

A mere ten months separated the acceptance of the Estienne-Schneider project in January 1916 and the creation of the first *groupe* of tanks on 7 October 1916. There were several reasons why this lead time was so short. Estienne was both a creator and an entrepreneur at the same time. Inventing something is not enough, for the 'vision' must then be adapted to reality. Estienne, as an engineer and an officer, played an active role in both these stages. He used the short-cut method.[9] On his desk was the motto: 'To accomplish anything entails consciously resigning yourself to doing less-than-perfect work.'[10] He reckoned it was better to build imperfect machines that could then be modified instantly using the experience gained when they were tried out for real, rather than wait for the construction of a series of prototypes that gradually incorporated a succession of improvements. Another reason why the project was so swiftly implemented was that its path was eased by its precursors. It was an adaptation of the Brillié machine, which itself was an extension of the ideas of Breton and of the 'Baby Holt' agricultural tractor, whose caterpillar tracks had in turn been inspired by the railway.

Yet the development of the new arm was hindered by the confrontation between the command of the Assault Artillery and the departments of the interior. The Minister of Armaments, Albert Thomas, was accountable for sparse resources for the use of the war effort as a whole. Estienne, on the other hand, wanted his organization to expand and reach its full potential. Until January 1918, the relevant bodies lacked clearly-defined limits to their respective responsibilities. (These bodies were the Assault Artillery and the Directorate of Motor-Transport Services, along with the Ministry of Armaments and the offices of its two under-secretaries of state: Inventions and War Production.) This contributed to many points of friction:

- a mismatch existed between the army's pace of time – urgency – and the pace of time in the country's interior, which was still infused with a bureaucratic mindset. The commission in charge of the tank project insisted on redoing trials that the Schneider company had just undertaken. This wasted six weeks;
- the commission placed a concurrent order. The Directorate of Motor-Transport Services managed to ensure that 400 tanks were ordered from the Saint-Chamond company, at the same time as the Schneider project was going ahead. The double order entailed a waste of resources that did nothing to favour the rapid creation of tank units;
- the key programmes saw constant clashes of opinion. In looking to the future, Estienne wanted to develop a light tank. But the Directorate of Motor-Transport Services preferred simply to extend the existing order, or else produce a super-heavy tank, which its engineers regarded as more prestigious;
- a failure to take an holistic view of the tank. The Ministry of Armaments strove to ensure that the 800 ordered tanks were delivered on schedule. But the production of spare parts was neglected, lest it held up the manufacture

of the core product. The consequences were catastrophic. On 1 April 1918, as many of the Assault Artillery's tanks were immobilized by a lack of spare parts as the number that had been destroyed by the enemy since its creation.[11]

Jules-Louis Breton, of the National Assembly, created an Assault Artillery advisory committee in order to reduce the conflicts. The committee included representatives from all the relevant bodies.

One result of the friction was that projections became virtually meaningless. A host of technical problems had the same effect. On the Schneiders, for example, it proved necessary to increase the thickness of the armour and to add an electric starter. The Saint-Chamond tank was even more problematic. On 25 November 1916, the Assault Artillery could count on just eight Schneiders instead of the expected 400. The first Saint-Chamond appeared only on 23 February 1917. Meanwhile, the new commander-in-chief, Nivelle, gave absolute priority to a programme for 850 artillery tractors – a decision that delayed the production of medium tanks and froze the light tank in its infancy. These artillery tractors were intended to transport artillery and ammunition across the old combat zone once the Germans had been dislodged by Nivelle's planned offensive, but as it turned out they would not be used.[12]

## Painful Apprenticeship
### The initial organizational structure

On 25 October 1916, Estienne was given a tactical assistant, Colonel Jean Monhoven, and also a technical assistant, Major Aimé Doumenc who had organized the *Voie sacrée* (the supply route to Verdun).

The Assault Artillery had three centres at its disposal:

- Fort Trou-d'Enfer, near Marly-le-Roi 18 km west of Paris, provided tank-driving training;
- Cercottes camp, 10 km north of Orléans, took delivery of the tanks fresh from production and formed the units;
- Champlieu camp, located 13 km south of Compiègne within the theatre of operations, was where the combat units were based and trained.

The men began to arrive in August 1916. They were volunteers who had come from every arm. Hence they were primarily 'migrants', whose motivation turned Champlieu camp into a 'tactical laboratory'. Within the officer corps, two types were dominant:

- mobilized civilians, reservist officers or officers who had risen from the ranks: finding themselves shunned by the professional officers, they were attracted to the new arms, where nobody could claim to be better than them. The first military use of tracked machines in France seems to have been the initiative of a reservist, Lieutenant Cailloux: two tractors on caterpillar tracks were brought back from Tunisia to pull heavy artillery pieces in spring 1915;

- cavalrymen: being unemployed, they were available. Hence they swarmed into the other arms, bringing with them their background culture and their frustrations. In both the aeronautics and the Assault Artillery, they came up once more with offensive-minded schemes consisting of charges or duels, and balked at cooperating with the other arms. They were bolstered by the Assault Artillery's initial doctrine, which favoured a massed tank charge in order to make the most of the technical surprise.

Most of the Assault Artillery's officers came from the cavalry. Among them, Major Louis Bossut was a 'star'. Even before the war, he had been famed for his horse-riding skills and he was a genuine hero who earned several official citations in 1914. Bossut was one of the first to join the Assault Artillery. He commanded a *groupe* of tanks in December 1916 and then the larger of the two *groupements* that were committed to battle in April 1917. His notion of how tanks should be used in combat remained a sudden and unexpected charge, which had been the dominant notion at the time he had arrived at Champlieu. On 15 April, the day before his death, he wrote to his brother that 'the tank is a horse with which you charge',[13] and he insisted on galloping at the head of his men instead of remaining as an adviser at the command post of the army to which he was attached, as any good artillery commander would have done. His posthumous citation conveys the mindset of many Assault Artillery officers of this time: 'Having given all his great gusto as a soldier and dauntless horseman, [he] fell gloriously while leading his tanks in an heroic cavalcade at the final enemy lines.'[14]

The Assault Artillery had two types of medium tank. The ways in which these tanks could be used were largely determined by their characteristics. The characteristics set out in Table 3 show that the tanks had only two possible uses:

- support: the machines advanced at the same rate as the infantry, in order to help it destroy any resistance. They could therefore be distributed among the infantry units.
- charge: the tanks exploited their armoured protection to thrust as deeply as possible into enemy positions. It was better in this case to use them in mass, so as to enhance their moral impact and enable them to support each other.

On the other hand, it was inconceivable that the Schneiders and Saint-Chamonds could exploit a breakthrough or undertake reconnaissance missions.

An information base about the tanks and their capabilities was initially created by exercises that began at Champlieu in December 1916. These exercises were held on training grounds where simulated defensive systems had been set up. They provided guidance on suitable combat methods and enabled certain technical problems to be identified. But it was difficult to do more than that in just a few weeks, and sometimes the training conditions lacked realism. Lieutenant Charles-Maurice Chenu commented later on the fanciful nature of the enemy trenches, 'an ideal and geometric system, easy for the tanks to cross'.[15]

This information base was enriched by knowledge gleaned from cooperation with Allied armies. Following Estienne's visit to Lincoln camp in June 1916, exchanges continued until the end of the war, with the British systematically

*Table 3: Comparison of the Schneider and the Saint-Chamond tank.*

| | | Schneider | Saint-Chamond | Remarks |
|---|---|---|---|---|
| Weight (tonnes) | | 13.5 | 24 | The heaviness of the tanks meant they had to be transported by railway, and that took time. |
| Length x width x height (metres) | | 6 x 2 x 2.4 | 7.9 x 2.7 x 2.4 | Big, but also imposing, targets. |
| Machine-guns | | 2 | 4 | The Schneider was suited only for action at close quarters, as its gun had an effective range of 200 metres. The Saint-Chamond could lend support from afar (700 metres). |
| Gun | | 75mm, short-barrelled | 75mm, ordinary barrel | |
| Armour (mm of steel) | sides | 11.5 | 17 | Invulnerable frontally, except to direct artillery fire. The Saint-Chamond had higher quality armour. |
| | front | 17 | 11.5 | |
| Crew | | 6 | 9 | Required large numbers of trained personnel. |
| Engine (horsepower) | | 70 | 90 | Low power-to-weight ratio: 5 hp/tonne for the Schneider, and less than 4 for the Saint-Chamond. The Saint-Chamond used the power more efficiently. |
| Operational range (hours) | | 6-7 | 7-8 | Distance covered in action could not exceed 20-30km, including the return leg. |
| Speed (km/hr) | max | 6 | 10 | The tanks progressed at the same speed as the infantry. |
| | all terrain | 2-3 | 3-4 | |
| Max slope that could be climbed (per cent) | | 55 | 70 / 80 | Problems with the undercarriage reduced the Saint-Chamond's capabilities in action. |
| Max trench width that could be crossed (metres) | | 1.50 | 1.80 | Many German trenches were wider than these figures. |

sharing the lessons of their tank actions, starting with those of late 1916. The Royal Tank Corps' great offensive at Cambrai in November 1917 was analysed in particular detail. Since the Germans had practically no tanks, the British provided the only possible source of imitation for the French. Their willingness to cooperate tactically led to the creation in August 1918 of the inter-Allied centre of Recloses, 60 km south of Paris, which grouped together several tank and infantry battalions from various Allied nations. Information was shared at Recloses and all sorts of experiments carried out. Every week, around thirty officers attended a training course.

The French were able to use the information they collected to decide how their combat units should be organized. The basic tactical unit was the battery, composed of four tanks. Four batteries formed a *groupe*. By 31 March 1917, the Assault Artillery had thirteen Schneider *groupes* available, along with two incomplete Saint-Chamond *groupes*.[16] Major Bossut suggested that a supporting infantry force should be specially trained to help the tanks advance more easily. Exercises carried out with a light infantry unit, the 17th Battalion of Foot *Chasseurs*, made it possible to identify effective methods. Each *groupe* of tanks taking part in an attack had an infantry company attached to it. The company was divided into élite *groupes* (three-man teams, for accompanying each individual tank), and into support *sections* (similar in size to British platoons, for creating points where trenches could be crossed).

Several stages can be seen in the way thinking developed about how the Assault Artillery should be used. In December 1915, Estienne originally envisaged troops being transported by armoured trailers. But he then abandoned that idea in favour of the concept of landships when he accepted Brillié's plan. The following month, GHQ's Third Department advocated using tanks for a rapid attack against the German second position, since conventional means were far less effective against this second position than against the first.

In the first *Note on the tactical use of tanks*, which was issued on 20 August 1916, Estienne imposed the notion of a great charge so the first two positions could be taken in a matter of hours. But the production delays meant it would be impossible to assemble a great mass of tanks anytime soon, and in any case their ability to cross obstacles proved limited. Furthermore, the prior use of tanks by the British precluded any surprise. The Germans could now be expected to take counter-measures. The discovery that they had adopted an armour-piercing bullet with a steel core triggered a decision to add an extra layer of armour to the Schneiders, but this made them heavier and slower and imposed further production delays. The Germans had therefore pulled off a sort of technical neutralization, even though they had not really taken much action. Apart from widening some of their trenches, they had merely created some anti-tank batteries of 77mm guns, which lacked any special training. Some other guns were concealed individually on the battlefield and had orders to open fire only if tanks appeared.

These changed circumstances brought about a return to the Third Department's initial concept of how the Assault Artillery should be used. The tanks would extend the action of the guns against those enemy positions whose distance behind the front line meant they escaped the brunt of the initial artillery preparation. The thorniest point of doctrine concerned the cooperation of tanks and infantry regiments. Although the need for cooperation was recognized, the means of implementing it remained vague. Instructions issued at the start of 1917 laid down the principle that 'one arm awaits the other only if unable to advance further by its own means'.[17] The subordination of tank units to large units was stated only grudgingly. As for their subordination to the infantry, it did not exist at all.

### Test of fire

The French tanks were committed to action for the first time as part of the Nivelle offensive. Nivelle intended his main attack, which was launched on 16 April 1917, to achieve a breakthrough between Laffaux and the northern side of Reims. The 5th Army, which formed the eastern wing of this attack, was reinforced by tanks. The tanks had the mission of supporting the infantry's advance during the attack on the enemy's second and third positions. The artillery preparation that preceded the attack lasted several days and therefore ruled out any surprise. The terrain was heavily cratered from the bombardments and was also surrounded by heights, which provided the Germans with plenty of observation points.

On 16 April, the Assault Artillery committed 132 Schneiders, which were divided into two forces led by Major Bossut (five *groupes*) and Major Louis Chaubès (three *groupes*). Chaubès' *groupement* came up behind the infantrymen who were assaulting the first position, turned into a congested mass and was unable to emerge into the open. *Groupement* Bossut managed with difficulty to pass the German intermediate position, so it could deploy into a line of attack. But so fierce was the German fire that the infantry – both the attacking regiments and those units earmarked to support Bossut's tanks – were left far behind as they struggled forward. The armoured *groupes* reached the second position, but were devastated by accurate artillery fire. They nevertheless repelled two counter-attacks and even managed to mount a couple of joint actions with the small amount of infantry that had been able to link up with them. At nightfall, the surviving tanks fell back, incurring further heavy losses, mostly from breakdowns.[18]

The losses in personnel came to 25 per cent, which was not a particularly high level for the circumstances of the time. But the losses in tanks were staggering. Out of the 121 that left the assembly positions, seventy-six were lost, fifty-seven of them to enemy action.[19] Hence the loss rate in tanks was 63 per cent, which would be regarded today as a 'tactical destruction', and there was little to show for it. This first engagement of the Assault Artillery destroyed one-third of its existing equipment resources, and inflicted disappointment and misgivings on its men. Their main misgiving concerned the reliability of the materiel. One tank in every four broke down in the combat zone for one reason or another. But the big surprise was that as many as thirty-five tanks caught fire. It was hardly surprising that enthusiasm declined, given that the crews faced the prospect of going back into action with a one-in-four chance of their tank going up in flames.

The German artillery provided a second surprise. The loss of fifteen tanks to direct hits was only to be expected, but the destruction of another thirty-seven as a result of shells exploding nearby was unforeseen. The artillery fire was extremely accurate because of the observation posts and airplanes that were available to the Germans. The accuracy of the fire was devastatingly effective as the tanks moved forward in close columns up to the intermediate position. The infantry that was meant to be supporting the tanks provided practically no help. The tank crews did not realize that the 17th Battalion of Foot *Chasseurs,* which had been specially trained for this role, had been replaced at the last moment by a unit that had received only the most basic instruction.[20]

Yet there was also cause for encouragement. The attack had managed to make some gains against troops in entrenched positions. The tanks' armour had proved impervious to small-arms fire. Some tanks had seen off counter-attacks with ease, although such actions amounted to no more than neutralizations that needed to be exploited at once by infantry – something that was impossible unless the infantry was near at hand.

The initial enthusiasm in the ranks of the Assault Artillery gave way to a more realistic outlook. It was decided not to produce any more medium tanks once the original order had been fulfilled. The cavalryman's dream of surprising the enemy with a great charge, while the 'pedestrians' of the infantry followed as best they could, had come to nothing. The men grasped that the various arms had to work together. The Assault Artillery's initial setback also demonstrated how difficult it was to anticipate the sheer complexity of using a new tactical system.

The failure of the tanks caused some resentment. General Louis Deville, the commander of the 42nd Infantry Division, reckoned in his report that 'the appearance of the tanks was the signal for an intense bombardment, which caused heavy losses in the 94th Infantry Regiment and above all in the 332nd ... The tanks had a rather harmful effect.'[21]

At a higher level, the check suffered by the Nivelle offensive resulted in the Assault Artillery being caught up in the disillusionment. Some men criticized Nivelle and completely rejected anything that appeared linked to his 'method'. Others, who had always been hostile to allocating resources to so audacious a weapons system, took advantage of the situation to argue once more about the funding of the tanks. An irrational atmosphere arose, in which the most exaggerated rumours circulated and many tank men became convinced that they were going to be returned to the regiments from which they had come. The production of the Schneiders almost ground to a halt. From 1 July to 30 September, only eighteen tanks emerged from the factories.[22] The first trials of the Renault light tanks were the subject of negative reports, which provided an excuse to suspend the programme. But Pétain, the new commander-in-chief and formerly Estienne's superior, staunchly defended the Assault Artillery. He was intent on waiting for 'the Americans and the tanks' in order to win the war.

As for the Germans, their success on 16 April strengthened their initial perceptions and hardly motivated them to innovate. They paid little attention to their concealed anti-tank guns, whose crews had a nerve-racking task, and instead focused on long-range, indirect fire, which seemed more effective.

### The learning process

The Assault Artillery may have won Pétain's protection, but still needed to restore widespread confidence in the usefulness of tanks. That required victories, even modest ones. Barely two weeks after the setback of 16 April, the Assault Artillery fought its second action in a starkly different way, and thereby demonstrated its capacity to learn and innovate. *Groupement* Lefebvre, which contained three armoured *groupes*, was attached to the 6th Army in order to take part in a renewed attempt to conquer the Chemin des Dames on 5 May 1917. It would go into action near the moulin de Laffaux, and this time it was to act in close support of the infantry rather than going it alone. Hence the tank batteries had the mission of supporting specially-designated units, and were to do so by neutralizing specific objectives. The command posts of the armoured *groupes* were located with those of the infantry divisions. *Groupement* Lefebvre was deployed in depth, with an element held in reserve at each echelon. The tanks were distributed by batteries between various attack positions close to the front line. Meticulous preparations were made for artillery fire to blind the enemy's observation posts and counter his batteries. An observation airplane, protected by six fighters, was responsible for keeping the command informed of the tanks' advance and locating the enemy anti-tank guns for the artillery.[23]

By the evening of 5 May, the 6th Army had made only limited gains, but those gains were largely due to the action of the tanks. Twelve Schneiders made repeated interventions, penetrating up to a depth of over 3 km from the infantry's jumping-off line. The Schneiders made it possible to breach barbed-wire entanglements, neutralize numerous machine-guns and repel several German counter-attacks. The 17th Battalion of Foot *Chasseurs*, used this time in its supporting role, proved highly useful. On the other hand, a *groupe* of Saint-Chamond tanks – which saw action for the first time this day – had a similar experience to the setback of 16 April. The *groupe* was able to field sixteen tanks, but only because sixteen others had been cannibalized at Champlieu owing to the shortage of spare parts. Twelve of the sixteen tanks managed to reach the assembly position. Nine of them actually set off for the attack, and just one crossed the first German trench.[24] The losses in personnel were proportionately similar to those of 16 April. But the final losses in tanks amounted to just three.[25] In terms of its psychological impact, the action at Laffaux restored confidence in the Assault Artillery, even if it was on too minor a scale to remove every misgiving.

After-action questionnaires were completed by all the tank commanders and the officers of units supported by tanks. These questionnaires helped the high command to put together the 'current best practice',[26] until the first real regulation was issued on 29 December 1917 (the *Interim instruction on the use of tanks*). Tactical problems were also addressed through horizontal communication between the combatants, who all lived together at Champlieu camp. For example, Captain Lefebvre's discussions with those of his comrades who had seen action on 16 April meant that he had already foreseen most of the innovations required for the attack at Laffaux even before his superiors sent him the lessons drawn from the first engagement.[27]

The realism of training was significantly improved from summer 1917 onwards. For instance, artillery barrages were represented using lines of cloth that were moved according to a strict timetable.[28] The technological problems that had been identified were considered by commissions, and the combatants took part in this process. The problem of tanks catching fire was quickly resolved in this way, with a whole raft of changes being made to the machines. This effective sharing of information was disrupted by the efforts of the enemy, who never stopped striving to come up with counter-measures against tanks. Thus arose a dialectic of parries and counter-parries.

When it was noticed that the Germans were saturating the observation slits of the tanks with small-arms fire, false slits were painted, and the real ones camouflaged. As a riposte to the widening of trenches, means of crossing them were developed. When Chenu learned that an armoured *groupe* had carried out an attack:

> We went the next day to interview the survivors. We learned that the enemy had put a new tactic into effect against the tanks. [The German infantry let themselves be passed and then attacked at close quarters.] We were therefore taught a counter-tactic: a line of tanks in staggered rows, covering each other's flanks and each firing on its neighbour to free it from its attackers.[29]

To make it as difficult as possible for the Germans to develop counter-measures, the French strove to leave no tank in enemy hands. At Laffaux, the French artillery destroyed two tanks that had been left abandoned on the battlefield. Estienne proposed the creation of a specialized *groupe* for recovering wrecked tanks.

The French were able, as a result of their learning process, to develop the ideas that had been tried out at Laffaux.[30] Infantry battalions that were to be supported by tanks did a week's course of manœuvres with them. The tank officers attended infantry rehearsals. Communications between tanks and infantrymen were improved by means of pigeons, movable panels that could be operated from inside the tanks and – most importantly of all – four wireless tanks, whose sets had a range of 12 km. Reconnaissances and the analysis of aerial photographs enabled an operation to be planned in extreme detail. The movement of each individual tank was arranged beforehand.

On 23 October 1917, two armoured *groupements* were committed to action in the Battle of La Malmaison, which conquered the western end of the Chemin des Dames. *Groupement II* (three Schneider *groupes*, with two wireless tanks) was to help reduce points of resistance as far as an objective that lay 3 km away. It was to do so in two stages: initially advancing behind the infantry and then taking the lead. *Groupement X* (two Saint-Chamond *groupes*, with two wireless tanks) was to help conquer the first kilometre and then adopt an overwatch position against counter-attacks. The *groupes* carried out these missions with varying degrees of success. Out of sixty-three tanks committed to action, just twenty fulfilled their mission. But their effect was decisive, and only nine tanks were lost as a result of enemy action, along with eighty-two men.[31]

The victory of La Malmaison is of interest mainly because it confirmed once and for all that tanks were useful. But neither could the limitations of this 'first Assault Artillery' be ignored. Breakdowns still accounted for at least 25 per cent of those tanks committed to action: although technological improvements had been made, their effect was offset by general wear-and-tear. The medium tanks were neither robust nor manœuvrable enough to cope with heavily-cratered ground. They found it difficult to move forward and reach their objectives, and became vulnerable once they halted.

The tanks provided yet another example of the S-shaped development curve: after a fairly slow start they experienced a rapid growth phase, before reaching a level where almost no further increase in effectiveness occurred. Only if new solutions were explored could the Assault Artillery grow in effectiveness once more.

# The Assault Artillery Reaches Maturity
## Successive generations

In total, the medium tanks had 231 engagements during 1917. (Each occasion on which any one tank saw action counted as one tank engagement.) The 'first Assault Artillery' now had a solid 'tactical memory' at its disposal. The question of how it should be used tactically had been more or less settled, but other, intractable problems presented themselves, namely the low mobility of the tanks and their high loss rate, which was never less than 40 per cent in any action.

The end of the year was used to develop the most recent innovations, with a thorough restructuring and the conversion of the 262nd Infantry Regiment into a permanent regiment of supporting infantry.[32] The decision was taken to create an Assault Artillery centre, under its own commander, for each army group. The centres were located at Mailly (140 km east of Paris) for the Central Army Group, and at Martigny-les-Bains in Lorraine for the Eastern Army Group. Each of these two centres received a couple of *groupements* of medium tanks. Champlieu served as the centre of the General Reserve of Assault Artillery with the four remaining *groupements*. Marly was disbanded and Cercottes was given the triple role of depot, organizational base and individual training centre.[33]

At the Ministry of War, a branch of the Directorate of Artillery was created for the Assault Artillery on 8 January 1918. The powers of this branch covered anything relating to tanks except their production, although the head of the branch did have the right to monitor production on behalf of the Minister of War. This much improved the situation, even if the Assault Artillery's interests did not necessarily coincide with those of the artillery. A private members' bill for creating a fully-fledged Directorate of the Assault Artillery was introduced in the National Assembly in May 1918, but was not passed.[34]

The final developments came when the tank units returned to action in March 1918 and found themselves in a new, defensive role. The combat units still had 245 Schneiders and 222 Saint-Chamonds available at this time.[35] The lack of spare parts meant that many tanks had been 'cannibalized' in order to keep the others in working order. In April 1918, a force of seven armoured *groupements* was formed south of Amiens, behind the 1st and 3rd Armies. Its mission was to help defend the French second position. This was a mission that had not previously been considered in detail. In order to fulfil it, an Assault Artillery staff was created within each of the relevant armies. Trailers were fitted up, towed by tracked vehicles, to enable tanks to be transported back and forth on the many lateral movements they were required to make by road.[36]

The medium tanks were employed in three different ways up until July. Firstly, they were used in four small-scale actions – in batteries or *groupes* – between March and May. The purpose of these actions was to gain local objectives, but the results were mixed.[37] Secondly, on 11 June, four infantry divisions and four armoured *groupements* (163 tanks) were committed to action to counter the enemy offensive in the Matz valley. By the end of that day, the German offensive had been slowed down, but at a cost to the Assault Artillery of seventy-three tanks and 355 men.[38] These figures amounted to 43 per cent of the tanks and 25 per cent of the men. The tank attack on 11 June was comparable to that of 16 April 1917 in terms of the scale of the resources used and the losses that were suffered. Yet whereas the earlier attack had appeared to be a failure, this latest one on 11 June was seen as a partial success. It was also the last action in which only the medium tanks were engaged.

A month later, the medium tanks were used in a third different way. On 18 July, Schneiders and Saint-Chamonds went into action alongside some light tanks, the Renault FTs, beyond the Villers-Cotterêts forest. Once again, nearly 40 per cent of the tanks were lost.[39] Despite efforts to repair machines and reconstitute units, the tanks contributed little to the action after the first day. This attack in July was the last effective action of the first generation of Assault Artillery. The medium tanks were kept in active service until the end of the war, but the return on the resources invested in them soon became marginal. Their monthly number of engagements, which was around 200 in June and July, fell to eighty or ninety in the final months of the war, compared with 1,640 engagements of Renault FTs. Nevertheless, the units and personnel of the 'first Assault Artillery' were kept in being, so they could receive the Mark V tanks that had been ordered from the British and also the heavy tanks that were intended to be built. In the meantime, the number of medium tanks per *groupe* was reduced. Certain *groupes* saw at least some of their medium tanks replaced by Renault FTs. Medium tanks might be used instead for resupply missions in the combat zone.[40]

*

As early as the start of 1916, Estienne had been considering the use of smaller tanks to complement the action of the medium ones. But he encountered resistance from the Directorate of Motor-Transport Services, which remained dubious about the idea of having a machine-gun operated by just one crew member, and producing a 5- or 6-tonne tank to bring this single, unreliable weapon up to the firing line for five minutes.[41] By November 1916, the designs were sufficiently advanced to consider industrial production, but such were the misgivings that the first order came only in March 1917. Even then, just 150 light tanks were ordered. An order for another 1,000 was placed the following month, only to be suspended by the Minister of Armaments in the changed mood that followed the setback of 16 April. Pétain's support enabled the order, which was revived, to be increased to more than 3,000 tanks in total. (The increased order was placed in September 1917, three months after being requested.)

In technological terms, the Renault FT was a marvel. As well as being the first operational tank to have a turret that rotated 360 degrees, it had an original design with the engine located at the rear. Except in terms of armament, its capabilities were superior to the medium tanks.[42] Above all, its weight of just 6.5 tonnes meant it could be loaded on to a lorry. The ability to transport the Renault FTs by road freed the Assault Artillery from the railway. Hence the Assault Artillery's use acquired an operational flexibility that had previously been lacking.

The initial delays and production problems with the Renault FTs meant that the first generation of tanks began its decline before the next had reached its growth phase. The result was a period of weakness:

> The French Assault Artillery, with reduced numbers of its old tanks and still not provided with its new ones, was far from being able to play the role for which it had been destined. It would find itself impotent and useless in the face of the enemy attack [in March 1918].[43]

The planned increase in material means meant that more personnel were needed to serve that equipment. Five thousand men were at Cercottes by the start of 1918, and their number grew at the same rate as the orders that were placed. Maintaining the quality of recruits under these conditions proved difficult. Many of the new arrivals had previously been wounded while serving in the other arms, or were men who, owing to the increased demands for manpower, were now deemed fit for military service despite their previous exemptions and who lacked proper military training. In April 1918, Estienne reckoned that the men as a whole were below average and in no way matched what the Assault Artillery needed.[44] Furthermore, out of 120 training tanks, forty-one were unavailable on 7 March and seventy-five on 14 June.[45] The acceleration in production resulted in a drop in the industrial quality, with many tanks having to be rejected owing to manufacturing flaws. The Assault Artillery also lacked some vital materiel, including the lorries that were intended to transport the Renault FTs.

The doctrine for using the new tanks was still tentative. The Royal Tank Corps' big attack at Cambrai in November 1917 had sparked much interest, but the Third Department remained cautious when it noted that during this operation a single 77mm gun had reportedly destroyed ten British tanks at Flesquières and had stopped any further advance that day. Although the ways in which tanks ought to be used was examined in detail, barely any consideration was given to their defensive roles, and yet until July 1918 the tanks would have to act predominantly on the defensive.

The success of the first German offensive, which was unleashed on 21 March 1918, made it necessary to move the Assault Artillery facilities from Champlieu, where they were too exposed. These movements, and the cramming of an extra 3,000 men and a mass of equipment into Cercottes, complicated the Assault Artillery's logistics.

### The new Assault Artillery takes off
The second Assault Artillery underwent four stages of growth:

- May-June 1918: adapting to challenges;
- the July counter-attack;
- August-September: the offensives to regain lost ground;
- September-November: the general offensive.

The organizational structure of this second Assault Artillery was based on light tank battalions. In November 1917, the Light Tank Training Company was created at Champlieu in order to speed up the creation of these battalions. It was no more than a provisional organization and was assigned some thirty unfinished Renault FTs. Its principal mission was to come up with recommendations as soon as possible concerning what technical changes were required.[46] On 1 January 1918, this Training Company was split between the Subsidiary Organization Park of Champlieu, which provided technical training, and the 1st Light Tank Company, which was responsible for tactical experimentation.[47] By 20 March, on the eve of the first German offensive, enough personnel were available to form a light tank battalion, but with just one Renault FT in a state ready to fight.[48]

In April, these improvisations began to give way to a complete reorganization. Three companies of US motor-mechanics and thousands of Chinese or Moroccan labourers created a vast complex in the area of Bourron, 63 km south-east of Paris, on the southern side of Fontainebleau forest.[49] The Grand Park of Bourron was assigned a reserve pool of several hundred light tanks. It kept the Assault Artillery centres at army group level supplied with tanks, and in exchange received badly-damaged ones for repair. The Grand Park also had a mobile section to support units that were too far away from the particular park to which they were attached.[50]

The management of personnel was rationalized. On 1 May 1918, the 500th Artillery Regiment at Cercottes took charge of the creation of the light tank battalions.[51] Once a light tank battalion was formed, it was sent to Villiers-sous-Grez, 5 km south-west of Bourron, for tactical training under the direction of the staff of the 508th Artillery Regiment. From August onwards, Grez-sur-Loing, 3 km south of Bourron, was where the Assault Artillery's Training Battalion handled individual reinforcements and sick and wounded men who were being sent to the rear. An additional echelon – that of the combat tank regiment – was created in May. Brigades were then created: two in July, followed by a third in October. These brigades replaced the Assault Artillery commands that existed at army group level. Being mobile staffs, they could be attached to an army entrusted with an operation, in order to organize the action of the tanks. Support was provided by the nearest Assault Artillery park.

The gains made by the German offensives obliged the light tanks to fight their first engagements at short notice. These engagements rarely conformed with the regulation in force, which had anticipated only massed, offensive actions. The 1st Light Tank Battalion was ordered to be committed to action at the start of April, even though it was barely trained. Despite the critical situation, Estienne managed to secure a delay to allow a full technical overhaul. Had he not done so, the result would have been a disaster since so many problems still existed. Even so, the first engagement of the light tanks – at Chaudun on 31 May – was more or less a repeat of the Assault Artillery's initial setback of April 1917. Amid the haste, out of three light tank battalions, only six sections managed to arrive in time to be sent into action. In order to reach the attack line, they first had to cross 1,500 metres of exposed plateau in full daylight, without the benefit of any smokescreen or artillery support.[52] With too little time available in which to prepare, the Assault Artillery reverted to the simplest method, a tank charge. But the men of the Moroccan Division found it difficult to follow. The tanks shuttled backwards and forwards to shepherd *groupes* of *tirailleurs* (indigenous light infantrymen) to the objectives. But when the tanks fell back at the end of the action, the infantrymen went with them. Hence the ground that had been gained was lost, and three abandoned tanks fell into German hands.[53]

Actions that involved both tanks and infantry had to be improvised by the combatants in the absence of any preliminary, joint exercises or a known doctrine of use. In June, when the 6th Army was defending the Retz forest with the 501st Combat Tank Regiment, it distributed the tanks between the infantry battalions for attacks with a depth of several hundred metres. Engaging tanks in penny packets like this was criticized by the Assault Artillery commanders, and yet it was undoubtedly the best way to use them at that particular time. The Renault FT sections took the place of inexistent reserves and provided important moral support simply by being there. They allowed short, sharp blows to be struck, each of which won a 'mini-victory' and made it easier 'to hold on'. In contrast to the fighting at Chaudun, this type of action was within the scope of infantry units that had lacked enough time to train with tanks.[54]

The lull in April-May finally made it possible to carry out combined-arms exercises involving both infantry and light tanks. By July, the 'tactical memory' had become sufficiently developed to allow the first tactical regulation for light tank units to be issued. The light tanks were normally to be used in large numbers, in regularly-mounted, offensive operations intended to conquer a deep zone. The ground over which the operations were to be conducted had to be fairly easy to cross, and this ruled out attacking first positions that had been heavily cratered by shelling. The concept of tanks fighting amidst the infantry was established. The light tank meant that the infantry finally had an effective support vehicle. Yet the use of the light tank also entailed some obligations. The infantrymen were to stick to the tanks in order to exploit opportunities that arose. They were not to leave a tank in enemy hands. Nor were they to fall back when they saw tanks returning to the rear.[55] All this required joint exercises and direct contacts. The artillery and aviation were to assist the light tank battalions by neutralizing the enemy's artillery, blinding his observation posts with smoke shells, and destroying or chasing away his aircraft.[56] One *groupe* of quick-firing, heavy artillery was designated to deal with the close-range, anti-tank guns, in response to reports that an observation airplane transmitted by radio. The attackers had to try and achieve surprise, and also to preserve the initial surprise effect. Hence the action had to be carefully prepared, and long, preliminary bombardments either reduced or omitted. Since the tanks quickly became worn out, they had to be used at the right moment, making the most of favourable circumstances such as fog. They also had to be relieved frequently, and reserves were to be kept in hand. Once the infantry was firmly established on the objective, it had to let the tanks withdraw.

The counter-offensive launched from the Villers-Cotterêts forest on 18 July 1918 provided an opportunity to put these principles into practice and to win back the initiative from the Germans. For the light tanks, it marked the start of the acceleration phase in the S-shaped developmental curve. For the medium tanks, in contrast, it signalled the end of that curve. Between 18 and 27 July, 185 Schneider tanks were engaged, along with 190 Saint-Chamonds and 585 Renaults. It was the first time that the tank units went into action without a preliminary artillery bombardment, and also the first time that they fought for several days on end. In total, within the 10th Army, 140 medium tanks (37 per cent) and 129 light tanks (22 per cent) were seriously damaged. The losses in men amounted to 891.[57]

The moral impact of the surprise use of massed tanks was clear, but so too was a slowness to assimilate tactical principles. Some divisional commanders hesitated to devote a sizeable part of their 'fire allocation'[58] to protect tanks that did not belong to them. Some artillerymen were reluctant to use smoke shells, regarding them as unworthy of their 'art'.[59] What also became apparent was that during the subsequent days of the action, the results achieved by the light tank battalions dropped off rapidly.

The counter-offensive of 18 July was followed by four attacks that sought to regain the ground that had been lost to the Germans since March and to occupy some important positions:[60]

- 1 August: attack on the plateau of Grand Rozoy (10th Army). One light tank battalion (forty-five tank engagements) took part in the conquest of the plateau, but an entire company was destroyed by two 77mm guns;
- 8-18 August: attack in the Montdidier region (1st and 3rd Armies). The initial attack was a major success, but the resumption of the action on 16 and 17 August proved less effective. Three light tank battalions were involved (182 tank engagements), along with a Schneider *groupement* (thirty-two). A total of fifteen tanks were lost;
- 20 August – 16 September: attack north of the Aisne river (10th Army). The Assault Artillery fielded a large force, with seven light tank battalions (429 tank engagements), twenty-eight Saint-Chamonds and twelve Schneiders. But the fighting was difficult, and losses heavy (109 Renault FTs and six Schneiders);
- 12-15 September: reduction of the Saint-Mihiel salient (US 1st Army). For the first time, French tank units were integrated into an Allied large unit. They took part in large numbers, with five light tank battalions (118 tank engagements) as well as two Saint-Chamond and two Schneider *groupes,* which respectively had twenty-five and thirty-six tanks in action. Two of the light tank battalions were US units. Yet the tanks intervened only intermittently, being hindered more by congestion than by the enemy.

In this first series of offensives, the tank units played a secondary, and not always happy, role. Many of them had been rebuilt after the hard fighting in July. They often suffered heavy losses during these offensives, primarily as a result of being used in a clumsy way.

The second offensive phase began in September. Its objective was to seize two great defence lines: the Hindenburg Line and the Hermann-Hunding-Brunhild Line. Five major attacks were launched, as well as two on a more modest scale:

- 26 September – 8 October: offensive in the Argonne and Champagne (US 1st Army and French 4th Army). This offensive was one of the biggest engagements in the history of French armour, involving twelve light tank battalions (852 tank engagements) and six *groupes* of medium tanks (seventy-seven Schneiders and twenty-five Saint-Chamonds). Two of the light tank battalions were US units. Tank losses were moderate: seventy-five Renault FTs and nine medium tanks;

- 30 September: attack by the 5th Army on the plateaux between the Vesle and Aisne rivers. The three Schneider *groupes* (twenty-four Schneiders and ten light tanks) managed to advance a mere 300 metres and lost six Schneiders and one Renault;
- 16 October: US raid on Haumont wood. The Americans attempted a raid against the enemy rear with a company of fifteen light tanks. It was a complete failure;
- 3-20 October: offensive by the Army of Flanders in Belgium. Four light tank battalions (181 tank engagements) played a vital role. They took part in actions in built-up areas and carried out cavalry missions, such as pursuit and exploitation, to a depth of 20 km, losing twenty Renault FTs. One *groupe* of fifteen Saint-Chamonds was present, but played no role;
- 17-30 October: offensive towards Guise by the 1st Army. After breaking through the Hindenburg Line, the offensive progressed 24 km. Three light tank battalions (311 tank engagements) were highly active during these two phases and lost thirty tanks;
- 3-20 October: attack by the British 2nd Army between the Lys and Scheldt rivers. For the first time, four light tank battalions (135 tank engagements) were integrated within a British army. The advance was rapid, and only ten tanks were destroyed;
- 25-30 October: attack on the Hunding position by the 5th Army. This final action was tough. Despite the presence of three light tank battalions (140 tank engagements), the breakthrough remained elusive and twenty-five tanks were lost.

For the light tanks, this second offensive phase of just over a month saw twenty-seven battalion engagements and 1,644 tank engagements. (Twenty-one light tank battalions were available at this time, and the number of tank engagements was as many as during the rest of 1918.) During operations, the action of tanks had become decisive. At the operational level, the mobility conferred on the light tank battalions as a result of their transport by lorry[61] enabled resources to be concentrated more rapidly than on the German side, for the Germans were dependent on their artillery. The Allies made a series of attacks with their various armies and thereby kept the initiative until the end of the war. Ludendorff had now lost any chance of organizing a final offensive that might have given him a stronger negotiating hand.

At the tactical level, an infantry regiment often had the support of a light tank company. By this stage in the war, an infantry regiment's strength had dwindled to just 600 or 700 combatants. For these men, the tank company's ten machine-guns and five 37mm guns – mobile, protected and operated 1.50 metres above the ground from a rotating turret with telescopic sights – were equivalent to the firepower of several machine-gun companies. The tanks also provided considerable moral support against Germans who lacked equivalent means. From now on, the light tank battalions were closely integrated into attacks on fortified positions. In addition, they tried out new missions during the pursuit phases, such as capturing key points in the enemy rear. Their growth was also quantitative. The Renault FT tank was built on a production line, like a motor-car, with a total of 2,653 being delivered. It was therefore possible to create nine combat tank regiments and twenty-six light tank battalions. Twenty-one of these battalions saw action.[62]

By analysing the evolution of these engagements, we can see that the increase in material means was accompanied by a growth in tactical memory:

*Table 4: French light tank engagements, 1918.*

| Phases | Available btns | Engagemts | Losses | | Eng'mts per btn | Losses per btn |
|---|---|---|---|---|---|---|
| | | | tanks | per cent | | |
| Defensive actions (31 May – 17 Jul) | 7 | 281 | 13 | 4.6 | 40 | 1.9 |
| Counter-attack (18-27 Jul) | 9 | 585 | 129 | 22.1 | 65 | 14.3 |
| Clearance offensives (1 Aug – 13 Sep) | 15 | 774 | 135 | 17.5 | 52 | 9.0 |
| General offensive (26 Sep – 2 Nov) | 21 | 1,644 | 163 | 7.7 | 78 | 7.8 |
| Total | | 3,284 | 440 | 13.5 | 156 | 21.0 |

Column headings:

Available btns:   number of available battalions of light tanks
Engagemts:   number of tank engagements
Losses:   tanks written off, or badly damaged. The percentages show the tank losses as a proportion of the number of tanks in action.
Eng'mts per btn:   average number of tank engagements in each battalion
Losses per btn:   average number of tanks lost in each battalion

Several lessons can be drawn from Table 4:
- the use of the light tanks during the July counter-offensive was unusual. The tanks were used in mass, and each battalion was engaged on average for one-and-a-half days out of the nine days of fighting. Losses were heavy, with one-third of the means being lost, which was largely a reflection of the lack of experience in using light tanks;
- if we set aside the exceptional way in which light tanks were used in July, we can identify several trends:
(1) a rising rate of tank engagements per light tank battalion. In each operational phase of about one-and-a-half months, the period during which each light tank battalion was in action rose from just under one day in June to nearly two days in October. The use of tanks was hence limited in time, but vital. Therefore, it had to be managed as effectively as possible

by the large units. During offensives, the light tank battalions tended to be used at a progressively later stage. They served less and less as a spearhead, acting instead as a support for the infantry when the infantry began to weaken;

(2) a doubling of the total number of tank engagements in the final phase. This increase is explained by the arrival of six new light tank battalions (a 40 per cent increase) and the rise in the rate of tank engagements ‘per unit (a 50 per cent increase);

(3) a steady fall, from August onwards, in losses per light tank battalion. This fall was all the more remarkable in that it coincided with the increase in strength of the German anti-tank defence;

• the steady rise in the rate of tank engagements, and the constant fall in losses, could have resulted only from the effect of experience and the proliferation of innovations in tactics and logistics (resupply and repairs). The effect of experience can be defined as the increase in return obtained by a better mastery of know-how over the course of time.

In October 1918, Colonel Pol Maurice Velpry had two light tank battalions available in Flanders. The older of them was able to remain in action for seven days and withstand losses of up to 50 per cent. The other battalion, which was newly-formed, had to be withdrawn after losses of 16 per cent.[63] The older battalion was more adept, not least at managing its strength by frequently relieving its first-line sections, which enabled the men to rest and maintain their equipment.

A reduction in the time required to make a battalion fit again for action meant it was possible to increase the number of battalions that were available to fight. Initially, a light tank battalion that had been fully engaged needed six weeks after being withdrawn from action to be restored to combat effectiveness. But this period became ever shorter as a result of the fall in losses, greater experience at maintenance, the formation of a battalion to manage individual replacements, and the creation of an equipment reserve at Bourron. From June 1918, the second Assault Artillery expanded at the rate of one light tank battalion every week and doubled its efficiency every three months. Its resources were increasing ever more rapidly.

The German reaction to the evolving threat followed it closely. Anti-tank defence became a priority only after the Allied attack at Villers-Cotterêts on 18 July 1918. Short-range defence underwent a rapid development. The Germans deployed greater numbers of direct-fire weapons against tanks, namely anti-tank rifles, guns and *Minenwerfer* ('mine-throwers', or trench-mortars). The main ridge-lines that the tanks had to cross were systematically targeted by batteries located between 1,000 and 1,500 metres away. Concentrations of fire were pre-registered on those zones where tanks were likely to appear. Defensive systems included more and more mines, traps and obstacles. Behind their lines, the Germans created ‘anti-tank forts’ to block axes of advance. The German infantry trained against mock-up tanks made from wood, so it would confidently use its own weapons against the real thing. A network of look-out posts watched for any signs that hostile tanks were being inserted, so the whole German disposition could be alerted.[64]

The effectiveness of these various German measures was mixed. In all, 753 French tanks were destroyed or badly damaged. Just four of them, including one light tank, fell victim to the German infantry's man-portable weapons. The ineffectiveness of these weapons seems to have stemmed from the limited penetrative capacity of the ammunition and also from the nerve-racking nature of combat against tanks at extremely close range. Even though the 13mm anti-tank rifle was effective up to 300 metres when used against Renault FTs on the firing range, it was worthless in actual action.[65] Mines (sixteen tanks destroyed) and obstacles had only a limited and indirect effect. In contrast, the artillery destroyed 301 medium tanks (97 per cent of their total losses) and 356 Renaults (81 per cent).[66] Clearly, the artillery was by far the most effective arm against tanks. It is also notable that the Renault FTs proved more difficult than the medium tanks to destroy, for one light tank was destroyed out of every eight engaged, compared with one medium tank out of every three.[67]

## Interrupted growth

The new generation of Assault Artillery, which was organized around the light tanks, was rapidly expanding when hostilities ended in November 1918. We can attempt to ascertain the point it had reached on the S-shaped development curve. What is absolutely clear is that additional resources could still have been drawn from many sides:

- the fulfilment of the production programme: on 11 November 1918, France had 2,700 Renault FTs in the field. Yet they amounted to just one third of the programme to produce 7,000 light tanks of all types by March 1919. These 7,000 tanks were to equip fifty-four light tank battalions, organized into eighteen combat tank regiments and six brigades;[68]
- the diversification of tanks: the Renault FT had been designed to spawn an entire family of some fifteen different tanks. Industrial problems and a shortage of time had prevented any of them from being produced apart from those versions that were armed with a machine-gun or a 37mm gun. But if hostilities had continued for several more months, the light tank battalions would have been reinforced by tanks mounting a 75mm gun and by command tanks equipped with wireless communications. The Assault Artillery was also waiting for a whole range of other innovations, such as projectiles for carrying messages, phosphorus smoke shells, resupply trailers and Orthlieb bridges for crossing cuttings;[69]
- the solving of certain technical problems: some technical faults, such as the fragility of the drive belts, had caused many breakdowns,[70] and there had not been enough time to resolve them all. Similarly, the under-estimation of the required number of spare parts had caused a bottleneck. The lull over the winter of 1918-19 would have enabled the French to solve some of these problems and reduce the number of tanks that were out of service;
- the diversification of missions: the use of Renault FT units by US forces, and to a lesser extent by the British, had an enhancing effect since the Allies had different tactical cultures. The Americans, who were not much steeped in the culture of positional warfare, often came up with dynamic ways

of using light tank units. On the third day of the Battle of Saint-Mihiel (14 September 1918), they mounted an audacious raid that created disorder in the enemy rear.[71] On 16 October, they tried doing so again, this time on the right bank of the Meuse river, but suffered a check;[72]

- the improvement of operational mobility: the Renault FT tank had been designed so it could be transported by lorry. But producing these transporter vehicles in time had proved impossible, so the Assault Artillery had been obliged to ask the Directorate of Motor-Transport Services for assistance for every operation. The creation of permanent sections equipped with purpose-built vehicles would have conferred greater mobility on the light tank battalions and made it easier to concentrate forces rapidly;
- the effect of experience: there was still much room for improvement when it came to mastering tactical know-how. Some large units remained ignorant of how best to use tanks. The officers of the light tank battalions complained that their units were often used too early, without any thought being given to the eventual exploitation. In particular, much time would have been needed before the planned fifty-four light tank battalions reached a state of tactical perfection.

In short, in November 1918 the second Assault Artillery still had many ways of increasing its resources. That process would have been slowed down by the demands for skilled personnel, the rapid wear-and-tear of equipment and the enemy's adaptations. It is therefore likely that the second generation would have reached its peak effectiveness during the summer of 1919. If we examine the Assault Artillery at the time of the Armistice, we can detect the early signs of a new cycle of innovation, a cycle based on organizational changes rather than on the technical leap of a new generation. Large, autonomous units began to emerge, as a result of two key trends.

The first of these trends was diversification. The Assault Artillery commanders strove to create a complete weapons system based on the complementary strengths of the light tanks, which specialized in accompanying the infantry, the medium tanks for providing support or gaining objectives, and super-heavy tanks, which were to be introduced. The 2C tank weighed 68 tonnes and had armour up to 45mm thick. This almost invulnerable landship was intended to serve as a spearhead during attacks against fortified positions.[73]

The second trend was a greater and greater integration of the arms. Increasingly, elements of other arms were integrated into an armoured action, rather than the tanks being integrated into the action of a different arm. Already, one infantry unit, the 262nd Infantry Regiment, was entirely motorized and trained to fight alongside the medium tanks. The increase in tank numbers made necessary a proportional expansion of this new type of infantry. The idea of an armoured, tracked vehicle for transporting troops was beginning to emerge. The British, with whom the French worked closely, tried out this concept with the Mark IX. By October 1918, when light tank battalions were in combat, they were often in radio communication with a *groupe* of quick-firing 155mm guns and with an observation airplane.[74] The Assault Artillery's officers pondered the quickest way of neutralizing any anti-tank resistance that might be encountered in 1919:

The possible solution is to protect the tanks with an accompanying artillery capable of advancing close to the tanks themselves and communicating instantly with them. The armoured artillery seems likely to fulfil this role.[75]

Some airplanes had operated for the sole benefit of the Assault Artillery from an early stage. They had begun by reporting the locations of anti-tank guns to the artillery, but had then seen their tasks become diversified. Laurent Eynac, an aviator and member of the National Assembly, highlighted this diversification when he described what happened on 28 August 1918:

The airplanes supplied information to the tank crews and eased their advance by bombing the strongpoints and redoubts. With the help of smoke bombs dropped along the fighting line, they managed to prevent the enemy from seeing the tanks approach, and thereby enabled surprise to take effect.[76]

All these various elements began to be linked by radio, with the wireless tanks playing a key role. They could therefore be commanded simultaneously and while the action was in progress.

By autumn 1918, the French already possessed all the material means necessary for forming large units that would surely have been termed 'motorized'. Some innovative, and at least partly motorized, units had already been created. Among them were the Air Division, the motorized artillery regiments and the two 'modernized' cavalry corps, all of which will be discussed in the next chapter. It would have been possible in 1919 to imitate the example set by the creation of the Air Division and devote some of the available resources to converting at least one tank brigade into an autonomous unit at the commander-in-chief's disposal. This brigade could have combined, under a single command, several combat tank regiments, some heavy or medium tanks, means of transport, some completely motorized infantry and artillery battalions, at least one squadron of airplanes, a *groupe* of armoured cars and a wealth of communications means. These units would have dealt punches, moving rapidly from one point to another of the front, but advancing on the battlefield in waves and at the same rate as the infantrymen, for 'the current era is that of rapid strategy but slow tactics'.[77]

On 24 February 1919, GHQ published a note called *General considerations on the artillery and tanks of the future*. Issued under Pétain's signature, it set out the state of current thinking at the end of the war. It anticipated a 'progressive transformation of today's infantry into a mobile, armoured infantry', and the 'appearance of tank-versus-tank combat'. It then listed the variety of tanks that were needed: light tanks, heavy tanks (to break pockets of resistance and to deal with the enemy's tanks and anti-tank guns), command tanks, supply tanks and artillery observation tanks. As for how the tanks would be used, it stated:

What will be required in future battles is the ability to bring armoured, tracked vehicles for infantry and artillery forward to certain points – preferably those points where the decision will be sought.[78]

The history of the Assault Artillery was typical of the life of most organizations. The arm had a difficult childhood, but its resources were then increased by two generations following one after the other. The key feature remained the exceptional speed of this expansion. The Assault Artillery, in common with the artillery or aviation, was an organization that acted within the theatre of operations – the theatre of real time – but was deeply rooted in the technical and industrial world of the 'interior' of the country, where a noticeably different mindset prevailed. The mindset in the interior was a combination of both a military bureaucracy that retained peacetime attitudes and an economic centralization that was a precursor to the great, planned economies. The points of contact between these two different ways of thinking saw a never-ending succession of confrontations and mediation. Hence human interactions played a key role, and the Assault Artillery's good fortune was to have had, in Estienne, a man perfectly suited to political in-fighting. His knowledge, in the broadest sense of the word, and even the immoderate nature of his personality, were assets that enabled him to solve a host of problems and help ensure that national resources were allocated to his endeavour.

Yet, despite the vision of its creator, the Assault Artillery was used in mass and as an offensive spearhead on just three occasions – firstly on 16 April 1917, and then again on 11 June and 18 July 1918 – and the results were mixed. So the idea of tanks took hold not by them acting as a spearhead, but rather by them winning a succession of 'mini-victories' in cooperation with the infantrymen. The Assault Artillery was not a miracle arm, but it did make itself indispensable. Its relative importance increased ever more steeply at a time when, while factories were producing 400 Renault FTs every month, the infantry units were dwindling to just half of their theoretical strength.

*

The Assault Artillery's growing importance sparked some adverse reactions at the end of the war. A desire to restrict the role of the tanks was deemed *de rigueur* among certain officers of the combat arms. Some of them regarded trench warfare as an aberration. Since tanks were a response to the problem of how to assault trenches, they were to be regarded as part of an interlude that was coming to a close. Others thought that the habit of using tanks might 'deaden the offensive spirit.'[79] They feared that the 'real infantry' – that of 1914 – was coming under the wing of these slow and dependent vehicles. Hence the drawbacks of the vehicles became the subject of mockery: 'The Renault tank is, by definition, a broken-down machine that nevertheless deigns to work on occasion!'[80]

As for the tank officers, many of the former pioneers had become conservative, being psychologically imprisoned by their victories. In 1922, Colonel Charles Chédeville, who had formerly commanded the Assault Artillery brigade attached to the 4th Army, suggested the Champagne offensive (26 September – 8 October 1918) as a relevant model for how to use tanks. He thought that the most reliable way of seizing fortified positions remained an artillery preparation followed by an attack that the infantry was to carry out as if it lacked any armoured support. Only then were the tanks to try and catch up with their infantry and fight alongside it.[81] In 1925, Lieutenant-Colonel Pol Maurice Velpry, another Assault Artillery brigade commander and a future tank inspector, reckoned that the tank of the future would be an improved Renault FT. These trends of thought were all bound up in some entrenched beliefs:

- the tank's only mission, the mission for which it had been created, was to 'ease the task of our own infantry'.[82] The tanks were therefore subordinated to the infantry by a decree of 13 May 1920;
- the tank was unsuited to mobile warfare: units that carried out a movement of 25 km on caterpillar tracks, in a single stretch, were then obliged to halt for half-a-day;[83]
- the tank was unfit for fighting in difficult terrain: woods, mountains, marshes or towns. 'All these are no-go areas for tanks and even more so for tank armies', stated General Emile Alléhaut in 1929 in *Motorization and tomorrow's armies;*[84]
- tanks could not be used in mass and without support. In 1935, the author of an article in the *Revue d'infanterie* closed his account of the attack on 16 April 1917 by expressing the wish that: 'the French tanks should preserve this guiding concept of being used in conjunction with the other arms, especially the infantry. They should adapt this concept to keep pace with technological advances rather than rejecting it as something outdated. Before letting themselves be carried away by dreams of mechanical cavalcades, they should recall the splendid, and yet bloody and fruitless, charge of the [armoured *groupes]* AS5 and AS9 towards the railway line, 2 km out in front of the leading infantrymen.'[85]

The transition to peacetime brought with it additional causes for a slowing down and a restriction of the imagination where the use of tanks was concerned. There was no longer any tactical problem to be solved. The current paradigm 'explained everything', and not for many years to come could it be challenged by an external threat. Intangible resources soon drained away. Combined-arms combat is complex and difficult to maintain at a peak of efficiency. The end of the fighting, demobilization and a shortage of training means left the Assault Artillery unable to maintain its know-how. It remained tied to a plethora of equipment. This equipment soon became obsolete as a result of developments in the automobile industry, and yet it was retained because the financial and industrial means needed to replace it were no longer available. Furthermore, the tanks were regarded as an offensive arm and as such they found themselves increasingly out of tune with public opinion. We can therefore see the extent to which history had a hand in shaping immediate post-war thinking about the future use of tanks.

# Chapter 11

# The Grand Army of 1918

The French army underwent a series of crises following the disastrous Aisne offensive of April-May 1917. There was a crisis of morale for the infantry, tactical and industrial crises for the technical arms and a cultural crisis for the cavalry. It took time to resolve these crises and to redefine an operational doctrine. The first step was to restore the confidence of the troops, which meant giving them some impressive victories. The army's materiel and tactics then had to be developed as rapidly as possible in order to withstand the Germans, who had acquired a temporary advantage of numbers and whose offensive methods were formidable. The years 1917 and 1918 saw the French and German armies of the next thirty years taking shape at the same time.

## Preparing for a New Form of Warfare

Pétain, the new commander-in-chief, set out his initial operational concepts in a series of pamphlets issued between May and July 1917. These pamphlets were: *Directive number 1* (19 May 1917); the *Instruction of 4 June 1917 for the implementation of directive number 1; Directive number 3* (4 July 1917); and the *Amendment of 27 July 1917 to the instruction of 16 December 1916.* They showed that Pétain remained true to his ideas of autumn 1915. To start with, he would increase both the amount of materiel and its mobility, with a particular focus on tanks and airplanes. Next, he would absorb the enemy reserves with repeated attacks on different fronts. Then, once he had the materiel he needed, he would make a general push.

For the immediate future, physical and moral constraints obliged Pétain to be prudent in conducting the defensive and offensive. He had to wear down the foe whilst incurring a minimum of losses. Attacks had to use as many material means as possible in order to spare the infantry. They had to be limited to the capture of the first German position, so the operation was more or less bound to succeed and so masses of artillery did not have to be moved forward.

Manœuvre was nonetheless restored – not by the scale of the attacks, but by their multiplication along the front. The French high command understood that from now on the art of war boiled down to rapid operations but slow engagements. It therefore developed the area behind the front, and put in place the means for transferring combat equipment from one sector of the front to another by rapid lateral movements. This meant that forces had to be arranged in depth, an elaborate transport organization set up and a number of construction projects carried out.

### Limited offensives

Strategy and tactics are closely linked not only to technology, but also to the morale of the combatants. The French army had grown increasingly frustrated after the failed attempts to break through in Artois, in Champagne, at the Somme and on the Aisne, and it had lost much of its faith in great, decisive operations. The 'mutinies' of May-June 1917 were the most dramatic expression of this mood within the units.

Opinion among the generals was more divided. Adherents of the offensive remained convinced that Nivelle's method had failed to work because of political reasons, bad luck and a shortage of means. They argued that the situation had now changed, for masses of modern equipment were reaching units, and the conjunctural causes of Nivelle's failure had vanished. Those who advocated the offensive found the defensive, and limited battles, unthinkable. But most generals took a different view and agreed with the commander-in-chief. In their opinion, they had to wear down the enemy, while at the same time rebuilding their own moral strength, before they could even think of trying to break through.[1] Once again, the school of firepower and method prevailed.

Several limited attacks were therefore prepared in meticulous detail. The attackers studied the defensive systems they had to take. Officers were able to fly over the front. Aerial and panoramic photographs were provided for the assault battalions, and the troops trained on simulated enemy defences.[2] The infantry's action was planned on a scientific basis: it was calculated that a battalion could penetrate to a depth of 1 km, and that a regiment could go up to 3 or 4 km. The artillery spent months preparing for its action and accumulated vast resources. Whereas 0.7 tonnes of shells had been needed for every 1 metre of the front attacked in Champagne in 1915, the figure was now 6 or 7 tonnes. Thirty-two days and 266 trains were required to stockpile the 80,000 tonnes of ammunition needed to feed the Battle of La Malmaison and gain 70 square km of ground.

For the operation of La Malmaison, five artillery *groupements* supported each assault division. Three of the *groupements* were to establish a barrage in front of each regiment, another was to provide the distant, standing barrage, and the fifth was to shell any assemblages of enemy troops that were reported by aircraft. The operation was closely coordinated, partly because of the use of airplanes for liaison and artillery spotting, and partly because a real web of telephone lines had been set up with combined-arms points of connection.[3] In earlier battles, which had sought to break through the enemy front, the biggest uncertainty had been the attack against the second position, which had required the artillery to be brought forward. But since this stage no longer existed, there was nothing to complicate planning. Nothing prevented planners from calculating what would happen throughout an entire operation, nor from prescribing the combatants' every move in the smallest detail from the start to finish of an action.[4]

These battles saw many innovations and experiments. They included not only contact aircraft for keeping track of the infantry's advance, but also the passage of lines, which involved one unit moving through another in order to take the lead. Another innovation was the 'square' disposition of a division, with its three infantry regiments side by side, and the three battalions of each regiment arranged one behind the other. Yet another experiment was the use of *groupements* of up to 120 machine-guns, firing indirectly so their mass of bullets plunged into the enemy rear. Stokes mortars, quick-firing artillery and tanks all began to be used in large numbers.

These principles were applied by the British in Flanders on 31 July 1917, and by the French at Verdun in August and at La Malmaison in October. In each of the operations of Verdun and La Malmaison, three to four army corps, with seven or eight infantry divisions in the first line, supported by tanks and by around 2,000 artillery pieces, attacked fronts that were 10-17 km wide. A six-day artillery preparation, followed by two or three days of fighting, produced a gain of 5 km. The Germans suffered heavily. They saw twenty-four of their infantry divisions ground down at Verdun, and lost a further 50,000 men at La Malmaison. In contrast, French losses were limited. At La Malmaison, they amounted to 12,000 men.

Yet the most important result of these battles was unquestionably the restoration of confidence at every level. General Jacques Elie de Fonclare, who commanded an army corps at Verdun, stated: 'In some previous offensives, we had planned and perfected everything, except the key tool – the men themselves. In the offensive of 20 August, we had the sense not to neglect this overriding factor.' General Fénelon François Germain Passaga added:

> Courage is needed to carry out an attack, but courage on its own is not enough. All too often a lack of wisdom and understanding of realities have caused us to squander valuable forces and allow success to slip through our fingers, and this is not sufficiently recognized.[5]

The losses of the second half of 1917 were the lowest of the entire war. Between August and December, they amounted to 38,000 men dead or missing and 128,000 sick or wounded.[6] The troops sensed their strength had returned. Once more they believed in victory, and this rediscovered confidence removed the restraints on change.

Nevertheless, these limited offensives had their flaws. They could work only in a few areas of the front where conditions were favourable. Surprise was still not complete. A rapid succession of offensives was out of the question, because of the time needed to shift the enormous mass of artillery from one point of the front and establish it at another. The key flaw was that the success of this type of operation depended on the use of a colossal amount of materiel. Fielding a similar density of resources for an offensive on a wide front would simply have been impossible.

The *Instruction on the offensive action of large units in battle* (31 October 1917) synthesized the methods used in these engagements and the lessons to be drawn from them. It set out a conception of the offensive that sought to solve the tactical problem by taking caution and method to an extreme. Fighting in open country was not even discussed. GHQ thereby turned into a system what should have remained just a temporary phenomenon. The *Instruction* thoroughly convinced the infantry that it was incapable of doing anything at all without powerful artillery support.[7]

In many ways, this was a return to the methods of the 'scientific conduct of the battle' – methods that had become established back in January 1916 after Pétain had helped instigate them. Yet far superior means were now available, and the emphasis placed on cooperation between the arms might make it possible to regain a certain tactical flexibility if units underwent lengthy training.[8] The 'red book' – a reference to the colour of the *Instruction*'s cover – was well received on the whole in the junior staffs and within units. But it provoked a certain scepticism among several generals who favoured shock. They complained that the infantry's role was limited to occupying what the shells had conquered, and they particularly criticized the abandonment of any hope of a quick victory. In their view, Nivelle's method remained valid.[9]

## The defensive organization of the front

The *Instruction* of 31 October 1917 had barely been issued before it became largely obsolete. The considerable increase in modern, military equipment, and the German adoption of new offensive methods, raised the prospect of a return to a war of movement. *Directive number 4* (22 December 1917) tried to organize the defence of the front in readiness for these new actions. The pamphlet generated many reservations. It was perceived to be both instituting and prescribing the primacy of the defensive in the high command's plans. This was a notion that many officers still found hard to stomach. Some even talked of 'a return to 1870', which showed just how strong the memory of that 'dreadful year' remained, even as late as 1918.[10] Yet the balance of strength at the end of 1917 was clear-cut. For the first time since the start of the war, the German army had the advantage of numbers. Since the Germans did not have time on their side, they were obviously going to be quick in bringing their new combat methods into play on the Western Front. To counter these methods, *Directive number 4* (and the *Instruction* of 24 January 1918 for its implementation), introduced the concept of defence-in-depth.

As an example to illustrate the concept, let's look at the arrangements made by the 36th Infantry Division. The division established itself on the defensive in the region of Courcelles-Méry, 20 km north-west of Compiègne, between 5 and 7 June 1918. It was arranged in two echelons. The first echelon contained two regiments, which divided the front between them. Each of these regiments used some of its strength to hold a forward zone, which had a couple of lines separated by an interval of 200 metres. The units occupying this zone had to dislocate the enemy attack, so the assault troops would become separated from their artillery support. They also had to gain time for reinforcements from the army corps to reach the division.

Extending up to 1 km to the rear of this forward zone was the battle zone. Here, *groupes de combat* (tactical subunits broadly equivalent to British sections) were arranged for mutual support in a pattern similar to the spots representing the number five on dice. The arrangement of these *groupes de combat* became progressively denser up to the main line of resistance. The division received about sixty machine-guns to supplement its normal allocation. The men needed to serve these additional guns were taken from the engineer companies, the cavalry squadron and the divisional training centre. The machine-guns were distributed throughout the disposition and carefully hidden. Anti-tank guns and some individual batteries were likewise established on the main line of resistance. The trench-mortars, the 37mm guns and the Stokes mortars were placed behind this line.

In the second echelon was a second position, which had both an intermediate line and a main line. This position was held by the third of the division's three infantry regiments. Two-thirds of this regiment's strength was on the main line. The artillery was either behind this position or distributed between the regiments of the first echelon.

Since the commander of the 36th Infantry Division knew the rough date of the German offensive, he aimed to achieve defensive surprise. The necessary construction work was done at night, and the carefully-concealed positions were occupied only at the last moment. Furthermore, the first lines were evacuated on the eve of the attack.

Another infantry division, the 11th, was in support of the 36th. On 8 June, the commander of the 11th organized a command-post exercise. This involved

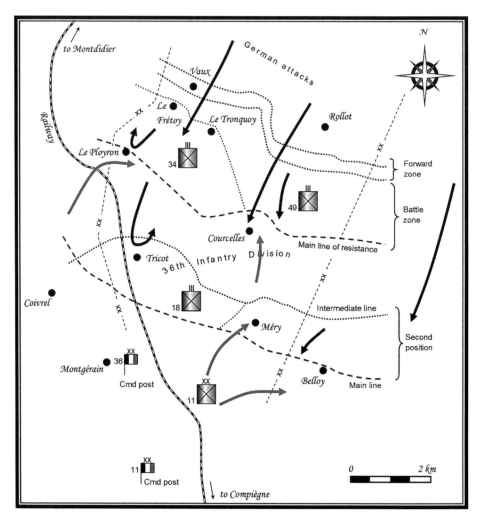

The 36th Infantry Division at Courcelles-Méry, 9 June 1918.

each unit sending a command group to occupy the actual place that had been earmarked for it in the second position of the 36th Division. Each command group had to set up its complete communications network. The 11th Division was therefore ready to intervene, should it be needed.

The German attack was unleashed as expected in the early hours of 9 June. It followed an artillery preparation, which relied heavily on gas shells. Much of the shelling hit empty ground, and the attack units became disorientated. The French troops in the forward zone fought furiously before falling back on the main line of resistance. The Germans were finally checked in front of this line, but we should note one flaw. Notwithstanding the efforts of the divisional and regimental commanders to ensure the implementation of the concept of defence-in-depth, enough troops had been left in the first line for the command posts of both the foremost battalions of the 34th Infantry Regiment to be surrounded in the early stages of the assault.[11]

*The organization of operational mobility*

Behind this deep defensive system, the French high command set up an entire network to allow a high degree of operational mobility. By doing so, it hoped to exploit the marked Allied superiority in motor-vehicles. During the course of the war, the French motor-transport service expanded to ten times its initial size. Starting with a park of 9,000 vehicles in 1914, it ended up with 88,000 in 1918, when the corresponding German figure was barely 40,000.[12] To make the most of these plentiful resources, the road network in the theatre of operations was tightly organized, along the same lines as the railways. Motor-Transport Regulatory Commissions were created in 1916, with responsibility for managing and supervising the traffic on a set of roads that could cope with intensive traffic. 'Policed roads' were created by dividing the road network into permanent operating zones called 'fixed cantons'. These zones were linked by telephone and could be reinforced by mobile 'cantons'.

The first achievements of this system were logistical in nature. The most famous 'policed road' was the *Voie sacrée*, or Sacred Way. In 1916, it enabled some 5,000 to 6,000 vehicles a day to drive between Bar-le-Duc and the troops fighting at Verdun.[13] By August 1918, roads were used to transport 456,000 wounded men and 1,040,000 tonnes of equipment in a single month.

The existence of these resources and organization meant that in 1918 large-scale, strategic movements could be made by road. These movements complemented those that were made by railway and had the advantage of being more flexible. Initially, they were carried out by the General Artillery Reserve, which was the first to prepare, in a rational manner, manœuvres by road using lorries. Movements of reserve divisions were also organized. The twenty *groupements* of the motor-transport service enabled one-fifth of the French large units to be conveyed from one point to another of the front in a few days. The German offensive of March 1918 was eventually checked by seventeen divisions transported by road from the 23rd to the 26th of that month. Later in the spring, between 27 May and 2 June inclusive, the motor-transport service conveyed the infantry of thirty-three divisions, along with the artillery of three divisions, to seal off the German breakthrough on the Aisne, whereas just nineteen divisions were brought up by railway.[14] Other units that intervened – the two modernized cavalry corps, the Air Division and the motorized artillery regiments – were totally unique. For its movements, the Air Division relied on an entire 'chessboard' of airfields that had been prepared behind the likely combat zones. In May, light tank battalions became available, and they, too, could be transported by lorry.

The ubiquity of the internal combustion engine in the French army enabled its units to 'stick' permanently to the enemy in both attack and defence. This was a stark contrast to the slow pursuits in September 1914 and during the German *Alberich* withdrawal in March 1917. Tactical mobility, which depended on the creation of entirely tracked units, had not yet become a reality by the Armistice. But strategic mobility on wheels was already a reality and conferred a significant advantage over the German army, which was far less advanced in this field.[15] This mobility was eased by another French advantage, namely in communications. The French army in 1918 had 200,000 telephones compared with 2,000 in 1914; 2 million km of telephone line compared with 600 km; and 28,000 wireless sets compared with fifty. The technology of the wireless sets, especially the continuous wave ones, was far in advance of those used by the Germans.[16]

## France's Shock Troops
### *The new infantry*

The high command had patched up the infantry's psychological make-up. But even after the restoration of morale, it remained difficult to conceive of any offensive undertakings as risky as those of 1917. The infantry was also suffering from a serious manpower crisis. Despite the disbandment of some units, this crisis persisted until the end of the war. In 1918, the infantry companies had to fight while chronically and increasingly understrength. By the middle of 1917 they had already received their full allocation of the new individual and crew-served weapons that had begun to be issued the previous year, so they could hardly count on any further increase in their firepower from that source. Besides, all these weapons – 37mm guns, automatic-rifles and light mortars – had been the result of improvisation and did not fully answer the infantry's needs. The one piece of equipment that should have made a real difference in enhancing the infantry's capabilities was the light tank, but its production was falling further and further behind.

Perhaps the answer instead lay in an improvement of combat methods. Many officers were tempted to do what the Germans had done and concentrate resources on élite divisions, which would be bigger versions of the *corps francs* and special *sections* that some units had created. Pétain took advantage of the thinking that was generated about the reorganization of the infantry company to launch a debate as to whether to create assault units. It was a vigorous debate, but in the end Pétain rejected the notion of having units of 'gladiators'. He reckoned that the *Stosstruppen* (assault troops) were 'an indication of the decline of the German high command's confidence in its infantry.'[17] In his view, implementing this élitist idea would lead to the creation of two armies, one rich and one poor.[18] In the French infantry, which was still 'convalescing', the 'poor' version would be highly fragile. Above all, Pétain was thinking at the operational level. He applied the principle of Verdun on a large scale: average units that spent spells at the front on a rotational basis were worth more than élite units that rapidly became worn out by being constantly in action.

We should note that the situation was a bit more complicated in reality, for the French did have a few 'assault divisions'. Six infantry divisions – the 11th, 37th, 38th, 39th, 43rd and 48th – were committed to action fifteen or sixteen times during the war, compared with the average of just seven times per division. These units, often composed of Colonial or North African troops, benefitted from having better men, equipment and training.[19]

Notwithstanding the existence of this handful of assault divisions, the high command preferred to embark on a sustained improvement of the overall standard of tactics. Training, which had previously been rather neglected, was now emphasized, with a particular focus on cooperation between the arms. Yet this did not truly transform infantry combat, since the Renault FT tank arrived in significant numbers only in May 1918, right at the time when the French army was fighting on the defensive.

Meanwhile, the abundance of automatic-rifles opened the way for a major organizational innovation. The *Fusil mitrailleur* 1915 'Chauchat' was a convenient, but unreliable, weapon. In order to complement and protect the automatic-riflemen, it was therefore necessary to form integrated tactical units smaller than a *section*. The result was the creation of the *groupe de combat*. Sergeants were given responsibility for the combination of weapons in these *groupes de combat*. This was a crucial qualitative leap, for it entailed an admission that the officers were unable to exercise direct control over all the combatants, and it was also a recognition that young NCOs were capable of directing an action without supervision.

The story of this radical innovation exemplifies the infantry's metamorphosis during the war. The starting point can be found in two phenomena that had been taking effect since August 1914. The first was the thinning-out of combat formations to reduce their vulnerability to fire as much as possible. The spacing between men in the skirmish line, as stipulated in the regulations, expanded from one pace in 1914 to four or five paces (between 2.5 and 3 metres) in September 1916. In other words, it took two years of war to accept something that had been evident since the end of the Russo-Japanese War in 1905. Much the same slowness had been seen before the war in decentralizing command first to captains and then to *section* leaders. A desire to cling on to power helps explain the delay, but it is also likely that changes to the regulations were simply belated, formal recognition of what units had already been doing from an early stage.

The second phenomenon was the issuing of a wide range of weaponry to the infantry companies: grenades, automatic-rifles and the discharger for the Viven-Bessières rifle-grenade. This technical transformation led to a greater specialization and interdependence of the men. Hand-grenades, for example, were now in such widespread use that team work was indispensable. The grenade-thrower was extremely vulnerable while he was throwing grenades. He needed comrades nearby to protect him and others to supply him with ammunition. It was much the same for all the new weapons. Hence a division of work came into being, which required a new solidarity. The result was the creation of a modern infantry, where the tactical unit became a machine for generating fire – a machine in which each of the combatants was a cog.

The thinning-out of formations, and the accumulation of different weapons, meant that the captain who commanded a company was deprived of any real ability to coordinate his men. An official note dated 27 September 1916 lowered the echelon of combined-arms coordination from the company to the *section* (the equivalent level of a British platoon). The *section* was divided into two specialized units. One half-*section* grouped together the infantry-support weapons and was the 'fire' element. The other half-*section* was the manœuvre element, composed of *voltigeurs* ('vaulters', or light infantrymen).

Even this structure proved too cumbersome to be commanded by word of mouth. In any case, a more generous allocation of automatic-rifles allowed other possibilities to be considered. The training section at GHQ orchestrated the thinking. The result was the *Note on the reorganization of the infantry company,* dated 10 September 1917. The infantry's basic tactical unit was organized definitively around the automatic weapon, by grouping together the men who served that weapon and those who protected it. This new half-*section,* which contained between fifteen and twenty men, was officially termed a *groupe de combat*. It gathered the whole provision of infantry light weapons and split them between two specialized squads. One squad contained *grenadiers-voltigeurs,* and the other the automatic-riflemen and rifle-*grenadiers*.

Before the war, a combination of different weapons had been found at battalion level and no lower. But the mixing of weaponry had then descended the echelons as command was decentralized from the level of captain to that of sergeant. By 1917, the *groupe de combat* commanders did not merely ensure that orders from above were carried out. They also had to issue orders of their own. This revolution in mentalities was eased by the democratization of the trenches, for the vast majority of the NCOs and *section* leaders were civilians who had been called up for active service. It was eased, too, by the increasing professionalization of the men and by the mutual trust generated as a result of shared ordeals. Major Emile Laure described how the new *groupes de combat* operated:

> The core consisted of automatic weapons that could rapidly come into action and let fly a vast number of bullets. These automatic-rifles were in the hands of the *fusiliers*. Around them were *grenadiers,* who used their hand- or rifle-grenades to keep the enemy at a distance. Lastly, *grenadiers-voltigeurs* were scampering about and searching any hiding places, agile, alert and ready at any moment to use either their rifle, their bayonet or some grenades.[20]

The new organizational structure allowed a wide range of formations to be adopted within the *section* to suit the situation. For example, units might be arranged abreast so as to form a line. Alternatively, they might be formed in column with a frontage of either one or two men. The general principle was that a unit tended to adopt the line when in contact with the enemy, but the column if it was in the second echelon or if it wanted to infiltrate rapidly.

When attacking a position, which was the infantry's main mission, the *groupe de combat* might be tasked with either assault or support. If given an assault role, it jumped off from a 'parallel' of trenches at Zero Hour and headed for its objective, sticking as closely as possible to the artillery barrage (or, from May 1918 onwards, in the wake of a tank). The *groupe de combat* would not hang about in reaching the objective, but would merely toss some grenades at any defenders and dugout entrances it might pass on its route. The vital point was that the *voltigeurs* had to arrive as soon as possible after the barrage had lifted away from the objective. If they arrived quickly, they would find the defenders still too stunned by the shelling to put up an effective defence. But if the defenders were given time to collect their wits and reorganize, they would resist.

The attackers would reduce resistance by a combination of fire and movement, pinning the enemy inside his dugouts with automatic-rifle fire, neutralizing him there with indirect-fire weapons (hand- or rifle-grenades) and outflanking him by means of the movement of *voltigeurs*. But if the resistance was too strong, the *groupe de combat* would employ all its means to try and pin the enemy down with fire, so either a neighbouring unit or a support unit could take the resistance in the flank and rear. Once the enemy position had been occupied, the sergeant would reorganize his *groupe de combat* and resume his forward march, or else dig in against counter-attacks.

If a *groupe de combat* had a support role, it was entrusted with filling gaps that might open in the assault wave, with helping to reduce individual pockets of resistance by outflanking them, or with holding the conquered positions in the face of counter-attacks. Alternatively, a *groupe de combat* might be given the mission of mopping-up trenches, as distinct from an attack mission. Its squad of *grenadiers-voltigeurs* would combine the action of its men: scouts armed with rifles would work their way along an enemy communication trench, blocking the exits from any holes and protecting the *grenadiers,* who from behind them would 'sprinkle' dugouts with grenades. Meanwhile, the rifle-grenadiers of the other squad would fire grenades to greater distances, in order to keep enemy reinforcements at bay.

The new regulations also anticipated that 1918 would see fighting in open ground, away from entrenched positions. In that case, the *groupe de combat* might receive a patrol mission to keep or obtain contact with the enemy, or else to support the manœuvre with fire. The movement would be carried out using the formations described earlier. It would be done at a walk in close terrain. But if the terrain was open and exposed to enemy fire, it would be done in rushes, by either the entire *groupe de combat* or by squad.

At the same time as the French were adopting these changes, the British and German infantry likewise organized themselves around an automatic weapon, the lightest one available. The Germans had adopted the Maxim 08/15 machine-gun, and the British the Lewis Gun (1915 model). Yet despite the effectiveness of these weapons, they were not really light enough to be used as automatic-rifles. (The Maxim weighted 16 kg.) They were therefore grouped together into light machine-gun sections or squads, which resulted in a sharp separation of the functions of fire and manœuvre within platoons. Only France adopted a light automatic-rifle, the Chauchat 1915, but it was a second-rate piece of equipment. The scrap metal used in its manufacture was of terrible quality, and the semi-circular magazine often became jammed or clogged with dirt. The Chauchat's flaws were offset by combining it with other weapons. The tactical unit that resulted from this combination of weapons may have been powerful, but it proved difficult to command, and ultimately its performance was uneven. The sergeant tended to focus – as he was directed to do by the regulation – on the automatic-rifle. He tended to neglect the shock element and used it primarily to protect the automatic-rifle. It was equally rare for all the weapons that composed the half-*section* to be used to their full potential, for they had different characteristics. The effectiveness of this combat depended on extensive training and personnel who knew exactly what they were doing. Not until the end of spring 1918 did the new structure become fully effective.

\*

In short, only after three years of war had it been recognized that decentralization of command offered the answer to the tactical problem posed by the increase in firepower. Yet the poor quality of the new weapons, and the fact that they were placed together in *groupes de combat*  of mixed composition, had initially impaired their performance. They were able to become fully effective only as a result of experience and training, and after they had been integrated into a complex, combined-arms combat.

The necessary competence acquired through experience and training declined quickly after the war. The *groupe de combat,* which was so effective at the end of 1918, soon became a core reason for the weakness of the French infantry in the inter-war period. Yet from today's perspective, the creation of the *groupe de combat* was one of the key innovations in infantry combat during the twentieth century. It lent its image to modern French infantry. Even now, in 2004, the French infantry is still organized on remarkably similar bases, including in terms of its weaponry and the difficulties of command. A sergeant in charge of a *groupe de combat* of 1918 has more in common with his counterpart of 2004 than that of 1914.

### The cavalry's incomplete transformation

To the rear of the infantry, the cavalry still had the specific role of preparing to exploit any breakthrough. On 8 December 1916, GHQ issued an *Instruction on the use of cavalry in battle.* This *Instruction* reorganized the cavalry and set out its mission, with a view to what was intended to be the decisive offensive of April 1917 on the Aisne:

> The cavalry will complete the success gained by the other arms, by turning the retreat of the defeated enemy elements into a rout, and by preventing them from recovering and rallying to form a new line of resistance.[21]

General Robert de Buyer, who commanded the 2nd Cavalry Corps, noted:

> In the battles that have been fought up to now, [the cavalry] has been unable to find a use for itself. This has prevented it from learning lessons as the other arms have done. No matter. When it does come to be used, it will have to distinguish itself from the very start with a master-stroke. It must do so. Its honour is at stake, as the complete success of the high command's plans will be resting on its shoulders.[22]

Yet all such endeavours between 1915 and 1917 came to nothing. Since there was no question of tampering with either the spirit of the cavalry or its missions, all that could be changed were its organizational structures and technical means. On 24 October 1917, General Félix Robillot, the new commander of the 2nd Cavalry Corps, proposed a plan for reorganizing and using the cavalry corps. Working from the assumption that victory was assured, he still saw the cavalry, 'maintained at great expense', as the instrument that could turn actions into decisive battles and convert the enemy's withdrawal into a rout. But he demanded much greater and more modern means for this purpose.[23] His plan became reality the following year. The cavalry corps of 1918 was endowed with a wealth of:

- means of command: an enlarged staff, two squadrons of airplanes, one balloonist company, one telegraph company;
- means of manœuvre support: two companies of sappers-and-miners, one bridging train company, two motor-transport *groupes* (120 lorries, capable of transporting one infantry battalion);
- combat elements: three cavalry divisions, one division of dismounted cavalry, two *groupes* of armoured cars.

The cavalry corps of 1918 had just one weak point, namely its organic artillery. Not until October 1918, when it received two *groupes* of 75mm guns and one *groupe* of 105mm, was this weakness resolved.[24]

The most innovative feature of the cavalry corps' equipment consisted of its ninety-six armoured cars. They carried both a 37mm gun and a machine-gun, and were organized into eight *groupes*. Two of the *groupes* were assigned to each of the three cavalry divisions of the corps, and the remaining two were under the direct control of the corps itself.[25] Strangely, these *groupes* had belonged to the Directorate of Artillery until January 1917, and in many cases had been manned by sailors. They had then been officially attached to the cavalry,[26] and as such were the only 'acquisition' that the cavalry made during the entire war.

## Mastery of the Deep Battle
### *The artillery: making things too complex*

Pétain's limited offensives in the second half of 1917 saw the artillery become hugely predominant. These offensives are referred to as 'artillery battles' and often involved more artillery personnel than infantrymen. Yet the artillery's supremacy was itself a catalyst for change, since it produced new deadlocks. The quantities of ammunition that were consumed became stupendous. At Verdun in August 1917, 6 tonnes of shells were needed for every linear metre of front attacked, compared with 1 tonne at the Somme.[27] The shells expended at La Malmaison in October 1917 cost more than 500 million *francs*[28] – or twice the total production cost of every tank that France made during the war[29] – and yet this was sum paid for attacking just 10 km of front. Similar extremes were reached in planning. Artillery fire plans became tens of pages long, and it might take over a month to put all the batteries in place. The action of the artillery grew so cumbersome and expensive that it provided an incentive to resort to other solutions, especially the use of tanks. Consequently, the artillery sought to safeguard its role by implementing three innovations that gave it a new flexibility. These innovations were modularity, motorization and the simplification of the preliminary registration.

Artillery preparations for major attacks lasted so long that they ruled out any chance of surprise, and thereby jeopardized success. The duration of the preparations resulted largely from the need to register all the artillery fires by direct observation. Since the number of observation posts on the ground was limited, this mission fell for the most part to the aviation. But from 1917, the aviation's performance became increasingly unreliable. The reasons included the vicissitudes of both the weather and the enemy, the congestion of radio frequencies as use of the wireless became widespread, and also the pre-eminence of the fighters, which absorbed more and more of the aviation's aircraft and skilled personnel. The solution to the problem was a radical one. The work that the heavy artillery had done to perfect the 'scientific preparation of fires' enabled the preliminary registration to be reduced to its most basic form. Accurate fires could now be delivered straightaway, and aerial observers had to do no more than provide simplified fire-control. This innovation, which was the result of an accumulation of minor improvements, transformed the artillery's role. From now on, batteries could arrive at the last moment, and effective fires could be delivered even at night or in bad weather. Above all, the shorter time needed for the preliminary registration meant that attacks regained an element of surprise. The first experiment, at La Malmaison, was a major success.[30]

The reduction in the duration of artillery preparations was also eased by the removal of another deadlock, this one psychological rather than technical. The French finally recognized – long after the Germans had reached the same conclusion – that trying systematically to destroy an enemy position required too much ammunition and, more importantly still, too much time. The benefits of destruction were more than offset by the extra time the enemy was given in which to react. The French therefore reckoned it was better, and more realistic, simply to try and neutralize the enemy's means for several hours, while still preserving the advantage of surprise. All these methods were disseminated by means of an *Instruction on artillery fire,* dated 19 November 1917, and a major innovation was adopted for implementing them, namely training exercises using live firing against the enemy. In short, it now became possible to concentrate masses of motorized artillery at a given point during the night so they could open fire the following day.[31]

Modularity was a further reason why the artillery was able to regain a certain flexibility. It had already been tried out at Verdun in 1916, when the *groupes* of divisional artillery had been separated from their infantry.[32] This had led to many problems, involving mutual misunderstandings and cases of clumsiness in using improvised *groupements.*[33] But by autumn 1917, training and the circulation of information had allowed methods to be standardised. The *groupes* of field artillery – especially those of the army corps – now gradually lost any permanent bond to their parent formation. Their organizational structure was standardized, and they could be removed at any time from the large units in response to temporary needs on certain parts of the front.[34] In spring 1918, the motorized *groupes* came under the direct, centralized control of the General Artillery Reserve, which from now on grouped together all those units that did not form an organic part of the divisions or army corps.[35]

The creation of the motorized artillery was primarily a response to the shortage of horses. The process began at the end of 1916, when several 75mm *groupes* belonging to army corps were motorized as an experiment. Such was the success of this 'lorry-borne artillery' that a programme was set up for 1918 to create forty regiments of this type.[36] By adding the heavy batteries and motorized (anti-aircraft) guns to these regiments, the motorized artillery ended up with a total of 584 batteries, whereas the number of horse-drawn batteries was 1,795.[37] It played a vital role during the German 1918 offensives. The motorization of the artillery had been fostered by a shortage of horses, just as a shortage of men had fostered innovations in the infantry. Yet so great did the dearth of horses become that in 1918 all the artillery *groupes* had to be reduced to three batteries, each containing three pieces. Thus the artillery found itself hindered at least as much by the scarcity of horses as by the enemy.

These were ground-breaking innovations, and yet the combined effect of them all was insufficient to adapt the artillery arm fully to the conditions of the new war of movement.

### The large-scale use of aviation

Everyone thought that the aviation was destined to play a major role in the battle of 1918. But at the end of 1917, it experienced its first major crisis – a growth crisis that manifested itself in industrial bottlenecks and tactical uncertainty. The branches of the aviation had expanded significantly, but the bomber branch reached its limits as early as 1915, followed by observation in 1916. Their growth was, in fact, stifled by that of the fighter branch. The enemy fighters were far superior to the French bombers in technical terms and prevented any deep raid. As for the French fighter branch, it tended to get a disproportionate share of the human and material resources. The pejorative phrase 'aristocracy of the air' began to be used in 1917 to designate the fighters. The rapid and unbalanced expansion of the aviation was accompanied by a degree of organizational anarchy that had to be overcome.

When Pétain became commander-in-chief, he began by setting out his conception of aerial action. The aeronautics were to act in mass in order to seek air superiority, carry out the strategic exploration of the battlefield, and attack the pressure points in the enemy disposition with bombs and machine-guns. The three subdivisions (fighters, bombers and observation) were to work closely together, in cooperation with the other arms, and daylight bombing was to resume.[38]

On 3 August 1917, Colonel Maurice Duval joined GHQ as the assistant chief-of-staff in charge of the aeronautics in the theatre of operations. To achieve the objectives set out by Pétain, Duval introduced a true management system, and in doing so he completely reorganized the aviation ahead of the great confrontations of 1918. The first step was to create a more coherent industrial and operational nexus, extending all the way from the 'factory to the front'. This entailed having to overcome the divergent interests of GHQ, the directorates of the arms, the ministries and civilian businesses. By the end of the war it had been achieved, as a result of Duval's experience of having worked previously at the Ministry of War and also owing to the appointment of Daniel Vincent to lead a new and more powerful under-secretariat of military aeronautics. Production increased, but the appearance of new technical deadlocks once again emperilled the expansion of the arm.[39] The problems were finally able to be resolved after an alarmist report from Pétain led to Colonel Paul Dé being appointed as Director of the Central Department of Aviation Production and, at the start of 1918, to Major Albert Caquot being made head of the aviation's technical branch. Thereafter, production increased spectacularly, and within a few months the aeronautics in the theatre of operations doubled in size.

The next step was to rationalize the environment in which the squadrons operated. As well as making units homogenous and bringing them fully up to strength, Duval created a real 'chessboard' of airfields along the entire front and set up a network of access roads. A comprehensive reorganization of logistics and maintenance made it possible to achieve high rates of aircraft availability. On 23 March 1918, at the start of the great battles of that year, all but seventeen of the 600 aircraft that constituted the Air Division's established strength were present.[40] Each subdivision of the arm was equipped with just a single type of aircraft, with the sole exception of night bombing. Furthermore, these were high-quality aircraft: Salmson for observation, Breguet XIV for daylight bombing and Spad VII (subsequently Spad XIII) for the fighter role. The difference in performance between these machines and those of 1914 was stupendous. The maximum speed had more than doubled (220 km/hour for the Spad XIII). The upper ceiling had almost tripled (6,500 metres with the Breguet XIV). The weight of bombs carried had risen from 100 to 500 kg (Farman F.50). The minimum time needed to reach an altitude of 2,000 metres was now a mere 4 minutes and 30 seconds (Spad XIII), compared with more than 25 minutes in 1914.

Increases were seen not merely in performance but also in numbers. On 1 January 1918, the aerial order of battle contained some 3,000 machines – more than twice as many as a year earlier and four times more than at the start of 1916. The French aviation doubled in size every year, despite the country's industrial problems. The abundance of aircraft permitted an expansion from six fighter *groupes* to eleven by 21 March 1918, and to thirteen by the Armistice. It also transformed aerial tactics. Each army involved in an operation had one or more fighter *groupes* at its disposal, and these *groupes* were integrated into the action as a whole. From now on, there was no place for individualism in the combat methods of the *groupes*. The death of the French ace Georges Guynemer on 11 September 1917 marked the end of an era. The observation aircraft had effective protection once more, owing to a system of permanent patrols at high and low altitudes, and then owing to massed actions by entire *groupes*. The number of available machines made it possible to create higher echelons: the *escadre* (wing) composed of three *groupes,* followed by the brigade of two *escadres* (one of fighters and the other of bombers). A distinction was now drawn between a fighter aviation, under the orders of each army and entrusted with protecting the observation aircraft, and a more offensive aviation under the orders of the Northern Army Group.

## The Combined-Arms Battlefield
### The tactical crisis of spring 1918
Despite all these innovations, the French struggled with the defensive actions of 1918, which were the first they had fought since July 1916. During the four months from 21 March to 17 July, they were constantly scrambling to contain German breakthroughs. Only one army, the 4th under General Henri Gouraud, managed to hold on to its positions in the face of the onslaught, by scrupulously applying *Directive number 4*. Despite the commander-in-chief's orders and his personal involvement, the preparation for defence and training for a war of movement proved inadequate. Many divisions, admittedly, were thrown against the enemy without warning: they had to 'unlearn' trench warfare in just a few days and try to manoeuvre in the face of assault troops who had been specially trained for that role. What saved the situation were the French army's modernity and spirit of sacrifice. It had motorized units – tank battalions, cavalry corps, motorized artillery, lorry-borne infantry and the Air Division – that the Germans lacked. These units enabled the French to create barriers of fire quickly and to set up counter-attacks, for example on the Matz river on 11 June and above

all in the Villers-Cotterêts forest on 18 July. The French army had once again improvised a new form of warfare, and had done so in spite of the efforts made to train it.

From September 1914 to March 1918, except for six months at Verdun, the French infantry was focused almost exclusively on breaking the German front. It lacked a zone where it could also wage a war of movement, as the German army was able to do on the Eastern Front. The *poilus* were therefore an 'infantry of the trenches'. They became increasingly adapted to their setting, but in doing so grew more and more incapable of changing it. Hence re-educating the troops in how to manœuvre remained difficult, even though everyone by the end of 1917 could see that the war of movement was going to resume.[41] The success of Pétain's limited offensives actually intensified this difficulty, for they were the antithesis of the combat methods that were desirable for the future. In October 1917, almost at the same time as the French prevailed at La Malmaison through extremes of planning, the Germans triumphed at Caporetto by boldness and movement. This was a far cry from pre-war theories of national culture, which had contrasted French flexibility with German rigidity.

The *Instruction on the offensive action of large units in battle* (31 October 1917) formalized the French tendency to be cautious. It stated, for example, that any advance beyond the *objectif éventuel* – the most forward objective that a unit was permitted to occupy should it find itself able to do so – should be 'cautious and methodical' and was to be undertaken solely on the orders of the army commander, 'who is the only person able to decide on its appropriateness, since he alone is able to see the overall picture.'

*Directive number 2b* issued a reminder of the imminence of battle in open country, and sought to rationalize the training needed to cope with it. Yet the directive struggled to win widespread acceptance. GHQ's liaison officers noted that there was a persistent tendency to prepare 'only trench warfare actions'.[42] A post-war study of the 13th Infantry Division recorded that 'training with a view to manœuvre was neglected. Tactical bonds became weaker, and the practice of operations in open terrain was completely forgotten. This had severe drawbacks, as the division would soon find to its cost.'[43]

In effect, the French infantry was surprised by the first actions of the new war of movement, which began at the end of March 1918. When the 13th Infantry Division intervened on the Vesle river in the evening of 27 May, it 'found itself unexpectedly faced once more with the practices of warfare in open country, to which it was totally unaccustomed.'[44] The superiority of the German assault infantry was immediately clear:

> Everywhere our troops complained of having been outflanked in their centres of resistance as a result of the infiltration of enemy skirmishers and machine-gunners. It was a deadly word, for it inspired a sort of superstition in our soldiers and left them unmanned. The reality was that the German infantry and machine-gunners manœuvred. It was necessary to do the same as them.[45]

The Germans – or at least their specialized units – were skilled at exploiting the terrain to infiltrate enemy positions, using small elements and squads of light machine-guns, under the protection of heavy machine-guns. They were always trying to undermine their opponents psychologically by firing into their flank or rear, and by subjecting them to brief but violent shelling.[46] The French infantrymen, 'whose ranks now included barely any veterans of 1914', had no memories of the war of movement and lost their nerve as soon as they thought they were cut off. In contrast, 'the engineers and the artillery, which had greater numbers of old soldiers, remained very calm'.[47] Paradoxically, the infantry found that its high proportion of automatic weapons actually put it at a disadvantage in this type of action. If it lacked enough ammunition to use its machine-guns, it abandoned them, for they were troublesome to carry. It did the same with its automatic-rifles, which it perceived as no match for the enemy's light machine-guns. It also readily abandoned rifles fitted with grenade dischargers. Furthermore, its accoutrements were out-of-date, which caused problems with stowing weapons and tools. As a result, the 13th Infantry Division lost practically half its crew-served infantry weapons. The division demonstrated a lack of discipline among the men, who were totally unused to carrying 'their gear' for long distances and for long periods of time, since 'movements were now made only in lorries'.[48] No longer did the infantry seem either able or willing to dispense with massive artillery support. Its action was marked by slowness and hesitation. The officers and NCOs remained disorientated if they encountered the unexpected, and they were unable to communicate once the telephone lines were cut.[49] Nor did it help that the infantry found the defensive actions so murderous. The 13th Infantry Division lost seven men per company in every day of defensive fighting, compared with five men at Verdun. Two-thirds of the division's infantry were out of action after two weeks.[50]

The artillery likewise struggled with the opening actions of 1918. French divisions were often flung into battle with urgent orders to re-establish a front line that the Germans were repeatedly breaking. The organic artillery of the divisions and army corps had trouble following the movements of the lorry-borne infantry, and frequently found itself caught off guard once it had arrived in place. The artillery had become set on doing one thing alone, namely striving to ensure its fire was accurate. The problem was that during the improvised actions that were now happening one after the other, there no longer existed either telephone lines or large-scale maps showing the distribution of targets. The artillerymen had to be content with maps on a scale of 1:80,000 and had to forget about formal fire plans.[51] Three things saved the situation. The first was the spontaneous decentralization of means down to the level of infantry regiments, so that fire support was immediately to hand. The second was the rapid intervention of the motorized artillery of the General Artillery Reserve, which made it possible to establish huge firing lines under the protection of cavalry units, and sometimes even to replace *groupes* of divisional artillery that had still not managed to rejoin their units. The third was the 'tactical memory' of the artillery, which enabled it to adapt quickly, thanks to the 'old lags' who had experienced the war of movement of 1914.

This period was General Duval's opportunity to impose his ideas on the need for a large aerial unit. From 21 to 25 March, the Féquant and Ménard *groupements*, or brigades, of fighters and bombers were sent out over the battlefield of Picardy.

The bombers were able to offset the artillery's impaired performance and to harass the German rear. The *groupes* of bombers attracted the German fighters, which were then crushed by the greater numbers of French aircraft. Having gained this success, Duval secured the creation of an Air Division on 15 May. Both the Féquant and Ménard brigades were grouped within this division, and Duval himself took command of it. No other country in the war had a similar unit. It had several original characteristics, including a flexible organizational structure that evolved as lessons were gleaned from the battle. It repeatedly combined fighters and bombers, and then separated them again. The network of landing grounds established along the front enabled the division to switch to a new base up to 150 km away in a single night.[52] It acted in mass with its 600 airplanes – three times the number in the aerial park of 1914 – and closely linked the action of its fighters and bombers.[53] Priority went to achieving air superiority and to bombing the battlefield or targets in its immediate rear such as railway lines, bivouacs and ammunition dumps. Strategic operations were limited to the industrial sites of eastern France, namely the Briey basin and the Moselle and Sarre valleys.[54] During the spring 1918 crisis, these 'flying firemen' achieved marvels at every critical point: Picardy, the Chemin des Dames and Compiègne, followed on 15 July by the German crossing points over the Marne river. Each time, the squadrons took advantage of the disorder into which the Germans inevitably fell in trying to exploit breakthroughs rapidly. They harassed any located German columns with bombs and machine-gun fire in order to slow them down. Similarly, the Air Division supported counter-offensives, such as the one made by General Charles Mangin south of Montdidier on 11 June.

## The new army of manœuvre

Once again, the French infantry had to adapt in haste, just as it had done after the defeats of the Battle of the Frontiers in August 1914 and after the German offensive at Verdun in February 1916. Following the initial setbacks of the March 1918 actions, GHQ sent a note to the units on 9 April. Essentially, it reminded them about the requirements for learning 'offensive manœuvre in open country', which had already been clearly set out in *Directive number 2b* issued on 30 December 1917. The infantry had to be retrained to be mobile, to combine fire and movement and to use flexible formations. Officers and NCOs had to be retaught to adopt uncomplicated command methods, brief orders, precision in designating objectives and the sensible use of the infantry's support arms – artillery, air power and tanks – for both preparing and supporting attacks.[55]

Yet this note appeared too late to have an immediate impact, as did the more general *Directive number 5* issued on 12 July 1918.[56] Units adapted to the new warfare to different degrees. Some were well prepared, notably in Gouraud's 4th Army, but most had to repeat the learning process, this time while facing the enemy. The process was eased by the determination of some generals, such as Mangin, to 'shake off the mud of the trenches'. On the eve of the attack of 8 August, General Eugène Debeney, the commander of the 1st Army, stated that he was giving his approval in advance to any act of initiative, regardless of its outcome. As in August 1914, changes were rapid and showed the French infantry's capacity to adapt.

The infantry fighting during the summer of 1918 was the antithesis of that practised four years earlier. In August 1914, large numbers of enthusiastic infantrymen charged in dense battalions, naïvely and without worrying too much about support. By 1918, units were rarely left with more than 50 per cent of their theoretical strength, and the men were worn out. But the *poilus* now operated within a well-integrated, combined-arms system. Airplanes were intervening more and more frequently to support them (three times more often than in 1917). The number of light tanks was rising (one for every 200 riflemen). The artillery had rediscovered flexibility and was firing more shells than the Germans. There was also the cavalry, especially the divisional squadron for seizing key points in the rear of a retreating enemy. The infantry no longer fought independent actions as in 1914. No longer was it subordinated to the action of artillery as it had been during positional warfare. It was now integrated into a modern, complex system that generated fifteen times more firepower around each rifleman than had been available to him in 1914, and three times more than in 1915.

This did not make the fighting any less murderous. The infantry companies of the 13th Infantry Division lost as many men per day in September-October 1918 as in August 1914.[57] But the periods of combat were much shorter. Furthermore, the 1918 offensives had a dual nature: positional warfare, followed by a pursuit of the enemy to the next position. What the Allies sought to achieve was not a breakthrough, but a continuous shaking of the enemy defence, 'by means of a hammering that would cease whenever the artillery became unable to extend its action any further, and would then continually resume on another point of the front'.[58] Each of these 'punches' was similar to the Battle of La Malmaison, with fewer means but greater flexibility, and was followed by a rapid redeployment made possible by the widespread motorization of forces. Once the Germans found their front had become untenable, they fell back to a new line. The Allies then began a pursuit that resembled a war of movement. A good example of this process is provided by the 13th Infantry Division in September-October. It launched a positional attack that gained 4 km in four days, at a cost of 2,000 men. Its subsequent pursuit lasted seven days and covered 45 km, for a loss of just 300 men.[59]

Unlike the Germans, the French infantry did not make large-scale use of infiltration. Its methods were undeniably slower. Yet in the end those methods not only cost fewer men but above all were safer in psychological terms – as was shown by the collapse of the German army once it had used up its assault troops. Nor were the French infantry's methods entirely lacking in sophisticated manœuvres. It learned, for example, to thwart the deep German defensive dispositions by likewise organizing itself in depth and sending only small detachments to lead the way. It thoroughly mastered both raids and the passage of lines, which were complicated procedures. One such raid was carried out in the evening of 14 July 1918 by a company of the 366th Infantry Regiment, strengthened by élite *grenadiers* who were specially trained for this sort of action. Five artillery *groupes* provided support. The raid penetrated four successive trenches to a depth of 5 or 6 km. The interrogation of captured prisoners revealed that a long-expected German attack would come in a few hours. The

French also found out the timing of the preliminary artillery bombardment and were able to counter the German offensive preparations with shelling of their own. They also abandoned their first position and prepared a barrage on that vacated position.[60]

The cavalry's high degree of operational mobility had made it outstanding during the defensive phase. But when the French attacked, the cavalry became impotent once more, since the necessary prerequisite for its action – the breaking of the front – never materialized. This was exemplified by the attack of General Mangin's 10th Army near Villers-Cotterêts on 18 July 1918. The 2nd Cavalry Corps was in the second echelon. Once the attack gained the first objective, the cavalry corps' mission (provided the enemy was no longer able to offer any organized resistance) was to move forward into the first echelon and fan out in several directions.[61] The cavalry corps had been reinforced with five battalions of lorry-borne infantry (although it would be joined by these battalions only on the actual day of the action) and five 75mm artillery *groupes*. Once it had passed through the infantry, it would be supported by a *groupe* of fighter aircraft.

What actually happened was that four hours after the start of the action, Mangin ordered the 2nd Cavalry Corps to pass through the divisions in the first line in order to march on Fère-en-Tardennois. He did so in the mistaken belief that the German front had disintegrated. The corps struggled to get through the congestion in the first echelon, only to find that the enemy was still resisting. It then received a paradoxical mission: to open the way for the infantry. The cavalrymen dismounted and attacked, but gained hardly any ground. After being relieved in place, the corps went back to the second echelon.[62]

In its two cavalry corps the French army had two large exploitation units that in spirit were forerunners of the large, mobile units of 1940. Yet these two corps marked the limit to the amount of modernity that the cavalry could swallow at this time. The *Instruction of 26 May 1918 on the use of cavalry* (complemented on 24 June by a note to the armies) sparked 'much discontent within an arm that was proud of its past and its traditions, by trying to tell it that fighting on foot was an almost normal mode of action, and by trying to reduce its role in many cases to no more than the transport of firepower'.[63]

The cavalrymen believed that the role of the horse remained crucial 'as a means of rapid transport', and favoured horse-drawn artillery 'so as not to be confined to the roads'. Cold steel – the *arme blanche* – was not abandoned.[64] In the same vein, the 7th and 10th Regiments of Foot *Cuirassiers* were intended to specialize in supporting tanks, doing so either on foot or in vehicles. Here was implicit recognition that a degree of overlap existed between the Assault Artillery's mission and that of the heavy cavalry with its focus on the charge. The use of *cuirassiers* in support of tanks was successfully tried out at La Malmaison, but this path was not subsequently followed. On the other hand, the *groupes* of armoured cars proved invaluable during the pursuit phases when the Germans were being chased back from one major defensive line to another. The armoured cars fulfilled all the traditional cavalry missions: harassment, reconnaissance, deep raids and the capture of key points by surprise.

## Fire from the sky

In the offensive, the artillery had entirely new characteristics compared to previous years:

- it was amply equipped with powerful, modern, long-range, quick-firing weapons;[65]
- it made large-scale use of the whole range of chemical shells (asphyxiating, lachrymatory, smoke, and above all mustard gas);
- it had a remarkable strategic mobility, owing to the use of the railway and, in particular, lorries;
- it possessed the techniques and training needed to carry out rapid fires with a minimum of adjustment.

The French no longer sought to achieve a breakthrough. Nor did they try to imitate the Germans and provoke a collapse of the opposing front by means of infiltration. Instead, the aim was to shake the enemy through a series of 'punches': attacks that were limited in depth and yet brutal and repeated. These tactics enabled the French artillery to make the most of its strengths. The artillery preparations lasted no more than a few hours, but were so sudden and intense that they were enough to neutralize a zone so it then fell to a combined-arms assault. Although smaller amounts of artillery tended to be used than in the battles of the second half of 1917, the artillery *groupements* were able to slip rapidly from one point of the front to another.

The story of the artillery's development during the war was one of a series of problems being solved by an organization with vast means at its disposal. Unlike the infantry, which suffered such slaughter, the artillery could rely on a tactical memory in order to make progress. But in contrast to the other technical arms, which were younger and more flexible, it was constantly in danger of becoming overly rigid and complex. It went through successive surges of complexity, followed by phases of rationalization. Despite its efforts, it proved unable to anticipate the drastic tactical changes that occurred, such as at Verdun in 1916 or in Picardy two years later. Yet it managed on each occasion to adapt to these changes, by radically transforming itself within a matter of months, and in this respect it symbolized the French army as a whole.[66]

The aviation made a substantial contribution to French fire supremacy. It was able to do so as a result of the Air Division being used on every offensive front. Not only did the division help secure mastery of the skies above the zone of action – something that eased all the other actions – it also harassed the enemy rear. The division shot down 637 German airplanes and 125 balloons. Yet the concept of the Air Division sparked much criticism. The six fighter *groupes* that remained at the disposal of the armies to protect the observation aviation proved insufficient. A *groupe* from the Air Division often had to be requested as a reinforcement, and this provoked recriminations. The Air Division's mixture of airplanes proved ineffective, for the bombers were heavier and slower than the single-seater fighters. As for the fighters, they were fast, but had a limited flying range and were clumsy in low-altitude combat. Since the bombers were poorly escorted, they ended up hardly ever being used beyond a range of 15 km. Their action was therefore superimposed on that of the artillery[67] instead of extending it.[68] What the French lacked was an aircraft of the sort available to the Germans: a two- or three-seater with armour plating, powerfully armed and capable of both escorting bombers properly and carrying out strikes against ground troops. But machines of this type, namely the Caudron R.XI, appeared in large numbers only in the final weeks of the war, for the fighter personnel were 'staunch single-seaters' and remained ill-disposed to the new type to the very end. Most seriously of all, the actions of the armies and that of the Air Division operating under Duval's direct command were often thought to be poorly coordinated.[69]

In 1918, the aviation also tried out new methods appropriate for the war of movement. After the shock inflicted by the German attack on 21 March, long-range reconnaissance, which had been rather neglected, received more attention. In Flanders that October, some ground units were resupplied by air after becoming cut off by a flooded swathe of shell-holes that was several km wide. In thirty-six hours, some 30,000 rations, weighing a total of 25 tonnes, were dropped at low altitude.[70] Before any major offensive, men were delivered inside enemy lines by air in order to carry out sabotage. A plan was even made, though not implemented, for four Voisin bombers to parachute an eight-man detachment under Major Evrard into a clearing in the Ardennes in October, for a sabotage mission in the Meuse valley.[71] It was also common for squadrons to work with tank units. They might neutralize anti-tank defences by strafing, creating smoke screens or correcting artillery fire, or they might make night flights to cover the noise made by tanks taking up position before an attack.

## The new operational doctrine

*Directive number 5* was issued on 12 July 1918, just days before the final, doomed German attack. The directive tried to raise awareness of the new concept of offensive operations. The outdated *Instruction* of 31 October 1917 was put aside. Limited objectives now gave way to distant ones. Short, precise orders were preferred to plans, and had to allow much scope for initiative to the subordinates who were tasked with carrying them out. The artillery preparation, brief and violent in nature, was now to try and neutralize the enemy rather than destroy him. The infantry was once again to play the principal role in battle. Equipped with powerful weaponry, it was to advance rapidly, even if temporarily deprived of artillery support.[72] The abundance of modern equipment that now existed made it possible to manœuvre once more.

After 18 July, the Allies held the undisputed initiative. Under the supreme command of Marshal Ferdinand Foch, they launched three series of offensives. The first, from 8 August to 13 September, sought to regain the ground that had been lost to the Germans. The second, at the end of September, tried to cross the Hindenburg Line, which extended from near Ypres to the vicinity of Reims. The third, at the end of October, had the objective of reaching the Hermann Line, some 30 km further back. Meanwhile, the Army of the Orient had begun a manœuvre on 15 September that broke through the Macedonian front. This was the French army's only decisive breakthrough during the whole war: as well as inducing Bulgaria to make peace, it carried the war on to Austro-Hungarian territory.

The Allied offensives on the Western Front had some new features. The big German offensives earlier that year had been separated by extensive intervals to allow masses of artillery to be put in place. In contrast, the Allies – and the French army in particular – used three series of 'punches'. Although less spectacular than the German infiltrations, these series of punches were far less spaced out in time. The French attacks were often made by one or two armies, generally in conjunction with the British or US forces. Each attack had the support of several hundred tanks, and often the Air Division was present with its 600 aircraft. Even though the artillery preparations were less massive than in 1916 or 1917, they were more effective owing to the use of mustard-gas shells and new methods. Since they were only a few hours in duration, they preserved surprise. Each attack was managed in a methodical way by combined-arms *groupements,* and in the course of a week's fighting carved out a salient in the enemy's combat dispositions, measuring an average of some 10 km in depth and 15 km in width. The multiplication of these salients produced a shaking of the line, followed by a German withdrawal. Positional warfare then gave way to a war of movement as far as the next line. Hence the attackers had to apply the techniques of these two forms of war in succession.[73] Ultimately, these methods proved as rapid and effective as those of the enemy, but were sounder since they did not rely on a limited number of élite combat soldiers who were difficult to replace. The Germans were also dependent on their artillery, which was slow to put in place, whereas the French were able to concentrate motorized units in a matter of days. In both attack and defence, the Germans had been left behind.

## The Model Battle

'The black day of the German army' was what Ludendorff called 8 August 1918 as a result of the success of the Allied offensive. Two days later, he submitted his resignation to the *Kaiser,* who refused it. This attack marked a strategic turning point. It symbolized the French tactical revival and illustrated the new capabilities of the arms. It would be used as a model in post-war military education.

This inter-Allied operation was commanded by the British commander-in-chief, Field Marshal Sir Douglas Haig. The aim was to free the Paris–Amiens railway line and also, for the French, to destroy the enemy on the Santerre plateau. The plateau, an undissected tableland, was covered with farmers' crops and dotted with woods and large villages. It lay between two marshy and flat-bottomed valleys: the Luce valley to the north (running from east to west) and the upper valley of the Avre to the south (running from the south-east to north-west). The two rivers joined each other some 12 km south-east of Amiens.

The French 1st Army, under General Debeney, was organized along the Avre river on a north-south axis. On its flanks were the British 4th Army to the north and the French 3rd Army to the south. The main offensive lasted from 8 to 10 August and was completely successful. It took a chunk out of the German front some 40 km wide and 15-20 km deep. These gains were extended by the offensives of the neighbouring French and British armies, and as a result the Germans fell back on their *Winterstellung* Line, abandoning the area they had conquered since 21 March.

The victory was remarkable on several counts. In the first place, the staff managed to mount a complex, offensive operation in a matter of days, instead of the weeks that had been required earlier in the war. The inter-Allied operation was launched just a fortnight after Foch issued his order of attack on 24 July. The speed of concentration was mainly the result of the offensive using the troops who were already in place: the three army corps that had been fighting in the sector for weeks under General Debeney. In contrast, the Germans had an army of manœuvre that was entirely separate from a static army for holding the line. If the Germans had been launching this offensive, they would have had to create a shock force behind their lines, resulting in delays and security leaks. Note that this was a complete reversal of the situation in 1914. Back then, the Germans with their homogenous active and reserve corps had enjoyed an advantage over the two-tiered French army.

In order to strengthen the offensive of 8 August, the French high command transferred to the 1st Army's control an army corps (belonging to the 3rd Army) that was on its southern flank. It also sent some mobile units. Four French infantry divisions reached the zone of operations by lorry or railway from 23 July onwards. The 2nd Cavalry Corps arrived, partly on horseback and partly in lorries. These combat units remained in the second echelon. The artillery *groupes*

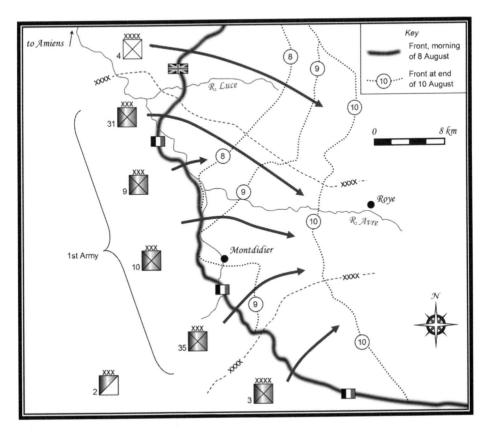

Battle of Montdidier, August 1918.

sent to reinforce the operation came by road, if they were motorized or towed, or else by railway. On 6 August, two light tank battalions were unloaded from their transport lorries. The Air Division was alerted on the same day and its 600 aircraft were ready to fight by 8 August after making a short hop to return to the installations from which it had been fighting a few weeks earlier. (These installations had been temporarily abandoned by the Air Division as a precautionary measure before the German offensive of mid-July, but had been carefully maintained during its absence.)

Another reason for the speed with which the operation could be mounted was the simplification of artillery procedures. All the preliminary steps for using 1,600 artillery pieces were done in a few days, in a 'topographical' way with no need for registration shots that might alert the enemy.

The speed with which units were put in place and preliminary measures were carried out helped ensure surprise. So, too, did strict security. The planning was done by officers specifically chosen by the army corps. These officers personally wrote or typed the orders. Use of the telephone was banned, and any indiscretion severely punished. All the movements involved in putting the units in place, including the artillery, were carried out during the two nights before the assault. Only on the eve of the attack did the forces of the first echelon take up their positions. Reconnaissances were reduced to a minimum and were made with special precautions. On the night before the attack, airplanes flew over the 37th Infantry Division to drown the noise of the tanks.[74]

The planned manœuvre was in itself original. The 31st Army Corps, which formed the northern wing of the 1st Army, had a small bridgehead on the right bank of the Avre, 4 km long and just 500 metres wide. Further south were three corps on the left bank: the 9th, 10th and 35th Army Corps. The action of these forces would consist of two phases. On 8 August, the 31st Corps was to enlarge its bridgehead in the wake of a brief artillery preparation and was to link up with the 9th Corps, which would cross the Avre a few hours later. Next day, the 10th and 35th Corps were to launch a pincer attack on either side of Montdidier. The 10th Corps would use the 9th's bridgehead to cross the Avre. The desired outcome was a general shaking of the enemy, rather than the breakthrough sought earlier in the war.

This lateral movement was coupled with a remarkable manœuvre of artillery fire. Only a limited amount of artillery was available for the operation: fourteen batteries for every kilometre, compared with forty at La Malmaison. The staff of the 1st Army therefore arranged a manœuvre of fire that would slide from north to south, keeping pace with the progress of the manœuvre as a whole. Additional artillery was concentrated in the north for 8 August, behind the 31st Corps. Once that corps was sure of success, it transferred some of its artillery resources to the neighbouring corps, which in turn gave them up at the end of its own mission. Meanwhile, another part of the artillery resources was shifted directly to the southern wing, into a zone behind the 35th Army Corps. In this zone, communications had been set up and emplacements provided for each battery, in readiness for a second big artillery preparation that was due to be unleashed on 9 August. At the same time, each corps needed to be capable of supporting its neighbours within a particular zone and with a particular number of artillery pieces, but without having to move any of its means.

The long-range artillery pieces were placed in the centre of the disposition, so they could act throughout the whole zone of action. At the level of each corps, resources were distributed in a rational manner. The field artillery and the heavy, short-range artillery (including the 220mm mortars) were distributed between the divisions. The field artillery was primarily to provide the rolling barrages, while the heavy, short-range artillery crushed any resistance that was encountered. The long-range pieces were at the disposal of the army corps for counter-battery or for targeting more distant objectives. The artillery's mobility and modularity were exploited as the battle progressed, with *groupes* being transferred from one division to another in accordance with those divisions' means. The 37th Infantry Division began the battle with ten *groupes* and ended it with three. On 11 August, the artillery of the 42nd Infantry Division found itself operating with four different divisions one after the other.[75]

Control of the third dimension allowed the lateral manœuvre to be combined with action in depth. The artillery was arranged in three tiers: in close proximity to the regiments, in the corps' zone of action and in the army zone. It was aided by a total of twenty-two observation airplane squadrons at corps level, three squadrons for the heavy or super-heavy artillery, three reconnaissance squadrons and thirteen balloons. These means of short-range intelligence-gathering were protected by three fighter *groupes,* or about 150 aircraft. The artillery's action was complemented by the Air Division's resources, especially its long-range reconnaissance *groupement* and three bomber squadrons. The 300 two-seaters of the bomber squadrons extended the effect of the heavy artillery's fire by hitting the arrival zones of enemy reinforcements, especially railway stations. The presence of the night bomber *groupes* of *Groupement* Laurens made it possible to harass the enemy around the clock. The Air Division's remaining five fighter *groupes,* which contained over 300 single-seaters, had a range of changing missions. They might be tasked with keeping watch, escorting bomber aircraft, attacking convoys and assemblages of troops, or attacking the kite balloons that the Germans used for observation.

The total of these air assets was roughly seven times greater than the entire French air service of 1914, and they were all operating within a rectangle 40 km long and 30 km deep. The favoured method was action in mass within a specific slot of time and space. Such action was generally made possible by intelligence provided by the reconnaissance squadrons. The information was transmitted either by the wireless, by messenger aircraft (in the case of photographs), or by messages dropped with attached weights on to a piece of ground designated for that purpose. All the intelligence was centralized by the aeronautics commander, who was in constant touch with the Air Division by means of either radio or a liaison officer. It was therefore possible to mount raids such as those carried out on 10 August against a convoy at the exit from the town of Roye, which was attacked by two full fighter *groupes*[76] or against the Lassigny–Noyon road with sixty-eight bombers escorted by nine Caudron R.XI airplanes. The second of these two actions saw 17.5 tonnes of explosives dropped in thirty minutes, despite the presence of German fighters. Not only did these fighters fail to shoot down any French aircraft, they also lost two of their own number. On this day alone, the Air Division discharged 50 tonnes of projectiles against the Germans, along with 20,000 rounds of ammunition. The results were analysed using photographs taken after each round of bombing. The photographs also revealed that on 10 August the Germans were starting to abandon their airfields, and this was a sure sign of an imminent withdrawal.

A protective bubble of shells and airplanes therefore existed. (One airplane actually collided with a shell in mid-air.) Under this protection, several ground units were to exploit in depth any opportunities that might arise. In the north, within the 31st Army Corps, the exploitation units were the 153rd Infantry Division, a provisional cavalry regiment (five squadrons and three machine-gun sections) and two light tank battalions. In the centre, the exploitation was assigned to a cavalry division. South of Montdidier, the task was given to the rest of the 2nd Cavalry Corps. But as it happened, these units were unable to fulfil their role. The cavalry found that the congestion on the battlefield precluded any mounted action.[77] The bottlenecks also hampered one of the light tank battalions, which reached the front line behind schedule and short of petrol. Just one of its companies, which had managed to refuel, actually intervened in the action and did so only in a limited way.[78] The other light tank battalion achieved more, as a result of excellent coordination between the tank sections and the infantrymen. (The battalion had been distributed so that each of the infantry's assault regiments had a tank company.) Nine out of eighty-nine tanks were destroyed or badly damaged.[79]

As for the infantry combat, it showed both a new boldness and close integration with the other arms. The 42nd Infantry Division, for example, formed part of the first assault wave of the 31st Army Corps. Its initial problem was that its zone was intersected by the Luce river and lay more than 1 km away from the Bavarian advanced posts. The solution adopted was for the infantry to cross the Luce quietly at night and establish itself just 300 metres from the enemy lines. At 4.20 am, the artillery preparation was unleashed. The use of smoke shells added to the density of the fog and concealed the infantry assault, which was launched just an hour after the start of the preparation. The infantrymen escaped the enemy barrage triggered by the assault, since they jumped off from ground far in front of their initial disposition. As they advanced, they stuck as closely as possible behind the rolling barrage, which lifted 100 metres every three minutes.

The first objective was gained after an hour. Part of the divisional artillery moved forward so it could continue to provide direct support. The second echelon passed through the first at the end of the morning and fought throughout the afternoon to seize the second objective. The exhausted division was relieved early that evening. In a single day, it had penetrated to a depth of 10 km, taking 2,100 prisoners, seventy-nine guns or mortars, 200 machine-guns and three villages. Never in forty-eight months of fighting had it gained a finer tally.[80]

Coordination between the infantry and the artillery was eased by the two-seaters of the divisional squadron, which were constantly flying over the ground troops. During the afternoon of the 8th, in thirty minutes, an aircraft of the 15th Colonial Infantry Division evicted some Germans from a position by machine-gunning them, before informing both the division by the wireless and the artillery by a message dropped from the air. It then chased the Germans once again, from the wood where they had established themselves. By dropping a message, as well as using machine-gun fire with tracer bullets, it indicated to the men of the 2nd

Colonial Infantry Regiment where their neighbouring units and the enemy were now in position.[81] I have already mentioned the 153rd Infantry Division fighting closely alongside tanks. Another innovation was the use of linking detachments between divisions, which prevented the loss of time in keeping the divisions aligned.[82] (These linking detachments consisted of a few *sections* and were sometimes multinational in composition.)

*

The victory of 1918 was won by surmounting the deadlocks that resulted from over-rapid growth in the tactical-industrial nexus. The army that Pétain wanted took shape with the pieces of the puzzle being put in place one after the other. The aviation was the first to resolve its industrial problems and organize itself for battle. Nevertheless, it was hampered by a failure to create squadrons early enough with the specific role of providing supporting fire for ground troops. This deficiency would persist until 1940 and was the result of the conservatism of the fighter branch, which had previously been a model of modernity and technical innovation. In all other respects, the French aviation was the foremost in the world at this time. It fielded 3,800 modern aircraft, which had the support of a powerful industry. There was a clear-cut division between the cooperation branch (156 squadrons) and the fighter branch (132 squadrons).

The artillery modernized itself in a remarkable and timely way. The only thing lacking was tracked artillery, which was in the planning stage. The widespread adoption of the internal combustion engine transformed the artillery from a powerful but rigid organization into a highly flexible arm within a matter of months. The artillery ended the war with 263 regiments and 1,100,000 men. It had almost tripled in size in four years. The field artillery in 1914 had accounted for more than 90 per cent of the pieces in the army's field forces. It did not grow much during the war – the number of its 75mm guns rose from 4,100 to 4,900 – although one in three of its regiments was now motorized. Hence the artillery's expansion occurred primarily in its other subdivisions: the anti-aircraft artillery (six regiments and 900 pieces) and in particular the heavy artillery which, with 5,000 pieces and its excellent technology, stole the limelight from the 75mm regiments. The overwhelming majority of the 156 squadrons of observation aircraft were at the heavy artillery's service. The artillery's relative importance in terms of manpower had risen from 18 to 36 per cent of the total number of men in the armies. Its tactical importance can be seen from the fact that it inflicted 70 per cent of enemy losses, compared with 25 per cent in previous conflicts.

The infantry had more difficulty in carrying out its transformation and did so incompletely. It had to relearn in a hurry how to fight a war of movement, and was obliged to wait for the light tank battalions that started to appear in large numbers only in September 1918. Its own combat, waged with skeletal units, included large-scale operational movements. These movements were made possible by motorization on a far greater scale than on the German side, and also by a fairly methodical manœuvre of fire. When 2,300 light tanks did belatedly arrive, they enabled something to be done to regenerate infantry combat, by finally giving the infantrymen the mobile support they needed. The infantry was no longer the 'queen of battles'. Its share of the army's manpower had shrunk from 70 to 50 per cent, and it inflicted only one-quarter of the enemy losses. Many of its companies were no stronger than fifty men. In October 1918, the battalions of *chasseurs* of the 47th Infantry Division had to reduce their *voltigeur* and machine-gun companies from four *sections* to three.[83] There can be no dispute that the French 'industrial infantry' was the most modern in the world. It was widely motorized, possessed its own aviation, its tanks and many light weapons, and was integrated into a complete, combined-arms framework. But, deeply scarred by its losses, it lacked confidence in its future.

The cavalry was the arm whose transformation was most delayed. Even though it created modern units, namely the cavalry corps and the *groupes* of armoured cars, its influence on the fighting remained limited. From now on, the French army had fewer cavalrymen than airmen (about 4 per cent of the total strength in each case), and this symbolized the transfer of missions between the two arms. The most forward-thinking of the cavalrymen had joined the motorized arms. But those cavalrymen who had the greatest reluctance to abandon the horse waited in vain for a breakthrough, and then came to think that the war in the trenches had been just an aberration.

# Conclusion

And so the French army of 1918 emerged victorious, with the growing help of its allies. But in order to win, it was obliged to carry out the deepest and fastest transformation in its history. In the process, it laid the foundations for a new military organization, whose broad outlines can still be seen today.

This transformation was not the achievement of an 'enlightened' high command working in the calm surroundings of staff offices. It was not a case of the high command constantly synthesizing information that arrived from units as far forward as the front, and then using that information to define a doctrine perfectly suited to the situation of the moment. The high command did not ensure that the doctrine then evolved harmoniously in response to change, nor translate it into requisite skills that the units immediately adopted. This notion of centralized control of change is largely an illusion. A centralized approach had been in place before the war, but even at that early stage had been incapable of grasping technical developments properly. In particular, the translation of doctrine into practical abilities down at unit level had been both protracted and incomplete, partly because of the filters through which the doctrine had to pass – the generals or the cultures of the arms – but above all because of the deficiencies of the training structure. The French army of 1914 was therefore characterized by a brilliant brain but clumsy movements, and this mismatch was cruelly shown by the opening actions, which were invariably disastrous.

Yet the early defeats also revealed a great moral strength, which enabled the French to withstand the shock of the challenges that would follow one after the other throughout the next four years. Furthermore, the defeats confirmed that the men and units who were actually in contact with the front were the main instigators of tactical innovations, owing to the pressure and urgency to which they were subjected. These tactical innovations constituted the 'raw material' of the changing of an army.

*

Following the opening stages of the war, the process of adaptation took shape as initiatives became more prolific. The introduction of new equipment, and the innovations of the Germans, acted as a constant stimulus for initiatives. The many changes combined in clusters to cause the capabilities of the arms to evolve. The arms had to deal with a succession of challenges, and always as a matter of urgency. These challenges included changes in the form of warfare – an offensive or defensive posture – as well as the need to confront changes in scale and master a growing complexity. Technical advances, and the sheer magnitude of the resources that were used, permitted an unprecedented growth and diversification of new branches, as well as a modernization of the traditional core elements. More specifically, the development of motorization made it possible to set up new forms of combat, such as the aeronautics or the tanks, and to create numerous, modern units such as the Air Division, motorized artillery, light tank battalions or the *groupes* of armoured cars. We must also emphasize the increase in the infantry and artillery's firepower and in the means of communication.

Every arm felt the effects of this technical modernization. Yet they all developed in their own way, at different speeds of transformation, and encountered specific problems of how to control their growth, or simply how to preserve what they already had, or even how to survive. Each arm experienced an average of one major change a year, but rarely at the same time as the other arms. The overall development of the French army resulted from these 'impulses' of its arms. Since these 'impulses' were rarely synchronized, the army's development was constantly jerky, and this helps to explain the frequent changes of doctrinal paradigms.

The high command's role in this 'organized chaos' was to master these powerful changes. Hence doctrinal thought, which seeks to guide the operational use of the various arms, remained a necessity. It kept its pre-war form, namely a confrontation between two schools of thought, one of which advocated boldness and shock while the other favoured method and firepower. Each school of thought was represented by a group of men, so whenever a paradigm temporarily gained the upper hand the result was a change of faces. But there were also some specific men – the experts – who served as links and as conveyors of ideas between all these stages in the process of change. These experts ranged from 'holders of doctorates in violent death', such as the air ace Lieutenant René Fonck, to managers of industrial warfare such as General Debeney, to entrepreneurs such as General Estienne, Major Saconney or Major de Rose, and to the godfathers, the benevolent patrons of the innovators.

*

One of the milestones in this process of adapting to the war was the appointment of the 'expert', General Pétain, as commander-in-chief. The pre-war generation at GHQ gave way to a pragmatic team that followed the commander-in-chief's lead in regarding the management of change as an integral function of command. A modern organization was established, which tapped the feelings and ideas of the troops, rationalized the way the arms were used and integrated them into an effective whole, as well as ensuring that ideas were disseminated through a coherent training structure. This new organization made it possible to assimilate the tripling of material means that occurred in the final eighteen months of the war. Above all, it allowed the French army to adapt to three forms of warfare: the 'extremely methodical approach' of the second half of 1917, followed by the mobile, defensive actions of 1918, and the mobile, offensive ones later that same year. These final transformations came to an abrupt stop in November 1918 before all the problems had been resolved.

*

The French army had reason to be proud of its modernity. In the end, it had managed to overcome all the challenges it had been obliged to take up. Yet the immediate post-war period provided glimpses of some new inflexibilities that did not augur well for the pursuit of this control of change. In 1918, one paradigm was completely dominant: that of the 'combined-arms battlefield'. It incorporated great strategic mobility with limited tactical actions. These actions took the form of punches and combined the artillery, infantry and aviation in a closely-knit trio. The effectiveness of this doctrine depended on significant material means, and above all on advanced training. Yet from the 1920s onwards, a shortage of funding resulted in a gradual lapse back into the bad habits seen before the war, and once again the French army found itself with inadequate means of training. The gap between a coherent doctrine and flawed practice soon opened up again.

As regards doctrinal thought, the pre-war debates were often over-simplified by being summed up in terms of the extreme ends of the argument, and they were largely invalidated because of their failure to foresee the technical developments that had occurred. After the Great War, one school, that of firepower and method, was dominant. It suited an infantry that had lost its taste for boldness and had become frustrated by multiple offensives that had no longer had any scope for surprise. It is true that the spread of motorization and the use of caterpillar tracks offered glimpses of new possibilities to the adherents of shock. But such dissenters were rare in a Forum that grew more and more conformist. As a result of the impoverishment of both the doctrinal debate and the training means, the French army gradually condemned itself to having to adapt in a hurry yet again. Yet rapid changes inevitably cause damage and, even more importantly, they need time and immense willpower. Although these prerequisites were present during the Great War, it was presumptuous of the French army to assume they would always exist.

*

German concepts likewise became fixed in 1918, despite today's widespread misconception that this was not so. The Germans had been impressed by the tactical prowess of their own assault troops and by the operational effectiveness of the French motorized units. They therefore tried to combine the two. On either side, therefore, the actions of 1940 appeared to be a continuation of those of 1918 with other means.

*Appendix 1*

# Timeline of Operations

## 1914

### Battle of the Frontiers

| | |
|---|---|
| Aug 3: | Germany declares war on France. |
| Aug 4: | The German army crosses the Belgian frontier. |
| Aug 5: | Attack on Liège by a German assault force. General Sordet's cavalry corps penetrates into Belgian Ardenne. It clashes with the German cavalry on the 8th. |
| Aug 7-25: | Battle of Alsace. Two French offensives (7 and 14 Aug) are repelled. |
| Aug 14-25: | French offensive in Lorraine and in the Vosges (1st and 2nd Armies). German counter-offensive on the 20th. French renewal of the offensive on the 25th. Stabilization in September. |
| Aug 22-25: | French offensive (3rd and 4th Armies) in the Ardennes. Actions of Paliseul, Neufchâteau, Bertrix, Virton, Ethe and Rossignol. French withdrawal. |
| Aug 16: | End of the Battle of Liège. French 5th Army moves forward in Belgium. |
| Aug 20: | Withdrawal of the Belgian divisions on Antwerp. Brussels occupied by the Germans. French 5th Army moves to the Sambre and confronts the Germans at Charleroi on the 22nd. |
| Aug 23: | General withdrawal of the French 5th Army. British action at Mons. |
| Aug 26: | The left-hand corps of the British Expeditionary Force is shaken by the German 1st Army. |
| Aug 29: | Battle of Guise. Temporary check to the German advance. |
| Aug 30: | Joffre gives the order for a general withdrawal on the Seine. |
| Aug 31: | March of the German 1st Army (von Kluck) swerves to the south-east. |

### Actions on the Marne and on the Aisne

| | |
|---|---|
| Sep 5: | Attack by the French 6th Army against the flank of the German 1st Army. |
| Sep 6: | Counter-offensive of the Marne. General battle along the whole front. |
| Sep 7: | Battle of the Saint-Gond marshes. Fall of the fortress of Maubeuge. |
| Sep 10-13: | General withdrawal of the Germans. |
| Sep 20: | German offensive north of Verdun and in the Woëvre. Capture of Saint-Mihiel. |
| Sep 26: | Check to a German general offensive between the Oise and Meuse. |

## Race to the sea

| | |
|---|---|
| Sep 18-24: | Battle of Picardy: the French 2nd Army is transferred from Lorraine towards the Somme. Stabilization of the front to the west of Péronne. |
| Oct 3: | Creation of the French 10th Army, for the defence of Arras. |
| Oct 9: | Belgian army falls back on Ostend. The British army takes up position north of Béthune. |
| Oct 16: | Offensive of the German 4th Army on the Yser. |
| Oct 27-30: | The locks of the Nieuport region are opened, flooding the lower valley of the Yser. German offensive on Ypres and the Monts des Flandres. |
| Nov 6-17: | New German onslaught against Ypres and Dixmude. The front now runs unbroken from the North Sea to the Swiss frontier. |
| Dec 16: | Start of the fighting for Notre-Dame de Lorette, north of Arras. |

# 1915

## Minor operations

| | |
|---|---|
| Dec 20 – Jan 12: | 'Fight for the observation posts' along the whole front. |
| Jan 19-22: | The French troops are thrown off the summit of the Hartmannswillerkopf (also known as the Viel-Armand) in the Vosges. |
| Feb 16 – Mar 15: | Multiple attacks by the French 4th Army in Champagne, on an 8-km front between Beauséjour and le Bois-Sabot. Gain of 1 km. |
| Feb 17: | French attack with mines on the ridge of Les Eparges. |

## Breakthrough attempts

| | |
|---|---|
| May 9: | French offensive in Artois. Attack by the 10th Army on Vimy Ridge. |
| Jun 16-24: | Resumption of the French offensive in Artois. |
| Sep 25-29: | French offensive in Champagne (2nd and 4th Armies). Franco-British offensive in Artois. |
| Oct 6 – Nov 1: | Renewal of the French offensive in Champagne and in Artois. |

## Balkans

| | |
|---|---|
| Feb 19: | Start of the Dardanelles campaign with the long-range bombardment of the Turkish defensive works of Kum Kale and of Sedd-ul-Bahr. |
| Mar 18: | The Allied naval squadron penetrates into the Dardanelles and continues its duel with the Turkish batteries. Three ships are sunk, including the French battleship *Bouvet*. |
| Apr 25: | Allied landings on both sides of the Dardanelles. |
| Oct 3: | Creation of the Army of the Orient, for supporting Serbia. |
| Dec 8: | Evacuation of the remnants of the Allied expeditionary corps from the Dardenelles to Salonika. |
| Dec 12: | The Army of the Orient falls backs on the entrenched camp of Salonika. |

# 1916

## Verdun

Feb 21-26:        Drumfire and German assault on the right bank of the Meuse. French resistance and withdrawal (24th). Capture of Fort Douaumont (25th). General Pétain receives command of the sector. Establishment of the *Voie sacrée* (Sacred Way).

Mar 6:            Attack by the German army on the left bank of the Meuse, between Béthincourt and the river. It reaches Hill 304 and the Mort-Homme, but the summits remain in French hands.

Apr 9:            German general attack on both banks of the Meuse.

May 1:            General Pétain replaces General de Langle de Cary at the head of the Central Army Group. General Nivelle replaces Pétain at Verdun.

May 4-29:         German offensive against Hill 304 and the Mort-Homme.

May 22:           General Mangin's offensive to retake Fort Douaumont.

Jun 7:            German army captures Fort Vaux after a seven-day siege.

Jun 23:           German summer offensive. Capture of the defensive work of Thiaumont, Fleury village and the crossroads of the Chapelle Sainte-Fine.

Jul 11:           New German offensive. Halted in front of Fort Souville.

Aug 1-6:          Final German offensive on the right bank of the Meuse.

Aug 18:           French army recaptures Fleury.

Oct 24:           Offensive by General Mangin on the right bank of the Meuse. Fort Douaumont is retaken.

Dec 15:           Offensive by General Mangin on the right bank of the Meuse. Capture of the Hardaumont massif.

## Somme

Jun 24:           Start of the Allied artillery preparation on the Somme.

Jul 1:            Franco-British offensive north of the Somme.

Jul 14:           New British offensive on the Somme. The German second position is taken.

Jul 18:           German counter-attack against Delville wood.

Sep 4:            Offensive of the French 10th Army (General Micheler).

Sep 12:           Offensive of the French 6th Army (General Fayolle).

Sep 15:           British offensive on the Somme. Capture of Flers, Martinpuich and Courcelette. First use of the tank on the battlefield (Flers and Courcelette).

Nov 20:           Halt of the offensive.

Dec 12:           General Nivelle replaces Joffre as commander-in-chief of the French armies on the Western Front.

# 1917

## Nivelle offensive

Mar 16:           Operation 'Alberich'. German withdrawal between the Somme and the Oise.

Apr 9-16:         British offensive at Vimy.

Apr 14:           Check of the French 3rd Army's attack on Saint-Quentin.

| | |
|---|---|
| Apr 16-20: | Offensive on the Aisne. Abandonment of the idea of a breakthrough. The operations continue until 15 May. |
| May-Jun: | 'Mutinies' in the French army. |
| May 15: | Pétain replaces Nivelle as commander-in-chief of the French armies on the Western Front. |

## Limited offensives

| | |
|---|---|
| May 28 – Jun 7: | The British reduce the Messines salient. |
| Jul 31: | Franco-British offensive in Flanders. The British persist until 10 November. |
| Aug 20-24: | Offensive north of Verdun. |
| Oct 23-26: | Battle of La Malmaison. |
| Nov 20-30: | British offensive at Cambrai with the massive use of tanks. |

# 1918

## German offensives

| | |
|---|---|
| Mar 21 – Apr 5: | *Michael* offensive against the British 3rd and 5th Armies, between Bapaume and Noyon in the direction of Amiens. Intervention of the French reserves. |
| Apr 9-30: | *Georgette* offensive in Flanders. French intervention. Half of the French army is north of the Oise. |
| May 27 – Jun 6: | *Blücher* offensive on the Aisne. French 6th Army suffers a disaster. |
| Jun 9-13: | *Gneisenau* offensive against the French 3rd Army. Battle of the Matz. French counter-attack on the 11th. |
| Jul 15 – Aug 2: | *Friedensturm* ('peace' offensive) in Champagne. The French 4th Army holds on north of Reims. The 5th and 6th Armies are driven in. Counter-attack by the 10th Army at Villers-Cotterêts. |

## Allied offensives

| | |
|---|---|
| Aug 8-10: | Start of the clearing offensives. Franco-British attack in Picardy and in the region of the Matz. |
| Aug 20 – Sep 3: | Second phase of the clearing operations. The French 10th Army attacks north of the Aisne. British offensives in Artois. Between Arras and Soissons, Germans fall back on the Hindenburg Line (20 km to the rear). The Line is reached on 10 September. |
| Sep 12-16: | A French and US offensive reduces the Saint-Mihiel pocket. |
| Sep 15: | In Macedonia, the Army of the Orient breaks the Bulgarian front. |
| Sep 29: | Bulgaria signs an armistice. |
| **Oct:** | The offensive of the Army of the Orient extends in three directions: Constantinople, Romania and Hungary. |
| Sep 26-30: | Allied general offensive in the face of the Hindenburg Line. |
| **Oct, start:** | South of the Oise, opposite the French, the Germans fall back between the 4th and 12th on the Hunding Line. Opposite the US, the Germans fall back from 9 October, and then resist foot by foot until November. North of the Oise, the Germans fall back on the Hermann Line on 8 October. |

| | |
|---|---|
| Oct 14-26: | Allied general offensive in the face of the Hermann-Hunding-Brunhild Line. Capture of the triangle Lille-Roubaix-Tourcoing. The Netherlands frontier is reached on the 20th. Capture of the Hermann-Hunding Line between the Escaut and the Argonne. |
| Oct 31 onwards: | General push between the Netherlands frontier and the Moselle. An offensive is planned in Lorraine for 14 November. |
| Nov 11: | Germany signs an armistice with the Allies. |

*Appendix 2*

# Analysis of the 13th Infantry Division's Actions

## Analysis

The 13th Infantry Division was at the front twenty-one times. It was present at the front for a total of 118 days, or 52 per cent of the total duration of the war. Between August 1914 and December 1915, the division spent as many days present at the front as during the next three years combined. Four periods can be clearly identified:

### The war of movement of 1914

Fifty days of engagement for four actions, for a total duration of seventy-five days, from the Battle of the Frontiers to the end of the Race for the Sea. Total losses amounted to 11,903 men, or the division's infantry strength. The whole infantry of the division was 'consumed' in three months, at a rate of about 230 MEN FOR EACH DAY OF FIGHTING. In each action, the division lost an average of one-fifth of its strength. AN ADVANCE OF 1 KM COST ABOUT TWENTY-SEVEN MEN. The average density was one battalion per km, supported by an average of two machine-guns and one 75mm battery. This was in line with the average of the available means of support within the division. There was no reinforcement from outside the division.

### The ferocity of 1915

The division was engaged in Artois for 352 days, or about 80 per cent of the period. It lost 37,232 men, or an average of 105 MEN FOR EVERY DAY OF FIGHTING. The percentage of losses varied widely, but reached the record of 61 per cent for the actions of Lorette (gaining a depth of 800 metres of ground). This was unarguably the division's most difficult period of the war. AN ADVANCE OF 1 KM COST MORE THAN 8,000 MEN. For every 1 km of ground, the division engaged an entire regiment. From April 1915, a major increase occurred in the available means of support. Each regiment was then supported by a regiment of 75mm guns, a *groupe* of heavy artillery pieces and a mass of machine-guns equivalent to twice the divisional allocation. The division was therefore reinforced by external means of support during offensives.

### 1916

For the 13th Infantry Division, the year can be divided into three main periods: (1) the big battles (Verdun and the Somme, ninety-three days, or 25 per cent of the year); (2) sector occupation (eighty-eight days, or 25 per cent); (3) rest and training (50 per cent). Losses amounted to 11,492 men, or sixty-three FOR EVERY DAY OF PRESENCE AT

THE FRONT, BUT 113 FOR EVERY DAY IT PARTICIPATED IN A BIG BATTLE. Yet the extreme violence of the two weeks spent at Verdun should be noted, since the division lost practically 40 per cent of its strength there. AT THE BATTLE OF THE SOMME, AN ADVANCE OF 1 KM COST 900 MEN. The norms of engagement differed between the two battles. The densities and means used at Verdun were similar to those of 1915. On the Somme, the density of engagement was less than one-third (two battalions instead of three per km). But the artillery support was of the same level as at Verdun and, above all, modern infantry weaponry had made its appearance. Hence far greater firepower was deployed per man.

### From June 1917 to May 1918
The division had a quiet spell, taking part in just one major action – that of La Malmaison, where the losses were low. In total, the unit lost 2,406 men, OR TWELVE MEN FOR EVERY DAY OF PRESENCE AT THE FRONT. AT LA MALMAISON, AN ADVANCE OF 1 KM COST FEWER THAN 100 MEN. The density was two battalions per km, and the firepower was enormous. Each battalion was supported by a regiment of heavy artillery and a regiment of 75mm guns, and in terms of its own resources between two and three times the normal allocation of infantry weaponry. The density of fire was equivalent to at least double that of the most violent of the previous actions.

### The new war of movement, from May to November 1918
The division took part in four major engagements, which amounted to a total of just twenty-four days of fighting. The total losses were 6,532 men, or an average of 272 MEN FOR EVERY DAY OF FIGHTING. If we set aside the final engagement, which sealed the German collapse, the average loss was 365 men per day, which was higher than the figure for 1914. Hence the 1918 actions were generally short but violent, as was the case during the first war of movement. AN ADVANCE OF 1 KM COST 700 MEN BEFORE THE END OF OCTOBER, AND 100 TIMES FEWER THEREAFTER. On average, the density of engagement was one battalion per km, or the equivalent of the 1914 actions, but with four or five times greater firepower. The units were not reinforced in infantry weaponry, but could have the benefit of the support of one or two 75mm *groupes* and of one heavy *groupe*. Each battalion had a squadron of airplanes flying overhead and the assistance of five or six tanks.

### Key to Tables 5 and 6:

### Table 5: The actions of the 13th Infantry Division
| | |
|---|---|
| Artillery losses: | Average losses of the field artillery, in men per day and per engaged battery |
| Attack: | Attack against fortified positions |
| Frontage: | Average frontage of the division, in km |
| Infantry losses: | Average losses of the infantry, in men per day and per engaged company |
| Movement: | Average movement, in km |
| Occupation: | Occupation of a sector of the front without a serious engagement |
| Offensive: | Mobile offensive manœuvre (movement longer than 10 km) |

| Percentage of strength: | Percentage of engaged numbers of troops (the division and attached units) |
|---|---|
| Retreat: | Mobile defensive manœuvre (movement longer than 10 km) |

Based on the statistics provided by *Lieutenant-colonel* Emile Laure and *Commandant* Jacottet in *Les étapes de guerre d'une DI*. Paris: Berger-Levrault, 1928, pp.299-382.

## Table 6: Density of the 13th Infantry Division's firepower per km of front and per day of engagement

| (a) | a few weapons (motorized-guns, 80mm mountain guns, trench mortars, 'line-throwing' guns (for throwing grappling-hooks against barbed-wire) |
|---|---|
| (b) | a few airplanes working on the front and for the benefit of the 13th Infantry Division |
| (c) | two squadrons for the three infantry divisions of the army corps |
| (d) | a few airplanes, but with no overall organization |
| (e) | total number of tanks |
| (f) | one squadron per day |
| Attack: | Attack against fortified positions |
| Auto-rifles: | Automatic-rifles |
| Occupation: | Occupation of a sector of the front without a serious engagement |
| Offensive: | Mobile offensive manœuvre (movement longer than 10 km) |
| Retreat: | Mobile defensive manœuvre (movement longer than 10 km) |
| Rifles | Men armed with rifles |
| VB | Rifles equipped with grenade-launchers |

The 'Firepower' column has been calculated by the author, based on the following empirical values:

| Rifle | 1 |
|---|---|
| Rifle equipped with grenade-launcher | 8 |
| Automatic-rifle | 10 |
| Machine-gun | 30 |
| 37mm gun | 50 |
| Trench-mortar | 50 |
| Stokes mortar | 50 |
| 75mm gun | 100 |
| Heavy artillery piece | 150 |
| Tank | 200 |

Based on the statistics provided in *Lieutenant-colonel* Emile Laure and *Commandant* Jacottet in *Les étapes de guerre d'une DI*. Paris: Berger-Levrault, 1928, pp.299-382.

**Table 5: The actions of the 13th Infantry Division.**

| | Actions | | Days of engagement | Average daily loss | Total losses |
|---|---|---|---|---|---|
| | Type of action | Period of engagement | | | |
| 1. | Offensive | 1914, Aug | 8 | 317.66 | 2,541 |
| 2. | Retreat | 1914, Aug | 13 | 275.4 | 3,480 |
| 3. | Offensive | 1914, Sep | 21 | 136 | 2,856 |
| 4. | Offensive | 1914, Oct | 8 | 400.85 | 3,026 |
| 5. | Attack | 1914, Oct-Dec | 58 | 100 | 5,800 |
| 6. | Attack | 1914, Dec – 1915, Jan | 44 | 72.7 | 3,198 |
| 7. | Attack | 1915, Mar-Apr | 50 | 66 | 3,300 |
| 8. | Attack | 1915, Apr-Jun | 53 | 257 | 13,621 |
| 9. | Attack | 1915, Jun-Sep | 100 | 47 | 4,700 |
| 10. | Attack | 1915, Sep-Oct | 20 | 305 | 6,100 |
| 11. | Attack | 1915, Nov-Dec | 27 | 19 | 513 |
| 12. | Defensive (Battle of Verdun) | 1916, Mar | 16 | 464 | 7,324 |
| 13. | Occupation | 1916, Apr-Jul | 88 | 10.72 | 943 |
| 14. | Attack (Battle of the Somme) | 1916, Aug-Dec | 77 | 41.89 | 3,225 |
| 15. | Occupation | 1917, Jun-Aug | 80 | 12 | 960 |
| 16. | Attack (Battle of La Malmaison) | 1917, Oct | 14 | 79.15 | 1,108 |
| 17. | Occupation | 1918, Jan-May | 117 | 3.57 | 418 |
| 18. | Retreat | 1918, May-Jun | 9 | 313.9 | 2,825 |
| 19. | Defensive | 1918, Jul | 4 | 341 | 1,364 |
| 20. | Attack | 1918, Sep-Oct | 4 | 507 | 2,028 |
| 21. | Attack | 1918, Oct-Nov | 7 | 45 | 315 |

| Percentage of strength | Frontage | Movement | Infantry losses | Artillery losses | Density of riflemen |
|---|---|---|---|---|---|
| 21.47 | 20 | 20 | 7.8 | 0.24 | 400 |
| 16.17 | 10 | 32 | 5.1 | 0.21 | 905 |
| 28.9 | 5 | 140 | 3.33 | 0.724 | 1,156 |
| 22 | 12 | 70 | 8.7 | 0.24 | 555 |
| 29.8 | 11 | - | 1.18 | 0.9 | 840 |
| 17.94 | 4 | 1 | 1.5 | 0.5 | 1,403 |
| 20 | 3.5 | - | 1.23 | 0.03 | 1,864 |
| 61 | 1 | 0.8 | 5.7 | 0.02 | 3,579 |
| 34.7 | 1 | 0.5 | 1.3 | 0.02 | 2,834 |
| 41 | 1 | 1.8 | 6.4 | 0.007 | 4,290 |
| 4.5 | 3-4 | - | 0.68 | 0 | 2,600 |
| 38 | 2.8 | - | 5.44 | 0.9 | 2,955 |
| 8.6 | 5 | - | 0.29 | 0.021 | 781 |
| 26 | 2.4 | 3.5 | 1.15 | 0.05 | 1,608 |
| 10.44 | 3.5 | - | 0.4 | 0.027 | 808 |
| 6.8 | 1.2 | 6.2 | 3.4 | 0.0031 | 1,400 |
| 0.26 | 22 | - | 0.9 | 0 | 195 |
| 25 | 9 | 22 | 7.2 | 0.87 | 514 |
| 11.3 | 8 | 3 | 7.3 | 1.2 | 520 |
| 23 | 2.3 | 4 | 7.3 | 3 | 520 |
| 4.2 | 4.5 | 45 | 1.6 | 0.08 | 415 |

Table 6: Density of the 13th Infantry Division's firepower per km of front and per day of engagement.

| Actions | | | Rifles | VB |
|---|---|---|---|---|
| | Type of action | Period of engagement | | |
| 1. | Offensive | 1914, Aug | 400 | - |
| 2. | Retreat | 1914, Aug | 905 | - |
| 3. | Offensive | 1914, Sep | 1,156 | - |
| 4. | Offensive | 1914, Oct | 555 | - |
| 5. | Attack | 1914, Oct-Dec | 840 | - |
| 6. | Attack | 1914, Dec – 1915, Jan | 1,403 | - |
| 7. | Attack | 1915, Mar-Apr | 1,864 | - |
| 8. | Attack | 1915, Apr-Jun | 3,579 | - |
| 9. | Attack | 1915, Jun-Sep | 2,834 | - |
| 10. | Attack | 1915, Sep-Oct | 4,290 | - |
| 11. | Attack | 1915, Nov-Dec | 2,600 | - |
| 12. | Defensive (Battle of Verdun) | 1916, Mar | 2,955 | - |
| 13. | Occupation | 1916, Apr-Jul | 781 | 46 |
| 14. | Attack (Battle of the Somme) | 1916, Aug-Dec | 1,608 | 96 |
| 15. | Occupation | 1917, Jun-Aug | 808 | 99 |
| 16. | Attack (Battle of La Malmaison) | 1917, Oct | 1,400 | 268 |
| 17. | Occupation | 1918, Jan-May | 195 | 36 |
| 18. | Retreat | 1918, May-Jun | 514 | 94 |
| 19. | Defensive | 1918, Jul | 520 | 96 |
| 20. | Attack | 1918, Sep-Oct | 520 | 104 |
| 21. | Attack | 1918, Oct-Nov | 415 | 69 |

| Auto-rifles | Machine-guns | 37mm guns | 75mm guns | Heavy guns | Trench mortars | Stokes mortars | Aircraft | Tanks | Firepower |
|---|---|---|---|---|---|---|---|---|---|
| - | 0.9 | - | 1.8 | - | - | - | - | - | 610 |
| - | 2.72 | - | 4.02 | - | - | - | - | - | 1,380 |
| - | 3.44 | - | 8.88 | - | - | - | - | - | 2,150 |
| - | 1.68 | - | 3.12 | - | - | - | - | - | 920 |
| - | 2.4 | - | 5.44 | 0.72 | - | - | - | - | 1,560 |
| - | 4 | - | 17.4 | 2.4 | - | (a) | (b) | - | 3,620 |
| - | 13.9 | - | 13 | 5 | 0.8 | - | - | - | 4,430 |
| - | 26 | - | 39 | 16 | 10 | - | - | - | 11,160 |
| - | 61 | - | 32 | 8 | 5 | - | - | - | 9,280 |
| - | 61 | - | 46 | 28 | 8 | - | - | - | 15,320 |
| - | 32 | - | 40 | 24 | 4 | - | - | - | 13,760 |
| - | 43.5 | - | 23.2 | 15.6 | 5.6 | - | 3.7 | - | 9,350 |
| 46 | 16.5 | 2 | 12 | 4.8 | 2.4 | - | 2 | - | 4,350 |
| 96 | 43.2 | 5 | 28 | 24 | 5 | - | 8 | - | 11,540 |
| 50 | 24 | 3 | 13 | 16 | 4 | 3 | 4-5 | - | 7,020 |
| 99 | 64 | 6 | 80 | 98 | 31 | 10 | 9 | - | 31,550 |
| 12 | 4.8 | 1 | 3.55 | 1.82 | - | - | (c) | - | 4,620 |
| 31 | 8.8 | 1 | 4.2 | 1.3 | - | 2.2 | (d) | - | 6,090 |
| 32 | 12 | 3 | 11 | 11 | - | 3 | 14 | - | 3,530 |
| 52 | 11.2 | 1.2 | 31 | 25 | - | 3 | 10 | 14(e) | 12,070 |
| 32 | 8.5 | 1 | 28 | 11 | - | 2 | (f) | 5 | 5,660 |

*Appendix 3*

# Statistical Data

## Table 7: Equipment allocations of the French armies

| Equipment | 1914 | 1918 | Production |
|---|---|---|---|
| Grenades | - | 150,000,000 | |
| Rifle rounds | 1,338,000,000 | 1,800,000,000 | 6,300,000,000 |
| 155mm shells | - | 5,000,000 | |
| Automatic-rifles | - | 120,000 | 225,000 |
| Machine-guns | 5,100 | 60,500 | 87,000 |
| 75mm guns | 3,840 | 4,968 | 17,300 |
| Heavy artillery pieces | 308 | 5,128 | 6,700 |
| Mortars | - | 18,000 | |
| Airplanes | 170 | 3,600 | |
| Tanks | - | 2,300 | 5,300 |
| Motorised vehicles | 180 | 53,800 | |
| Telephones | 2,000 | 200,000 | |
| Radio sets | 50 | 28,000 | |

Source: Fouquet-Lapar, Philippe. *Histoire de l'armée française*. Paris: Presses universitaires de France, 1986, p.68.

## Table 8: Relative importance of the arms
(in per cent)

| Arm | 1914 | 1918 |
|---|---|---|
| Infantry | 72 | 50 |
| Cavalry | 5 | 4 |
| Artillery | 18 | 36 |
| Engineers | 5 | 7 |
| Aeronautics | 0.5 | 3 |

Source: Fouquet-Lapar, Philippe. *Histoire de l'armée française*. Paris: Presses universitaires de France, 1986, p.68.

## Table 9: Losses of each arm
(killed and missing, as a percentage of the total strength of the arm).

| Arm | Officers | Other ranks |
|---|---|---|
| Infantry | 29.0 | 22.9 |
| Cavalry | 10.3 | 7.6 |
| Artillery | 9.2 | 6.0 |
| Engineers | 9.3 | 6.4 |
| Aeronautics | 21.6 | 3.5 |
| Aerostation | 5.7 | 2.7 |
| Train | 4.4 | 3.6 |
| Motor-transport services | 1.9 | 1.7 |
| Other services | 4.1 | 3.0 |
| Overall | 18.9 | 16.1 |

Source: Larcher, Maurice (lieutenant-colonel). 'Données statistiques sur les forces françaises de 1914-1918', in *Revue militaire française* (Apr-Jun 1934), numéro 156, p.358.

# References

**Note:**
SHAT refers to the *Service historique de l'armée de terre* (the historical branch of the French army, at the Château de Vincennes). In 2005, the various historical branches of the French armed forces were amalgamated into the *Service historique de la défense*.

**Preface**
(pages xii-xiv)
1. For these interpretative templates, I began by re-reading James March, Herbert Simon and Michel Crozier. The books by each of these individual authors about organizations are now regarded as classics. I then took an interest in recent business theories, especially evolutionary theory. Studies on innovation, with the notable inclusion of Norbert Alter's French-language publications, formed another fertile source. Nor could I fail to draw inspiration from such authors as Williamson Murray, Barry Posen or Stephen Rosen and their work on military innovation in the US or German armies.
2. Having seen from personal experience how much distance can exist between regulations and their actual implementation, I established the hypothesis that the same held true during the period I was studying. I tested this hypothesis against the historical sources. Similarly, it was while I was observing Infantry Battalion Number 4 at Sarajevo in 1993 that the idea occurred to me of change brought about by the micro-actions of units grappling with tangible problems.

**Chapter 1: The Masterminds of *La Revanche***
(pages 1–31)
1. Laure, Emile (lieutenant). *L'offensive française*. Paris: Lavauzelle, 1912, p.129.
2. *Ibid*, pp.6-7.
3. Billard, Marie Marcel André (capitaine). *Education de l'infanterie*. Paris: Chapelot, 1913, p.1.
4. A record year was 1898, when five different men held the post of Minister of War. Each of the crucial years 1911-14 saw a succession of two to five Ministers of War a year.
5. Bonnal, Henri (général). *Questions militaires d'actualité*. 1re série: *La prochaine guerre [etc]*. Paris: Chapelot, 1906, p.59.
6. They included in particular the Second Department, which was responsible for intelligence, and the Third Department, which was entrusted with operations.
7. Hoff, Pierre (contrôleur général). 'Le ministère de la Guerre de 1871 à 1914', in *Revue historique des armées* (1983), numéro 153.
8. Bonnal. *Questions militaires d'actualité*. 1re série. *op. cit.*, p.84.
9. Hoff. *op. cit.*
10. *Ibid.*
11. *Ibid.*

12. Delmas, Jean (général). 'L'Ecole supérieure de guerre, 1876-1940', in *Revue historique des armées* (Sep 2002), numéro 228.

13. Kessler, Charles (général). *Tactique des trois armes.* Paris: Chapelot, 1902, pp.102-3.

14. France: Ministère de la guerre. *Annuaire officiel de l'armée française pour 1914.* Paris: Berger-Levrault, 31 décembre 1913.

15. Bonnal, Henri (général). *Infanterie: méthodes de commandement, d'éducation et d'instruction.* Paris: Chapelot, 1900, p.7.

16. See Bach, André (général). *Fusillés pour l'exemple, 1914-1915.* Paris: Tallandier, 2003.

17. The cavalry committee met only four times in 1910. Hoff. *op. cit.*

18. Lemay, Benoît. 'Les relations entre le corps des officiers et le pouvoir politique en France. Le temps de la revanche, 1870 à 1914', on www.hist.montreal.ca.

19. For more on these notions, see d'Iribarne, Philippe. *La logique de l'honneur: gestion des entreprises et traditions nationales.* Paris: Seuil, 1989.

20. Saint-Maixent for the infantry, Saumur for the cavalry, and Versailles for the scientific arms, namely the artillery, engineers and train. (Train in this sense meant the men, animals and vehicles for transporting the army's baggage, ammunition, supplies and other materials.) Vincennes remained the school of administration.

21. Except for the colonial army, which was more open, especially in its artillery. See Klotz, Lucien (député). *L'armée en 1906: considérations générales à propos du budget de la guerre.* Paris: Lavauzelle, 1906, pp.166-9.

22. Delmas. *op. cit.*

23. Messimy, Adolphe. *L'armée et ses cadres.* Paris: Chapelot, 1908, p.18.

24. Percin, Alexandre (général). *Le massacre de notre infanterie, 1914-1918.* Paris: Albin Michel, 1919, p.71.

25. Porch, Douglas. *The march to the Marne: the French army, 1871-1914.* Cambridge: Cambridge University Press, 1981, p.84.

26. Delmas. *op. cit.*

27. Girardet, Raoul. *La société militaire de 1815 à nos jours.* Paris: Perrin, 1998, pp.205-6.

28. Montaigne, Jean-Baptiste (lieutenant-colonel). *Vaincre: esquisse d'une doctrine de la guerre, basée sur la connaissance de l'homme.* Paris: Berger-Levrault, 1913, p.ix.

29. Titeux, Eugène (lieutenant-colonel). *Saint-Cyr et l'Ecole spéciale militaire en France.* Reissued Paris: Firmin-Didot, 1914, p.538.

30. In 1912, the school was split. The Applied School of Engineers was transferred to Versailles, while the Applied School of Artillery remained at Fontainebleau.

31. Delmas. *op. cit.*

32. Bonnal. *Questions militaires d'actualité.* 1re série. *op. cit.*, p.35.

33. Porch. *op. cit.*, p.219.

34. Bonnal. *Questions militaires d'actualité.* 1re série. *op. cit.*, p.79.

35. *Ibid,* p.82.

36. *Ibid,* p.55.

37. Gambiez, Fernand (général); and Suire, Maurice (colonel). *Histoire de la première guerre mondiale,* 2 vols. Paris: Fayard, 1968, p.96.

38. Porch. *op. cit.*, p.151.

39. Just 6 per cent of colonial officers had a surname with a particle. (The particle 'de', or its variants, often but not invariably indicated noble origins.) In contrast, 21 per cent of Saint-Cyr cadets in 1883 bore surnames with a particle. Whereas just one-third of

Saint-Cyr cadets studied on scholarships, a full 68 per cent of men who opted for a colonial career were scholarship students. *Ibid*, p.152.

40. *Ibid*, p.155.
41. Bonnal, Henri (général). *L'art nouveau en tactique*. Paris: Chapelot, 1904, p.16.
42. Bonnal. *Questions militaires d'actualité*. 1re série. *op. cit.*, p.66.
43. Porch. *op. cit.*, p.165.
44. Laure. *L'offensive*. *op. cit.*, p.111.
45. Percin, Alexandre (général). *Le combat*. Paris: Alcan, 1914, p.161.
46. Fugens (lieutenant-colonel). *La guerre de 1870 et ses répercussions sur les débuts de 1914*. Conférence du 6 janvier 1932 à l'Ecole supérieure de guerre, p.36.
47. Laure. *L'offensive*. *op. cit.*, p.25.
48. France: Ministère de la guerre. *Annuaire officiel de l'armée française pour 1914*. *op. cit.*
49. Montaigne. *Vaincre*. *op. cit.*, p.x.
50. Boucher, Arthur (colonel). *La France victorieuse dans la guerre de demain*. Paris: Berger-Levrault, 1911, p.5.
51. Laure. *L'offensive*. *op. cit.*, p.50.
52. Colin, Jean (général). *Les transformations de la guerre*. 1911. Reissued Paris: Economica, 1989, p.74.
53. Billard. *op. cit.*, p.4.
54. France: Ministère de la guerre. *Décret du 3 décembre 1904 portant règlement sur les manœuvres d'infanterie*. Paris: Lavauzelle, 1910, p.78. Article 252.
55. *Ibid*, p.46. Article 126.
56. Mousset (commandant). *Cours d'histoire militaire de l'Ecole spéciale militaire*, juin 1937, p.243.
57. France: Ministère de la guerre. *Décret du 3 décembre 1904*. *op. cit.*, p.76. Article 266.
58. *Ibid*, p.78. Article 252.
59. France: Ministère de la guerre. *Décret du 20 avril 1914 portant règlement sur les manœuvres d'infanterie*. Paris: Lavauzelle, 1914, p.132. Article 348.
60. Laure. *L'offensive*. *op. cit.*, p.131.
61. Billard. *op. cit.*, p.32.
62. Montaigne. *Vaincre*. *op. cit.*, p.66.
63. Foch, Ferdinand (colonel). *Des principes de la guerre: conférences faites à l'Ecole supérieure de guerre*, 2nd ed. Paris: Berger-Levrault, 1906, p.30.
64. General Langlois took a similar line. So did 'Captain Jibé': 'The increase in firepower, therefore, will always benefit the attack.' Colin's view was much the same: 'Thus the defensive seems destined to lose even more of its advantages.'
65. Kessler. *op. cit.*, p.131.
66. Bonnal: 'At the same rate as advances are made in weaponry, battles are becoming less murderous.' (Bonnal. *Questions militaires d'actualité*. 1re série. *op. cit.*, p.46.) Grandmaison: 'Since combat is more difficult than before, one would have thought it would be more murderous, and yet statistics show that the opposite is the case.' (de Grandmaison, Louis (colonel). *Deux conférences faites aux officiers de l'Etat-major de l'armée, février 1911: la notion de sûreté et l'engagement des grandes unités*. Paris: Berger-Levrault, 1911, p.3.) Colin went further: 'The rate of losses has declined continuously, ever since weapons were adopted.' (Colin. *op. cit.*, p.21.)
67. Colin. *op. cit.*, p.130.

68. *Revue militaire des armées étrangères* (Jan-Jun 1906), p.17.

69. *Ibid*, p.31.

70. Herr, Frédéric-Georges (général). *L'artillerie: ce qu'elle a été, ce qu'elle est, ce qu'elle doit être.* Reissued Paris: Berger-Levrault, 1924, p.231. Based on the work of Surgeon-General Toubert, published in the *Revue d'infanterie* (15 Sep 1921).

71. de Grandmaison, Louis (commandant). *Dressage de l'infanterie en vue du combat offensif.* Reissued Paris: Berger-Levrault, 1908, p.18.

72. Griffith, Paddy. *Forward into battle: fighting tactics from Waterloo to the near future.* Reissued Novato (California): Presidio Press, 1991, p.63.

73. *Ibid*, p.66.

74. Berger-Levrault (publisher). *Le livre du gradé d'infanterie: à l'usage des élèves caporaux, caporaux et sous-officiers de l'infanterie et du génie, contenant toutes les matières nécessaires à l'exercice de leurs fonctions et conforme à tous les règlements parus jusqu'à ce jour.* Paris: Berger-Levrault, November 1914, p.1.

75. Montaigne. *Vaincre. op. cit.*, p.115.

76. Herrmann, David G. *The arming of Europe and the making of the First World War.* Princeton (New Jersey): Princeton University Press, 1997, p.80.

77. de Maud'huy, Louis-Ernest (colonel). *Infanterie.* Paris: Lavauzelle, 1911, p.37.

78. Montaigne. *Vaincre. op. cit.*, p.71.

79. Maud'huy. *op. cit.*, p.9.

80. Griffith. *Forward into battle. op. cit.*, p.87.

81. Maud'huy. *op. cit.*, p.37.

82. *Ibid*, p.97.

83. Joffre, Joseph (maréchal). *Mémoires du maréchal Joffre, 1910-1917*, 2 vols. Paris: Plon, 1932, vol. 1, p.15.

84. Gascouin, Firmin-Emile (général). *Le triomphe de l'idée.* Paris: Berger-Levrault, 1931, p.16.

85. *Ibid*, p.119.

86. *Ibid*, p.22.

87. *Ibid*, p.125.

88. Wanty, Emile. *L'art de la guerre*, 3 vols. Verviers (Belgium): Editions Gérard, 1967-8, vol. 2, p.83.

89. SHAT. 7 N 1108, 2; and 7 N 1130, 1. Lettres de Laguiche et Girodou au ministre de la Guerre. An unusual system was put in place to ensure that lorries were available on mobilization. Any civilian who bought a lorry that met certain standards was paid a subsidy equivalent to one-third of the purchase price. The lorry was then entered on a register.

90. Among the hundreds of military works in the Berger-Levrault catalogue were just three monographs about the motor-car (including one that was devoted to breakdowns). This was twelve times fewer than for hippology (the study of horses). Aviation, with twenty-one texts, was beginning to arouse a degree of interest. The same gaps existed in the most important regulatory documents, such as the 1913 *Field service regulation* (just two of its articles concerned aviation) and the 1914 *Infantry training regulation*. Yet all these authors were qualified staff officers. They held field officer rank, were mostly still young and were fairly open to new ideas.

91. Jibé (capitaine) (pseud). [Mordacq, Henri-Jean-Jules]. *L'armée nouvelle: ce qu'elle pense, ce qu'elle veut.* Paris: Plon, [c.1905], p.88.

92. Quoted in Cru, Jean Norton. *Témoins: essai d'analyse et de critique des souvenirs de combattants édités en francais de 1915 à 1928*. Reissued Nancy: Presses universitaires de Nancy, 1993, p.367. The original can be found in Maugars, Maurice (capitaine). *Avec la Marocaine*. Paris: Albin Michel, 1920.

93. Girardet. *op. cit.*, p.147.

94. Jibé. *op. cit.*, p.88.

95. Joffre. *op. cit.*, vol. 1, p.34.

96. *Ibid*, vol. 1, p.33.

97. Percin, Alexandre (général). *1914: les erreurs du haut commandement*. Paris: Albin Michel, 1919, p.29.

98. Debeney, Marie-Eugène (général). *La guerre et les hommes: réflexions d'après-guerre*. Paris: Plon, 1937, p.281.

99. 'The Russo-Japanese war demonstrates that frontal attacks by brute force are both necessary and possible, and thus exempts us from any discussion.' de Grandmaison. *Deux conférences. op. cit.*, p.31

100. de Grandmaison. *Dressage. op. cit.*, p.42.

101. Griffith. *Forward into battle. op. cit.*, p.90.

102. de Grandmaison. *Deux conférences. op. cit.*, p.28.

103. *Ibid*, p.69.

104. See Contamine, Henry. *La revanche, 1871-1914*. Paris: Berger-Levrault, 1957.

105. Laure. *L'offensive. op. cit.*, p.7

106. Montaigne. *Vaincre. op. cit.*, p.106.

107. *Ibid*, p.xiii.

108. Laure. *L'offensive. op. cit.*, p.111.

109. *Ibid*, pp.69 and 86. See also p.91: 'There is a limit to the increase of artillery. That is an undeniable fact, and public opinion must be warned about it.'

110. Percin. *Le combat. op. cit.*, p.161.

111. This is a reference to a statement made by the Minister of War, Marshal Edmond Le Bœuf, at the start of the Franco-Prussian war in 1870. He said that the French army was ready, and that even if the war should last two years, 'our soldiers would not lack a single gaiter button'. *Ibid*, p.246.

112. Montaigne. *Vaincre. op. cit.*, p.130.

113. Billard. *op. cit.*, p.399.

114. *Ibid*, p.3.

115. Laure. *L'offensive. op. cit.*, p.83.

116. Gascouin, Firmin-Emile (général). *L'évolution de l'artillerie pendant la guerre*. Reissued Paris: Flammarion, 1921, p.143.

117. Gascouin. *Le triomphe de l'idée. op. cit.*, p.116.

118. *Ibid*, p.120.

119. *Ibid*, p.112.

120. *Ibid*, p.201.

121. Laure. *L'offensive. op. cit.*, p.8.

122. Porch. *op. cit.*, p.227.

123. Laure. *L'offensive. op. cit.*, pp.9 and 51.

124. Billard. *op. cit.*, p.30.

125. Laure. *L'offensive. op. cit.*, p.259.

126. de Grandmaison. *Deux conférences. op. cit.*, p.9.

127. Laure. *L'offensive. op. cit.,* p.107.

128. Chalmandrey, André (capitaine). *Le règlement de manœuvres de l'avenir: infanterie.* Paris: Alcan-Lévy, 1904, p.vii.

129. Foch. *op. cit.,* p.25.

130. Laure. *L'offensive. op. cit.,* p.138.

131. de Lardemelle, Charles (général). *1914: le redressement initial.* Paris: Berger-Levrault, 1935, p.29.

132. Larcher, Maurice (commandant). 'Le 10e corps à Charleroi (20 au 24 août 1914)', in *Revue militaire française* (Oct-Dec 1930), numéro 38.

133. Debeney. *La guerre et les hommes. op. cit.,* p.12.

134. *Ibid,* p.278.

135. Gascouin. *L'évolution de l'artillerie. op. cit.,* p.53.

## Chapter 2: In Search of a Doctrine
(pages 32–60)

1. Foch, Ferdinand (colonel). *Des principes de la guerre: conférences faites à l'Ecole supérieure de guerre,* 2nd ed. Paris: Berger-Levrault, 1906, p.1.

2. 'The universally recognized scientific achievements that, for a time, provide model problems and solutions for a community of practitioners.' See Kuhn, Thomas Samuel. *La structure des révolutions scientifiques.* Trans Laure Meyer. Paris: Flammarion, 1983, p.11.

3. Definition used by Major Gourmen. See Gourmen (commandant). 'Lewal, Maillard et Bonnal, leur influence sur la doctrine militaire française', in France: Ecole supérieure de guerre. *Centenaire de l'Ecole supérieure de guerre 1876-1976* (conference proceedings, 13-14 May 1976). Paris: ESG-SHAT, 1976.

4. Foch. *op. cit.,* p.7.

5. *Ibid,* p.12.

6. Bonnal, Henri (général). *Questions militaires d'actualité.* 1re série: *La prochaine guerre [etc].* Paris: Chapelot, 1906, pp.64-8. Not until 1908 were realistic umpiring rules introduced in France. The rules included weighting factors, with entrenchments, artillery support and use of the terrain increasing the strength of units.

7. Montaigne, Jean-Baptiste (lieutenant-colonel). *Vaincre: esquisse d'une doctrine de la guerre, basée sur la connaissance de l'homme.* Paris: Berger-Levrault, 1913, p.240.

8. Percin, Alexandre (général). *Le combat.* Paris: Alcan, 1914, p.122.

9. Laure, Emile (lieutenant). *L'offensive française.* Paris: Lavauzelle, 1912, p.221.

10. Monteilhet, Joseph. *Les institutions militaires de la France, 1814-1924.* Paris: Alcan, 1926, p.310.

11. Bonnal. *Questions militaires d'actualité.* 1re série. *op. cit.,* p.69.

12. Henrionnet, C. (commandant). *Le jeu de la guerre en France.* Paris: Lavauzelle, 1898, p.10.

13. Gascouin, Firmin-Emile (général). *Le triomphe de l'idée.* Paris: Berger-Levrault, 1931, p.36.

14. Joffre, Joseph (maréchal). *Mémoires du maréchal Joffre, 1910-1917,* 2 vols. Paris: Plon, 1932, vol. 1, p.35.

15. Alexandre, Georges-René (général). *Avec Joffre d'Agadir à Verdun: souvenirs, 1911-1916.* Paris: Berger-Levrault, 1932, p.18.

16. Joffre. *op. cit.,* vol. 1, p.36

17. Gamelin, Maurice-Gustave (général). *Manœuvre et victoire de la Marne*. Paris: Grasset, 1954, p.106.

18. This is the origin of the *pas chasseur ('chasseur* step') or the brisk jog of the Italian *Bersaglieri* on parade.

19. France: Ministère de la guerre. *Règlement du 12 juin 1875 sur les manœuvres de l'infanterie (modifié par l'instruction du 20 avril 1878)*. Paris: Dumaine, 1880, pp.vii-viii.

20. *Ibid*, p.viii.

21. *Ibid*, p.xiii.

22. *Ibid*, p.xxxvii.

23. *Ibid*, p.12.

24. Bonnal, Henri (général). *L'art nouveau en tactique*. Paris: Chapelot, 1904, p.9.

25. Bails (lieutenant-colonel). 'Evolution des idées sur l'emploi tactique de l'organisation du terrain, de Napoleon à nos jours', in *Revue militaire française* (Jul-Aug-Sep 1926), p.208.

26. *Ibid*, pp.207-8.

27. Rocolle, Pierre. *L'hécatombe des généraux*. Paris: Lavauzelle, 1980, pp.268-9.

28. Foch. *op. cit.*, p.6.

29. de Maud'huy, Louis-Ernest (colonel). *Infanterie*. Paris: Lavauzelle, 1911, p.202.

30. Boucher, Arthur (général). *Les doctrines dans la préparation de la grande guerre*. Paris: Berger-Levrault, 1925, p.98.

31. *Ibid*.

32. Bonnal's father, an artillery major, had served with officers of the First Empire. Bonnal. *Questions militaires d'actualité. op. cit.*, p.282.

33. Boucher. *Les doctrines. op. cit.*, p.105.

34. Bonnal. *L'art nouveau en tactique. op. cit.*, p.44.

35. Foch. *op. cit.*, p.37

36. Wanty, Emile. *L'art de la guerre*, 3 vols. Verviers (Belgium): Editions Gérard, 1967-8, vol. 2, p.72.

37. Foch. *op. cit.*, p.37.

38. Debeney, Marie-Eugène (général). *La guerre et les hommes: réflexions d'après-guerre*. Paris: Plon, 1937, pp.265-6.

39. *Ibid*, p.265.

40. Wanty. *op. cit.*, vol. 2, p.74.

41. Bonnal. *L'art nouveau en tactique. op. cit.*, p.124.

42. *Ibid*.

43. Foch. *op. cit.*, p.322.

44. Gourmen. *op. cit.*

45. Nachin (commandant). 'Les règlements de manœuvre d'infanterie d'avant-guerre', in *Revue militaire française* (Oct-Dec 1922), vol. 6, pp.238-9.

46. Bonnal. *L'art nouveau en tactique. op. cit.*, p.9.

47. Pétain, Philippe (colonel). *Cours d'infanterie de l'Ecole supérieure de guerre*. np: 1911, p.232.

48. *Ibid*, p.236.

49. *Ibid*, p.234.

50. Buat, Edmond (commandant). *Etude théorique sur l'attaque décisive*. Paris: Chapelot, 1909, p.48.

51. Pétain. *op. cit.*, p.237.

52. Bonnal, Henri (général). *Infanterie: méthodes de commandement, d'éducation et d'instruction.* Paris: Chapelot, 1900, pp.205-6.

53. Under pressure from the Minister of War, General Georges Boulanger.

54. ed. Corvisier, André. *Histoire militaire de la France,* 4 vols. Paris: Presses universitaires de France, 1992-4, vol. 3, p.20.

55. France: army. 72nd Infantry Regiment. *Note sur les modifications qui semblent devoir être apportées à la tactique de l'infanterie.* Amiens: Presse régimentaire, 72e RI, 1903, p.3.

56. *Ibid,* p.5.

57. Kessler, Charles (général). *Tactique des trois armes.* Paris: Chapelot, 1902, p.48.

58. Bonnal. *L'art nouveau en tactique. op. cit.,* p.166.

59. Montaigne, Jean-Baptiste (lieutenant-colonel). *Etudes sur la guerre.* Paris: Berger-Levrault, 1911, p.123.

60. France: Ministère de la guerre. *Décret du 3 décembre 1904 portant règlement sur les manœuvres d'infanterie.* Paris: Lavauzelle, 1910, p.6.

61. *Ibid,* pp.7-8.

62. *Ibid,* p.8.

63. *Ibid,* p.60. Article 188.

64. Kessler. *op. cit.,* p.110.

65. France: Ministère de la guerre. *Décret du 3 décembre 1904. op. cit.,* p.45. Article 122.

66. Kessler. *op. cit.,* p.100.

67. France: Ministère de la guerre. *Décret du 3 décembre 1904. op. cit.,* p.7.

68. Bonnal. *L'art nouveau en tactique. op. cit.,* p.58.

69. France: Ministère de la guerre. *Décret du 3 décembre 1904. op. cit.,* p.72. Article 239.

70. *Ibid,* p.72. Article 240.

71. Montaigne. *Etudes sur la guerre. op. cit.,* p.136.

72. Nachin. 'Les règlements de manœuvre d'infanterie d'avant-guerre'. *op. cit.,* p.247.

73. 'Quelques enseignements de la guerre russo-japonaise', in *Revue militaire des armées étrangères* (Jan-Jun 1906), p.36.

74. *Ibid.*

75. *Ibid,* p.304.

76. SHAT. 7 N 670. Deuxième bureau. Enseignements de la guerre russo-japonaise. Note numéro 7. Habillement, janvier 1905.

77. 'Quelques enseignements de la guerre russo-japonaise'. *op. cit.,* p.36.

78. de Grandmaison, Louis (commandant). *Dressage de l'infanterie en vue du combat offensif.* Reissued Paris: Berger-Levrault, 1908, p.54.

79. *Ibid,* p.38.

80. Montaigne. *Etudes sur la guerre. op. cit.,* p.40.

81. Billard, Marie Marcel André (capitaine). *Education de l'infanterie.* Paris: Chapelot, 1913, p.97.

82. de Grandmaison. *Dressage. op. cit.,* p.vi.

83. *Ibid,* p.136.

84. General Langlois, in the preface to de Grandmaison. *Dressage. op. cit.,* p.vii.

85. France: Ministère de la guerre. *Décret du 2 décembre 1913 portant règlement sur le service des armées en campagne.* Paris: Berger-Levrault, 1914, p.14.

86. 'Quelques enseignements de la guerre russo-japonaise'. *op. cit.,* pp.21-2.

87. *Ibid,* p.307.

88. Colin, Jean (général). *Les transformations de la guerre*. 1911. Reissued Paris: Economica, 1989, p.42.

89. *Ibid*, p.54.

90. de Grandmaison. *Dressage. op. cit.*, p.31.

91. *Ibid*.

92. *Ibid*, p.42.

93. *Ibid*, p.66.

94. Debeney, Marie-Eugène (colonel). *Cours d'infanterie*. Paris: Ecole supérieure de guerre, 1913, 2e conférence.

95. Buat. *Etude théorique. op. cit.*, pp.2-3.

96. France: Ministère de la guerre. *Décret du 20 avril 1914 portant règlement sur les manœuvres d'infanterie*. Paris: Lavauzelle, 1914, p.16.

97. *Ibid*, p.29.

98. *Ibid*, p.138. Article 337.

99. Contamine, Henry. *La revanche, 1871-1914*. Paris: Berger-Levrault, 1957, p.85.

100. Fayolle, Marie-Emile (maréchal). *Cahiers secrets de la grande guerre*. Ed. Henry Contamine. Paris: Plon, 1964, p.46.

101. Revol, Joseph (général). 'Souvenirs: à l'Ecole supérieure de guerre (1903-1905)', in *Revue historique des armées* (3/1979), numéro 136, pp.130-44.

102. Fuller, J.F.C. (John Frederick Charles). *L'influence de l'armement sur l'histoire*. Trans Lionel-Max Chassin. Paris: Payot, 1948, p.144.

103. Joffre. *op. cit.*, vol.1 , p.31.

104. *Ibid*, p.32.

105. Wanty. *op. cit.*, vol. 2, p.71.

106. Joffre. *op. cit.*, vol. 1, p.32. It is interesting to note that Lanrezac and Boudériat were dismissed in 1914 by none other than Joffre.

107. Montaigne. *Vaincre. op. cit.*, p.105.

108. Montaigne. *Etudes sur la guerre. op. cit.*, p.111.

109. *Ibid*, pp.112-13.

110. *Ibid*, p.120.

111. de Grandmaison, Louis (colonel). *Deux conférences faites aux officiers de l'Etat-major de l'armée, février 1911: la notion de sûreté et l'engagement des grandes unités*. Paris: Berger-Levrault, 1911, p.30.

112. *Ibid*, p.23.

113. *Ibid*, p.51.

114. *Ibid*, p.ix.

115. *Ibid*, p.48.

116. Laure. *L'offensive française. op. cit.*, p.126.

117. *Ibid*, p.7.

118. de Grandmaison. *Deux conférences. op. cit.*, p.69.

119. *Ibid*, p.25.

120. de Grandmaison. *Dressage. op. cit.*, p.147.

121. *Ibid*.

122. *Ibid*, p.35.

123. *Ibid*, p.146.

124. Mack was the Austrian general encircled by Napoleon I at Ulm in October 1805.

125. Laure. *L'offensive française. op. cit.*, p.126.

126. Joffre. *op. cit.*, vol. 1, p.35.

127. France: Ministère de la guerre. *Décret du 28 octobre 1913 portant règlement sur la conduite des grandes unités*. Paris: Lavauzelle, 1913, p.48. Rapport au ministre.

128. *Ibid.*

129. *Ibid.*

130. *Ibid,* p.6. Article 2.

131. *Ibid,* p.6. Article 4.

132. *Ibid,* pp.7-8. Article 9.

133. *Ibid,* p.7. Article 6.

134. *Ibid,* p.57. Rapport au ministre.

135. *Ibid,* p.6. Article 5.

136. *Ibid,* p.7. Article 7.

137. *Ibid,* p.49. Rapport au ministre.

138. *Ibid,* p.7. Article 8.

139. *Ibid,* p.9. Article 15.

140. de Grandmaison. *Deux conférences. op. cit.*, p.x.

## Chapter 3: The Flaws in the Learning Process
(pages 61–78)

1. Joffre, Joseph (maréchal). *Mémoires du maréchal Joffre, 1910-1917*, 2 vols. Paris: Plon, 1932, vol. 1, p.33.

2. Jibé (capitaine) (pseud). [Mordacq, Henri-Jean-Jules]. *L'armée nouvelle: ce qu'elle pense, ce qu'elle veut*. Paris: Plon, [c.1905], p.167.

3. Chalmandrey, André (capitaine). *Le règlement de manœuvres de l'avenir: infanterie*. Paris: Alcan-Lévy, 1904, p.32.

4. *Ibid,* p.64.

5. *Ibid,* p.47.

6. Buat, Edmond (commandant). *Etude théorique sur l'attaque décisive*. Paris: Chapelot, 1909, pp.125-6.

7. France: Ministère de la guerre. *Décret du 3 décembre 1904 portant règlement sur les manœuvres d'infanterie*. Paris: Lavauzelle, 1910, p.16. Article 15.

8. Monteilhet, Joseph. *Les institutions militaires de la France, 1814-1924*. Paris: Alcan, 1926, p.8.

9. Laure, Emile (lieutenant). *L'offensive française*. Paris: Lavauzelle, 1912, p.54.

10. *Ibid,* p.55.

11. *Ibid,* p.187.

12. *Ibid,* p.192.

13. *Ibid,* p.192.

14. Billard, Marie Marcel André (capitaine). *Education de l'infanterie*. Paris: Chapelot, 1913, p.16.

15. Alexandre, Georges-René (général). *Avec Joffre d'Agadir à Verdun: souvenirs, 1911-1916.* Paris: Berger-Levrault, 1932, p.78.

16. *Ibid,* p.80.

17. Rocolle, Pierre. *L'hécatombe des généraux*. Paris: Lavauzelle, 1980, p.59.

18. *Ibid,* p.40.

19. *Ibid,* p.52.

20. *Ibid,* p.22.

21. Percin, Alexandre (général). *Le combat.* Paris: Alcan, 1914, p.213.
22. *Ibid*, p.214.
23. Treignier, Eugène (député). *L'infanterie de demain: rapport fait au nom de la commission de l'armée sur le projet de loi des cadres de l'infanterie.* Paris: Lavauzelle, 1912, p.108.
24. *Ibid*, p.87.
25. Billard. *op. cit.*, p.257.
26. Bonnal. *Questions militaires d'actualité.* 3e série. Paris. Chapelot, 1908, pp.59-60.
27. Kessler, Charles (général). *Tactique des trois armes.* Paris: Chapelot, 1902, p.122.
28. Porch, Douglas. *The march to the Marne: the French army, 1871-1914.* Cambridge: Cambridge University Press, 1981, p.201.
29. Treignier. *op. cit.*, p.184.
30. de Grandmaison, Louis (commandant). *Dressage de l'infanterie en vue du combat offensif.* Reissued Paris: Berger-Levrault, 1908, p.101.
31. Herrmann, David G. *The arming of Europe and the making of the First World War.* Princeton (New Jersey): Princeton University Press, 1997, p.82.
32. *Ibid*, p.83.
33. Laure. *L'offensive française. op. cit.*, p.26.
34. Jibé. *op. cit.*, p.175.
35. Monteilhet. *op. cit.*, p.310.
36. Porch. *op. cit.*, p.201.
37. Joffre. *op. cit.*, vol. 1, pp.79-80.
38. *Ibid*, p.84.
39. Alexandre. *op. cit.*, p.84.
40. Percin. *Le combat. op. cit.*, p.154.
41. Treignier. *op. cit.*, p.108.
42. Monteilhet. *op. cit.*, p.313.
43. Russo-Turkish war of 1877-8.
44. Foch, Ferdinand (colonel). *Des principes de la guerre: conférences faites à l'Ecole supérieure de guerre,* 2nd ed. Paris: Berger-Levrault, 1906, p.318.
45. France: Ministère de la guerre. *Décret du 3 décembre 1904. op. cit.*, p.61. Article 192.
46. de Grandmaison. *Dressage. op. cit.*, pp.59, 101.
47. Montaigne, Jean-Baptiste (lieutenant-colonel). *Etudes sur la guerre.* Paris: Berger-Levrault, 1911, p.191.
48. Allemand, Thierry. *Evolution des sections d'infanterie de 1871 à 1982.* Ecole des hautes études en sciences sociales. Thèse de 3e cycle sous la direction du professeur Alain Joxe, p.186.
49. Laure. *L'offensive française. op. cit.*, p.97.
50. Montaigne. *Etudes. op. cit.*, p.192.
51. *Ibid*, p.188.
52. de Grandmaison. *Dressage. op. cit.*, p.50.
53. *Ibid*, p.53.
54. *Ibid*, pp.53-4.
55. *Ibid*, p.65.
56. Porch. *op. cit.*, p.207.
57. Treignier. *op. cit.*, p.102.
58. Klotz, Lucien (député). *L'armée en 1906: considérations générales à propos du budget de la guerre.* Paris: Lavauzelle, 1906, p.178.

59. ed. Corvisier, André. *Histoire militaire de la France,* 4 vols. Paris: Presses universitaires de France, 1992-4, vol. 3, p.105.
60. *Ibid,* vol. 3, p.106.
61. Bonnal. *Questions militaires d'actualité.* 3e série. *op. cit.,* p.68.
62. Porch. *op. cit.,* p.192.
63. Treignier. *op. cit.,* p.51.
64. Revol, Joseph (général). 'Souvenirs: à l'Ecole supérieure de guerre (1903-1905)', in *Revue historique des armées* (3/1979), numéro 136, pp.130-44.
65. Laure. *L'offensive française. op. cit.,* p.61.
66. Treignier. *op. cit.,* p.155.
67. de Grandmaison. *Dressage. op. cit.,* p.ix.
68. Laure. *L'offensive française. op. cit.,* p.199.
69. *Ibid,* p.69.
70. Billard. *op. cit.,* p.13.
71. *Ibid,* p.19.
72. de Grandmaison. *Dressage. op. cit.,* p.82.
73. Larcher, Maurice (lieutenant-colonel). *Le 1er corps à Dinant, Charleroi, Guise, août 1914.* Paris: Berger-Levrault, 1932, p.2.
74. *Idem.*

## Chapter 4: The Choice of Arms
(pages 79–98)

1. SHAT. *Inventaire sommaire des archives de guerre.* Série N, 1872-1919. Vincennes: Service historique de l'armée de terre, 1995, p.116.
2. Larcher, Maurice (commandant). 'Le 10e corps à Charleroi (20 au 24 août 1914)', in *Revue militaire française* (Oct-Dec 1930), numéro 38, pp.174, 175.
3. *Ibid,* p.176.
4. The last of these thirty-one battalions had been formed in December 1912.
5. Le Pichon, Yann; and Deleuze, Benoît. *Les alpins.* Paris: Berger-Levrault / Didier Richard / Lavauzelle, 1988, p.15.
6. *Ibid,* p.27.
7. Jibé (capitaine) (pseud). [Mordacq, Henri-Jean-Jules]. *L'armée nouvelle: ce qu'elle pense, ce qu'elle veut.* Paris: Plon, [c.1905], p.256.
8. Mordacq, Henri-Jean-Jules (commandant). *Les cyclistes combattants.* Paris: Fournier, 1910, pp.16-22.
9. Treignier, Eugène (député). *L'infanterie de demain: rapport fait au nom de la commission de l'armée sur le projet de loi des cadres de l'infanterie.* Paris: Lavauzelle, 1912, pp.147-8.
10. Mordacq. *op. cit.,* p.93.
11. SHAT. *Inventaire sommaire. op. cit.,* p.153.
12. Blin (colonel). *Histoire de l'organisation et de la tactique des différentes armes: 1610 à nos jours.* Paris: Lavauzelle, 1931, p.18.
13. To be more exact, six caissons in every thirteen were filled with high-explosive shells, compared with just one in thirteen previously. See Alexandre, Georges-René (général). *Avec Joffre d'Agadir à Verdun: souvenirs, 1911-1916.* Paris: Berger-Levrault, 1932, p.55.
14. Herr, Frédéric-Georges (général). *L'artillerie: ce qu'elle a été, ce qu'elle est, ce qu'elle doit être.* Paris: Berger-Levrault, 1923, p.7.

15. SHAT. *Inventaire sommaire. op. cit.,* p.143.

16. *Ibid.*

17. Percin, Alexandre (général). *Le combat.* Paris: Alcan, 1914, p.164.

18. Montaigne, Jean-Baptiste (lieutenant-colonel). *Vaincre: esquisse d'une doctrine de la guerre, basée sur la connaissance de l'homme.* Paris: Berger-Levrault, 1913, p.37.

19. Percin. *Le combat. op. cit.,* p.175.

20. Gascouin, Firmin-Emile (général). *L'évolution de l'artillerie pendant la guerre.* Reissued Paris: Flammarion, 1921, p.68.

21. *Ibid,* p.59.

22. *Ibid,* p.62.

23. Herr. *op. cit.,* p.7.

24. A gun had a barrel length twenty times greater than its calibre, and its fire had a flat trajectory. A mortar had a barrel length less than ten times greater than the calibre, and a very high trajectory. The barrel length of an howitzer was between ten and twenty times the calibre, and the trajectory was arced.

25. Porch, Douglas. *The march to the Marne: the French army, 1871-1914.* Cambridge: Cambridge University Press, 1981, p.237.

26. Herr. *op. cit.,* p.265.

27. *Ibid,* pp.265-6.

28. Alexandre. *op. cit.,* p.49.

29. *Ibid,* p.29, using data abstracted from *Le Temps* (16 Jul 1914).

30. Buat, Edmond (commandant). *Etude théorique sur l'attaque décisive.* Paris: Chapelot, 1909, p.34.

31. SHAT. 7 N 48, 2. Général André. Note de présentation numéro 2 pour la question du renforcement de l'artillerie de campagne, 28 juin 1904. SHAT. 1 N 9, 1. Conseil supérieur de la guerre. Procès-verbal, 30 janvier 1904, pp.49-60.

32. Percin. *Le combat. op. cit.,*p.265.

33. Porch. *op. cit.,* p.235.

34. Percin. *Le combat. op. cit.,* p.262.

35. de Grandmaison, Louis (commandant). *Dressage de l'infanterie en vue du combat offensif.* Reissued Paris: Berger-Levrault, 1908, p.9.

36. Percin. *Le combat. op. cit.,* p.252.

37. Herr. *op. cit.,* pp.16-17.

38. *Ibid,* p.19.

39. Alexandre. *op. cit.,* p.47.

40. *Ibid,* p.50.

41. *Ibid,* p.38.

42. *Ibid,* p.44.

43. Percin. *Le combat. op. cit.,* p.161.

44. Kessler, Charles (général). *Tactique des trois armes.* Paris: Chapelot, 1902, p.8.

45. Gazin, Fernand (capitaine). *La cavalerie française dans la guerre mondiale, 1914-1918.* Paris: Payot, 1930, p.45.

46. *Ibid,* p.38.

47. Buat. *Etude théorique. op. cit.,* p.45.

48. Percin. *Le combat. op. cit.,* p.164.

49. de Lardemelle, Charles (général). *1914: le redressement initial.* Paris: Berger-Levrault, 1935, p.25.

50. Villatoux, Marie-Catherine. 'De l'inspection permanente de l'aéronautique à la direction de l'aéronautique', in *Revue historique des armées* (4/2003), numéro 233, pp.15-26.

51. *Ibid.*

52. Facon, Patrick. 'Août 1914, les aéronautiques européennes s'en vont en guerre', in *14-18* (Jun-Jul 2002), numéro 8.

## Chapter 5: The Test of Fire
(pages 99–116)

1. On the Eastern Front, a German force destroyed two Russian armies by manœuvre in the Battle of Tannenberg. At Lemberg, the Russians surrounded the Austrian positions.

2. de Langle de Cary, Fernand (général). *Souvenirs de commandement, 1914-1916.* Paris: Payot, 1935, pp.11-22. Rocolle, Pierre. *L'hécatombe des généraux.* Paris: Lavauzelle, 1980, Chapter 4.

3. Wanty, Emile. *L'art de la guerre,* 3 vols. Verviers (Belgium): Editions Gérard, 1967-8, vol. 2, p.110.

4. Joffre, Joseph (maréchal). *Mémoires du maréchal Joffre, 1910-1917,* 2 vols. Paris: Plon, 1932, vol. 1, p.302.

5. Rocolle. *op. cit.,* p.262.

6. *Ibid,* p.352.

7. *Ibid,* p.89.

8. *Ibid,* p.90.

9. Larcher, Maurice (commandant). 'Le 10e corps à Charleroi (20 au 24 août 1914)', in *Revue militaire française* (Oct-Dec 1930), numéro 38.

10. Joffre. *op. cit.,* vol. 1, p.421.

11. Larcher, Maurice (lieutenant-colonel). *Le 1er corps à Dinant, Charleroi, Guise, août 1914.* Paris: Berger-Levrault, 1932, p.53.

12. Fayolle, Marie-Emile (maréchal). *Cahiers secrets de la grande guerre.* Ed. Henry Contamine. Paris: Plon, 1964, pp.24-5.

13. Rocolle. *op. cit.,* p.101.

14. Laure, Emile (lieutenant-colonel); and Jacottet (commandant). *Les étapes de guerre d'une division d'infanterie: 13e division.* Reissued Paris: Berger-Levrault, 1932, p.28.

15. *Ibid,* p.31.

16. *Ibid,* p.61.

17. France: Ministère de la guerre. *Les armées françaises dans la grande guerre,* 11 tomes. Paris, 1922-37, tome 1, vol 2, annexes vol 1, p.576. Annexe numéro 864.

18. Herr, Frédéric-Georges (général). *L'artillerie: ce qu'elle a été, ce qu'elle est, ce qu'elle doit être.* Paris: Berger-Levrault, 1923, p.31.

19. Gascouin, Firmin-Emile (général). *Le triomphe de l'idée.* Paris: Berger-Levrault, 1931, p.115.

20. *Ibid,* p.197.

21. *Ibid,* p.131.

22. Contamine, Henry. *La victoire de la Marne: 9 septembre 1914.* Collection 'Trente journées qui ont fait la France'. Paris: Gallimard, 1970, p.298.

23. Gascouin. *Le triomphe de l'idée. op. cit.,* p.120.

24. Gascouin, Firmin-Emile (général). *L'évolution de l'artillerie pendant la guerre.* Reissued Paris: Flammarion, 1921, p.73.

25. Rocolle. *op. cit.,* p.13.

26. Herr. *op. cit.*, p.28.
27. Gascouin. *Le triomphe de l'idée. op. cit.*, p.206.
28. Herr. *op. cit.*, p.27.
29. Gascouin. *Le triomphe de l'idée. op. cit.*, p.106.
30. *Ibid*, p.132.
31. Alléhaut, Emile (colonel). *Le combat de l'infanterie: étude analytique et synthétique d'après les règlements, illustrée de cas concrets de la guerre 1914-1918.* Paris: Berger-Levrault, 1924, p.9.
32. *Ibid*, p.96.
33. Six out of ten *généraux de division* of the cavalry would be dismissed.
34. Rocolle. *op. cit.*, p.199.
35. *Groupement* Cornulier-Lucinière.
36. Gambiez, Fernand (général); and Suire, Maurice (colonel). *Histoire de la première guerre mondiale,* 2 vols. Paris: Fayard, 1968, vol. 1, p.207.
37. Laure and Jacottet. *op. cit.*, pp.58-9.
38. Gazin, Fernand (capitaine). *La cavalerie française dans la guerre mondiale, 1914-1918.* Paris: Payot, 1930, p.308.
39. *Ibid*, p.310.
40. *Ibid*, p.309.
41. *Ibid*, p.311.
42. France: Ministère de la guerre. *Décret du 28 octobre 1913 portant règlement sur la conduite des grandes unités.* Paris: Lavauzelle, 1913, p.43. Article 130.
43. Gazin. *op. cit.*, p.312.
44. SHAT. *Inventaire sommaire des archives de la guerre.* Série N, 1872-1919. Vincennes: Service historique de l'armée de terre, 1995, p.140.
45. Boullaire, François-René (général). *Histoire du 2e corps de cavalerie du 1er octobre au 1er janvier 1919, après les archives du ministère de la guerre.* Paris: Lavauzelle, 1923, p.472.
46. Bouvard, Henri (commandant). *Les leçons militaires de la guerre.* Paris: Masson, 1920, p.159.
47. Gazin. *op. cit.*, p.317.
48. Orthlieb, Jean (commandant). *L'aéronautique: hier, demain.* Paris: Masson, 1920, p.21.

## Chapter 6: The Pressure of the Front
(pages 117–36)

1. Flichy, Patrice. *L'innovation technique: récents développements en sciences sociales, vers une nouvelle théorie de l'innovation.* Paris: La Découverte, 1995, p.21.
2. Corda, H. (lieutenant-colonel). *L'évolution des méthodes offensives de l'armée française. La recherche de la surprise pendant la grande guerre, 1914-1918.* (Conférences faites les 9 et 11 mars 1921 aux sociétés d'officiers suisses de Zurich et de Lausanne.) Paris: Gauthier-Villars et Cie, 1921, p.4.
3. Laure, Emile (commandant). *Au 3e bureau du troisième GQG, 1917-1919.* Paris: Plon, 1921, p.36.
4. *Ibid*, p.57.
5. Miquel, Pierre. *La grande guerre.* Paris: Fayard, 1983, p.215.
6. Bédier, Joseph. *L'effort français: quelques aspects de la guerre.* Paris: La renaissance du livre, 1919, p.4.

7. Gascouin, Firmin-Emile (général). *Le triomphe de l'idée*. Paris: Berger-Levrault, 1931, p.162.

8. Sorman, Guy. *Les vrais penseurs de notre temps*. Paris: Fayard, 1989, pp.261-2.

9. Kimpflin, René-Georges. *Le premier souffle: un fantassin sur la Trouée de Charmes, août-septembre 1914*. Paris: Perrin, 1920. Quoted in Cru, Jean Norton. *Témoins: essai d'analyse et de critique des souvenirs de combattants édités en francais de 1915 à 1928*. Reissued Nancy: Presses universitaires de Nancy, 1993.

10. Caron, François. *Le résistible déclin des sociétés industrielles*. Paris: Perrin, 1985, p.201.

11. www.theaerodrome.com

12. Bouchacourt, Louis (commandant). *L'infanterie dans la bataille: étude sur l'attaque, étude sur la défense*. Paris: Lavauzelle, 1927, pp.121-2.

13. SHAT. 16 N 2090. Projets d'inventions transmis au 3e bureau du GQG.

14. Joffre, Joseph (maréchal). *Mémoires du maréchal Joffre, 1910-1917*, 2 vols. Paris: Plon, 1932, vol. 2, p.18.

15. de Pierrefeu, Jean. *GQG secteur 1: trois ans au Grand quartier général, par le rédacteur du 'communiqué'*, 2 vols. Paris: L'Edition française illustrée, 1920, vol. 1, p.163.

16. Dubail, Augustin Yvon Edmond (général). *Quatre années de commandement, 1914-1918*, 3 vols. Paris: Fournier, 1920-1, vol. 1, pp.106-7.

17. *Ibid*, vol. 1, p.183.

18. *Ibid*, vol. 1, p.213.

19. *Ibid*, vol. 1, p.226.

20. Gaudin, Thierry; and Aubert, Jean-Eric. *De l'innovation*. Paris: Editions de l'Aube, 1998, p.35.

21. ed. Corvisier, André. *Histoire militaire de la France*, 4 vols. Paris: Presses universitaires de France, 1992-4, vol. 3, p.222.

22. Gaudin and Aubert. *op. cit.*, p.26.

23. Deygas, Ferdinand-Joseph (commandant). *Les chars d'assaut: leur passé, leur avenir*. Paris: Lavauzelle, 1937, p.49.

24. Herr, Frédéric-Georges (général). *L'artillerie: ce qu'elle a été, ce qu'elle est, ce qu'elle doit être*. Reissued Paris: Berger-Levrault, 1924, p.286.

25. de La Chapelle, Raoul. *Hors du cadre: souvenirs d'un artilleur de tranchée K. Ki.* Paris: Berger-Levrault, 1923. Quoted in Cru. *op. cit.*, pp.445-6.

26. Gazin, Fernand (capitaine). *La cavalerie française dans la guerre mondiale, 1914-1918*. Paris: Payot, 1930, p.151.

27. Debeney, Marie-Eugène (colonel). *Cours d'infanterie*. Paris: Ecole supérieure de guerre, 1913, 3e conférence.

28. SHAT. 7 N 670. 2e bureau. Enseignements de la guerre russo-japonaise, note numéro 2, mitrailleuses, décembre 1905.

29. *Revue militaire des armées étrangères*. Jan-Jun 1906, p.186.

30. SHAT. 1 N 9, 11. Conseil supérieur de la guerre, procès-verbal, 7 juin 1905.

31. Chenu, Charles-Maurice. *Du képi rouge aux chars d'assaut*. Paris: Albin Michel, 1932, p.112.

32. Nachin (commandant). 'Les règlements de manœuvre d'infanterie d'avant-guerre', in *Revue militaire française* (Oct-Dec 1922), vol. 6.

33. Bonnal, Henri (général). *L'art nouveau en tactique*. Paris: Chapelot, 1904, p.54.

34. Montaigne, Jean-Baptiste (lieutenant-colonel). *Vaincre: esquisse d'une doctrine de la guerre, basée sur la connaissance de l'homme*. Paris: Berger-Levrault, 1913, p.7.

35. SHAT. 6 N 42. Note sur l'emploi tactique des sections de mitrailleuses dans les troupes d'infanterie, par le général Lyautey, commandant le 10e corps d'armée, le 7 novembre 1911.

36. Debeney. *Cours d'infanterie. op. cit.*, 3e conférence.

37. France: Ministère de la guerre. *Décret du 20 avril 1914 portant règlement sur les manœuvres d'infanterie.* Paris: Lavauzelle, 1914, p.127. Article 336.

38. Chenu. *op. cit.*, p.91.

39. Bouvard, Henri (commandant). *Les leçons militaires de la guerre.* Paris: Masson, 1920, p.46.

40. Nachin. 'Les règlements'. *op. cit.*

41. Gaudin and Aubert. *op. cit.*, p.20.

42. Daille, Marius (général). *Histoire de la guerre mondiale*, vol. 2: *Joffre et la guerre d'usure, 1915-1916.* Paris: Payot, 1936, p.229.

43. Serrigny, Bernard (général). *Trente ans avec Pétain.* Paris: Plon, 1959, p.98.

44. Bloch, Marc. 'Les inventions médiévales', in *Les annales d'histoire économique et sociale* (1935), numéro 36, p.831. Cited in Flichy. *op. cit.*, p.47.

45. Ballé, Catherine. *Sociologie des organisations.* Paris: Presses universitaires de France, 1990, p.76.

46. Orthlieb, Jean (commandant). *L'aéronautique: hier, demain.* Paris: Masson, 1920, p.23.

47. Corvisier. *op. cit.*, vol. 3, p.222.

48. Gaudin and Aubert. *op. cit.*, p.129.

49. de Pierrefeu. *op. cit.*, vol. 2, p.178.

50. Lucas, Pascal-Marie-Henri (colonel). *L'évolution des idées tactiques en France et en Allemagne pendant la guerre de 1914-1918.* Reissued Paris: Berger-Levrault, 1932, p.304.

51. *Ibid*, p.49.

52. Fayolle, Marie-Emile (maréchal). *Cahiers secrets de la grande guerre.* Ed. Henry Contamine. Paris: Plon, 1964, p.79.

53. Lucas. *L'évolution. op. cit.*, pp.79-80.

54. Fayolle. *op. cit.*, p.140.

55. Laure, Emile (lieutenant-colonel); and Jacottet (commandant). *Les étapes de guerre d'une division d'infanterie: 13e division.* Paris: Berger-Levrault, 1928, p.85.

56. *Ibid*, p.34.

57. *Ibid*, p.68.

58. Fayolle. *op. cit.*, p.90.

59. Note numéro 2663 du 3e bureau du GQG en date du 12 novembre 1914.

60. Joffre. *op. cit.*, vol. 2, p.6.

61. Daille. *Histoire de la guerre mondiale*, vol. 2. *op. cit.*, p.76.

62. Laure. *Au 3e bureau. op. cit.*, p.vi.

63. Pedroncini, Guy. *Pétain: général en chef, 1917-1918.* Paris: Publications de la Sorbonne / Presses universitaires de France, 1974, p.40.

64. Laure. *Au 3e bureau. op. cit.*, p.vii.

65. *Ibid*, p.vi.

66. Miquel, Pierre. *Le gâchis des généraux: les erreurs de commandement pendant la guerre de 14-18.* Paris: Plon, 2001, pp.175-6.

67. Laure and Jacottet. *op. cit.*, p.217.

68. *Ibid*, p.218.

69. Pedroncini. *Pétain: général en chef. op. cit.*, p.212.

70. Bédier. *op. cit.*, p.4.

71. Gascouin, Firmin-Emile (général). *L'évolution de l'artillerie pendant la guerre.* Reissued Paris: Flammarion, 1921, p.282.

72. Toffler, Alvin. *Future shock.* New York: Random House, 1970.

73. Lucas. *L'évolution. op. cit.*, p.220.

74. Drucker, Peter. *Les entrepreneurs.* Paris: L'Expansion / Hachette / J.-C. Lattès, 1985, p.238.

75. Herr. *op. cit.*, p.268.

## Chapter 7: GHQ and Tactical Change
(pages 137–63)

1. Gambiez, Fernand (général); and Suire, Maurice (colonel). *Histoire de la première guerre mondiale,* 2 vols. Paris: Fayard, 1968, vol. 1, p.184.

2. de Pierrefeu, Jean. *GQG secteur 1: trois ans au Grand quartier général, par le rédacteur du 'communiqué',* 2 vols. Paris: L'Edition française illustrée, 1920, vol. 1, p.39.

3. Alexandre, Georges-René (général). *Avec Joffre d'Agadir à Verdun: souvenirs, 1911-1916.* Paris: Berger-Levrault, 1932, p.122.

4. Serrigny, Bernard (général). *Trente ans avec Pétain.* Paris: Plon, 1959, p.42.

5. de Pierrefeu. *op. cit.*, vol. 1, p.40.

6. *Ibid*, p.48.

7. Gascouin, Firmin-Emile (général). *L'évolution de l'artillerie pendant la guerre.* Reissued Paris: Flammarion, 1921, p.268.

8. Ferro, Marc. *La grande guerre.* Paris: Gallimard, 1990, p.117.

9. Fayolle, Marie-Emile (maréchal). *Cahiers secrets de la grande guerre.* Ed. Henry Contamine. Paris: Plon, 1964, p.142.

10. Pedroncini, Guy. *Pétain: général en chef, 1917-1918.* Paris: Publications de la Sorbonne / Presses universitaires de France, 1974, p.86.

11. Pedroncini, Guy (ed.) *Journal de marche de Joffre, 1916-1919.* Vincennes: Service historique de l'armée de terre, 1990, p.101.

12. Pedroncini. *Pétain: général en chef. op. cit.*, p.77.

13. de Pierrefeu. *op. cit.*, vol. 2, p.45.

14. Laure, Emile (commandant). *Au 3e bureau du troisième GQG, 1917-1919.* Paris: Plon, 1921, p.29.

15. Lucas, Pascal-Marie-Henri (colonel). *L'évolution des idées tactiques en France et en Allemagne pendant la guerre de 1914-1918.* Reissued Paris: Berger-Levrault, 1932, p.185.

16. Pedroncini. *Pétain: général en chef. op. cit.*, p.78.

17. Laure. *Au 3e bureau. op. cit.*, p.16.

18. *Ibid*, p.19.

19. *Ibid*, p.34.

20. *Instruction of 26 January 1916 on the offensive combat of large units,* and *Instruction of 16 December 1916 regarding the aim and the conditions of a general offensive action.*

21. SHAT. 16 N 2092. Etudes de la section instruction du 3e bureau du GQG, août 1917.

22. The draft included standard models of plans and operational orders, so as 'to create unity of wording and use it to mitigate the effects of the constant *noria* [rotating relief] of units'. See Laure. *Au 3e bureau. op. cit.*, p.44.

23. SHAT. 16 N 2094. Expérimentation de l'emploi des mitrailleuses en tir indirect, note numéro 979 du 3e bureau du GQG du 1er août 1917.

24. Laure. *Au 3e bureau. op. cit.,* p.34.

25. SHAT. 16 N 2094. Projet de réorganisation de la compagnie d'infanterie, 3e bureau du GQG, note numéro 18671, 18 juillet 1917.

26. SHAT. 16 N 2091. Réorganisation de la compagnie d'infanterie, 3e bureau du GQG, note numéro 9897, 10 septembre 1917.

27. Laure. *Au 3e bureau. op. cit.,* p.11.

28. de Pierrefeu. *op. cit.,* vol. 2, p.43.

29. Laure. *Au 3e bureau. op. cit.,* p.83.

30. Bédier, Joseph. *L'effort français: quelques aspects de la guerre.* Paris: La renaissance du livre, 1919, p.72.

31. See Appendix 2.

32. de Gaulle, Charles. *La France et son armée.* Paris: Plon, 1938. Reissued Livre de poche, 1973, p.273.

33. Dubail, Augustin Yvon Edmond (général). *Quatre années de commandement, 1914-1918,* 3 vols. Paris: Fournier, 1920-1, vol. 1, p.213.

34. *Ibid,* p.250.

35. *Ibid,* p.243.

36. Campana, Louis-Charles-Roger. *Les enfants de la grande revanche: carnet de route d'un saint-cyrien.* Paris: Marcel Gilly. 1920. Quoted in Cru, Jean Norton. *Témoins: essai d'analyse et de critique des souvenirs de combattants édités en francais de 1915 à 1928.* Reissued Nancy: Presses universitaires de Nancy, 1993, p.103.

37. Laure, Emile (lieutenant-colonel); and Jacottet (commandant). *Les étapes de guerre d'une division d'infanterie: 13e division.* Reissued Paris: Berger-Levrault, 1932, p.100.

38. Bédier. *op. cit.,* p.47.

39. Daille, Marius (général). *Histoire de la guerre mondiale,* vol. 2: *Joffre et la guerre d'usure, 1915-1916.* Paris: Payot, 1936, p.110.

40. *Ibid,* p.239.

41. Laure and Jacottet. *op. cit.,* p.127.

42. Fayolle. *op. cit.,* p.128.

43. Serrigny. *op. cit.,* p.97.

44. *Ibid,* p.98.

45. Laure and Jacottet. *op. cit.,* p.222.

46. Laure. *Au 3e bureau. op. cit.,* p.8.

47. France: Etat-major de l'armée. Service historique. *Notice historique sur les inspecteurs généraux,* juin 1927, p.21.

48. SHAT. 16 N 2093. Note 2350 du 4 septembre 1916 sur l'organisation de l'instruction dans les armées.

49. A note from GHQ, dated 12 July 1917, asked each army to provide a summary of its training structure (description of schools, sites, those in charge, programmes).

50. From 11 to 18 June, the 4th Army, which led the way in training within the Central Army Group, hosted the training directors from the various armies, in order to set out its methods and exchange opinions.

51. Laure. *Au 3e bureau. op. cit.,* pp.24-7.

52. *Ibid,* p.61.

53. Fayolle. *op. cit.,* p.40.

54. *Ibid,* p.44.

55. Lucas. *L'évolution des idées tactiques. op. cit.,* p.49.

56. *Ibid*, p.51.

57. *Ibid*, pp.50-1.

58. de Pierrefeu. *op. cit.*, vol. 1, p.163.

59. Daille. *Histoire de la guerre mondiale*, vol. 2. *op. cit.*, p.228.

60. *Ibid*, p.75.

61. Fayolle. *op. cit.*, p.70.

62. Dubail. *op. cit.*, vol. 1, p.207.

63. Laure and Jacottet. *op. cit.*, p.86.

64. de Langle de Cary, Fernand (général). *Souvenirs de commandement, 1914-1916*. Paris: Payot, 1935, p.74.

65. Lucas. *L'évolution des idées tactiques. op. cit.*, pp.55-6.

66. Fayolle. *op. cit.*, p.76.

67. Morel-Journel, Henry. *Journal d'un officier de la 74e division d'infanterie et de l'Armée française d'Italie, 1914-1918*. Montbrison: E. Brassart, 1922. Cited in Cru. *op. cit.*, p.214.

68. Daille. *Histoire de la guerre mondiale*, vol. 2. *op. cit.*, p.228.

69. de Langle de Cary. *op. cit.*, p.81.

70. Daille. *Histoire de la guerre mondiale*, vol. 2. *op. cit.*, p.228.

71. Lucas. *L'évolution des idées tactiques. op. cit.*, p.65.

72. *Ibid*, p.69.

73. SHAT. 16 N 1677. Dossier 33. Pièce 3322.

74. Daille. *Histoire de la guerre mondiale*, vol. 2. *op. cit.*, p.127.

75. Lucas. *L'évolution des idées tactiques. op. cit.*, p.90.

76. Daille. *Histoire de la guerre mondiale*, vol. 2. *op. cit.*, p.229.

77. Fayolle. *op. cit.*, p.138.

78. *Ibid*, p.141.

79. Daille. *Histoire de la guerre mondiale*, vol. 2. *op. cit.*, p.81.

80. *Ibid*, p.229.

81. Fayolle. *op. cit.*, p.142.

82. Daille. *Histoire de la guerre mondiale*, vol. 2. *op. cit.*, p.397.

83. *Ibid*, p.235.

84. SHAT. 16 N 1679. Dossier 39. Pièce 4704.

85. Lucas. *L'évolution des idées tactiques. op. cit.*, p.109.

86. Daille. *Histoire de la guerre mondiale*, vol. 2. *op. cit.*, p.394.

87. *Ibid*, p.396.

88. *Ibid*, p.416.

89. Note from the commander of the 6th Army, dated 8 June 1916. Quoted in Lucas. *L'évolution des idées tactiques. op. cit.*, p.139.

90. *Ibid*, p.151.

91. *Ibid*.

92. Daille. *Histoire de la guerre mondiale*, vol. 2. *op. cit.*, p.397.

93. See Appendix 2.

94. Lucas. *L'évolution des idées tactiques. op. cit.*, p.167.

95. *Ibid*, p.147.

96. SHAT. 16 N 1683. Dossier 52. Pièce 7090.

97. SHAT. 16 N 1683. Dossier 55. Pièce 7684 bis.

98. Lucas. *L'évolution des idées tactiques. op. cit.*, p.163.

99. *Ibid*, p.173.

100. Daille. *Histoire de la guerre mondiale*, vol. 2. *op. cit.*, p.151.

## Chapter 8: Confronting the Trenches
(pages 164–84)

1. Bédier, Joseph. *L'effort français: quelques aspects de la guerre*. Paris: La renaissance du livre, 1919, p.3.

2. Joffre, Joseph (maréchal). *Mémoires du maréchal Joffre, 1910-1917*, 2 vols. Paris: Plon, 1932, vol. 2, p.24.

3. Joffre carried a notebook in his pocket in which he kept track of the number of shells rather than the number of men.

4. de Langle de Cary, Fernand (général). *Souvenirs de commandement, 1914-1916*. Paris: Payot, 1935, p.70.

5. Alléhaut, Emile (colonel). *Le combat de l'infanterie: étude analytique et synthétique d'après les règlements, illustrée de cas concrets de la guerre 1914-1918*. Paris: Berger-Levrault, 1924, pp.32-40.

6. Fayolle, Marie-Emile (maréchal). *Cahiers secrets de la grande guerre*. Ed. Henry Contamine. Paris: Plon, 1964, p.114.

7. See Appendix 2.

8. Lucas, Pascal-Marie-Henri (colonel). *L'évolution des idées tactiques en France et en Allemagne pendant la guerre de 1914-1918*. Reissued Paris: Berger-Levrault, 1932, p.166.

9. Bouvard, Henri (commandant). *Les leçons militaires de la guerre*. Paris: Masson, 1920, p.108.

10. Laure, Emile (lieutenant-colonel); and Jacottet (commandant). *Les étapes de guerre d'une division d'infanterie: 13e division*. Reissued Paris: Berger-Levrault, 1932, p.258.

11. *Ibid*, pp.281-3.

12. *Ibid*, p.153.

13. SHAT. *Inventaire sommaire des archives de guerre*. Série N, 1872-1919. Vincennes: Service historique de l'armée de terre, 1995, p.122.

14. *Ibid*, p.324.

15. *Ibid*, p.139.

16. Gazin, Fernand (capitaine). *La cavalerie française dans la guerre mondiale, 1914-1918*. Paris: Payot, 1930, p.324.

17. SHAT. *Inventaire sommaire. op. cit.*, p.138.

18. Gazin. *op. cit.*, p.152.

19. *Ibid*, p.433.

20. Pedroncini, Guy. *Pétain: général en chef, 1917-1918*. Paris: Publications de la Sorbonne / Presses universitaires de France, 1974, p.61.

21. *Ibid*.

22. Boullaire, François-René (général). *Histoire du 2e corps de cavalerie du 1er octobre au 1er janvier 1919, après les archives du ministère de la guerre*. Paris: Lavauzelle, 1923, p.460.

23. Gazin. *op. cit.*, p.250.

24. SHAT. *Inventaire sommaire. op. cit.*, p.147.

25. The old generation of heavy guns had a rate of fire of one round every two minutes. The modern guns could fire a round every thirty seconds. Herr, Frédéric-Georges (général). *L'artillerie: ce qu'elle a été, ce qu'elle est, ce qu'elle doit être*. Reissued Paris: Berger-Levrault, 1924, p.151.

26. Nine hours on 21 February 1916 at Verdun.

27. The French used chemical shells for the first time in August 1916. They used mustard gas for the first time in April 1918, six months after the Germans. In all, the French produced just one-third of the amount of chemical agents produced by the Germans.

28. Gascouin, Firmin-Emile (général). *L'évolution de l'artillerie pendant la guerre.* Reissued Paris: Flammarion, 1921, p.127.

29. SHAT. *Inventaire sommaire. op. cit.,* p.150.

30. Maître (général). 'Evolution des idées sur l'emploi de l'artillerie pendant la guerre', in *Revue militaire française* (Jan-Mar 1924), vol. 11. Tableau 10.

31. Herr. *op. cit.,* p.145.

32. Daille, Marius (général). *Histoire de la guerre mondiale,* vol. 2: *Joffre et la guerre d'usure, 1915-1916.* Paris: Payot, 1936, p.235.

33. Pedroncini. *Pétain: général en chef. op. cit.,* p.80.

34. SHAT. *Inventaire sommaire. op. cit.,* pp.151-2.

35. Service historique de l'armée de l'air. Note au sujet du fonctionnement de l'aviation, direction du Service aéronautique, numéro 4386, GQG, 10 novembre 1914, fonds 1914-1918. Quoted in Facon, Patrick. 'Aperçus sur la doctrine d'emploi de l'aéronautique militaire française, 1914-1918', in *Revue historique des armées* (1988), numéro 3.

36. Orthlieb, Jean (commandant). *L'aéronautique: hier, demain.* Paris: Masson, 1920, pp.218-19.

37. In all, 16,500 pilots and 2,000 observers were trained. See: ed. Corvisier, André. *Histoire militaire de la France,* 4 vols. Paris: Presses universitaires de France, 1992-4, vol. 3, p.233.

38. Orthlieb. *op. cit.,* pp.64-5.

39. Corvisier. *op. cit.,* vol. 3, p.219.

40. Laure and Jacottet. *op. cit.,* p.131.

41. Grandhomme, Jean-Noël; and Krempp, Thérèse. *Charles de Rose: le pionnier de l'aviation de chasse.* Strasbourg: La nuée bleue, 2003, p.193.

42. Voisin, André (général). *La doctrine de l'aviation française de combat au cours de la guerre, 1915-1918.* Paris: Berger-Levrault, 1932, p.36.

## Chapter 9: In the Death Zone
(pages 185–203)

1. Gaudy, Georges. *Souvenirs d'un poilu du 57e régiment d'infanterie: l'agonie du Mont-Renaud, mars-avril 1918.* Paris: Plon, 1921, pp.162-3.

2. Jünger, Ernst. *Feu et sang: bref épisode d'une grande bataille.* Trans Julien Hervier. Paris: Christian Bourgeois, 1998, pp.101, 107, 112.

3. Galtier-Boissière, Jean. *Un hiver à Souchez.* Paris: Les Etincelles, 1930, p.28.

4. Jünger. *Feu et sang. op. cit.,* pp.25, 96.

5. Armengaud, Jean (lieutenant-colonel). *L'atmosphere du champ de bataille.* Paris: Lavauzelle, 1940, p.39.

6. Dupont, Marcel. *Impressions d'un officier de légère, 1915-1917.* Paris: Plon, 1918. Quoted in Masson, Philippe. *L'homme en guerre, 1901-2001: de la Marne à Sarajevo.* Paris/Monaco: Editions du Rocher, 1997, p.87.

7. Chenu, Charles-Maurice. *Du képi rouge aux chars d'assaut.* Paris: Albin Michel, 1932, p.274.

8. Jünger. *Feu et sang. op. cit.,* p.91.

9. *Ibid*, p.65.

10. Armengaud. *op. cit.*, p.15.

11. Pinguet, Jean. *Trois étapes de la brigade des marins*. Paris: Perrin, 1918. Quoted in Cru, Jean Norton. *Témoins: essai d'analyse et de critique des souvenirs de combattants édités en francais de 1915 à 1928*. Reissued Nancy: Presses universitaires de Nancy, 1993, p.400.

12. Coste, Charles (commandant). *La psychologie du combat*. Paris: Berger-Levrault, 1929, p.173.

13. *Ibid*, p.170.

14. Cru. *op. cit.*, p.142.

15. Galtier-Boissière, Jean. *Un hiver à Souchez*. Paris: Les Etincelles, 1930. Quoted in Cru. *op. cit.*, pp.139-40.

16. des Vignes Rouges, Jean (pseud). *Bourru, soldat de Vauquois*. Paris: Perrin, 1917. Quoted in Armengaud. *op. cit.*, p.111.

17. d'Arnoux, Jacques. *Paroles d'un revenant*. Paris: Plon, 1925. Quoted in Armengaud. *op. cit.*, p.119.

18. Holmes, Richard. *Acts of war: the behaviour of men in battle*. New York: The Free Press, 1989, p.170.

19. Armengaud. *op. cit.*, p.36

20. Naegelen, René. *Les suppliciés: histoire vécue*. Paris: Baudinière, 1927. Quoted in Armengaud. *op. cit.*, p.123.

21. Armengaud. *op. cit.*, p.52.

22. Cru. *op. cit.*, p.28.

23. Delvert, Charles. *Carnets d'un fantassin*. Paris: Albin Michel, 1935, p.22.

24. Holmes. *op. cit.*, p.150.

25. Rommel, Erwin (lieutenant-colonel). *L'infantry attaque: enseignements et expérience vécue*. Montpellier: Ecole d'application de l'infanterie, nd, p.46.

26. *Ibid*, p.60.

27. Chenu. *op. cit.*, p.153.

28. Cru. *op. cit.*, p.28.

29. *Ibid*, pp.28-9, 210.

30. Chaine, Pierre. *Les mémoires d'un rat*. Paris: Payot, 1921. Quoted in Cru. *op. cit.*, p.426.

31. Coste. *op. cit.*, pp.184-5.

32. Galtier-Boissière, Jean. *La fleur au fusil*. Paris: Baudinière, 1928. Quoted in Armengaud. *op. cit.*, p.140.

33. Chenu. *op. cit.*, pp.227-8.

34. Jünger. *Feu et sang. op. cit.*, p.93.

35. Armengaud. *op. cit.*, p.51.

36. Rommel. *op. cit.*, p.46.

37. Jünger, Ernst. *Orages d'acier: souvenirs du front de France*. Trans F. Grenier. Paris: Payot, 1930, p.184.

38. Gaudy. *op. cit.*, p.185.

39. Bouchacourt, Louis (commandant). *L'infanterie dans la bataille: étude sur l'attaque, étude sur la défense*. Paris: Lavauzelle, 1927, pp.121-2.

40. Jünger. *Orages. op. cit.*, p.256.

41. Coste. *op. cit.*, p.31.

42. Gaudy. *op. cit.*, p.42.

43. Genevoix, Maurice. *Ceux de 14*. Paris: Flammarion, 1950, p.94.

44. Morel-Journel, Henry. *Journal d'un officier de la 74e division d'infanterie et de l'Armée française d'Italie*. Montbrison: Eleuthère-Brassart, 1922. Quoted in Cru. *op. cit.*, p.215.

45. Coste. *op. cit.*, p.30.

46. Marot, Jean. *Ceux qui vivent*. Paris: Payot, 1919. Quoted in Cru. *op. cit.*, p.450.

47. Jünger. *Feu et sang. op. cit.*, p.49.

48. Gaudy. *op. cit.*, p.182.

49. Jünger. *Orages. op. cit.*, p.226.

50. Chenu. *op. cit.*, p.67.

51. Dorgelès, Roland. *Les croix de bois*. Paris: Albin Michel, 1919. Quoted in Coste. *op. cit.*, p.26.

52. Maisonneuve, Paul-Henri (capitaine). *L'infanterie sous le feu: étude critique sur le combat de la compagnie*. Paris: Berger-Levrault, 1925, p.18.

53. Monod, Gabriel. *Soldat français et soldat allemand*. Quoted in Armengaud. *op. cit.*, p.145.

54. Armengaud. *op. cit.*, p.51.

55. Jünger. *Feu et sang. op. cit.*, pp.90, 121.

56. *Ibid*, p.97.

57. *Ibid*, p.106.

58. *Ibid*, pp.168, 172.

59. Coste. *op. cit.*, p.105.

60. Genevoix. *op. cit.*, p.33.

61. *Ibid*, pp.91-2.

62. Pézard, André. *Nous autres à Vauquois*. Paris: La Renaissance du livre, 1918. Quoted in Armengaud. *op. cit.*, p.140.

63. Genevoix. *op. cit.*, p.138.

64. Rommel. *op. cit.*, p.67.

65. Galtier-Boissière, Jean. *La fleur au fusil*. Paris: Baudinière, 1928. Quoted in Armengaud. *op. cit.*, p.134.

66. Chenu. *op. cit.*, p.89.

67. Holmes. *op. cit.*, p.156.

68. Jünger. *Feu et sang. op. cit.*, p.13.

69. Delvert. *op. cit.*, p.150.

70. Jünger. *Orages. op. cit.*, p.18.

71. Mairet, Louis. *Carnet d'un combattant*. Paris: Crès, 1919. Quoted in Cru. *op. cit.*, p.192.

72. Holmes. *op. cit.*, p.277.

73. Marot, Jean. *Ceux qui vivent*. Paris: Payot, 1919. Quoted in Cru. *op. cit.*, pp.450-1.

74. Galtier-Boissière, Jean. *La fleur au fusil*. Paris: Baudinière, 1928. Quoted in Armengaud. *op. cit.*, p.134.

75. Jünger. *Feu et sang. op. cit.*, p.51.

76. Delvert. *op. cit.*, p.293.

## Chapter 10: The Steel Fist
(pages 204–29)

1. Bloch (commandant). 'L'avenir du char de combat', in *Revue militaire française* (Jan-Mar 1922), vol. 3, p.91.

2. Deygas, Ferdinand-Joseph (commandant). *Les chars d'assaut: leur passé, leur avenir*. Paris: Lavauzelle, 1937, pp.53-8.

3. *Ibid*, p.91.

4. SHAT. 16 N 2120. Documents du général Estienne adressés au ministre de la Guerre le 26 juin 1916.

5. Alter, Norbert (ed). *Les logiques de l'innovation: approche pluridisciplinaire*. Paris: La Découverte, 2002, p.80.

6. The theatre of operations, under the commander-in-chief's control, was set apart from the country's interior, which was the government's responsibility.

7. Company of forges and steelworks of the Navy and of Homécourt, known as 'Saint-Chamond'. It was Schneider's competitor.

8. Perré, Jean (capitaine). 'Le commandement allemand et les chars', in *Revue militaire française* (Apr-Jun 1925), vol. 15, p.222.

9. Peters, Thomas J.; and Waterman, Robert H. *Le prix de l'excellence*. Trans Michèle Garène and Chantal Pommier. Paris: Interéditions, 1983. Chapter 5.

10. Deygas. *op. cit.*, p.88.

11. Perré, Jean (lieutenant-colonel); and Le Gouest (capitaine). 'Chars et statistique', in *Revue d'infanterie* (1 July 1935), numéro 514.

12. Deygas. *op. cit.*, pp.116-20.

13. www.chronicus.com

14. *Idem.*

15. Chenu, Charles-Maurice. *Du képi rouge aux chars d'assaut*. Paris: Albin Michel, 1932, p.213.

16. SHAT. 16 N 2121. Notes du GQG, AS du 8 janvier 1917 et du 20 février 1917 sur l'organisation des unités tactiques.

17. SHAT. 16 N 2120. Ordre général numéro 1 du général commandant l'AS du 1er janvier 1917.

18. Perré, Jean (général). *Batailles et combats des chars français: l'année d'apprentissage, 1917*. Paris: Lavauzelle, 1937, pp.47-62.

19. SHAT. 16 N 2120. Carton 3, Dossier 4. Tableau des pertes en chars et personnels, GQG, 9 septembre 1919.

20. SHAT. 16 N 2124. Note du 3e bureau du GQG en date du 17 juin 1917.

21. SHAT. 22 N 1721. 32e CA.

22. Deygas. *op. cit.*, p.122.

23. Perré. *Batailles et combats ... l'année d'apprentissage. op. cit.*, pp.89-90, 93, 129.

24. Deygas. *op. cit.*, p.138.

25. SHAT. 16 N 2120. Carton 3, Dossier 4. Tableau des pertes en chars et personnels, GQG, 9 septembre 1919.

26. SHAT. 16 N 2124. Carton 15, Dossier 2. Directives d'emploi des chars.

27. Perré. *Batailles et combats ... l'année d'apprentissage. op. cit.*, p.87.

28. Gagneur, Maurice (capitaine); and Fourier, Marcel (lieutenant). *Avec les chars d'assaut*. Paris: Hachette, 1919, p.177.

29. Chenu. *op. cit.*, p.265.

30. Perré. *Batailles et combats ... l'année d'apprentissage. op. cit.*, pp.143-61.

31. SHAT. 16 N 2120. Rapport au sujet de la participation de l'AS aux opérations des 23 et 25 octobre 1917.

32. Dutil, Léon (capitaine). *Les chars d'assaut: leur création et leur rôle pendant la guerre, 1915-1918*. Paris: Berger-Levrault, 1919, p.115. Each of the three battalions that had composed the 262nd Infantry Regiment was attached to an Assault Artillery centre.

33. Dutil. *op. cit.*, p.97.

34. *Ibid*, pp.115, 139.

35. Perré and Le Gouest. *op cit.*, p.81.

36. Dutil. *op. cit.*, p.143.

37. *Ibid*, p.142.

38. SHAT. 16 N 2120. Carton 3, Dossier 4. Tableau des pertes en chars et personnels, GQG, 9 septembre 1919.

39. *Idem*.

40. Dutil. *op. cit.*, p.207.

41. Deygas. *op. cit.*, p.142.

42. Armour: between 6 and 16mm. Speed: between 2 and 8 km/hour. Capable of climbing slopes of up to 119 per cent (more than 45 degrees). Armament: either Hotchkiss machine-gun or 37mm gun. Dutil. *op. cit.*, p.83.

43. Dutil. *op. cit.*, p.118.

44. Deygas. *op. cit.*, p.190.

45. *Idem*.

46. Dutil. *op. cit.*, p.104.

47. *Ibid*, p.110.

48. *Ibid*, p.116.

49. *Ibid*, pp.126-30.

50. *Ibid*, pp.130-1.

51. *Ibid*, pp.132-3.

52. Lafitte, Raymond (lieutenant-colonel). *L'artillerie d'assaut de 1916 à 1918*. Paris: Lavauzelle, nd, p.43.

53. *Ibid*, p.45.

54. SHAT. 16 N 2150. Rapport du chef de corps du 501e RCC, 19 juin 1918.

55. Lafitte. *op. cit.*, pp.56-7.

56. *Ibid*, p.58.

57. SHAT. 16 N 2120. Carton 3, Dossier 4. Tableau des pertes en chars et personnels, GQG, 9 septembre 1919.

58. Number of artillery fires at the direct disposal of the divisional commander.

59. Dutil. *op. cit.*, pp.175-6.

60. The numbers of tank engagements and losses are from: SHAT. 16 N 2120. Carton 3, Dossier 4. Tableau des pertes en chars et personnels, GQG, 9 septembre 1919.

61. About 100 lorries, or three trains, were enough to transport a light tank battalion. Chédeville (colonel). 'Les chars de combat actuels et le haut commandement', in *Revue militaire française* (Jan-Mar 1922), vol. 3, p.332.

62. SHAT. *Inventaire sommaire des archives de guerre*. Série N, 1872-1919. Vincennes: Service historique de l'armée de terre, 1995, p.164.

63. Alléhaut, Emile (colonel); and Goubernard (commandant). 'A propos d'un jugement allemand', in *Revue militaire française* (Apr-Jun 1925), vol. 15, p.63.

64. Dutil. *op. cit.*, pp.255-9.

65. Bloch (commandant). *op. cit.*, p.97.

66. Perré and Le Gouest. *op. cit.*, p.103.

67. *Idem*.

68. 3,050 tanks armed with 37mm guns, 3,050 tanks armed with machine-guns, 600 tanks armed with 75mm guns and 300 wireless tanks. Deygas. *op. cit.*, pp.194-5.

69. *Ibid*, p.198.

70. Dutil. *op. cit.*, pp.222-4.

71. Stallings, Laurence. *Les Sammies*. Trans Michel Deutsch. Paris: Stock, 1963, p.185.

72. Dutil. *op. cit.*, p.208.

73. The intention was to use 300 Mark V tanks (which would replace the Schneiders and Saint-Chamonds) and also two regiments of 2C tanks and three *groupes* of US Liberty tanks. Deygas. *op. cit.*, pp.215, 220.

74. Chédeville. *op. cit.*, p.339.

75. SHAT. 16 N 2142. Carton 15. Dossier 4. Comptes rendus d'officiers des RCC, 24 juin 1920.

76. Paillat, Claude. *Dossiers secrets de la France contemporaine,* 8 vols. Paris: Robert Laffont, 1979-92, vol. 1, p.90.

77. Camon, Hubert (général). 'La motorisation', in *Revue militaire française* (Apr-Jun 1925), vol. 11, p.21.

78. Paillat. *op. cit.*, vol. 1, pp.98-100.

79. Alléhaut and Goubernard. *op. cit.*, p.58.

80. *Ibid.*

81. Chédeville. *op. cit.*, p.194.

82. Alléhaut and Goubernard. *op. cit.*, p.166.

83. Chédeville. *op. cit.*, p.331.

84. Alléhaut, Emile (général). *Motorisation et armées de demain.* Paris: Lavauzelle, 1929, p.53.

85. Compagnon (général), 'La chevauchée héroïque de Berry-au-Bac', in *Revue historique des armées* (1984), numéro 2, p.63.

## Chapter 11: The Grand Army of 1918
(pages 230–58)

1. Lucas, Pascal-Marie-Henri (colonel). *L'évolution des idées tactiques en France et en Allemagne pendant la guerre de 1914-1918.* Reissued Paris: Berger-Levrault, 1932, p.221.

2. Laure, Emile (lieutenant-colonel); and Jacottet (commandant). *Les étapes de guerre d'une division d'infanterie: 13e division.* Reissued Paris: Berger-Levrault, 1932, p.141.

3. *Ibid*, pp.145-6.

4. Lucas. *L'évolution des idées tactiques. op. cit.*, p.184.

5. Pedroncini, Guy. *Pétain: général en chef, 1917-1918.* Paris: Publications de la Sorbonne / Presses universitaires de France, 1974, p.99.

6. Lucas. *L'évolution des idées tactiques. op. cit.*, p.198.

7. *Ibid*, p.208.

8. Pedroncini. *Pétain: général en chef. op. cit.*, p.64.

9. Laure, Emile (commandant). *Au 3e bureau du troisième GQG, 1917-1919.* Paris: Plon, 1921, p.164.

10. Laure (général). *Cinq directives du Général Pétain, mai 1917 – juillet 1918.* Centre des hautes études militaires, 1939, p.15.

11. de Ripert d'Alauzier (colonel). 'La bataille de Courcelles-Méry', in *Revue militaire française* (Jul-Sep 1925), vol. 16.

12. ed. Corvisier, André. *Histoire militaire de la France,* 4 vols. Paris: Presses universitaires de France, 1992-4, vol. 3, p.178.

13. During the Battle of the Somme, the Motor-Transport Regulatory Commission of the main road linking Amiens and Proyart exceeded even this figure, with a total on 22 July of 3,500 lorries and 4,500 horse-drawn vehicles. See Lucas. *L'évolution des idées tactiques. op. cit.*, pp.151-2.

14. Pellegrin, Fernand-Louis-Lucien (colonel). *La vie d'une armée pendant la grande guerre*. Paris: Flammarion, 1921, p.289.

15. Corvisier. *op. cit.*, vol. 3, p.178.

16. See Appendix 3 and de Gaulle, Charles. *La France et son armée*. Paris: Plon, 1938. Reissued Livre de poche, 1973, p.277.

17. Pedroncini. *Pétain: général en chef. op. cit.*, p.79.

18. SHAT. 16 N 2092.

19. Larcher, Maurice (lieutenant-colonel). 'Données statistiques sur les forces françaises de 1914-1918', in *Revue militaire française* (Apr-Jun 1934), numéro 156, pp.351-63.

20. Laure. *Au 3e bureau. op. cit.*, p.35.

21. Boullaire, François-René (général). *Histoire du 2e corps de cavalerie du 1er octobre au 1er janvier 1919, après les archives du ministère de la guerre*. Paris: Lavauzelle, 1923, p.464.

22. *Ibid*, p.462.

23. *Ibid*, p.467.

24. *Ibid*, p.457.

25. Poli, Ange (colonel). 'Les groupes mixtes d'automitrailleuses et d'autocanons de la marine pendant la guerre de 1914', in *Revue historique des armées* (3/1988), numéro 172, pp.91-100.

26. SHAT. 16 N 45, Dossier 15, Pièce 136. Rattachement des unités d'automitrailleuses à la direction de la cavalerie.

27. Deygas, Ferdinand-Joseph (commandant). *Les chars d'assaut: leur passé, leur avenir*. Paris: Lavauzelle, 1937, p.302.

28. Herr, Frédéric-Georges (général). *L'artillerie: ce qu'elle a été, ce qu'elle est, ce qu'elle doit être*. Paris: Berger-Levrault, 1923, p.89.

29. Deygas. *op. cit.*, p.302.

30. Corda, H. (lieutenant-colonel). *L'évolution des méthodes offensives de l'armée française. La recherche de la surprise pendant la grande guerre, 1914-1918*. (Conférences faites les 9 et 11 mars 1921 aux sociétés d'officiers suisses de Zurich et de Lausanne.) Paris: Gauthier-Villars et Cie, 1921, p.44.

31. Maître (général). 'Evolution des idées sur l'emploi de l'artillerie pendant la guerre', in *Revue militaire française* (Jan-Mar 1924), vol. 11.

32. The two arms were moved, and became worn down, at completely different rates. The infantry reached the front earlier, 'melted' much faster, and left earlier. This was why the artillery *groupes* were split up from the infantry regiments.

33. The 2nd Army command issued an *Instruction on the use of artillery in the defensive* (27 May 1916). This brief instruction was given to any unit that arrived in the sector, but it became regulatory for the whole army. Herr. *op. cit.*, p.53.

34. Note from the commander-in-chief, 8 August 1917.

35. SHAT. *Inventaire sommaire des archives de guerre*. Série N, 1872-1919. Vincennes: Service historique de l'armée de terre, 1995, p.147.

36. Thirty-seven had been created by November 1918.

37. Maître. *op. cit.*
38. Corvisier. *op. cit.*, p.225.
39. *Ibid*, p.226.
40. Voisin, André (général). *La doctrine de l'aviation française de combat au cours de la guerre, 1915-1918*. Paris: Berger-Levrault, 1932, p.68.
41. Laure and Jacottet. *op. cit.*, p.155.
42. Laure. *Au 3e bureau. op. cit.*, p.80.
43. Laure and Jacottet. *op. cit.*, p.187.
44. *Ibid*, p.190.
45. Laure. *Au 3e bureau. op. cit.*, p.114.
46. Laure and Jacottet. *op. cit.*, pp.197-8.
47. *Ibid*, p.194.
48. *Ibid*, p.192.
49. *Ibid*, p.195.
50. See Appendix 2.
51. Lucas. *L'évolution des idées tactiques. op. cit.*, p.254.
52. Facon, Patrick. 'La division aérienne ou l'emploi en masse de l'aviation en 1918', in *14-18* (Aug-Sep 2001), numéro 3.
53. Service historique de l'armée de l'air. Fonds 1914-1918. Note sur l'emploi des escadres et groupes de combat dans la bataille. GQG, 3e bureau, Service aéronautique, 2 mars 1918. Cited by Facon, Patrick. 'Aperçus sur la doctrine d'emploi de l'aéronautique militaire française, 1914-1918', in *Revue historique des armées* (1988), numéro 3.
54. SHAT. *Inventaire sommaire. op. cit.*, p.176.
55. Laure. *Au 3e bureau. op. cit.*, p.115.
56. Lucas. *L'évolution des idées tactiques. op. cit.*, p.225.
57. See Appendix 2.
58. SHAT. *Inventaire sommaire. op. cit.*, p.129.
59. See Appendix 2.
60. Huguenot (colonel). 'Un coup de main historique', in *Revue militaire française* (Apr-Jun 1923).
61. Boullaire. *op. cit.*, p.376.
62. *Ibid*, pp.374-82.
63. Laure. *Au 3e bureau. op. cit.*, p.156.
64. Boullaire. *op. cit.*, p.467.
65. From now on, each infantry division had at its disposal one *groupe* of short-barrelled Schneider 155mm pieces. This was in addition to its 75mm regiment. Each army corps had two or three *groupes* of long-barrelled 105mm or 155mm pieces.
66. Situation of the French artillery on 11 November 1918: 105 horse-drawn regiments of field artillery, thirty-three lorry-borne regiments of field artillery, three regiments of mountain artillery, six *groupes* of horse artillery, sixty-four horse-drawn regiments of heavy artillery, twenty tractor-towed regiments of heavy artillery, three regiments of super-heavy artillery, five regiments of railway artillery, five regiments of trench-mortars, thirteen regiments of foot artillery, six regiments of anti-aircraft artillery, nine regiments and seven *groupements* of Assault Artillery, as well as some *groupes* in North Africa. All this amounted to a total of 4,968 75mm guns and 5,128 heavy pieces, served by 26,000 officers and 1,093,000 men. SHAT. *Inventaire sommaire. op. cit.*, pp.152-3.

67. The sortie of a bomber *groupe* (twenty to thirty airplanes) at the end of the war was the rough equivalent of an artillery bombardment with 500 155mm shells. See Orthlieb, Jean (commandant). *L'aéronautique: hier, demain.* Paris: Masson, 1920, p.164.

68. Voisin. *op. cit.,* p.131.

69. *Ibid,* pp.74-91.

70. *Ibid,* p.202.

71. *Ibid,* p.204.

72. Accompanying batteries were therefore tried out, at the direct disposal of the infantrymen.

73. Lucas. *L'évolution des idées tactiques. op. cit.,* p.265.

74. Daille, Marius (général). *La bataille de Montdidier.* Paris: Berger-Levrault, 1922, p.52.

75. *Ibid,* p.81.

76. *Ibid,* p.272.

77. *Ibid,* p.242.

78. *Ibid,* p.107.

79. SHAT. 16 N 2120. Carton 3. Dossier 4. Tableau des pertes en chars et personnels, GQG, 9 septembre 1919.

80. Cousine, André. *La vie d'une division française pendant la guerre 1914-1918.* Mémoire d'histoire pour la maîtrise spécialisée ès-lettres, sous la direction du professeur Duroselle. Paris: Sorbonne, 1969, p.231.

81. Daille. *La bataille de Montdidier. op. cit.,* p.269.

82. Cousine. *op. cit.,* p.229.

83. Mangin, Charles (général). *Les chasseurs dans la bataille de France: 47e division, juillet-novembre 1918.* Paris: Payot, 1935, p.175.

# Sources

Archives of the *Service historique de l'Armee de Terre*

## Conseil supérieur de la guerre

1 N 9/1      pp.49-60, 91.
              Procès-verbal de la réunion du CSG, 30 janvier 1904.
1 N 9/11     Procès-verbal de la réunion du CSG, 7 juin 1905.

## Fonds Galliéni

6 N 42      Emploi du temps du CHEM: note sur l'emploi tactique des sections de mitrailleuses dans les troupes d'infanterie, par le Général Lyautey commandant le 10e corps d'armée, 7 novembre 1911.
6 N 43      Etude sur l'infanterie dans la guerre de siège, rapport du 20e corps d'armée, 20 juin 1912.

## Archives des 1er et 2e bureaux de l'état-major de l'armée

7 N 48/2     Général André: note de présentation numéro 2 pour la question du renforcement de l'artillerie de campagne, 28 juin 1904.
7 N 404     TEDG (Tableau d'effectifs et de dotation de guerre) du 12 novembre 1916 et rectificatif numéro 17223-1-11 du 7 août 1918.

7 N 670     Enseignements de la guerre russo-japonaise: notes numéros 2, 7 et 10, 2e bureau, janvier 1905 – février 1906.
7 N 670     Enseignements de la guerre russo-japonaise: note numéro 7, 2e bureau, habillement.
7 N 1108/2 numéro 340; and 7 N 1130/1 numéro 248
              Emploi des camions automobiles pendant les manœuvres de 1909.

## Archives du 3e bureau du GQG

16 N 45      Dossier 15. Pièce 136.
              Composition des groupes d'automitrailleuses; rattachement des unités d'automitrailleuses à la direction de la cavalerie.
16 N 51      Registre 35. Pièce 98.
              Tableau des effectifs du 26 août 1916.
16 N 1677    Dossier 33. Pièce 3322.
              Note du commandant en chef sur les enseignements à tirer des combats récents, 3e bureau du GQG, 20 mai 1915.
16 N 1679    Dossier 39. Pièce 4704.
              Note sur le combat défensif, 3e bureau du GQG, 8 juillet 1915.
16 N 1683    Dossier 52. Pièce 7090.
              Note annexe provisoire à l'instruction du 8 janvier 1916 sur le combat offensif des petites unités, 3e bureau du GQG, 27 décembre 1916.

16 N 1683   Dossier 55. Pièce 7684 bis.
            Instructions visant le but et les conditions d'une action collective d'ensemble, 3e bureau du GQG, 16 décembre 1916.

16 N 1692   Dossier 83. Pièce 13142.
            Directive du général en chef numéro 4, 22 décembre 1917.

16 N 1995   Instructions sur l'action offensive des grandes unités dans la bataille, 3e bureau du GQG le 31 octobre 1917.

16 N 2090   Compte-rendu de mission du Lieutenant-colonel Picot auprès de l'artillerie de la 1re armée, 3e bureau du GQG, 7 octobre 1917; projets d'inventions transmis à la section instruction du 3e bureau du GQG.

16 N 2091   Réorganisation de la compagnie d'infanterie: note numéro 98887, 3e bureau du GQG, 10 septembre 1917.

16 N 2092   Notes et études de la section instruction, 3e bureau du GQG, août 1917.

16 N 2093   L'organisation de l'instruction dans les armées: note numéro 2350, 3e bureau du GQG, 4 septembre 1916.

16 N 2094   Expérimentation de l'emploi des mitrailleuses en tir indirect: note numéro 979, 3e bureau du GQG, 1er août 1917; projet de réorganisation de la compagnie d'infanterie: note 18671, 3e bureau du GQG, 18 juillet 1917.

16 N 2095   Rapport du Général Passaga, commandant la 133e DI. Observations relatives à l'engagement du 15 décembre 1916 (Verdun): note numéro 14652, 3e bureau du GQG, 20 janvier 1917.

16 N 2120   Ordre général numéro 1 du général commandant l'AS du 1er janvier 1917. Rapport au sujet de la participation de l'AS aux opérations du 23 et 25 octobre 1917.
            Carton 3. Dossier 4. Tableau des pertes en chars et personnels, GQG, 9 septembre 1919.

16 N 2121   Notes du GQG/AS du 8 janvier 1917 et du 20 février 1917 sur l'organisation des unités tactiques.

16 N 2124   Note du 3e bureau du GQG en date du 17 juin 1917.
            Carton 15. Dossier 2. Directives d'emploi des chars.

16 N 2142   Carton 15. Dossier 4.
            Comptes-rendus d'officiers des régiments de chars de combat, 24 juin 1920.

16 N 2150   Rapport du chef de corps du 501e Régiment de chars de combat, 19 juin 1918.

24 N 994    42e DI.

24 N 1721   32e CA.

# Printed Sources

Details of English translations are given in brackets at the end of the relevant entries.

## Printed archives

Berger-Levrault (publisher). *Le livre du gradé d'infanterie: à l'usage des élèves caporaux, caporaux et sous-officiers de l'infanterie et du génie, contenant toutes les matières nécessaires à l'exercice de leurs fonctions et conforme à tous les règlements parus jusqu'à ce jour.* Paris: Berger-Levrault, November 1914.

France: Ministère de la guerre. *Annuaire officiel de l'armée française pour 1914.* Paris: Berger-Levrault, 31 décembre 1913.

---- *Décret du 28 mai 1895 portant règlement sur le service des armées en campagne.* Paris: Berger-Levrault, 1895.

---- *Décret du 3 décembre 1904 portant règlement sur les manœuvres d'infanterie.* Paris: Lavauzelle, 1910.

---- *Décret du 28 octobre 1913 portant règlement sur la conduite des grandes unités.* Paris: Lavauzelle, 1913.

---- *Décret du 2 décembre 1913 portant règlement sur le service des armées en campagne.* Paris: Berger-Levrault, 1914.

---- *Décret du 20 avril 1914 portant règlement sur les manœuvres d'infanterie.* Paris: Lavauzelle, 1914.

---- *Règlement du 12 juin 1875 sur les manœuvres de l'infanterie (modifié par l'instruction du 20 avril 1878).* Paris: Dumaine, 1880.

Laffargue, André (capitaine). *Etude sur l'attaque dans la période actuelle de la guerre: impressions et réflexions d'un commandant de compagnie.* Paris: Plon, 1916.

## Contemporary publications (by author and by date of publication)

Ardant du Picq, Charles. *Etudes sur le combat: combat antique et combat moderne.* Paris: Chapelot, 1903. Reissued Paris: Editions Champ Libre, 1978. [*Battle studies.* Trans John Nesmith Greely and Robert Christie Cotton. New York: Macmillan Company, 1921.]

Billard, Marie Marcel André (capitaine). *Education de l'infanterie.* Paris: Chapelot, 1913.

Bonnal, Henri (général). *Infanterie: méthodes de commandement, d'éducation et d'instruction.* Paris: Chapelot, 1900.

---- *L'art nouveau en tactique.* Paris: Chapelot, 1904.

---- *Questions militaires d'actualité.* 1re série: *La prochaine guerre [etc].* Paris: Chapelot, 1906.

---- *Questions militaires d'actualité.* 3e série. Paris: Chapelot, 1908.

Boucher, Arthur (colonel). *La France victorieuse dans la guerre de demain.* Paris: Berger-Levrault, 1911.

Buat, Edmond (capitaine / commandant). *Etude théorique sur l'attaque décisive.* Paris: Chapelot, 1909.

----; and de Lacroix, Henri. *Un voyage d'état-major de corps d'armée: compte rendu détaillé.* Paris: Chapelot, 1908.

Cardot, Lucien (général). *Education et instruction des troupes: essais sur la doctrine.* Paris: Berger-Levrault, 1903.

---- *Hérésies et apostasies militaires de notre temps.* Paris: Berger-Levrault, 1908.

Chalmandrey, André (capitaine). *Le règlement de manœuvres de l'avenir: infanterie.* Paris: Alcan-Lévy, 1904.

Colin, Jean (général). *Les transformations de la guerre.* 1911. Reissued Paris: Economica, 1989. [*The transformations of war.* Trans Ladislas Herbert Richard Pope-Hennessy. London: Hugh Rees, 1912.]

Debeney, Marie-Eugène (colonel). *Cours d'infanterie.* Paris: Ecole supérieure de guerre, 1913.

Foch, Ferdinand (colonel). *Des principes de la guerre: conférences faites à l'Ecole supérieure de guerre,* 2nd ed. Paris: Berger-Levrault, 1906. [*The principles of war.* Trans Hilaire Belloc. London: Chapman and Hall, 1918.]

France: army. 72nd Infantry Regiment. *Note sur les modifications qui semblent devoir être apportées à la tactique de l'infanterie.* Amiens: Presse régimentaire, 72e RI, 1903.

Gamelin, Maurice-Gustave (capitaine). *Etude philosophique sur l'art de la guerre.* Paris: Chapelot, 1906.

Gilbert, Georges (capitaine). *Essais de critique militaire.* Paris: Librairie de la 'Nouvelle revue', 1890.

de Grandmaison, Louis (commandant / colonel). *Dressage de l'infanterie en vue du combat offensif.* Reissued Paris: Berger-Levrault, 1908.

---- *Deux conférences faites aux officiers de l'Etat-major de l'armée, février 1911: la notion de sûreté et l'engagement des grandes unités.* Paris: Berger-Levrault, 1911.

Henrionnet, C. (commandant). *Le jeu de la guerre en France.* Paris: Lavauzelle, 1898.

Jaurès, Jean. *L'armée nouvelle.* 1911. Reissued Paris: Imprimerie nationale, 1985. [*Democracy and military service: an abbreviated translation of the 'Armée nouvelle'.* Ed George Gordon Coulton. London: Simpkin, Marshall and Co, 1916. Reissued London: Forgotten Books, 2015.]

Jibé (capitaine) (pseud). [Mordacq, Henri-Jean-Jules]. *L'armée nouvelle: ce qu'elle pense, ce qu'elle veut.* Paris: Plon, [c.1905].

Kessler, Charles (général). *Tactique des trois armes.* Paris: Chapelot, 1902.

Klotz, Lucien (député). *L'armée en 1906: considérations générales à propos du budget de la guerre.* Paris: Lavauzelle, 1906.

Langlois, Hippolyte (colonel). *L'artillerie de campagne en liaison avec les autres armes,* 3 vols. Paris: Baudoin, 1892.

Laure, Emile (lieutenant). *L'offensive française.* Paris: Lavauzelle, 1912.

Lewal, Jules-Louis (colonel / général). *La réforme de l'armée.* Paris: Dumaine, 1871.

---- *Le combat complet.* Paris: Baudoin, 1898.

Lucas, Pascal-Marie-Henri (colonel). *La section et le chef de section au combat: ouvrage à l'usage des chefs de section.* Paris: Lavauzelle, 1913.

Maillard (général). (Goujat dit Maillard, Louis-Adolphe). *Eléments de la guerre.* Paris: Baudoin, 1891.

Marty-Lavauzelle, Roger. *Les manœuvres de l'Est en 1911.* Paris: Lavauzelle, 1911.

de Maud'huy, Louis-Ernest (colonel). *Infanterie.* Paris: Lavauzelle, 1911.

Messimy, Adolphe. *L'armée et ses cadres.* Paris: Chapelot, 1908.

Montaigne, Jean-Baptiste (lieutenant-colonel). *Etudes sur la guerre*. Paris: Berger-Levrault, 1911.

---- *Vaincre: esquisse d'une doctrine de la guerre, basée sur la connaissance de l'homme*. Paris: Berger-Levrault, 1913.

Mordacq, Henri-Jean-Jules (commandant). *Les cyclistes combattants*. Paris: Fournier, 1910.

Pédoya, Gustave (général). *L'armée n'est pas commandée*. Paris: Lavauzelle, 1902.

---- *L'armée évolue*, 3 vols. Paris: Chapelot, 1908-9.

Percin, Alexandre (général). *Le combat*. Paris: Alcan, 1914.

Pétain, Philippe (colonel). *Cours d'infanterie de l'Ecole supérieure de guerre*. np: 1911.

Ragueneau, Camille-Marie (lieutenant-colonel). *Les études militaires en France et la préparation du haut commandement*. Paris: Berger-Levrault, 1913.

Thoumas, Charles (général). *Les transformations de l'armée française: essais d'histoire et de critique sur l'état militaire de la France*. Paris: Berger-Levrault, 1887.

*Treignier, Eugène (député). L'infanterie de demain: rapport fait au nom de la commission de l'armée sur le projet de loi des cadres de l'infanterie*. Paris: Lavauzelle, 1912.

# Bibliography

Details of English translations are given in brackets at the end of the relevant entries.

## Publications on the period as a whole

Alexandre, Georges-René (général). *Avec Joffre d'Agadir à Verdun: souvenirs, 1911-1916.* Paris: Berger-Levrault, 1932.

ed. Corvisier, André. *Histoire militaire de la France,* 4 vols. Paris: Presses universitaires de France, 1992-4.

Debeney, Marie-Eugène (général). *La guerre et les hommes: réflexions d'après-guerre.* Paris: Plon, 1937.

Doise, Jean; and Vaïsse, Maurice. *Diplomatie et outil militaire, 1871-1969.* Paris: Imprimerie nationale, 1987.

Ferro, Marc. *La grande guerre.* Paris: Gallimard, 1990. [*The Great War, 1914-1918.* Trans Nicole Stone. Reissued London: Routledge, 2002.]

Fouquet-Lapar, Philippe. *Histoire de l'armée française.* Paris: Presses universitaires de France, 1986.

France: Ministère de la guerre. *Les armées françaises dans la grande guerre,* 11 tomes. Paris, 1922-37.

Fuller, J.F.C. (John Frederick Charles). *L'influence de l'armement sur l'histoire.* Trans Lionel-Max Chassin. Paris: Payot, 1948. [*Armament and history: a study of the influence of armament on history from the dawn of classical warfare to the Second World War.* London: Eyre and Spottiswoode, 1946.]

Gambiez, Fernand (général); and Suire, Maurice (colonel). *Histoire de la première guerre mondiale,* 2 vols. Paris: Fayard, 1968.

de Gaulle, Charles. *La France et son armée.* Paris: Plon, 1938. Reissued Livre de poche, 1973.

Jauffret, Jean-Charles. 'L'officier français, 1871-1919', in ed. Croubois, Claude. *Histoire de l'officier français: des origines à nos jours.* Saint-Jean-d'Angély: Editions Bordessoules, 1987.

Joffre, Joseph (maréchal). *Mémoires du maréchal Joffre, 1910-1917,* 2 vols. Paris: Plon, 1932. [*The memoirs of Marshal Joffre,* 2 vols. Trans Thomas Bentley Mott. London: Geoffrey Bles, 1932.]

Masson, Philippe. *Histoire de l'armée française: de 1914 à nos jours.* Reissued Paris: Perrin, 2002.

Miquel, Pierre. *La grande guerre.* Paris: Fayard, 1983.

Monteilhet, Joseph. *Les institutions militaires de la France, 1814-1924.* Paris: Alcan, 1926.

Renouvin, Pierre. *La crise européenne et la première guerre mondiale,* 3rd ed. Paris: Presses universitaires de France, 1948.

Wanty, Emile. *L'art de la guerre,* 3 vols. Verviers (Belgium): Editions Gérard, 1967-8.

## The years before the war

Boucher, Arthur (général). *Les doctrines dans la préparation de la grande guerre.* Paris: Berger-Levrault, 1925.

Contamine, Henry. *La revanche, 1871-1914.* Paris: Berger-Levrault, 1957.

Delbos, Jean-François. *La formation des officiers de l'armée de terre de 1802 à nos jours.* Paris: L'Harmattan, 2001.

Ehrenberg, Alain. *Le corps militaire: politique et pédagogie en démocratie.* Paris: Aubier, 1983.

Filloux, Jean-Claude; and Maisonneuve, Jean. *Anthologie des sciences de l'homme,* 2 vols. Paris: Dunod, 1991-3.

ed. Gambiez, Fernand (général). 'L'influence de l'Ecole supérieure de guerre sur la pensée militaire française de 1876 à nos jours', in France: Ecole supérieure de guerre. *Centenaire de l'Ecole supérieure de guerre 1876-1976* (conference proceedings, 13-14 May 1976). Paris: ESG-SHAT, 1976.

Girardet, Raoul. *La société militaire de 1815 à nos jours.* Paris: Perrin, 1998.

Herrmann, David G. *The arming of Europe and the making of the First World War.* Princeton (New Jersey): Princeton University Press, 1997.

Kuntz, François. *L'officier français dans la nation.* Paris: Lavauzelle, 1960.

Le Pichon, Yann; and Deleuze, Benoît. *Les alpins.* Paris: Berger-Levrault / Didier Richard / Lavauzelle, 1988.

Porch, Douglas. *The march to the Marne: the French army, 1871-1914.* Cambridge: Cambridge University Press, 1981.

Titeux, Eugène (lieutenant-colonel). *Saint-Cyr et l'Ecole spéciale militaire en France.* Reissued Paris: Firmin-Didot, 1914.

**The war**

Bach, André (général). *Fusillés pour l'exemple, 1914-1915.* Paris: Tallandier, 2003.

Bédier, Joseph. *L'effort français: quelques aspects de la guerre.* Paris: La renaissance du livre, 1919.

Bouvard, Henri (commandant). *Les leçons militaires de la guerre.* Paris: Masson, 1920.

Contamine, Henry. *La victoire de la Marne: 9 septembre 1914.* Collection 'Trente journées qui ont fait la France'. Paris: Gallimard, 1970.

Daille, Marius (général). *La bataille de Montdidier.* Paris: Berger-Levrault, 1922.

---- *Histoire de la guerre mondiale,* vol. 2: *Joffre et la guerre d'usure, 1915-1916.* Paris: Payot, 1936.

Dubail, Augustin Yvon Edmond (général). *Quatre années de commandement, 1914-1918,* 3 vols. Paris: Fournier, 1920-1.

Fayolle, Marie-Emile (maréchal). *Cahiers secrets de la grande guerre.* Ed. Henry Contamine. Paris: Plon, 1964.

Gallini, Jacques (lieutenant-colonel). *Les opérations de la 1re armée française du 1er au 8 août 1918: préparation de la victoire de Montdidier.* Paris: Lavauzelle, 1938.

Gamelin, Maurice-Gustave (général). *Manœuvre et victoire de la Marne.* Paris: Grasset, 1954.

Grasset, Alphonse (commandant). *Préceptes et jugements du maréchal Foch.* Reissued Paris: Berger-Levrault, 1920. *[Precepts and judgments: with a sketch of the military career of Marshal Foch.* Trans Hilaire Belloc. London: Chapman and Hall, 1919. Reissued 1921.]

Griffith, Paddy. *Forward into battle: fighting tactics from Waterloo to the near future.* Reissued Novato (California): Presidio Press, 1991.

---- *Battle tactics on the Western Front: the British army's art of attack, 1916-18.* New Haven and London: Yale University Press, 1994.

Koeltz, Louis (commandant). *La bataille de France, 21 mars – 5 avril 1918.* Paris: Payot, 1928.

Laffargue, André. *Foch et la bataille de 1918.* Paris: Arthaud, 1966.

de Langle de Cary, Fernand (général). *Souvenirs de commandement, 1914-1916*. Paris: Payot, 1935.

Larcher, Maurice (lieutenant-colonel). *Le 1er corps à Dinant, Charleroi, Guise, août 1914*. Paris: Berger-Levrault, 1932.

de Lardemelle, Charles (général). *1914: le redressement initial*. Paris: Berger-Levrault, 1935.

Lucas, Pascal-Marie-Henri (colonel). *L'évolution des idées tactiques en France et en Allemagne pendant la guerre de 1914-1918*. Reissued Paris: Berger-Levrault, 1932.

Mangin, Charles (général). *Les chasseurs dans la bataille de France: 47e division, juillet-novembre 1918*. Paris: Payot, 1935.

Miquel, Pierre. *Les poilus: la France sacrifiée*. Collection 'Terre humaine'. Paris: Plon, 2000.

Mordacq, Henri (général). *Les leçons de 1914 et la prochaine guerre*. Paris: Flammarion, 1934.

Stallings, Laurence. *Les Sammies*. Trans Michel Deutsch. Paris: Stock, 1963. *[The Doughboys: the story of the AEF, 1917-1918*. New York: Harper and Row, 1963.]

Watt, Richard M. *Trahison*. Trans Martin Kieffer. Paris: Presses de la Cité, 1964. *[Dare call it treason*. New York: Simon and Schuster, 1963.]

## Commanders

Autin, Jean. *Foch, ou le triomphe de la volonté*. Reissued Paris: Perrin, 1998.

Destremau, Bernard. *Weygand*. Paris: Perrin, 1989.

Grasset, Alphonse (commandant). *Préceptes et jugements du maréchal Foch*. Reissued Paris: Berger-Levrault, 1920. *[Precepts and judgments: with a sketch of the military career of Marshal Foch*. Trans Hilaire Belloc. London: Chapman and Hall, 1919. Reissued 1921.]

Hanotaux, Gabriel. *Le Général Mangin*. Paris: Plon, 1925.

Laure, Emile (commandant). *Au 3e bureau du troisième GQG, 1917-1919*. Paris: Plon, 1921.

Miquel, Pierre. *Le gâchis des généraux: les erreurs de commandement pendant la guerre de 14-18*. Paris: Plon, 2001.

Pedroncini, Guy. *Pétain: général en chef, 1917-1918*. Paris: Publications de la Sorbonne / Presses universitaires de France, 1974.

---- (ed.) *Journal de marche de Joffre, 1916-1919*. Vincennes: Service historique de l'armée de terre, 1990.

de Pierrefeu, Jean. *GQG secteur 1: trois ans au Grand quartier général, par le rédacteur du 'communiqué'*, 2 vols. Paris: L'Edition française illustrée, 1920. *[French headquarters, 1915-1918*. Trans Cecil Street. London: Geoffrey Bles, 1924.]

Percin, Alexandre (général). *1914: les erreurs du haut commandement*. Paris: Albin Michel, 1919.

Rocolle, Pierre. *L'hécatombe des généraux*. Paris: Lavauzelle, 1980.

Serrigny, Bernard (général). *Trente ans avec Pétain*. Paris: Plon, 1959.

## Evolution of the arms

Ailleret, Charles (colonel). *Histoire de l'armement*. Collection 'Que sais je?', numéro 301. Paris: Presses universitaires de France, 1948.

Alléhaut, Emile (colonel). *Le combat de l'infanterie: étude analytique et synthétique d'après les règlements, illustrée de cas concrets de la guerre 1914-1918*. Paris: Berger-Levrault, 1924.

Alléhaut, Emile (général). *Motorisation et armées de demain*. Paris: Lavauzelle, 1929.

Blin (colonel). *Histoire de l'organisation et de la tactique des différentes armes: 1610 à nos jours*. Paris: Lavauzelle, 1931.

Bouchacourt, Louis (commandant). *L'infanterie dans la bataille: étude sur l'attaque, étude sur la défense.* Paris: Lavauzelle, 1927.

Boullaire, François-René (général). *Histoire du 2e corps de cavalerie du 1er octobre au 1er janvier 1919, après les archives du ministère de la guerre.* Paris: Lavauzelle, 1923.

Bourget, Pierre-André (général). *Le Général Estienne: penseur, ingénieur et soldat.* Paris: Berger-Levrault, 1956.

Deygas, Ferdinand-Joseph (commandant). *Les chars d'assaut: leur passé, leur avenir.* Paris: Lavauzelle, 1937.

Doumenc, Aimé (général). *Les transports automobiles sur le front français, 1914-1918.* Ed. Paul Heuzé. Paris: Plon, 1920.

Dutil, Léon (capitaine). *Les chars d'assaut: leur création et leur rôle pendant la guerre, 1915-1918.* Paris: Berger-Levrault, 1919.

von Eimannsberger, Ludwig. *La guerre des chars.* Trans Louis-Georges Rousseau. Paris: Berger-Levrault, 1936.

Gagneur, Maurice (capitaine); and Fourier, Marcel (lieutenant). *Avec les chars d'assaut.* Paris: Hachette, 1919.

Gascouin, Firmin-Emile (général). *L'évolution de l'artillerie pendant la guerre.* Reissued Paris: Flammarion, 1921.

---- *Le triomphe de l'idée.* Paris: Berger-Levrault, 1931.

Gazin, Fernand (capitaine). *La cavalerie française dans la guerre mondiale, 1914-1918.* Paris: Payot, 1930.

Grandhomme, Jean-Noël; and Krempp, Thérèse. *Charles de Rose: le pionnier de l'aviation de chasse.* Strasbourg: La nuée bleue, 2003.

Herr, Frédéric-Georges (général). *L'artillerie: ce qu'elle a été, ce qu'elle est, ce qu'elle doit être.* Reissued Paris: Berger-Levrault, 1924.

Heuze, Paul. *Les camions de la victoire.* Paris: La renaissance du livre, 1920.

Lafitte, Raymond (lieutenant-colonel). *L'artillerie d'assaut de 1916 à 1918.* Paris: Lavauzelle, nd.

Laure, Emile (lieutenant-colonel); and Jacottet (commandant). *Les étapes de guerre d'une division d'infanterie: 13e division.* 1928. Reissued Paris: Berger-Levrault, 1932.

Maisonneuve, Paul-Henri (capitaine). *L'infanterie sous le feu: étude critique sur le combat de la compagnie.* Paris: Berger-Levrault, 1925.

Navarre, Albert-J. *Les services automobiles pendant la guerre.* Paris: Delagrave, 1919.

Orthlieb, Jean (commandant). *L'aéronautique: hier, demain.* Paris: Masson, 1920.

Paillat, Claude. *Dossiers secrets de la France contemporaine,* 8 vols. Paris: Robert Laffont, 1979-92.

Pellegrin, Fernand-Louis-Lucien (colonel). *La vie d'une armée pendant la grande guerre.* Paris: Flammarion, 1921.

Percin, Alexandre (général). *Le massacre de notre infanterie, 1914-1918.* Paris: Albin Michel, 1919.

Perré, Jean (général). *Batailles et combats des chars français: l'année d'apprentissage, 1917.* Paris: Lavauzelle, 1937.

----; and Aussenac, Louis Simon (commandant); and Suire, Maurice (capitaine). *Batailles et combats des chars français: la bataille défensive, avril-juillet 1918.* Paris: Lavauzelle, 1940.

Rimailho, Emile. *Artillerie de campagne.* Paris: Gauthier-Villars, 1924.

Rouquerol, Gabriel (général). *Le canon artisan de la victoire.* Paris: Berger-Levrault, 1920.

Rouquerol, Jean (général). *Les crapouillots, 1914-1918.* Paris: Payot, 1935.

Voisin, André (général). *La doctrine de l'aviation française de combat au cours de la guerre, 1915-1918*. Paris: Berger-Levrault, 1932.

### Behaviour of the combatants

Armengaud, Jean (lieutenant-colonel). *L'atmosphere du champ de bataille*. Paris: Lavauzelle, 1940.

Chenu, Charles-Maurice. *Du képi rouge aux chars d'assaut*. Paris: Albin Michel, 1932.

Coste, Charles (commandant). *La psychologie du combat*. Paris: Berger-Levrault, 1929.

Cru, Jean Norton. *Témoins: essai d'analyse et de critique des souvenirs de combattants édités en francais de 1915 à 1928*. Reissued Nancy: Presses universitaires de Nancy, 1993.

Delvert, Charles. *Carnets d'un fantassin*. Paris: Albin Michel, 1935.

Ducasse, André. *La guerre racontée par les combattants*, 2 vols. Paris: Flammarion, 1932.

Galtier-Boissière, Jean. *Un hiver à Souchez*. Paris: Les Etincelles, 1930.

Gaudy, Georges. *Souvenirs d'un poilu du 57e régiment d'infanterie: l'agonie du Mont-Renaud, mars-avril 1918*. Paris: Plon, 1921.

Genevoix, Maurice. *Ceux de 14*. Paris: Flammarion, 1950.

Holmes, Richard. *Acts of war: the behaviour of men in battle*. New York: The Free Press, 1989.

Jünger, Ernst. *Orages d'acier: souvenirs du front de France*. Trans F. Grenier. Paris: Payot, 1930. *[Storm of steel*. Trans Michael Hofmann. London: Allen Lane, 2003.]

---- *Feu et sang: bref épisode d'une grande bataille*. Trans Julien Hervier. Paris: Christian Bourgeois, 1998. (Revised extract of *Orages d'acier.)*

de Ligonnès, Bernard. *Un commandant bleu-horizon: souvenirs de guerre de Bernard de Ligonnès, 1914-1917*. Paris: Editions de Paris, 1998.

Masson, Philippe. *L'homme en guerre, 1901-2001: de la Marne à Sarajevo*. Paris/Monaco: Editions du Rocher, 1997.

Miquel, Pierre. *Les poilus: la France sacrifiée*. Collection 'Terre humaine'. Paris: Plon, 2000.

Meyer, Jacques. *Les soldats de la grande guerre*. Paris: Hachette, 1998.

Rommel, Erwin (lieutenant-colonel). *L'infanterie attaque: enseignements et expérience vécue*. Montpellier: Ecole d'application de l'infanterie, nd. *[Infantry attacks*. Reissued London: Greenhill Books, 1990.]

### Innovation theory; organizational sociology

Alter, Norbert. *La gestion du désordre en entreprise*. Paris: L'Harmattan, 1990.

---- *L'innovation ordinaire*. Paris: Presses universitaires de France, 2000.

---- (ed). *Les logiques de l'innovation: approche pluridisciplinaire*. Paris: La Découverte, 2002.

Ballé, Catherine. *Sociologie des organisations*. Paris: Presses universitaires de France, 1990.

Bernoux, Philippe. *La sociologie des organisations: initiation théorique suivie de douze cas pratiques*. Paris: Seuil, 1985.

Caron, François. *Le résistible déclin des sociétés industrielles*. Paris: Perrin, 1985.

Coriat, Benjamin; and Weinstein, Olivier. *Les nouvelles théories de l'entreprise*. Paris: Librairie générale française, 1995.

Crozier, Michel. *Le phénomène bureaucratique: essai sur les tendances bureaucratiques des systèmes d'organisation modernes et sur leur relations en France avec le système social et culturel*. Paris: Seuil, 1963. *[The bureaucratic phenomenon*. Trans by the author. Chicago: University of Chicago Press, 1964. Reissued Transaction Publishers, 2009.]

----; and Friedberg, Erhard. *L'acteur et le système: les contraintes de l'action collective.* Paris: Seuil, 1977. *[Actors and systems: the politics of collective action.* Trans Arthur Goldhammer. Chicago: Chicago University Press, 1980.]

Drucker, Peter. *Les entrepreneurs.* Paris: L'Expansion / Hachette / J.-C. Lattès, 1985. *[Innovation and entrepreneurship: practice and principles.* New York: Harper and Row, 1985. Reissued London: Butterworth-Heinemann, 2007.]

Flichy, Patrice. *L'innovation technique: récents développements en sciences sociales, vers une nouvelle théorie de l'innovation.* Paris: La Découverte, 1995. *[Understanding technological innovation: a socio-technical approach.* Trans Liz Carey-Libbrecht. Cheltenham: Edward Elgar, 2007.]

Gaudin, Thierry; and Aubert, Jean-Eric. *De l'innovation.* Paris: Editions de l'Aube, 1998.

d'Iribarne, Philippe. *La logique de l'honneur: gestion des entreprises et traditions nationales.* Paris: Seuil, 1989.

Kuhn, Thomas Samuel. *La structure des révolutions scientifiques.* Trans Laure Meyer. Paris: Flammarion, 1983. *[The structure of scientific revolutions.* Chicago: University of Chicago Press, 1962. Reissued 2012.]

March, James Gardner. *Décisions et organisations.* Trans Marie Waquet. Ed Alain-Charles Martinet. Reissued Paris: Editions d'organisation, 1991. *[Decisions and organizations.* Oxford: Blackwell, 1988.]

----; and Simon, Herbert Alexander. *Les organisations.* Trans J.-C. Rouchy. Paris: Dunod, 1964. *[Organizations.* New York: John Wiley, 1958. Reissued 1993.]

Mintzberg, Henry. *Le pouvoir dans les organisations.* Trans Paul Sager. Paris: Les Editions d'organisation, 1986. *[Power in and around organizations.* Englewood Cliffs (New Jersey): Prentice-Hall, 1983.]

---- *Le management: voyage au centre des organisations.* Trans Jean-Michel Béhar. Reissued Paris: Les Editions d'organisation, 1998. *[Mintzberg on management: inside our strange world of organizations.* Reissued New York: The Free Press, 2011.]

Peters, Thomas J.; and Waterman, Robert H. *Le prix de l'excellence.* Trans Michèle Garène and Chantal Pommier. Paris: Interéditions, 1983. Chapter 5. *[In search of excellence: letters from America's best-run companies.* Reissued London: Profile Books, 2015.]

Posen, Barry R. *The sources of military doctrine: France, Britain and Germany between the world wars.* Ithaca (New York): Cornell University Press, 1984.

Rosen, Stephen Peter. *Winning the next war: innovation and the modern military.* Ithaca (New York): Cornell University Press, 1991.

Shils, Edward A.; and Janowitz, Morris. 'Cohésion et désagrégation de la Wehrmacht pendant la deuxième guerre mondiale'. Reissued in *Les champs de mars* (2001), numéro 9, 1er semestre. ['Cohesion and disintegration in the Wehrmacht in World War II', in *Public opinion quarterly* (1948), vol. 12, issue 2, pp.280-315.]

Sorman, Guy. *Les vrais penseurs de notre temps.* Paris: Fayard, 1989.

Toffler, Alvin. *Le choc du futur.* Trans Sylvie Laroche and Solange Metzger. Paris: Denoël, 1971. *[Future shock.* New York: Random House, 1970.]

## Dissertations and monographs

Allemand, Thierry. *Evolution des sections d'infanterie de 1871 à 1982.* Ecole des hautes études en sciences sociales. Thèse de 3e cycle sous la direction du professeur Alain Joxe.

Corda, H. (lieutenant-colonel). *L'évolution des méthodes offensives de l'armée française. La recherche de la surprise pendant la grande guerre, 1914-1918.* (Conférences faites les 9 et 11 mars 1921 aux sociétés d'officiers suisses de Zurich et de Lausanne.) Paris: Gauthier-Villars et Cie, 1921.

Cousine, André. *La vie d'une division française pendant la guerre 1914-1918.* Mémoire d'histoire pour la maîtrise spécialisée ès-lettres, sous la direction du professeur Duroselle. Paris: Sorbonne, 1969.

Delmas (lieutenant-colonel). *Aperçu historique des méthodes de l'ESG.* Direction des études, cours d'histoire, octobre 1972.

France: Etat-major de l'armée. Service historique. *Notice historique sur les inspecteurs généraux,* juin 1927.

Fugens (lieutenant-colonel). *La guerre de 1870 et ses répercussions sur les débuts de 1914.* Conférence du 6 janvier 1932 à l'Ecole supérieure de guerre.

Huyon (colonel). *Les inspections de l'armée de terre de l'origine à nos jours.* SHAT, June 2000.

Laure (général). *Cinq directives du Général Pétain, mai 1917 – juillet 1918.* Centre des hautes études militaires, 1939.

Mousset (commandant). *Cours d'histoire militaire de l'Ecole spéciale militaire,* juin 1937.

## Articles

Alléhaut, Emile (colonel); and Goubernard (commandant). 'A propos d'un jugement allemand', in *Revue militaire française* (Apr-Jun 1925), vol. 15.

Aubert (capitaine). 'Emploi d'une section de chars dans le premier engagement des chars Renault, mai 1918', in *Revue d'infanterie* (Aug 1935).

Aubert (lieutenant-colonel). 'L'artillerie française de 1914 à 1918', in *Revue militaire française* (1929).

Bails (lieutenant-colonel). 'Evolution des idées sur l'emploi tactique de l'organisation du terrain, de Napoleon à nos jours', in *Revue militaire française* (Jul-Aug-Sep 1926).

Bloch (commandant). 'L'avenir du char de combat', in *Revue militaire française* (Jan-Mar 1922), vol. 3.

Camon, Hubert (général). 'La motorisation', in *Revue militaire française* (Apr-Jun 1925), vol. 11.

Chalmin, Pierre. 'Les écoles militaires françaises jusqu'en 1914', in *Revue historique des armées* (1954), 2.

Chédeville (colonel). 'Les chars de combat actuels et le haut commandement', in *Revue militaire française* (Jan-Mar 1922), vol. 3.

Compagnon (général). 'La chevauchée héroïque de Berry-au-Bac', in *Revue historique des armées* (1984), numéro 2.

Cornic (capitaine); and Delacommune (capitaine). 'Les chars Renault à Villers-Cotterêts en 1918', in *Revue d'infanterie* (Aug 1932).

Defrasne (colonel). 'La prévention de la peur et de la panique dans l'armée française de la 3e République (avant la guerre de 1914-1918)', in *Revue historique des armées* (1978), 1er trimestre.

Delmas, Jean (général). 'L'Ecole supérieure de guerre, 1876-1940', in *Revue historique des armées* (Sep 2002), numéro 228.

Duchêne (colonel). 'Comment naquit l'artillerie de tranchée française', in *Revue militaire française* (1925).

Facon, Patrick. Communication au colloque Air, 1984.

---- 'Aperçus sur la doctrine d'emploi de l'aéronautique militaire française, 1914-1918', in *Revue historique des armées* (1988), numéro 3.

---- 'La division aérienne ou l'emploi en masse de l'aviation en 1918', in *14-18* (Aug-Sep 2001), numéro 3.

---- 'Août 1914, les aéronautiques européennes s'en vont en guerre', in *14-18* (Jun-Jul 2002), numéro 8.

Gourmen (commandant). 'Lewal, Maillard et Bonnal, leur influence sur la doctrine militaire française', in France: Ecole supérieure de guerre. *Centenaire de l'Ecole supérieure de guerre 1876-1976* (conference proceedings, 13–14 May 1976). Paris: ESG-SHAT, 1976.

Gros-Long (colonel). 'La connaissance de la guerre', in *Revue universelle*. Abstract in *Revue militaire française* (Oct-Dec 1922).

Henninger, Laurent. 'Nouvelles armes, guerres nouvelles', in *Armées d'aujourd'hui* (May 2001), numéro 258.

Hoff, Pierre (contrôleur général). 'Le ministère de la Guerre de 1871 à 1914', in *Revue historique des armées* (1983), numéro 153.

Huguenot (colonel). 'Un coup de main historique', in *Revue militaire française* (Apr-Jun 1923).

Jourquin, Jacques. 'La vie au GQG de Chantilly', in *14-18* (Oct-Nov 2001), numéro 4.

Larcher, Maurice (commandant / lieutenant-colonel). 'Le 10e corps à Charleroi (20 au 24 août 1914)', in *Revue militaire française* (Oct-Dec 1930), numéro 38.

---- 'Données statistiques sur les forces françaises de 1914-1918', in *Revue militaire française* (Apr-Jun 1934), numéro 156, pp.351-63.

Maître (général). 'Evolution des idées sur l'emploi de l'artillerie pendant la guerre', in *Revue militaire française* (Jan-Mar 1924), vol. 11.

Nachin (capitaine). 'Les règlements de manœuvre d'infanterie d'avant-guerre', in *Revue militaire française* (Oct-Dec 1922), vol. 6.

Nachin, L. (capitaine). 'Ardant du Picq', in *Revue militaire française* (Oct-Dec 1925), vol. 17.

Normand (colonel). 'Fortifications françaises et allemandes', in *Revue militaire française* (Apr-Jun 1925), vol. 15.

Paquet (lieutenant-colonel). 'L'usure des effectifs allemands en 1918', in *Revue militaire française* (Jul-Sep 1925), vol. 16.

Peraldi-Fiorella. 'Exemples d'emploi des chars dans la guerre de 1914-1918. La contre-offensive de la 10e armée, juillet 1918', in *Revue d'infanterie* (May 1923).

Perré, Jean (capitaine / lieutenant-colonel / général). 'Le commandement allemand et les chars', in *Revue militaire française* (Apr-Jun 1925), vol. 15.

---- 'Le premier engagement des chars Renault en mai-juin 1918', in *Revue d'infanterie* (Dec 1932).

---- 'Naissance et évolution du char en France pendant la guerre de 1914-1918', in *Revue d'infanterie* (Jan 1935).

---- 'Activité comparée des chars anglais et français pendant la guerre de 1914-1918', in *Revue d'infanterie* (Apr 1935).

---- 'Chars et statistiques', in *Revue d'infanterie* (Jul and Sep 1935).

---- 'Chars contre chars', in *Revue d'infanterie* (Aug 1936).

---- 'Les chars allemands pendant la guerre', in *Revue d'infanterie* (Feb 1936).

---- 'Les chars dans la défensive. Avec la 1re armée (avril-mai 1918)', in *Revue d'infanterie* (Jan 1938).

----; and Le Gouest (capitaine). 'Chars et statistique', in *Revue d'infanterie* (Jul-Aug 1935), numéro 514.

Picot (colonel). 'A propos des plans d'emploi de l'artillerie', in *Revue militaire française* (Jul-Sep 1925), vol. 16.

Poli, Ange (colonel). 'Les groupes mixtes d'automitrailleuses et d'autocanons de la marine pendant la guerre de 1914', in *Revue historique des armées* (3/1988), numéro 172, pp.91-100.

Revol, Joseph (général). 'Souvenirs: à l'Ecole supérieure de guerre (1903-1905)', in *Revue historique des armées* (3/1979), numéro 136, pp.130-44.

de Ripert d'Alauzier (colonel). 'La bataille de Courcelles-Méry', in *Revue militaire française* (Jul-Sep 1925), vol. 16.

Velpry (lieutenant-colonel). 'Le char, moyen de guerre économique', in *Revue militaire française* (Jul-Sep 1925), vol. 16.

Villatoux, Marie-Catherine. 'De l'inspection permanente de l'aéronautique à la direction de l'aéronautique', in *Revue historique des armées* (4/2003), numéro 233, pp.15-26.

Yunker, Stephen. 'I have the formula, the evolution of the tactical doctrine of General Robert Nivelle', in *Military review* (Jun 1974).

## Internet

'Expérimentation et innovation dans les force canadiennes': on the Canadian army website, www.journal.forces.gr.ca

The phenomenon of the 'aces': www.the aerodrome.com

Alter, Norbert. 'Innovation et institution, concurrence ou convergence?' Lecture at the Forum de Toulouse, 25 Apr 2001. www.ac-toulouse.fr/innovalo/rencontres

Lemay, Benoît. 'Les relations entre le corps des officiers et le pouvoir politique en France. Le temps de la revanche, 1870 à 1914', on www.hist.montreal.ca.

Roux, Alain. 'Guerre future' and 'Littérature populaire' www.stratisc.org

Sweet, Frank. 'Evolution of infantry assault tactics, 1850-1918'. American Military University, Jul 1997. www.consimworld.com

Williamson, Murray. 'Thinking about Revolutions in Military Affairs', in *Joint force quarterly* (Summer 1997), pp.67-79; and ed. Williamson, Murray; and Millet, Allan R. *Military innovation in the interwar period*. Cambridge: Cambridge University Press, 1996. Abstract on the website of the Defense Technical Information Center, Department of Defense: www.dtic.mil/doctrine/jel/jfq

Williamson, Murray. 'Does military culture matter', in *Orbis* (Winter 1999). www.fpri.org

# Index

Abonneau, Gen Adalbert, 112
Ader, Clément, 96
Alexandre, Gen René, 63, 88, 92, 137, 138
Alkan, Sgt-Mechanic Robert, 183
Alléhaut, Gen Emile, 111
André, Gen Louis, 3–4, 5, 103
Ardant du Picq, Col Charles, 21, 77
Armengaud, Lt-Col Jean, 187–8, 192
Arnoux, Jacques d', 191
Arvers, Maj Paul, 81

Baquet, Gen Louis Henry Auguste, 87
Barail, Gen François-Charles du, 2
Barès, Maj Edouard, 121, 140, 180
Barescut, Gen Maurice de, 143
Barthou, Louis, 96
Bédier, Joseph, 118, 134, 165
Bel, Capt Ferréol-François, 36
Bellenger, Capt Georges, 97
Berge, Gen Henri, 87
Bergson, Henri, 24
Bernard, Col, 97
Bernhardi, Friedrich von, 19
Bernis, Capt Raymond de, 182, 183
Berthaut, Gen Jean-Auguste, 36
Besse, Col, 92
Billard, Capt Marie Marcel André, 1, 2, 20, 28, 50, 63, 66, 77
Blériot, Louis, 96
Bloch, Jan, 53, 54
Bloch, Marc, 129, 201
Boë, Gen Elie, 31, 77
Boelcke, Capt Oswald, 120
Bonnal, Gen Henri, 4, 6–7, 8–9, 15–16, 16–17, 22, 31, 33, 35, 40–3, 46, 47, 55, 58, 60, 74–5, 77, 126
Bonnier, Gen, 31
Bossut, Maj Louis, 123, 209, 211, 212
Bouchacourt, Maj Louis, 120, 195
Boucher, Col Arthur, 19, 40
Boulanger, Gen Georges, 3

Boullaire, Gen François-René, 174
Bourbaki, Gen Charles, 81
Bourdériat, Col Frédéric-Edmond, 7, 54
Bouvard, Maj Henri, 127,
Breton, Jules-Louis, 205, 206, 207–8
Bridoux, Gen Marie Joseph Eugène, 112
Brillié, Eugène, 205, 207, 211
Bro, Gen Joseph, 109
Brocard, Capt Antonin, 122, 182
Brun, Gen Jean, 96, 125
Buat, Gen Edmond, 44, 52, 62, 88, 178
Bugeaud, Gen Thomas Robert, 37
Burstyn, Gunther, 204
Bussche-Ippenburg, Maj Erich von dem, 204
Buyer, Gen Robert de, 240

Cailloux, Lt, 122, 208
Campana, Lt Roger, 145
Campenon, Gen Jean-Baptiste Marie Edouard, 3
Caquot, Maj Albert, 243
Cardot, Capt Lucien, 39, 50, 54, 60
Carence, Col, 158
Castelnau, Gen Edouard de Curières de, 105, 109, 139, 148, 150–1
Castelnau, Gen Henri, 6
Cézanne, Ernest, 81
Chaine, Lt Pierre, 193
Chalmandrey, Capt André, 29, 62
Chaubès, Maj Louis, 212
Chautemps, Félix, 66
Chédeville, Col Charles, 228–9
Chenot, Col, 106
Chenu, Sgt Charles-Maurice, 125, 127, 187, 193, 194, 197, 201, 209, 215
Cherfils, Col Pierre-Joseph-Maxime, 7
Cissey, Gen Ernest Courtot de, 2, 6, 8
Clausewitz, Carl von, 19, 24, 41
Clemenceau, Georges, 67, 96
Clerc, Col, 106

Clerc, Capt François, 81
Colin, Gen Jean, 19, 51
Combes, Emile, 67
Conneau, Gen Louis, 112, 175
Coste, Maj Charles, 194
Cru, Jean Norton, 192, 193

Daille, Gen Marius, 129
Darwin, Charles, 21
Debeney, Gen Eugène, 8, 26, 31, 41–2, 50,
    52, 60, 126, 142, 247, 252, 253
Deloule, Monsieur, 206
Deloye, Gen Denis François Félix, 87
Delvert, Capt Charles, 192–3, 202, 203
Derrécagaix, Gen Victor-Bernard, 36
Deville, Gen Louis, 213
Dhé, Col Paul, 243
Doumenc, Maj Aimé, 208
Doumenjou, Capt, 82
Doumer, Paul, 96
Dragomirov, Gen Mikhail Ivanovich, 39
Dubail, Gen Auguste, 121, 138–9, 144,
    145, 152
Duchêne, Maj, 121
Duchêne, Gen Denis Auguste, 134
Duval, Gen Maurice, 121, 141, 142, 243,
    246–7, 251

Estienne, Gen Jean, 83, 89, 97, 109, 121,
    121–2, 130, 136, 140, 141, 142, 179,
    204, 205–8, 209, 211, 213, 215, 217,
    218, 219, 228
Evrard, Maj, 251
Eynac, Laurent, 227

Fallières, Armand, 22
Faure, Capt André, 115
Fayolle, Gen Emile, 31, 65, 105, 131,
    132, 140, 150, 151, 152, 153, 157, 158,
    160, 264
Ferber, Capt Ferdinand, 96, 121
Ferrié, Col Gustave, 121
Ferrus, Maj Léonce, 205, 206
Fetter, Col Marie Hippolyte Alfred, 121
Foch, Marshal Ferdinand, 6, 20, 29, 31,
    32, 33, 40, 41, 43, 54, 60, 65, 71, 134,
    150, 156, 157, 158, 160, 251, 253

Fokker, Anthony, 122, 128, 182–3
Fonck, Lt René, 120
Fonclare, Gen Jacques Elie de, 106, 232
Franchet d'Espèrey, Gen Louis, 17, 31, 77,
    95, 104, 182
Frantz, Sgt Joseph, 115
Freud, Sigmund, 24
Freycinet, Charles de, 3–4, 10, 96

Galliéni, Gen Joseph, 10, 14, 17
Galtier-Boissière, Jean, 186, 190, 194
Garros, 2/Lt Roland, 115, 182
Gascouin, Gen Firmin Emile, 28, 31,
    109, 139
Gaudy, Cpl Georges, 185, 195, 197
Genevoix, Lt Maurice, 196, 200
Gérard, Lt Henri, 81, 121
Gervais, Auguste, 64
Gilbert, Capt Georges, 19
Girardet, Raoul, 14
Goltz, Colmar von der, 19
Gouraud, Gen Henri, 17, 146–7, 148,
    244, 247
Goÿs, Maj Louis de, 181
Gramsci, Antonio, 300
Grandmaison, Gen Louis Loyzeau de, 10,
    20, 21, 23, 25, 26–7, 29, 31, 49, 50, 51,
    56, 57, 60, 72, 76–7, 90, 105, 124
Guillaumat, Gen Adolphe, 148
Guynemer, Georges, 122, 182

Hagron, Gen Alexis Auguste
    Raphaël, 89
Haig, Field Marshal Sir Douglas, 252
Happe, Capt Maurice, 181
Hayek, Friedrich von, 119
Herbinger, Col Paul-Gustave, 17
Hérouville, Col d', 106
Herr, Gen Frédéric Georges, 87–8, 91, 109,
    141, 178
Hicks, John R., 129
Hirschauer, Col Auguste Edouard, 97
Hutier, Gen Oskar von, 130–1

Jacottet, Maj, xv
Jibé, Capt, 25, 61, 68
Joan of Arc, 27, 29

Joffre, Marshal Joseph, 10, 22, 25, 27, 36, 54, 58, 61, 63–4, 65, 91, 103, 106, 112, 118, 138, 140, 141, 145, 146, 156, 160, 163, 174, 206, 262, 264
Jones, 2/Lt H., 193
Joppé, Gen Maurice, 144–5
Jouinot-Gambetta, Gen François, 174
Jünger, Lt Ernst, 185–6, 187, 195, 197, 199, 201, 202, 203

Kessler, Gen Charles, 7, 8, 20, 54, 93
Kimpflin, Capt Georges, 119
Kluck, Gen Alexander von, 112, 115, 262
Kondratiev, Nikolai Dmitrievich, 117
Kuhn, Thomas, 149

Lacroix, Gen Henri de, 8, 75, 82
Laffargue, Capt André, 121
Lamothe, Gen Léon Jean Benjamin de, 90, 91
Langle de Cary, Gen Fernand de, 100, 153, 167, 264
Langlois, Gen Hippolyte, 7, 8, 28, 32, 36, 46, 54, 55, 60, 77, 85
Lanrezac, Gen, 31, 54
Larcher, Lt-Col Maurice, 31, 78, 80, 105
Lardemelle, Gen Charles de, 153
Lattre, Capt Jean de, 123
Laure, Maj Emile, xv, 1, 2, 18, 19, 27–8, 29, 30, 35, 57, 63, 68, 72, 76, 77, 112–13, 131–2, 148, 171–2, 238, 269
Le Bon, Gustave, 21, 22
Lebas, Gen Albert, 150
Lewal, Gen Jules-Louis, 3, 6, 36
Lombard, Gen Lombard, 87
Louis-Philippe I, King of the French, 50
Lucas, Col Pascal, xv, 141, 151, 170
Ludendorff, Gen, 222, 252
Lyautey, Gen Hubert, 16, 126

Maillard, Maj Louis-Adolphe Goujat dit, 6–7, 19, 40, 45, 60
Maistre, Gen Paul, 155
Malassenet, 2/Lt, 121
Mangin, Gen Charles, 17, 90, 110, 160, 247, 249, 264
Marion, Gen Charles Louis Raoul, 30
Martin, Pte-Mechanic, 183

Mathieu, Gen Charles Philippe Antoine, 87
Maud'huy, Col Louis de, 8, 22, 23, 31, 40, 53, 63, 77, 105, 126
Maugars, Capt Maurice, 24
Maunoury, Gen Michel-Joseph, 112
Mayer, Lt-Col Emile, 53
Mengin, Gen Justin, 91
Messimy, Adolphe, 12, 28, 65, 96, 112
Micheler, Gen Joseph Alfred, 160, 264
Millerand, Alexandre, 91
Minié, Claude-Etienne, 37
Mole, Lancelot de, 204
Moltke the Elder, Field Marshal Helmuth von, 19, 41, 55
Monhoven, Col Jean, 208
Montaigne, Lt-Col Jean-Baptiste, 14, 19, 20, 22, 23, 27, 28, 50, 54, 71, 72, 85, 126, 167
Monteilhet, Joseph, 35, 63, 69
Mourret, Gen Léon-Augustin, 206
Mutius, Gerhard von, 68

Napoleon I, Emperor of the French, 40–2, 46, 58
Négrier, Gen François-Oscar de, 7, 16, 43, 54, 60
Neznamov, Lt-Col Alexander Alexandrovich, 49, 51
Nivelle, Gen Robert, 132, 136, 140, 150, 160, 162, 178, 184, 208, 212, 213, 231, 232, 264, 265

Orthlieb, Maj Jean, 180–1, 225

Paillé, Lt-Col, 142
Passaga, Gen Fénelon François Germain, 232
Pavlov, Ivan, 21
Pedroncini, Guy, 134
Percin, Gen Alexandre, 25, 28, 34–5, 65, 69, 84, 86, 89, 90, 93, 95, 191
Pétain, Marshal Philippe, 8, 18, 31, 43, 44, 65, 73, 77, 104, 105, 109, 122, 132, 133134, 136, 138, 139–43, 146, 147–8, 149, 150, 154, 157, 162, 163, 174, 178, 205, 206, 213, 217, 227, 230, 232, 236, 241, 243, 245, 257, 264, 265

Peucker, Gen Eduard von, 40
Peuty, Maj Paul du, 184
Pézard, Lt André, 200
Pierrefeu, Jean de, 152
Pierron, Gen Edouard, 36
Poincaré, Henri, 32
Psichari, Lt Ernest, 24

Quénault, Air Mechanic Louis, 115

Raffray, Pte, 121
Ratzel, Friedrich, 21–2
Reffye, Gen Jean-Baptiste Verchère de, 24
Renard, Capt Charles, 95, 96, 121
Réveilhac, Gen Géraud François
    Gustave, 153
Revol, Capt Joseph, 75
Ribot, Théodule, 21
Rimailho, Lt-Col Emile, 87, 91–2, 156, 206
Rimbault, Capt, 195
Roberts, David, 204
Robillot, Gen Félix, 240
Rocolle, Pierre, 103
Rommel, Lt Erwin, 193, 195, 201
Roques, Gen Pierre Auguste, 96, 97, 102
Rose, Maj Charles de Tricornot de, 97,
    115, 122, 123, 130, 182, 183
Rouquerol, Gen Gabriel, 178
Russell, Bertrand, 24

Saconney, Maj Jacques, 110, 121
Saulnier, Raymond, 97

Schmettow, Gen Eberhard *Graf* von, 174
Schumpeter, Joseph, 117
Séré de Rivières, Gen Raymond, 2, 24, 39
Serrigny, Col Bernard, 129, 138
Shapero, Albert, 122
Silvestre, Gen Marie Félix, 87
Soloviev, Capt, 49, 51
Sordet, Gen Jean François André, 112, 113,
    114, 175, 262

Thomas, Albert, 206, 207
Toffler, Alvin, 135
Treignier, Eugène, 67, 70, 75

Urbal, Gen Victor d', 157

Vatry, Lt-Col Marc-Joseph-Edgard
    Bourdon de, 19, 41
Velpry, Col Pol Maurice, 224, 229
Verraux, Lt-Col Martial Justin, 53
Vincent, Daniel, 243
Voisin, Gabriel, 115

Wanty, Émile, 103
Watson, John B., 68
Wilhelm II, Emperor of Germany, 41, 92
Wisse, Maj, 86
Wright brothers (Orville and Wilbur),
    23, 96
Württemberg, Albrecht, Duke of, 101

Zédé, Lt-Col Charles, 81